the
LYNCH
complete

David Hughes

Virgin

For Stevie

This edition first published in 2001 by
Virgin Publishing Ltd
Thames Wharf Studios
Rainville Road
London
W6 9HA

A catalogue record for this book is available from the British Library.

ISBN 0 7535 0598 3

Phototypeset by Intype London Ltd

Printed and bound in Great Britain by Mackays of Chatham PLC

Contents

Acknowledgements

Firstly to Joanne Brooks and Dane McMaster, who got me off on the right foot and only tripped me up when I needed it; Chelsey Fox, who has all of the good qualities of an agent, and none of the bad ones; David Willing, Gordon and everyone at Picture Production Co; Fraser Bensted and Julia Delmas for diligent research; Angus Spottiswoode; Seamus A. Ryan and Alex Blair for coffee and sympathy; Jonathan Clements for his mentat-like *Dune* knowledge; Jimmy, Martin, Jo, Simon, Chris and the rest of the Beautiful Southmartins; Ian Freer, *Hotdog* and *SFX* for stunning reviews; Simon and Gary at *DreamWatch*, Caroline and Mark at *Empire*; Tim at *Timecode*; Maggie Monteith; Michael Barrs; Lynchians like Johnny Angel, Mike Dunn, Brian A. Gross, Ben Halligan, Craig Ranapia, Mike Hartmann, Anthony Kanizaj, Dominic Kulcsar, Adam Walter, The City of Absurdity and Craig Miller, John Thorne and John J. Pierce from *Wrapped in Plastic*; K. George Godwin; Hilary Humphrey Pitts and Cheryl Lieblod @ PAFA; Richard Beymer; John Mitchell; John Neff; Holly McGovern for a promise kept; American Spirits and Starbucks lattes; and to all of my willing interview subjects: Dana Ashbrook, Angelo Badalamenti, Trevor Beattie, Catherine Coulson, Peter Deming, Duwayne Dunham, Miguel Ferrer, Dexter Fletcher, Michael Horse, Michael Ontkean, Kimmy Robertson, Jonathan Sanger and Mary Sweeney. And especially to David Lynch, Barry Gifford, my wife Zahida and incredible children Harry and Jenna; Jackie and Pelham; and finally my own parents, who thankfully fit none of the Lynchian archetypes. Except maybe Mr and Mrs X.

Fuzzy Sandwiches, or There Is No Speed Limit on the Lost Highway: Reflections on David Lynch
by Barry Gifford

In 1997, when David Lynch, who had directed the film version of my novel *Wild at Heart*, and also had directed my two plays, 'Tricks' and 'Blackout', for a television production entitled *Hotel Room*, came to me and asked me to write with him the screenplay for a new film, I could hardly say no. After all, *Wild at Heart* had won the Palme D'Or at the Cannes Film Festival and propelled the book onto bestseller lists all over the world. Besides, we were good friends by now. The problem was that I was busily engaged writing a novel and was scheduled to leave for Spain in two weeks. How could we get a screenplay done *right now*, as Dave asked. In fact, he insisted. So I put aside the novel manuscript and agreed to work hard for two weeks and see what we came up with. If it seemed to be working after my return from Spain, if we both felt good about the project, then we would continue and work straight through until we had it finished.

David had optioned for film my novel *Night People*, and we had talked for a year or more about how that could be done, but nothing happened. (He told me his daughter, Jennifer, wanted to play the role of one of the two lesbian serial killers.) He fell in love with a couple of sentences in the book in particular, one of which was when one woman says to another, 'We're just a couple of Apaches ridin' wild on the lost highway.' What did it mean? he wanted to know. What was the *deeper* meaning of the phrase 'lost highway'? He had an idea for a story. What if one day a person woke up and he was another person? An entirely different person from the person he had been the day before. OK, I said, that's Kafka, *The Metamorphosis*. But we did not want this person to turn into an insect. So that's what we had to start with: a title, *Lost Highway*; a sentence from close to the end of the book *Night People* ('You and me, mister, we can really out-ugly the sumbitches, can't we?'); the notion of irrefutable change; and a vision Dave had about someone receiving videotapes of his life from an unknown source, something he had thought of following the wrap of the shooting of *Twin Peaks: Fire Walk with Me*. Now all we had to do was make a coherent story out of this.

A few years ago, when David, the producer Monty Montgomery, my friend Vinnie Deserio and I were sitting around talking about another story, Dave, in an effort to explain to me an effect he was after, said, 'You know that feeling you get when you've just gotten back from the dry cleaners a pair of slacks, dacron slacks, and you reach your hand in a pocket and you feel those *fuzzy sandwiches* with your fingers? Well, that's the feeling I'm looking for.' I just nodded and replied, 'Okay, Dave, I know *exactly* what you mean.'

I kept this incident in mind while he and I sat across from one another and puzzled out the scenario for *Lost Highway*, which I like to call *Orpheus and Eurydice Meet Double Indemnity*. We made it work – at least for each other – and I love the result, fuzzy sandwiches and all. That being said, it's important to understand that David and I work similarly, very hard, long hours, with time out only for coffee – in Dave's case, *lots* of coffee. Working with Dave is, for me, a great treat, because I know that as the director he's going to add an extra dimension to whatever we come up with on the page. Visually, it will take one giant step beyond. This gives me the confidence to let everything loose, a great privilege for a writer.

Both Lynch and I believe that films are, or should be, as dreams. When you enter the movie theatre the 'real' world is shut out. Now you are in the thrall of the filmmakers, you *must* surrender and allow the film's images to wash over you, to drown in them for two hours or so. And David is relentless in his use of imagery. *Lost Highway*, like *Blue Velvet* or *Eraserhead*, especially, is filled with unforgettable images. And we are set in a place, a city, a landscape, that is neither here nor there, a timeless form, presented within a non-linear structure – a Möbius strip, curling back and under, running parallel to itself before again becoming connected, only there's a kind of coda – but that's how it goes with psychogenic fugues. Figure it out for yourself, you'll feel better later; and if you don't figure it out, you'll feel even *better*, trust us. Trust is what it's all about with filmmakers like David Lynch, one of the very, very few true visionaries in the history of cinema. I once asked David, who is a painter, why he decided to make movies, and he told me (echoing many others, including Elia Kazan who said, 'The camera is such a beautiful instrument. It paints with motion'), 'Because I wanted to see my paintings move.'

Vinnie Deserio once said that the reason Dave and I work so well together is that he takes the ordinary and makes it seem extraordinary, and I take the extraordinary and make it seem ordinary. Maybe so; it sounds good, anyway. But there are no easy explanations for what occurs in *Lost Highway* or *Eraserhead*, nor should there be. When you go on a journey with David Lynch it's a trip you've never been on before – and may never want to take again – but it's unforgettable. Time to fasten your seat belt, as Bette Davis so memorably instructed (words by Joseph Mankiewicz) in *All About Eve*, because there is no speed limit on the lost highway.

San Francisco, August 2000

Barry Gifford wrote the novel *Wild at Heart* upon which David Lynch's film is based; two plays directed by Lynch in the HBO programme *Hotel Room*; and he co-wrote the screenplay of *Lost Highway*. His novel *Perdita Durango* was made into a feature film by the director Alex de la Iglesia, with whom Gifford also co-wrote the screenplay. Gifford's most recent book is *Wyoming*, a novel.

Welcome to Lynchworld

'HI, IS THAT DAVID?' booms the voice from the other end of the phone. The connection is so clear, and the voice so loud and familiar, for a sleep-befuddled moment I think it must be Gordon Cole. Then I remember: it's a little after 9.30, Prague time, and my interview with David Lynch is due to start in five hours' time. It must be Lynch calling to confirm, and here I am standing in my hotel room half-naked, trying to sign the room service bill with one hand, and rub sleep out of my eyes with the other. 'WE COULD DO THE INTERVIEW NOW, IF YOU WANT!' the booming voice continues. 'BUT WE HAVE TO DO IT IN THE BAR! 'CAUSE I'M A SMOKER, SEE?'

Something tells me meeting Lynch will live up to my expectations.

My only regret about my earlier volume, *The Complete Kubrick*, was that I did not get to meet the subject of the book, who passed away before the project was even pitched. Setting out to write this follow-up, I was not about to let the same thing happen twice. A one-to-one interview with Lynch was, I felt, fundamental to the book, despite the fact that it would be broken up and scattered throughout, so that each chapter – and boy, there were a lot of them this time – would contain a few fresh quotes from Lynch himself. What I didn't realise was how fundamental the interview would be to *everything* about the book. Meeting Lynch allowed me to see first-hand the unique way in which his mind works, and led me to create new boundaries for the areas covered by the book: not to over-analyse, or rationalise, or demystify those many projects of his whose power lies in subjective interpretation. After all, as David himself told me, 'you can't get the complete Lynch.'

The specific format of this book makes it particularly well suited to being read out of sequence, favourite projects first. (Funny how the book never seems to fall open at the *On the Air* section!) Seeing the relevant film or TV show *before* tackling the associated chapter is the wisest move – by now, you may have forgotten who did actually kill Laura Palmer. The section breakdowns build on the style established by the earlier books in this series, with each chronological entry featuring such basic information as title, year of release (or first broadcast), medium, format and running time(s), as well as drawing on the following categories as appropriate:

CAST / CREDITS: A full cast list, but only the key members of the crew. For full credits, check the end of the film, or the IMDb (**http://uk.imdb.com**).

UNCREDITED CAST/CREW: Belatedly giving credit where it's due.

TITLE SEQUENCE: Including title styles, music, opening shots and sometimes narration.

SUMMARY: The bit that, in the interest of completism, gives the plot away – in some cases, my own interpretation of what the heck is going on, for which I take full responsibility.

SOURCE: Background on the relevant source material of adaptations, or the gestation of a project if it evolved from, or was inspired by, another source.

ALTERNATIVE TITLES: *Labyrinth Man*, *Sailor and Lula* and others.

PRODUCTION HISTORY: The making of the movies.

CASTING: Who's who among the cast, and how they came to be there.

THE LYNCH MOB: Lynch's own unofficial repertory company, both behind and in front of the camera, cross-referenced with projects in which they have previously appeared.

MEMORABLE QUOTE(S): A personal choice of the most relevant, repeatable or resonant quotes from each of Lynch's films.

SOUND AND MUSIC: Lynch says that sound represents fifty per cent of his films. In this section, the other fifty per cent is music – usually Angelo Badalamenti's, but let's not forget Tractor and, er, Toto.

INFLUENCED BY: 'You don't know where things come from,' says Lynch. 'They could come from memories, they could be triggered, they could come to you from the ether. And if they are in the memory, if they're stored away, one day, for some reason, they're released, and it seems like a brand new idea.'

LEGACY: The influences of Lynch's films on everything from entire trends (*Twin Peaks* changing the face of television) to, uh, potato crisp commercials.

DÉJÀ VU: Didn't I see that shot of a highway at night in an earlier Lynch film? Did I already ask that?

THEMES AND MOTIFS: An attempt to unravel some of the mysteries, meanings and multiple layers in Lynch's films.

CUT SCENE(S)/ALTERNATIVE VERSION(S): A fairly detailed look at deletions, additions and amendments between script and screen, and different versions of the film, where relevant.

POSTER/TAG-LINE/TRAILER: 'A film is its own thing, and in an ideal world I think a film should be discovered knowing nothing.' Studio marketing departments tend not to agree with Lynch.

WHAT THE PAPERS SAID: A representative cross-section of critical appraisal from both sides of the Atlantic.

BOX OFFICE/RATINGS: Box office grosses in US dollars, and US TV ratings where appropriate.

AWARDS: Two Oscar nominations for Best Director, over a dozen Emmy nominations for *Twin Peaks*, a Palme D'Or for *Wild at Heart*, and more.

CONTROVERSY: Notes from a critical backlash, including 'Ban this sick film!' (*The Straight Story*).

EPISODE LOG: A breakdown of the episodes from Lynch's TV projects.

TRIVIA: Bore your friends! Be a pariah at parties! Win film quizzes! It's all the stuff that wouldn't fit comfortably into any other section.

APOCRYPHA: Did you know that Lynch wanted to remake *Lolita* with John Hurt as Humbert Humbert? No, neither did he.

AVAILABILITY: A round-up of the rather sorry state of Lynch's output on video, DVD and laserdisc, proving why we should all have a friend in Japan.

FINAL ANALYSIS: My own two cents' worth, Kent Brockman-style.

EXPERT WITNESS: A key player on the relevant project dishes.

LYNCH ON ... Finally, a few *bons mots* from the man himself.

Six Figures Getting Sick (1967)

Short / 1 min / colour / animation
Produced, directed and animated by David Lynch

UNCREDITED CREW: Lynch's friend and fellow art student Jack Fisk made the three plaster casts of Lynch's head onto which the film was projected.

ALTERNATIVE TITLE(S): *Six Figures Getting Sick* is often referred to, erroneously, as *Six Men Getting Sick*, or simply *Six Figures*. 'It's *Six Figures Getting Sick*,' Lynch confirms. In fact, the piece was originally untitled; Lynch gave it a name in order to make it easier to reference.

SUMMARY: A siren wails as three distended, animated figures – whose images are projected onto three sculpted heads, making six figures in all – catch fire as candles are lit. The bodies and stomachs begin to grow, and they vomit a bright red liquid. The film returns to the beginning and repeats itself.

PRODUCTION HISTORY: 'I was at the Pennsylvania Academy of Fine Arts in Philadelphia,' Lynch told Jonathan Ross about the period in the mid-1960s when he, a fledgling painter, first became interested in film. 'I was painting these kind of large, dark paintings, and it wasn't quite so nice when the painting was just still. It needed just to move a little bit, so this idea of animation came up. I kind of started to fall in love with film during that time.' As Lynch's first wife, Peggy Reavey, told Toby Keeler: 'He wanted his paintings to move, [that's] really what it came out of. He wanted his paintings to do more. He wanted them to make sounds. He wanted them to move.'

Lynch created *Six Figures Getting Sick* during his second year of attendance at the Pennsylvania Academy of Fine Arts, which he had joined in 1965 upon the advice of his artist friend Jack Fisk. 'It was a great time to be at the Academy,' Lynch told *Cinefantastique*, despite the fact that he hated living in Philadelphia. 'Schools have waves, and it just happened that I hit on a really rising, giant wave. There were so many good people at the school. And that really started everything rolling. I kind of got a feeling for things in terms of painting, and my own style kicked in.' In practical terms, Lynch was encouraged by the Academy's sponsorship of an annual experimental painting competition, for which Lynch decided to make something which was a cross between a moving painting and a looped animated film.

Lynch purchased a 16mm camera that could hold fifty feet of film and could also photograph single frames – an essential capability for animation. From the same Philadelphia dealer, he bought two floodlights that he was told to set at 45° angles to the action. Lynch soon discovered, however, that the camera's Cook lens could not be adjusted; instead, he was forced to fix the camera to a dresser in the seventh-floor downtown hotel room that would act as his makeshift studio, and to set up his makeshift animation stand – a board taped to a radiator – in such a place that the camera's viewfinder would capture all of the action.

Unfortunately, upon developing his film when the animation was complete, Lynch discovered that the viewfinder had picked up too *much* information: the animation board was in frame, but so was the radiator and the wall. To solve this problem, Lynch devised an ingenious sculpted screen, made from three plaster casts of his own head, onto which the film would be projected from such a distance that the extraneous images – the radiator and the wall – would fall away beyond the projection surface. Thus, as Peggy Reavey later explained: 'He projected it onto the screen, [and] these heads that he animated which went through all these contortions, and he had little birthday candles stuck on the canvas that he was using, and he lit them, and there was all these streaks of burning, and then at the very end all these heads vomited and . . . that was the end. And then it played over and over again.' Lynch evidently did not think much of his first film-making effort, telling *Cinefantastique*, 'It was much nicer to paint than [to] make those movies.'

SOUND AND MUSIC: There was no music in *Six Figures Getting Sick*; only the sound of a wailing siren was looped along with the film.

LEGACY: The most important legacy of *Six Figures Getting Sick* was that it prompted a wealthy artist, H. Barton Wasserman, to order a similar 'moving painting' that he could project at home any time he felt like it. Lynch did not wait to be asked twice. *The Alphabet* was the result.

THEMES AND MOTIFS: Sickness (or disease) and fire are two themes to which Lynch would return continually throughout his films. Disease, in particular, plays a major role in *Eraserhead* (the 'baby' is sick), *The Elephant Man* ('John' Merrick has a disfiguring disease of the skin and bones), *Dune* (Baron Harkonnen appears diseased) and *Blue Velvet* (Dorothy talks of men 'putting their disease' in her). Fire plays an important part in *Twin Peaks* (a fire destroys the sawmill; Laura Palmer liked 'playing with fire' and leaves a note that reads 'FIRE WALK WITH ME' at the scene of her murder, copied from something her killer says) and *Fire Walk With Me* (the title itself is a reference to the note); *Wild at Heart* (Lula's father is killed in a fire, an element which is a strong leitmotif throughout; Chris Isaak's 'Wicked Game' opens with the words 'The world was on fire and no one could save me but you'); *Lost Highway* (the house in the desert explodes in flames); even *The Straight Story* (one of Rose's children was badly burned in a fire; a house burns as Alvin's tractor careens out of control).

TRAILER: US talk show host Jay Leno once asked Lynch about his shortest film. Upon learning that it was 'plotless', and a mere one minute in duration, Leno asked him how one would go about making a trailer for a film like that. 'That's a problem,' Lynch replied, laughing.

AWARDS: *Six Figures Getting Sick* won the Pennsylvania Academy of Fine Arts's second annual Dr W. S. Biddle Cadwalder Memorial Prize.

AVAILABILITY: Although *Six Figures Getting Sick* is not available in its entirety, a short clip of the 'film' is shown as part of Toby Keeler's 1997 documentary *Pretty as a Picture: The Art of David Lynch*, which is available in the US as an NTSC VHS (FLV 1327) and Region 1 DVD (ID4810TKDVD).

FINAL ANALYSIS: A crucial step in the transformation of painter to film-maker, *Six Figures Getting Sick* strikes me as a playfully perverse work that, while undoubtedly of its time, could hold up against anything in today's contemporary art market. Sadly, its multi-media nature makes it one of the most difficult Lynch projects to reproduce, and it will probably endure as Lynch's greatest 'lost' work – lost to the general public, at least.

LYNCH ON *SIX FIGURES GETTING SICK*: 'That was going to be the end of my film-making experience. The entire "film" cost me two hundred dollars, and that was just too expensive.'

The Alphabet (1968)

16mm short / 4 mins / colour & b/w / live action & animation

Written, directed, photographed and edited by David Lynch
Produced by H. Barton Wasserman
Sound by David Lynch

Title song by David Lynch
Sung by Bob Chadwick
'Alphabet Song' sung by Peggy Lynch

CAST: Peggy Lynch (*The Girl*)

UNCREDITED CREW: Bob McDonald (Sound Effects Editor), Bob Cullum (Sound Mixing)

SUMMARY: A girl lies in bed as we hear children chanting the alphabet. On abstract animated landscapes, letters from A to Z appear as a man with an authoritative voice (like that of a teacher) sings indistinctly; a capital 'A' appears to give birth to several lower case 'a's; a distorted female figure reacts in shock as letters force their way into her head. The girl seen in bed earlier reacts violently. Blood streams from the eyes and mouth of her animated counterpart. The girl in bed attempts to reach various letters floating just beyond her grasp, as a female voice chants the 'Alphabet Song'. Finally, she falls back on the bed, writhing and vomiting blood.

SOURCE: Lynch has sometimes said that his ideas originate in his own dreams – often, in his case, daydreams. *The Alphabet*, however, began as someone *else*'s dream, as Peggy Reavey – then married to Lynch – has explained: 'I was home for Christmas, and I sat in the same room with my niece, who I think was about six. And she had a dream that night, a nightmare that woke me up, and she was just jumping around in bed reciting the alphabet: "A-B-C-D-E-F-G! A-B-C-D-E-F-G!" I was telling David about this, and his eyes just got as big as saucers. You know, I thought it was an interesting story. But to him, right away, this was material.'

PRODUCTION HISTORY: Almost immediately following his first foray into film-making, *Six Figures Getting Sick*, Lynch was commissioned by a wealthy associate, H. Barton Wasserman, to make what the director described as 'a similar type of thing, that would be like a painting you could turn on and run for a while and then turn off.' With $1,000 now at his disposal, Lynch set to work on the new piece, designed to be projected onto a sculptured screen, like *Six Figures Getting Sick*.

It took Lynch two months to shoot the two minutes and twenty-five seconds of film. But when the developed film came back from the lab, it was blank. 'I remember holding the film up to the light to see frames, and I saw no frames.' The director was not depressed, however; merely curious to know what had gone wrong. 'I remember someone asking, "Aren't you upset?" I said, "No." The hindsight part came in later,' he added. 'If that had come out and I had sent that to the American Film Institute, it wouldn't have been good enough to get me the grant I got later. And of course, that grant I *had* to have, if I was going to get into film. So fate was smiling on me.'

More surprisingly, Wasserman was also smiling: unfazed by the fate of his commission, he gave Lynch *carte blanche* to take the rest of the money and do whatever he wanted. Thus, armed with what remained of his patron's money, a small contribution from his father and an idea born out of a child's dream – the nocturnal alphabet-recital of his wife's niece – Lynch set about making what would become his third film, *The Alphabet*. The first thing the director did was paint the walls of his bedroom black, much to his wife's bemusement. 'He set up on the second floor,' Reavey said later, '[in] the room where he shot the scene in *The Alphabet* where I'm bouncing around the bed.'

Having seen the completed film, Lynch's artist friend Bushnell Keeler told the young film-maker about the American Film Institute (AFI), a brand new film school that Keeler's brother-in-law had helped establish in Washington, DC. Keeler encouraged Lynch to apply for a grant. Lynch did so, and submitted a print of *The Alphabet*, along with a short script he described as 'very weird . . . it was just little images and stuff, sort of like shorthand and poetry'. Lynch's application was initially unsuccessful, but when AFI director George Stevens Jr called to ask if the proposed budget of $7,118 could be reduced to $5,000, Lynch's reply was swift: 'You got it.'

CASTING: Peggy, Lynch's first wife and soon to be the mother of his first child, played the little girl who recited *The Alphabet*.

MEMORABLE QUOTE(S)
Voice: 'Remember, you're dealing with a human form.'

SOUND AND MUSIC: Aside from the singing, there is no music in *The Alphabet*, though the sound effects include a crying child, a siren, whistling and rushing wind. According to legend, Lynch tried to record the effects himself, using a rented Uher tape recorder; the machine was broken, however, resulting in a certain distortion of sound that Lynch, true to form, loved. Armed with his own peculiar brand of effects, Lynch approached a Philadelphia industrial film company, Calvin Productions, which agreed to edit and mix the soundtrack.

DÉJÀ VU: The siren heard in *The Alphabet* recalls the single sound effect in *Six Figures Getting Sick*, while the girl's sickness – here, as a direct consequence of rigidly enforced learning – is a clear reference to Lynch's earlier work.

THEMES AND MOTIFS: *The Alphabet* arguably encapsulates a single theme – in this case, fear of learning – more succinctly than any of Lynch's subsequent films. The girl's resistance to learning reflects that of a young David Lynch, who by his own admission was far more comfortable drawing than writing during his early school life. 'For me, back then, school was a crime against young people,' he remembered. 'It destroyed the seeds of liberty. The teachers didn't encourage knowledge or a positive attitude.' Besides, he added, 'the people who interested me didn't go to school.' The fact that Lynch's own mother taught English did not change his attitude to language, which *The Alphabet* clearly illustrates. 'I think that films should have a surface story,' he said in 1987, 'but underneath it there should be things happening that are abstract . . . things that resonate, and areas that words can't help you find out about.'

AVAILABILITY: Although it is occasionally screened on television, *The Alphabet* is currently unavailable on any format. Nevertheless, Lynch says that he plans to make this and his other short films available through his website, davidlynch.com.

FINAL ANALYSIS: Lynch's first fully-fledged animated film is an extraordinarily vivid portrait of the constricting effects of learning linguistic forms. Although it seems surprising that the director of *The Alphabet* would go on to write or co-write almost every one of his future films, Lynch's mistrust of language would be a recurring motif in his future work, from the letters found under the fingernails of BOB's victims to the clipped-out letters that litter his paintings (for instance, 'Sputnik Over City, Featuring the Letter A'), often communicating far less than the reader might imagine.

LYNCH ON *THE ALPHABET*: '*The Alphabet* is a little nightmare about the fear connected with learning. It's very abstract – a pretty dense little film.'

The Grandmother (1970)

16mm short / 34 mins / colour / live action & animation

Written, directed, produced, animated and photographed by David Lynch
Assistant Script Consultants Margaret Lynch, C.K. Williams

Still Photography Doug Randall
Music and Music Effects by Tractor
Sound Editing and Mixing by Alan R. Splet
Sound Effects by David Lynch, Margaret Lynch, Robert Chadwick, Alan R. Splet
Produced by American Film Institute

CAST: Richard White (*The Boy*), Dorothy McGinnis (*The Grandmother*), Virginia Maitland (*Mother*), Robert Chadwick (*Father*)

TITLE SEQUENCE: The titles, in white on a black background, state simply: 'THE GRANDMOTHER a film by DAVID LYNCH.'

SUMMARY: The earth spews forth two adults, a male and a female, who huddle together, making animal noises. The male seems disturbed by the arrival of a child, a young boy grown in the same organic fashion. Alone in a sparsely furnished room, the boy sits forlornly, playing with a plant, while his parents search, or forage, on all fours. At home, the 'father' drinks and the 'mother' preens. The boy wakes to find he has wet the bed, and his angry father punishes him by savagely rubbing his face in it. His mother beckons him, tries to kiss him, and shakes him when he rejects her. Alone in his room, he hears a whistling sound and follows it upstairs to its source: a seed, which he plants on a bed in a mound of earth and waters. Days pass, and the seed grows, eventually giving birth to a fully grown elderly woman, whom the boy adopts as his 'grandmother'. Now, whenever his slovenly parents mistreat him, he escapes to the sanctuary of his grandmother's love, and has childish fantasies in which he kills his parents. One night, she grows sick. The boy tries to get his parents to help him, but they laugh at him, and he returns upstairs to find his grandmother dead. Later, visiting a cemetery, he has a vision of her, but she appears not to recognise him, and her head snaps back in death. He wails in anguish and returns home to bed, trying to dream a way out of his miserable existence, and imagining himself joined to the pod that produced his grandmother.

PRODUCTION HISTORY: Having been accepted for the inaugural year of the American Film Institute (AFI), Lynch began combining his formal studies with his practical education: the making of his next short film, *The Grandmother*. 'He got five thousand dollars,' Lynch's first wife Peggy recalled, 'and he again proceeded to paint the inside of the house black.' Although Lynch explained that he had painted these makeshift sets black 'so that you'd see what was there, and not look at the walls', it was also because, while he was shooting in colour, he wanted the film to look black and white.

Lynch had originally projected a budget of $7,118 for the production of *The Grandmother*, although the AFI had agreed to fund it to a maximum of $5,000. With the money almost gone, and *The Grandmother* still some way from completion, Lynch prudently invited one of the Institute's founders, Tony Vellani, to Philadelphia to view the work in progress. Vellani was so impressed by Lynch's unfinished work that he not only agreed to grant Lynch an extra $2,200 to complete the project, but he also strongly recommended that Lynch apply for admission to the AFI's brand new Center for Advanced Film Studies, located in Los Angeles. Lynch readily agreed and, although he was too late to win a place among the Center's first applicants, the combination of *The Grandmother* and a script for a further short, *Gardenback* [see 'In Dreams,' page 245], was good enough to get him accepted for year two.

There was only one problem now facing the fledgling film-maker: how to explain to his parents the origin of the disturbing imagery of the dysfunctional family at the heart of the film. 'When my parents saw *The Grandmother*, they were very upset,' he told *Cinefantastique*, 'because they didn't know where it came from.'

CASTING: Looking for the quartet of actors who would bring *The Grandmother* to life, Lynch did not have to cast his net far. Richard White (*The Boy*) was a neighbour; Dorothy McGinnis (*The Grandmother*) was the mother-in-law of a former employer, Roger La Pelle; Virginia Maitland (*Mother*) and Robert Chadwick (*Father*) were both acquaintances.

THE LYNCH MOB: Robert Chadwick (*Father*) had, as Bob Chadwick, previously recorded vocal effects for *The Alphabet*.

SOUND AND MUSIC: The film's atmospheric music was provided by Tractor, a group to which Lynch's friend Ronnie Culbertson belonged. *The Grandmother* was particularly important in the development of Lynch's stylised sound, because it marked his first collaboration with sound effects engineer Alan R. Splet, who would work with the director on *Eraserhead*, *The Elephant Man*, *Dune* and *Blue Velvet* (he died in 1994). For the second time, Lynch approached industrial film company Calvin Productions, whose effects library he would need access to. But Bob Cullum was unavailable, and Lynch was referred instead to his assistant, Splet. At the time, Lynch thought, 'Oh, brother, I'm being shunted off to his assistant.'

For the next seven weeks, however, the pair worked ten- or eleven-hour days, usually seven days a week, experimenting with the company's effects library, all for the bargain price of $250 per reel of film. 'So that's an awfully good deal,' Lynch noted appreciatively. 'Otherwise, it would have [cost] thousands of dollars.' Where Lynch's desired effects could not be accomplished with the company's limited equipment, necessity proved to be the mother of invention – most notably where the Grandmother's whistle was concerned. With no reverb facility available, Lynch and Splet found a piece of aluminium heat ducting, through which the whistle was recorded. As Splet recalled, 'We rerecorded it maybe fifteen times through this piece of ducting to get the little bit of echo on it that we wanted.'

THEMES AND MOTIFS: *The Grandmother* expands upon the theme of communication (or lack of it) in *The Alphabet* by reducing the characters' language to a series of unintelligible sounds: barks, grunts, whistles, moans, groans and wails. Only the boy and his grandmother seem able to communicate, and then only using wordless and even soundless methods. The sense of alienation that would be crucial to Lynch's first feature, *Eraserhead*, is also in evidence here, along with the unhealthy relationship between selfish parents and an apparently unwanted child. Lynch also deals with the idea of an attic as a mental space, which was to have recurred in the abandoned *Gardenback* project: in *The Grandmother*, the borders between real and fantasy worlds are deliberately muddied, so that it is unclear whether the grandmother is a real or imagined presence in the boy's life.

WHAT THE PAPERS SAID: Although one cannot expect short films to create much press, it is surprising that, following the critical acclaim that greeted *Eraserhead* and *The Elephant Man*, Lynch's short subjects were not widely re-examined. One of the few critics to do so was Lloyd Rose, who, in 1984, had this to say about *The Grandmother*: 'The blacks are so rich that you feel you could sink your arms into them up to the elbows. Against this black, which is the backdrop to most of the scenes, Lynch's other colours stand out with hallucinatory sharpness: they almost hurt your eyes. The boy's dreadful mother wears a dress with a green-and-pink floral pattern, bright as a tropical bird's plumage. The boy wets his bed frequently, and the urine stain is a rich yellow-orange, like egg yolk.

'Lynch is one of the great movie sensualists,' Rose continued, 'but his is an odd sort of sensuality, because there's no overt sexual charge to it. Even when he's dealing with directly sexual symbols, there's something cool and dry, clinical, in his attitude. And his technique has no lush pleasures. There is no languorous camera movement, and none of the high excitement of vivid editing. We aren't swept along by Lynch's camera; we're caught by his images. Our memory of his work is likely to be a series of mysterious, iconographic compositions – as if we had been looking at an exhibition of paintings rather than at a film.'

AWARDS: *The Grandmother* won prizes at several film festivals – including those held in San Francisco, Belleview and Atlanta – and the Critics' Choice Award of an AFI panel voting on the twelve best film-makers to have been awarded grants.

AVAILABILITY: Although it is occasionally screened on television or at festivals, *The Grandmother* is currently unavailable on any format.

FINAL ANALYSIS: *The Grandmother* is a key work in Lynch's oeuvre, not only because its shows a maturing and developing film-maker at work and illustrates Lynch's surrealist tendencies (albeit with a relatively comprehensible narrative structure), but also because it demonstrates his increasing reliance on live action as a means to express his ideas. The film may seem like a baptism of fire to those unfamiliar with Lynch's more outlandish works, but the themes that underlie his work would be recognisable to anyone familiar with, in particular, *Eraserhead*, *Twin Peaks* and *Fire Walk With Me*. As a work of experimental film-making, it continues to succeed more than thirty years after its creation, largely due to its timeless themes, otherworldly colour saturation, extraordinary central performances, and – above all – its indication of a raw and powerful talent at work.

LYNCH ON *THE GRANDMOTHER*: 'There's something about a grandmother. I had two great – not *great* – they were *fantastic* grandmothers! And two fantastic grandfathers. And they were close to each other. But the film didn't come from that, I'm sure it didn't. It came from this particular character's need – a need that that prototype can provide. Grandmothers get playful. And they relax a little, and they have unconditional love. And that's what this kid conjured up.'

The Amputee (1974)

Short videotape / 5 mins / black and white / live action
Written, directed, photographed and edited by David Lynch
Photography by Frederick Elmes

CAST: Catherine Coulson (*Woman*), David Lynch (*Doctor*)

SUMMARY: A woman with both legs amputated at the knees sits, going over a letter she has written concerning a number of people involved in a tangled web of relationships. As her re-reading of the letter continues in voiceover, a male nurse enters, sits down in front of her and, without speaking, begins to treat the stumps of her legs. This involves snipping, copious amounts of spurting blood and bandaging, yet the woman continues to work on her letter, failing to acknowledge either the doctor or the treatment she is undergoing.

PRODUCTION HISTORY: While still at the American Film Institute (AFI) in 1974, with production on *Eraserhead* suspended due to lack of financing, cinematographer Frederick Elmes casually informed Lynch that he had been asked to shoot a test of two different stocks of black-and-white videotape. Elmes was planning to shoot a simple test pattern, but Lynch had a better idea: 'I said, "Would they object if you shot something else? What if I wrote something and we shoot two different versions of the same thing? Then they could see the stock, but we'll have shot something."' Elmes liked the proposal, believing that a simple live-action set-up might highlight the lighting contrasts between the stocks better than a test pattern. Lynch stayed up all night with Catherine Coulson, working on the set-up and the simple but effective special effects, and by the next day was ready to make his most rarely screened short film.

CASTING: *The Amputee* marked the acting debuts of both Lynch and Coulson, who were in the midst of working on *Eraserhead* at the time *The Amputee* was made.

THE LYNCH MOB: Both Catherine Coulson (*Twin Peaks*'s Log Lady) and Frederick Elmes were working, at the time, on Lynch's *Eraserhead*.

SOUND AND MUSIC: The videotape stock the AFI was testing did not allow Lynch to record synchronised sound; therefore, he was given his first experience of the Foley process, in which dialogue and sound effects recorded after production are added to the picture. 'We shot it and ran it back and Foleyed the whole thing live to picture,' Lynch explained. 'It was pretty exciting to do sound effects on the fly.'

THEMES AND MOTIFS: *The Amputee* marked the first appearance in a Lynch film of a physically disabled individual, an element that would recur in many future productions – including *The Elephant Man* (Merrick's disfigurement), *Eraserhead* (the deformed baby), *Blue Velvet* (the blind store clerk), *The Cowboy and the Frenchman* (Slim is deaf), *Twin Peaks* (Nadine Hurley has one eye; Philip Gerard is an amputee; Gordon Cole is mostly deaf), *Wild at Heart* (Juana wears leg braces; the hotel clerk has a bandaged foot; the disabled witness at the road accident), *The Straight Story* (Alvin's hip) and *Mulholland Drive* (the vagrant's deformed face) – though, perhaps significantly, no more, per capita, than such physical abnormalities occur in life.

AVAILABILITY: 'I'm gonna put them out on the Internet,' Lynch says of *The Amputee* and his other short films, which are intended as one of the centrepieces of his official website, davidlynch.com. 'For a short time, my short films were released non-theatrically, but they were never supposed to be released on video. But now you can get 'em in a video store, completely illegally, and this kills me,' he says, referring to *The Amputee* and several others of his widely bootlegged short films. 'I've not made one penny on my short films, but somebody's making money.' Lynch has no time for the argument that the films are often traded freely or at cost between fans, giving greater access to his early work and feeding the interest in his later commercial work. 'I'm not happy with the bootleggers,' he states firmly. 'They're the scum of the earth. Let them try to make something themselves, and then they can put it out.'

FINAL ANALYSIS: When *The Amputee* finally sees the light of day, audiences will at last have the chance to see one of Lynch's most minimalist creations, proving that the director who, a decade later, would mobilise a medium-sized army in order to make *Dune* could also tell a concise, efficient and above all effective story within a single camera set-up. The fact that the film was photographed by Frederick Elmes and co-starred Catherine Coulson and a young Lynch himself makes its current scarcity doubly frustrating.

LYNCH ON *THE AMPUTEE*: 'Catherine is in a chair and she's a double amputee. And she is going over a letter that she has written. She's reading it aloud to herself, in her head. And a doctor comes in – that's me – just to clean the ends of the stumps, and that's it. It's very minimal!'

Eraserhead (1977)

16mm feature / 100 mins (original version), 89 mins (release version) / black and white / live action & animation

Written, produced and directed by David Lynch
Camera and Lighting by Frederick Elmes, Herbert Cardwell

Location Sound and Re-recording by Alan R. Splet
Assistant to the Director Catherine Coulson
Production Manager Doreen G. Small
Picture Editing by David Lynch
Sound Editing by Alan R. Splet
Sound Effects by David Lynch, Alan R. Splet
Lady in the Radiator Song Composed and Sung by Peter Ivers
Pipe Organ by 'Fats' Waller
Crew Jeanne Field, Michael Grody, Stephen Grody, Toby Keeler, Roger Lundy, John
Lynch, Dennis Nance, Anatol Pacanowsky, Carol Schreder
Production Design and Special Effects by David Lynch
Special Effects Photography by Frederick Elmes
Assistant Camera Catherine Coulson
Special Thanks to Ron Barth, Mars F. Baumgardt, Ron Culbertson, Frank Daniel,
Richard Einfeld, Jack Fisk, Mary Fisk, Ken Fix, Andre Guttfreund, Marvin Goodwin
MD, Randy Hart, Roman Harte, George T. Hutchison, David Khasky, Jim King, Margit
Fellegi Laszlo, Paul Leimbach, David Lunney, Mr & Mrs D. W. Lynch, Peggy Lynch,
Sarah Pillsbury, Sidney P. Solow, Sissy Spacek, George Stevens Jr, Antonio Vellani
Produced with the co-operation of The American Film Institute Center For Advanced
Film Studies

CAST: John Nance (*Henry Spencer*), Charlotte Stewart (*Mary X*),
Allen Joseph (*Mr X*), Jeanne Bates (*Mrs X*), Judith Anna Roberts
(*Beautiful Girl Across the Hall*), Laurel Near (*Lady in the Radiator*),
V. Phipps-Wilson (*Landlady*), Jack Fisk (*Man in the Planet*), Jean
Lange (*Grandmother*), Thomas Coulson (*The Boy*), John Monez
(*Bum*), Darwin Joston (*Paul*), Neil Moran (*The Boss*), Hal Landon Jr
(*Pencil-Machine Operator*), Jennifer Lynch (*Little Girl*), Brad Keeler
(*Little Boy*), Peggy Lynch, Doddie Keeler (*People Digging in the
Alley*), Gill Dennis (*Man with Cigar*), Toby Keeler (*Man Fighting*),
Raymond Walsh (*Mr Roundheels*)

ALTERNATIVE TITLE: In France, *Eraserhead* was finally released
(following the success of *The Elephant Man*) in 1981, under the name
Labyrinth Man.

TITLE SEQUENCE: An ominous rushing sound builds as a caption
fades up on black: 'DAVID LYNCH presents'. The image switches to that
of a mottled sphere (the planet), seemingly resting on the head of what
appears to be a man (Henry Spencer), lying on his side in the
foreground. A large rendering of the title appears above this image,
stretching the full width of the screen. The planet remains motionless
as the man's head, still viewed sideways on, slowly lifts into frame,
revealing a furrowed brow and a sad look in his single exposed eye.
The title fades from view as the planet and the man's head merge in
double exposure, before the head returns to its original position and
rises again, this time above the planet, a dreamy look on the man's

face. His head continues to moves around the planet, which seems to grow larger in our view, pulsating in a grotesque and unnatural manner, as the man's head moves out of frame. The camera continues to move in on the planet, down through its rugged, organic surface, until a crusty-faced man (The Man in the Planet) is revealed, sitting by a window with its glass broken. Henry slowly opens his mouth as the image of a spindly, misshapen foetus appears in double exposure, gyrating as The Man in the Planet stirs and begins pulling his levers. As he does so, the foetus pictured in Henry's thoughts leaves Henry's mind and drops into a puddle of liquid. Henry's baby is about to be born.

SUMMARY: Henry Spencer, a young man with unusually tall hair and a dark suit with a pocket protector full of writing implements, arrives home at his apartment. A beautiful woman across the hall gives him a phone message from a girl named Mary, who is expecting Henry at her parents' house for dinner. Henry, who seems to have thought the relationship was over, braves the frightening sounds of the city and heads for Mary's place where, after surreal exchanges with her parents, and an even more bizarre dinner, he is shocked to be told that he and Mary have a baby. Later, at Henry's apartment, Mary feeds the deformed and bandaged infant, which mews and spits until she can stand no more. She leaves Henry and the baby to it. Alone with the pathetic creature that is growing sicker with each passing day, Henry finds no escape from the responsibility of looking after it; every time he tries to leave the apartment, it cries forlornly, forcing him to remain by its side. His only comfort comes from the presence he imagines in the room's radiator – a dancing girl who smiles and sings for him while wormlike organisms fall around her – and the beautiful neighbour, with whom he has a brief but cathartic tryst. Following his adultery, Henry's guilt preys on his mind, until he imagines himself meeting the Lady in the Radiator, placed in the dock for his thoughtless 'crime', decapitated, his head sold to a pencil factory, where it will be made into penciltop erasers. Emerging from his nightmare, Henry realises what he must do: he cuts the baby's bandages, exposes its innards, and kills it out of mercy. Electricity is in the air as Henry's world disintegrates, but the warmth of the Lady in the Radiator's smile seems to offer Henry hope, salvation, redemption. After all, she tells him, 'In heaven, everything is fine.'

PRODUCTION HISTORY: Having won his place at the American Film Institute's (AFI) recently opened Center of Advanced Film Studies in Beverly Hills, California – thanks in part to his short film script *Gardenback* [see **'In Dreams,'** page 245] – Lynch now found himself with a new project that interested him more, tentatively entitled *Eraserhead*. 'My original image was of a man's head bouncing on the ground, being picked up by a boy and taken to a pencil factory,' he told *Time*. 'I don't know where it came from.'

Having tried unsuccessfully to adapt *Gardenback* into feature form, Lynch ultimately abandoned the idea and, with the tacit approval of the AFI, borrowed the main characters and the germ of the story for his new project. 'I was excited about *Eraserhead* because it was something to do with *Gardenback* but it was so much more,' Lynch explained. 'I don't like films that are a one-thing film, and since the theme of *Gardenback* was adultery, all the scenes had to be tailored so that theme could be explored. Life isn't that way to me.'

Lynch considered his twenty-one-page 'script', which was like a free-form poem, to be a suitable basis for a feature-length film. Given that the general rule of thumb is that each page of a script translates to roughly one minute of film, the AFI could be forgiven for taking the view that *Eraserhead* would be around twenty minutes in duration; however, they had failed to reckon on Lynch's propensity for pause and effect, and to realise that minutes might pass between dialogue lines separated on the page by a single paragraph. After some negotiating, Lynch was given ten thousand dollars for a forty-two-minute film, shot in black and white, on 35mm film. (It was a measure of Lynch's commitment to *Eraserhead* that he was willing to proceed for a fifth of the money he had been offered, by an independent producer, to turn *Gardenback* into a feature.) The production was scheduled to last six weeks.

Preparation began in early 1972, with Lynch looking to stretch his allocated budget as far as possible, by recruiting friends and family to help out with everything from set construction (Lynch's brother, John) to hair styling (Jack Nance's wife, Catherine Coulson). Necessity was the mother of invention, but fate also played a part. First, Lynch found that in the grounds of the Center were several vacant outbuildings, including what would once have been stables, garages, greenhouses, servants' quarters and a huge hayloft. Second, Lynch managed to purchase, for a hundred dollars, a 'job lot' of 'flats' – two-dimensional backdrops – from a motion-picture studio that was going out of business. Now Lynch had his studio, and the materials to build his sets. As filming progressed, the 'flats' would be repeatedly removed, repainted (often by Lynch himself) and reused, turning the hayloft from one location to another.

Slowly but surely, Lynch gathered his crew, many of whom would take as many as five or six unofficial roles in the production. Lynch's long-time friend Jack Fisk introduced him to Doreen G. Small, with whom Fisk had worked on a 'blaxploitation' film, *Cool Breeze* (1972), and who would act as production manager during *Eraserhead*'s first year of production. Lynch was introduced to cinematographer Herbert Cardwell through Calvin Productions, the industrial film company which had assisted with sound for *The Alphabet* and *The Grandmother*, and for whom Alan R. Splet had worked before being invited to join the permanent staff of the Center. The final member of the crew, Catherine Coulson, became involved simply by being around the set as much as her husband, lead actor Jack Nance.

'We worked very meticulously,' Nance understated. 'Every reaction, every look, everything that was happening inside Henry's head . . . we had to get into that in great detail. I don't think it was ever *analysed*,' he told *Cinefantastique*, '[but] we had these long, strange conversations – "skull sessions" – and things would reveal themselves to us as we were going along.' Lynch had similar memories of rehearsals. 'Jack [Nance] and I would rehearse every move. Jack was like the most expert actor I have ever worked with,' he added. 'He would go into minute detail on an arm move.'

During this protracted pre-production period, two key elements of the film's enduring iconography were determined. The first was Henry's signature hairstyle, which Lynch wanted short at the back and sides, and teased up on top. The second was Henry and Mary's malformed progeny, a relatively unsophisticated but highly convincing animatronic that Nance promptly nicknamed 'Spike'. Although other members of the crew have credited Lynch with both creations, the director has steadfastly resisted talking about the design of the baby in particular, seeking, successfully, to retain the mystery of its design and functionality, since Lynch believes that to explain special effects is to reduce their magic, mystery and power to a mere technical accomplishment. The reality, of course, was that the design and function of the creature was probably much simpler than audiences imagined. 'It rose for a while and then it went down for a while,' he has said of the mewing, eye-rolling mutant whose malformed body is wrapped in bandages like the swaddling clothes of yore. In fact, 'Jack [Nance] always used to say it might as well just be a sock with a couple of buttons,' he added. 'That's what I loved about the whole *Eraserhead* thing,' he told *Cinefantastique*: 'faking it, but still taking the time to get it right and get the mood.'

Shooting began on 29 May 1972, on which day several senior AFI personnel – Frank Daniel, Antonio Vellani and others – dropped by to check on things, and left satisfied that all was under control. The day shoots did not last, however. Since the grounds around the makeshift studio were used during the day by the Beverly Hills parks department, even the ingenious soundproofing devised by Lynch and Splet failed to buffer the noise of parks department vehicles. Instead, Lynch decided to switch to night shoots, allowing him greater control over the variables and the crew to continue their day jobs. A year later, they were still shooting.

The extended production period took its toll on the crew. Conflicting professional duties and financial demands led Herb Cardwell to leave the production after nine months, to be replaced by Lynch's fellow AFI student Frederick Elmes. Elmes recalls being shown a couple of reels so that he could decide what he thought. 'They started with the real tame stuff . . . and then they got to the baby, which they saved for the end. And – *God!* – I didn't know what to make of it. It was bizarre, but captivating at the same time. I just didn't know what I was getting involved in. But I really was hooked right from the beginning.'

Such personnel changes – Doreen Small also left after a year – added to *Eraserhead*'s already extended production schedule, which ran into months, and then years. 'After a film's going for a couple of years, you sort of find your rhythm,' Lynch said, as though all film-makers should enjoy such scheduling luxury. 'We normally did about one shot a night. A "master shot" would definitely be lighting all night.' 'It just turned into this monster we couldn't finish,' Nance told the *Los Angeles Times* in 1990. 'It was a killer, but Lynch wouldn't give it up. We couldn't give it up. We had almost all of the script, but we couldn't put any of it together. So we kept shooting.' There were times, Lynch admits, when he thought the film would never be completed. 'At one time,' he told Jonathan Ross, 'I was thinking about building a small, eight-inch-tall Henry and stop-motioning him through some small cardboard sets, just to fill in the blanks, just to get it finished.'

Ideas would sometimes present themselves just as production seemed finally to be drawing to a close, most notably when Lynch was looking for a way to lighten the film's mood, and perhaps provide a more optimistic dénouement than his original ending, in which Henry's killing of the baby leads to the destruction of his world. Lynch recalls how one day he was sitting in the makeshift canteen where Catherine Coulson would prepare three meals per night for the cast and crew, 'and I just drew this little lady, and little foetuses were falling out of her. And I thought she would live in the radiator, where it's nice and warm, and this would be a real comfort for Henry.' Lynch immediately ran to the radiator on the set of Henry's room, and noticed a little square in it, which he felt would be perfect to house what would become known as 'the Lady in the Radiator'.

There were also more practical reasons why a film originally supposed to shoot for six weeks wound up taking several *years* from script to screen. 'To put it simply, we were broke,' Nance told *Wrapped in Plastic*, the *Twin Peaks* fanzine. 'We would shoot and we'd go broke. We would have to steal raw stock. We had to build a set and shoot, then tear down the set and build another set on top of it. There was sometimes no more than three or four of us working on the picture.' Although Nance somehow managed to keep his hair in the same style for four years, the extended production period led to some bizarre continuity challenges, such as the eighteen-month interval between one shot and another. 'I was sitting at the edge of the bed,' Nance told the *Los Angeles Times*, 'and I got up and went through the door in one scene, and it was a year and a half before I walked out the other side.'

CASTING: The principal discovery of *Eraserhead* was actor Jack Nance, who had appeared in a single film (1969's *Bushman*) by the time he was introduced to Lynch in 1970 via a mutual friend, who thought that Nance might be the perfect actor for Lynch's partly scripted short-film project, *Eraserhead*. 'He gave me several pages of this script,' Nance told *Wrapped in Plastic* in 1995, a year before his death. 'It was kind of confusing . . . a little unorthodox. I mean, there were these strange characters, and I didn't quite get it. He was talking about this weird world that these characters lived in.' Lynch left the script with Nance overnight, and screened *The Grandmother* for him the next day. 'Suddenly I saw what *Eraserhead* was all about,' Nance continued, 'what Lynch's "eye" was like. It was, like, all of a sudden there was nothing more in the world I wanted to do than *Eraserhead*.'

Lynch was introduced to Charlotte Stewart (later *Little House on the Prairie*'s schoolteacher) through her room-mate, production manager Doreen G. Small. The director found his other cast members among friends and family: Jack Fisk as The Man in the Planet; Lynch's wife Peggy and two of their progeny; three members of the Keeler family; Jack Nance's wife, Catherine Coulson; her cousin Thomas Coulson; and so on. Three other members of the cast – Judith Roberts (The Beautiful Woman Across the Hall), Allen Joseph (Bill X) and Jeanne Bates (Mrs X) had all belonged to a local theatre workshop, Theatre West.

THE LYNCH MOB: *Eraserhead*'s leading actor would, as Jack Nance, become one of Lynch's living trademarks, appearing in *Dune*, *Blue Velvet*, *The Cowboy and the Frenchman*, *Twin Peaks* (with Charlotte Stewart), *Wild at Heart*, *Fire Walk With Me* and *Lost Highway*. His friendship with Lynch continued until his death on 30 December 1996. 'Two months before his death,' Lynch recalled, 'we organised a little *Eraserhead* reunion. He looked to me to be in good shape. We joked, laughed – it was the last time that I saw him.'

Behind the scenes, the relationships were equally important. Jack

Fisk (The Man in the Planet) had originally sculpted Lynch's head for his first venture into film, *Six Figures Getting Sick*, and would go on to direct an episode of *On the Air*, and serve as production designer for *The Straight Story* and *Mulholland Drive*; Alan R. Splet had worked on the extraordinary sound effects for *The Grandmother*, and would collaborate with Lynch on *The Elephant Man*, *Dune* and *Blue Velvet*; cinematographer Frederick Elmes would photograph *Blue Velvet*, *The Cowboy and the Frenchman* and *Wild at Heart*; Catherine Coulson would play the popular Log Lady, Margaret Lanterman, in *Twin Peaks*; even Sissy Spacek (who provided unofficial production funding for *Eraserhead*, and is duly thanked in the credits), would go on to co-star in *The Straight Story*.

MEMORABLE QUOTES
Mary X: 'You're late, Henry.'
Henry: 'I didn't know if you wanted me to come or not! Where have you been? You never come around any more.'

Mrs X: 'Mary tells me you're a very nice fellow. What do you do?'
Henry: 'Oh, oh, I'm on vacation.'

Mr X: 'We've got chicken tonight. Craziest damn' things – they're man-made! Little damn' things! Smaller than my fist! Th-they're new!'

Mrs X: 'Have you and Mary had sexual intercourse?'

Mrs X: 'There's a baby. It's at the hospital. And you're the father.'
Henry: 'That's impossible, it's only been –'
Mary X: 'Mother, they're still not sure it *is* a baby!'

SOUND AND MUSIC: Lynch has often said that the element of sound is fifty per cent of each of his films, and this attitude was clearly in place by the time he set to work with Alan R. Splet on the extraordinary sound of *Eraserhead*. This time, the sound elements would be less organic than they had been in *The Grandmother*; instead, Lynch and Splet opted for a constant industrial sound, so that even sounds that should be organic – rolling thunder, suckling puppies, the rubbing of an eye, the Lady in the Radiator squashing the wormlike organisms – have the ominous presence of warped machinery. 'Alan Splet and I worked together in a little garage studio, with a big console and two or three tape recorders, and worked with a couple of different sound libraries for organic effects,' Lynch explained. 'Then we fed them through the console. It's all natural sounds. No Moog synthesisers. Just changes like a graphic equaliser, reverb, a Little Dipper filter set for peaking certain frequences and dipping out things, or reversing and cutting things together.'

At the beginning of the film, the prevailing sound was an atmospheric 'rushing', like an amplified version of the normal sound that exists in any open space, recordings of which are normally held by sound libraries for use in studios. 'I just took this one "presence" [recording] that we had in the library, called "Early Morning Presence",' Splet told *Cinefantastique*, 'and while we were sitting there, I started fiddling around with it, and I just stuck it through this one-third-octave graphic equaliser that I had, and opened it up. The sound started to open out, and we said, "My God, that's it!"' This kind of accidental discovery was typical of Lynch's working method. 'You don't know how something like that happens,' Splet said, wondering whether it was a conscious decision or a lucky accident, 'but it was the right sound.'

Finding just the right sound took many months, and it was only when Lynch decided that the film might have a chance of selection at the 1976 Cannes Film Festival that he and Splet began working around the clock, spending some six weeks on sound editing, before the music and dialogue were added in the final sound mix, which remains one of the most remarkable ever put to film.

Eraserhead's highly unusual soundtrack album (70027) contains this and many other industrial sounds, as well as excerpts from 'Digha's Stomp', 'Lennox Avenue Blues' and 'Messin' Around with the Blues' by Thomas 'Fats' Waller, 'Stompin' the Bug' by Phil Worde and Mercedes Gilbert, and 'In Heaven (Lady in the Radiator Song)', with lyrics by Lynch and music by Peter Ivers.

A cover version of 'In Heaven' was recorded by Boston-based rock group the Pixies for a BBC John Peel Show on 3 May 1988, and transmitted a fortnight later. The recording appears on the group's 1998 compilation album, *Pixies at the BBC* (GAD 8013 CD).

INFLUENCED BY: In her review of *Eraserhead*, *New Yorker* critic Pauline Kael noted the influence of Fritz Lang's *M* (1931), Luis Buñuel's *Un Chien Andalou* (1928) and Jean Cocteau's *Le Sang d'un Poète* (aka *Blood of a Poet*, 1930) on Lynch's film. Acknowledging his admiration for the latter, Lynch said, 'In my opinion, Cocteau is the heavyweight of surrealism. In this film, certain fears and uneasy feelings and questions manifest themselves in this phyiscal world, and [Cocteau] gets right off to this uneasy feeling right from the beginning.' The sequence in which Henry loses his head recalls two other surrealist films: René Clair's *Entr'acte* (1924) and Hans Richter's *Ghosts Before Breakfast* (1928), both of which Lynch had seen and admired. The latter film's central figure bears a striking physical resemblance to Henry in *Eraserhead*, even having the same unusual haircut.

Nevertheless, as Lynch has pointed out on many occasions, the greatest influence on his work in general, and on *Eraserhead* in particular, was the city of Philadelphia, to which Lynch moved at the age of nineteen, leaving behind his idyllic, small-town, white-picket-fence-and-droning-aeroplanes upbringing. 'Philadelphia was a city filled with fear, filled with twisted behaviour,' he recalled. 'There was sort of a sickness in the air, a twisted, infectious sickness, and it became the city. But it was very powerful, and a lot of Philadelphia seeped into me.' Lynch admits that '*Eraserhead* is the real *Philadelphia Story*.'

LEGACY: In the years following its initially limited exposure, as it steadily gained a wider audience, *Eraserhead* became shorthand for anything abstract, experimental, or avant-garde. Nevertheless, the film was more widely talked about than it was screened, and it was not until Lynch found more mainstream success with *Twin Peaks* that emergent independent film distributor Miramax Films stepped in to announce that it was planning a theatrical re-release of *Eraserhead*, described in Miramax publicity as 'an eerily erotic sci-fi parable of the responsibilities of parenthood', on a comparatively massive scale. 'There's a lot of interest in David Lynch,' Miramax's executive vice president Russell Schwartz told the *Los Angeles Times* in August 1991. 'And we think it would be fun taking a cult classic which for years played only at midnight shows and turning it into a mainstream picture.' Lynch was evidently enthusiastic. 'Those people who are familiar with David are more in touch with *Blue Velvet* and *Wild at Heart* than his earlier work,' his assistant, Gaye Pope, commented. 'Bringing *Eraserhead* out again for a whole new audience who've never seen it before is a great idea.'

Earlier, in 1985, gravel-voiced blues singer Tom Waits spoke of *Eraserhead*'s influence on his stage play and album *Frank's Wild Years*, in which his stage persona is a ne'er-do-well named Frank. 'It actually starts out with Frank at the end of his rope, despondent, penniless, on a park bench in East St Louis in a snowstorm, having a going-out-of-business sale on the whole last ten years of his life,' he told *Spin* magazine. 'Then he falls asleep and dreams his way back home. I've been saying that it's a cross between *Eraserhead* and *It's a Wonderful Life*.'

According to Howard Sounes's biography of Charles Bukowski, the cult writer 'could count on the fingers of one hand the films he liked,' but 'his all-time favourite film was *Eraserhead*.' Sounes further claimed that, during the filming of *Barfly* (1987), scripted by Bukowski from his own novel, and co-starring Jack Nance, Sounes claimed that Lynch and Isabella Rossellini 'visited the set and chatted to Bukowski about *Eraserhead*'.

Many observers compared writer-director Darren Aronofsky's startling first feature, π (1998), to *Eraserhead*: in addition to the cinematography and sound, the central character, Max, leads the same kind of fractured life as Henry, betrayed and perplexed by the world surrounding him. But while Aronofsky admits to an admiration of Lynch, he claims that π was not directly influenced, as many suggested, by *Eraserhead*. 'I always have seen Lynch as an expressionist,' he says. 'He's about emotions and mood very much like Fellini. The first film I saw of his was actually *Blue Velvet*. It touched me in a very deep way and I remember how off we all felt for days afterwards. I think that his work makes you live very profoundly in each and every moment, kinda like music, and that the effect of it stays with you for a very long time.'

DÉJÀ VU: Several moments in *Eraserhead* recall Lynch's earlier short *The Grandmother*: Henry sitting on his bed in solitude, the plant growing out of the mound of earth by Henry's bed, and especially Mrs X, who attempts to seduce Henry in a similar way to the boy's mother in *The Grandmother*.

THEMES AND MOTIFS: The reluctance of a new father to accept his parental responsibilities is one of the significant themes of *Eraserhead*, and the film was certainly conceived at a time when Lynch was just coming to terms with the unplanned birth of his daughter, Jennifer, in April 1968. As Lynch's long-time friend Jack Fisk told Jonathan Ross, 'He was in art school, wanting to take on the world with his painting, and found out suddenly that his girlfriend was pregnant, and got stuck with a baby. And I think it was, "Oh, no, my life has ended, I've got to become an adult." That experience, to my own mind, is probably what inspired the whole of *Eraserhead*.' Jennifer herself admitted as much. 'It was, without a doubt, inspired by my conception,' she told Ross, 'because David, in no uncertain terms, did *not* want a family. It was not his idea to get married, nor was it his idea to have children. But it happened.' Jennifer feels that too much of a connection has been made between *Eraserhead*'s deformed baby and the fact that she was born with club feet. 'Certainly it had a lot to do [with that] subconsciously, as any event that takes place in life has to do with things,' she admitted, 'but I don't think David credits that directly to where *Eraserhead* comes from. If I had to interpret it solely, I'd have to say yes, that was influential. But a lot of it was, as it is in the film, [about] a very simple man who has been thrown into a relationship and parenthood, is confused, and everything around him seems so immediately dark and strange, and he longs for this sort of clean, pure childhood image that he had before all this happened.'

Although Lynch admitted that the theme of a young man facing up to his responsibilities was a major element of *Eraserhead*, he believes that such simple explanations do the film an injustice. 'That's definitely in there,' he told *Rolling Stone*, '[but] *Eraserhead* is an abstract film. It's hopefully not just about one thing.' Besides, Lynch claims not to have been overly disturbed by Jennifer's conception, and his resulting marriage to Peggy Reavey. 'Sometimes a jolt of electricity at a certain point in your life is helpful,' he suggested. 'It forces you a little bit more awake. It makes something happen inside you. I didn't really understand what was happening, but because I had these new responsibilities, I think it really helped – it overlapped into the work. I was just starting to make films, and it made me focus in and take things more seriously.'

In his insightful book *David Lynch*, *Cahiers du Cinema* critic Michel Chion introduced another insightful observation, suggesting that Henry's (Lynch's) relationship to the child in *Eraserhead* went beyond the issue of a husband's monopoly on his wife's attention being usurped by the birth of a child. 'As the eldest of three children, [Lynch] must have experienced the first-born's drama of being deprived by an intruder of the exclusive love of his parents,' he observed. 'The dreadful baby in *Eraserhead*, whom everyone wants to kill and get rid of, represents what a first-born child can feel as it sees the wrinkled, screaming thing which comes to the family and steals its place.' Both of these themes are related to another, however: that of alienation, a feeling with which Lynch was familiar following his move to Philadelphia at the age of nineteen.

ALTERNATIVE VERSION / CUT SCENES: The appearance of several characters among the credits – Landlady, Little Girl, Little Boy, and People Digging in the Alley – which do not appear in the release version of *Eraserhead* is an obvious clue to the existence of a longer version. 'We wound up with enough film to circle the equator,' Nance told the *Los Angeles Times*, 'and David said, "I think we're just going to have to cut."' In fact, the version Lynch screened for the AFI, and later at the Filmex Film Festival, was around one hundred minutes in duration, perhaps even longer. Immediately after the screening, Lynch made a decision as painful as Henry's cutting open of the baby's bandages: to cut several scenes – three or four, as he recalls – from the film. 'A film isn't finished till it's finished,' he says, 'and *Eraserhead* didn't have to be finished till after that festival. The festival forced me to see what needed to be done.'

Details of several of the excised scenes remain sketchy. Certainly,

Lynch cut the scene in which Mr and Mrs X bring Mary and the baby home from hospital, as well as those of Henry receiving a telephone call, and Mary having a seizure in Henry's apartment. Another deleted scene was one for which Lynch had apparently found it necessary to dissect a cat. 'Some kids use wire and do a cat in, and Henry trips on the wire,' he recalled. 'It's just underneath the frame line, where he walks through those oil tanks – the cast was there.'

In another lost scene, Henry looks out of his window and, seeing two children digging for dimes in an alleyway, leaves his room and heads downstairs. Halfway down the hallway, the baby starts crying, but this time Henry doesn't stop; he goes all the way down the stairs (he cannot call the lift, because the landlady has propped the door open with a mop) but can still hear the sound of the baby crying coming down the lift shaft. Angrily kicking a couch leg, he is caught by the landlady, who scolds him and sends him back upstairs to his room. Lynch recalled that when Henry returns to his room, he sees that the kids are gone and some adults are alternately fighting over the dimes and digging. Only a brief glimpse of the men (one of whom is Lynch's friend Toby Keeler) fighting remains.

A further deleted scene was one in which Henry peers into a room next to his and sees two women (Catherine Coulson and V. Phipps-Wilson) in short white dresses, tied to a bed, while a man (Gill Dennis) with a complex piece of electrical apparatus that is sparking and fizzing moves towards them menacingly, smoking a cigar. Lynch took out this scene, he says, because it was too disturbing – not to the audience, but to the film. 'I didn't want anyone even to think about what was next door,' he explained.

Coulson – whose only other intended scene, playing a disgusted nurse who hands the baby over to its parents, was never filmed – was sorry to see her fleeting on-screen appearance go. 'I think it would be fun to say I acted in *Eraserhead*,' she told *Cinefantastique*. 'I wished that sometime David would show these scenes that he cut.' In fact, at the tenth-anniversary *Twin Peaks* fan festival in 2000, Coulson allegedly gave birth to the rumour that Lynch was planning to release the original hundred-minute cut of *Eraserhead*, probably on DVD, and almost certainly through his own website, davidlynch.com. Nonsense, says Lynch. 'It's like a guy with a hunchback growth, and you meet a pretty good surgeon, [who] takes it off, cleans it up, hardly any scars, and you go away. And you're very thankful that that's gone.'

TRAILER: The most widely screened trailer for *Eraserhead* was a series of images, each intercut with black, and accompanied by the rhythmic pulsing from the film's soundtrack. The images are as follows: Henry, as seen in the title sequence; the Man in the Planet;

Henry looking over his shoulder; the two halves of Mary X's picture being placed together; Mr X gesturing; a close-up of the baby's eye; a long shot of the stage, with Henry's head lying in a pool of blood; the couple across the hall; the Lady in the Radiator squashing things underfoot; the boy with Henry's head; Henry recoiling in horror; and finally, as the sound changes, the classic shot of Henry with eraser particles billowing about his head, followed by the title. No dialogue or synchronised sound is heard.

POSTER: A single image defines almost every poster for *Eraserhead*, in every format, in every country: a monochrome head-shot of Henry (Jack Nance), with illuminated powder billowing about his head.

TAG-LINE: The line 'In heaven, everything is fine,' taken from The Lady in the Radiator's song, was sometimes used during *Eraserhead*'s re-release.

WHAT THE PAPERS SAID: The original, hundred-minute version of *Eraserhead* received its first public screening on 19 March 1977, at the Filmex Film Festival in Los Angeles. 'There was this real pregnant pause,' Nance, who was present, said of the audience's reaction. 'There was this stunned silence. Then this applause started. [The audience] just stood up, and it was beautiful.'

However, one member of the audience was not applauding: a critic from industry bible *Variety*, dispatched to Filmex for the purpose of reviewing the many new films being unveiled there. '*Eraserhead* is a sickening bad-taste exercise,' began *Variety*'s withering review. 'Set, apparently, in some undefined post-apocalyptic future era, *Eraserhead* consists mostly of a man sitting in a room trying to figure out what to do with his horribly mutated child. Lynch keeps throwing in graphic close-ups of the piteous creature, and pulls out all gory stops in the unwatchable climax. Like a lot of AFI efforts, the pic has good tech values (particularly the inventive sound mixing), but little substance or subtlety.'

Most reviewers, including the *New Yorker*'s formidable film critic, Pauline Kael, took a different view. '[Lynch] seems to have reinvented the experimental-film movement,' she wrote. 'Watching this daringly irrational movie, with its interest in dream logic, you almost feel that you're seeing a European avant-garde gothic of the '20s or early '30s . . . The slow, strange rhythm is very unsettling and takes some getting used to, but it's an altogether amazing, sensuous film.'

The wide international re-release of *Eraserhead* gave the film its best notices of all. 'A masterpiece of a kind of film-making that reeks of the terror of creation,' enthused the *Guardian*'s Richard Combs, who insightfully noted that, whereas most horror films try to activate a fear of death, 'the brilliance of *Eraserhead* is that its horror is ante-natal, its characters are the pre-alive, and the limbo they inhabit isn't conventionally terrifying but has an airless, oppressive nothingness (vaguely fifties-ish).' In a five-star ('UNMISSABLE') review in *Empire*, Steve Beard celebrated the fact that 'no matter how many cheesy pop video or arty horror flicks rip off its (very late-seventies) aesthetic of slimy industrial decay, this film remains as powerful, original and disturbing as ever.'

BOX OFFICE: Following its debut at the Los Angeles Film Festival, *Eraserhead* began to creep out on the 'midnight movie' circuit courtesy of New York's prominent underground film distributor Ben Barenholtz, who had propelled films like Dennis Hopper's *Easy Rider* (1969), Alexandro Jodorowsky's *El Topo* (1971), Perry Henzell's *The Harder They Come* (1973) and John Waters's *Pink Flamingos* (1972) to success. Indeed, during publicity for his latest film, *Desperate Living* (1977), Waters fuelled interest in *Eraserhead* by championing Lynch's film at his own press conference. Slowly but surely, *Eraserhead* began to earn a cult following of its own, playing in one Los Angeles cinema every week for four years, its successful run continuing through the release of *The Elephant Man*.

It is difficult to quantify how much money the film earned during its initial release, and even during its successful re-issue in the early 1990s. But the fact that it continues to make money for all of the cast and crew members to whom Lynch generously gave a share of the profits would seem to be a good sign.

AWARDS: *Eraserhead* had taken four years to make, and several years to find an audience of any real size; Lynch could wait for the film to win its first awards. Having failed to qualify for film festivals in Cannes and New York prior to its theatrical distribution, word of mouth began to spread worldwide and *Eraserhead* found itself accepted into festivals like Edinburgh, Scotland, and Avoriaz, France, where a jury presided over by William Friedkin (*The Exorcist*) awarded it the Golden Antenna and Jurors' Choice awards. (The film was also nominated for Best Film at the Fantasporto International Fantasy Film awards in 1982 – a clear indication of the length of time it took the film to reach many European territories.)

In 1991, Lynch became the first recipient of the American Film Institute's Franklin J. Schaffner Alumni Medal, an acknowledgement of one of the AFI's most successful students.

CONTROVERSY: The only real controversy surrounding *Eraserhead* concerns the nature of the baby, which for more than a quarter of a century has remained a mystery. Conspiracy theories abound: after all, if Lynch shaved a mouse, dissected a cat and did God-knows-what-else to give verisimilitude to various peripheral props, might he not have gone a stage further for the most important 'prop' of all? Lynch was first grilled on the topic in 1978, while *Eraserhead* was playing at weekend midnights at New York's Cinema Village. The *SoHo Weekly News*'s Stephen Saban asked Lynch if he had used a calf foetus. 'That's what a lot of people think it is,' Lynch replied evasively. Was it battery-operated? Saban pressed. 'I really don't . . .' Lynch credits a doctor in the film, Saban observed. Was that related? 'Well, I was looking into different ways, you know, in the beginning . . .' After a long silence, Saban asked if Lynch was loath to reveal the secret behind the creation because it would be giving away a technical secret, or because it would get him arrested. 'You know,' Lynch replied, 'there's no promotional photos of the baby because people, like, uh . . . you know . . . it's, like, nice to discover along in the film and to not know, like, much about it.'

TRIVIA: In 1977, the actor who would become familiar – especially, over the coming years, to Lynch fans – as Jack Nance, preferred to be credited as *John* Nance, a contraction of his real name, Marvin John Nance.

During the making of *Eraserhead*, Lynch divorced his first wife, Peggy Reavey, the mother of his daughter, Jennifer. In 1977, he married Jack Fisk's sister, Mary. (They divorced in 1982, the year that their son, Austin Jack, was born.)

In 1979, Lynch was thrilled to learn that Stanley Kubrick, one of his all-time favourite directors, had screened *Eraserhead* for the cast and crew of *The Shining*, in order to put them in the mood for the film he was making.

APOCRYPHA: Just how long *did Eraserhead* take to make? Some say five years, some say six. In fact, from pre-production in the spring of 1972 to the completion of post-production around April 1976 was 'only' four years. It was fitting, then, that the film should remain on release in its native Los Angeles for the same length of time.

The gaffe squad – that loosely-formed and self-appointed cabal whose *raison d'être* is to spot unimportant errors in important movies – is fond of pointing out that, early in the film, Henry puts his right foot in a puddle, yet by the time he gets to his apartment, his left foot is wet. A subgroup of the gaffe squad – those who read great meaning into trivial mistakes – wonders whether this detail has any significance. None, according to Lynch. 'We couldn't remember which shoe went into the puddle,' he admitted to *Cinefantastique*. As Jack Nance would put it, with an exasperated look more Pete Martell than Henry, 'People write all this stuff about *Eraserhead*, and they get real psychological about it.'

Swiss artist and designer H. R. Giger, who toiled on Alexandro Jodorowsky and Ridley Scott versions of *Dune* (1984), denied the alleged influence of the *Eraserhead* baby on the baby alien 'chestburster' in *Alien* (1979), for which Giger won an Academy Award. 'I've been told that [Lynch] thinks we stole his *Eraserhead* baby for the alien chestburster, but that's not true,' Giger, whose designs for *Dune* were rejected by Lynch, told *Fear* magazine. 'I told Ridley Scott that he should see [*Eraserhead*], though he never did. David Lynch said that it was filmed exactly as his was, but it couldn't have been, because Ridley hadn't seen it!'

AVAILABILITY: *Eraserhead*'s theatrical re-release across Europe, using a new telecine transfer and Dolby soundtrack, in turn led to an improvement in the quality of the existing PAL video (051 8003). In the UK, *Eraserhead* is also available as a full screen (4:3) Region 2 DVD (078 069 2), also including the theatrical trailer.

The Japanese (Region 2) DVD (BBBF-1256), also available as part of The Lynch Box (BBBF-1210), features a near-perfect 'letterboxed' transfer, the US and Japanese theatrical trailers, a strange isolated version of 'In Heaven, Everything is Fine', and a Japanese television advertisement. Lynch had no involvement with this edition, claiming that 'it would probably make me sick if I saw it, for a lot of reasons. I'm trying to get a really good *Eraserhead* DVD, clean and perfect,' he adds. 'But I haven't got it yet.'

FINAL ANALYSIS: The term 'cult movie' is as overused and misapplied as the term 'genius', but *Eraserhead* defines the former term as surely as it defines its auteur as the latter. The problem with cults, however, is that they pass; looking at the other so-called 'cult' films of the 1970s it is hard to find one that has retained as much power, and remained as timeless, as Lynch's first feature. The black-and-white photography, anonymity of its setting and agelessness of its themes have allowed *Eraserhead* to stand the test of time, while its pioneering use of sound and ingenious special effects mark it as truly something special. Many of the images in the film are not merely unforgettable (another overused term), but wholly *indelible*. Played in a cinema, with the almost unbearable sound turned up to almost unbearable levels, the film does not merely take its audience captive, but rivets them to their chairs, their faces expressing that mixture of fascination and horror usually reserved for traffic accidents.

Despite more than two decades of conjecture about what it means to Lynch, it hardly matters; for, as with any truly great work of art, *Eraserhead*'s meaning and importance should be derived, subjectively, from the viewer, serving as a kind of Rorschach test that provokes both an immediate reaction and a lasting one, remaining imprinted on the memory long after the credits have rolled – whether you like it or not.

EXPERT WITNESS: 'I was there all day . . . you know, pulling levers, and it was hard work. I was used to like painting this plastic stuff on my face and making sores because he asked me to play The Man on the Planet. It looked great but it wasn't removable. I sort of did a combination of soaking and scraping and shaving and I think that about three days later my face was clean-shaven and free of all the make-up of that film.' – actor Jack Fisk (The Man in the Planet)

LYNCH ON *ERASERHEAD*: 'I [once] said it was a perfect film. Well, it was just that one day. I might have been very relaxed, and it was a long time ago, and it just struck me as, you know, perfect. But nothing is perfect. And you can shoot for it – you've *got* to shoot for it – but there's just no such thing as a perfect film.'

The Elephant Man (1980)

35mm feature / 125 mins / black and white / live action

Directed by David Lynch
Produced by Jonathan Sanger
Executive Producer Stuart Cornfeld
Screenplay by Christopher De Vore, Eric Bergren, David Lynch
Based on *The Elephant Man and Other Reminiscences* by Sir Frederick Treves and in part on *The Elephant Man: A Study in Human Dignity* by Ashley Montagu
Music by John Morris
Edited by Anne V. Coates
Production Designed by Stuart Craig
Director of Photography Freddie Francis

CAST: Anthony Hopkins (*Frederick Treves*), John Hurt (*John Merrick*), Anne Bancroft (*Madge Kendal*), John Gielgud (*F. C. Carr-Gomm*), Wendy Hiller (*Mrs Mothershead*), Freddie Jones (*Bytes*), Michael Elphick (*Night Porter*), Hannah Gordon (*Anne Treves*), Helen Ryan (*Alexandra, Princess of Wales*), John Standing (*Fox*), Dexter Fletcher (*Bytes's Boy*), Lesley Dunlop (*Nora Ireland*), Phoebe Nicholls (*Merrick's Mother*), Pat Gorman (*Fairground Bobby*), Claire

Davenport (*Fat Lady*), Orla Pederson (*Skeleton Man*), Patsy Smart (*Distraught Woman*), Frederick Treves (*Alderman*), Stromboli (*Fire Eater*), Richard Hunter (*Hodges*), James Cormack (*Pierce*), Robert Bush (*Messenger*), Roy Evans (*Cabman*), Joan Rhodes (*Cook*), Nula Conwell (*Nurse Kathleen*), Tony London (*Young Porter*), Alfie Curtis (*Charles, the Milkman*), Bernadette Milnes (*1st Fighting Woman*), Brenda Kempner (*2nd Fighting Woman*), Carole Harrison (*Tart*), Hugh Manning (*Broadneck*), Dennis Burgess (*1st Committee Man*), Morgan Sheppard (*Man in Pub*), Fanny Carby (*Mrs Kendal's Dresser*), Kathleen Byron (*Lady Waddington*), Gerald Case (*Lord Waddington*), David Ryall (*Man with Whores*), Deirdre Costello (*1st Whore*), Pauline Quirke (*2nd Whore*), Kenny Baker (*Plumed Dwarf*), Chris Greener (*Giant*), Marcus Powell (*Midget*), Gilda Cohen (*Midget*), Lisa Scoble (*Siamese Twin*), Teri Scoble (*Siamese Twin*), Eiji Kusuhara (*Japanese Bleeder*), Robert Day (*Little Jim*), Patricia Hodge (*Screaming Mum*), Tommy Wright (*First Bobby*), Peter Davidson (*Second Bobby*), John Rapley (*King in Panto*), Hugh Spight (*Puss in Panto*), Teresa Codling (*Princess in Panto*), Marion Betzold (*Principal Boy*), Caroline Haigh (*Tree*), Florenzio Morgado (*Tree*), Victor Kravchenko (*Lion/Coachman*), Beryl Hicks (*Fairy*), Michele Amas (*Horse*), Luci Alford (*Horse*), Penny Wright (*Horse*), Janie Kells (*Horse*), Lydia Lisle (*Merrick's Mother*)

UNCREDITED CAST: Co-writers Christopher De Vore and Eric Bergren were both given tiny, non-speaking roles in the film; neither are credited. Lesley Dunlop's name appears twice in the credits, misspelled 'Leslie' on one occasion.

UNCREDITED CREW: Despite the fact that he more than fulfilled the duties of a producer, Mel Brooks's name does not appear in the credits of *The Elephant Man* since, as writer and director of such films as *The Producers* (1968), *Blazing Saddles* (1974) and the black-and-white *Young Frankenstein* (1974), Brooks felt that his long association with comedy might give audiences the wrong impression about the serious nature of what would be the first film from his newly formed production company, Brooksfilms.

TITLE SEQUENCE: As John Morris's gentle title music plays, the simplest of white credits appear in sequence on a black background, the only elaboration being the slightly Victorian styling of the title itself.

SUMMARY: In Victorian England, eminent physician Frederick Treves discovers a seriously deformed man being exhibited as 'The Elephant Man' by a freak-show proprietor named Bytes. Treves borrows the wretched man, whom he assumes to be an uneducated imbecile, and presents him to fellow members of the Pathological Society, before returning him to Bytes, who savagely beats him. When the so-called Elephant Man, whose name is John Merrick, is admitted to hospital under Treves's care, the doctor discovers that he can talk and is educated. After initial difficulties, the incurable Merrick – who can only sleep safely sitting up, supported by pillows – is accepted into the hospital as a permanent patient, his care paid for by the generosity of philanthropists like celebrated thespian Mrs Kendal, alerted to Merrick's plight by a letter to *The Times*. Treves even introduces the grotesquely disfigured but sweet-natured man into London society, causing self-doubt about his own motives. Merrick's torments continue, however, as a heartless night porter regularly invites drunken crowds to gawp at him in his hospital sanctuary. One night, Bytes joins the paying customers, kidnaps Merrick and takes him abroad, where he returns to his pathetic existence as part of Bytes's circus show. The other 'freaks' engineer his escape, however, and after a harrowing and humiliating journey to London, Merrick, now terminally ill, returns to Treves's care, finding peace at last. After a night of wish-fulfilment at the theatre, Merrick discards the pillows from his bed and assumes a normal sleeping position, even though he knows it will kill him. He dies in his sleep, and is reunited in death with the mother he worships.

SOURCE: Although credited as being based on two separate works – *The Elephant Man and Other Reminiscences*, the celebrated memoir of surgeon Sir Frederick Treves (1853–1923), first published in the year of his death; and *The Elephant Man: A Study in Human Dignity* by Ashley Montagu, which first appeared in 1971 – writers Christopher De Vore and Eric Bergren used only the Montagu book, which reprinted Treves's romanticised, fanciful and occasionally melodramatic memoir in full.

PRODUCTION HISTORY: Producer and assistant director Jonathan Sanger, then working with Mel Brooks (*Silent Movie*, 1976), first encountered Christopher De Vore and Eric Bergren's two-hundred-page adaptation of Treves's memoir when De Vore's girlfriend – Sanger's babysitter – passed him the script in the summer of 1978. Knowing nothing about Merrick, but immediately recognising his story's potential, Sanger took a one-year option on the script before heading to New York with Anne Bancroft to scout locations for her 1980 film *Fatso*. During Sanger's absence, Brooks read the script, suggesting that it would make an ideal first venture for his own production company, Brooksfilms.

Sanger had held the option for barely a month when he and Brooks signed a deal to make the film and began thinking about possible directors. By this time, quite independently of the Elephant Man project, Sanger had been advised to see Lynch's *Eraserhead* by another Brooks employee, Stuart Cornfeld, whose enthusiasm for the film was shared by Sanger. 'I said, "Jeez, it's amazing,"' Sanger recalls, '"really unusual and strange. I'd love to meet this guy."' Cornfeld arranged a meeting, at which Lynch told him about *Ronnie Rocket* [see 'In Dreams,' page 248], and Sanger told Lynch about *The Elephant Man*. 'He said, "Oh, I like the sound of that." He didn't know anything about it; he just liked the name.'

Having realised that nobody was going to give him the money to make *Ronnie Rocket*, but having written nothing else of his own, Lynch evidently realised that he was going to have to consider filming somebody else's script if he wanted to direct another picture before *Eraserhead* erased itself from the memories of the few who had seen it. Thus, two days after their meeting, Lynch called to express his enthusiasm for the project. If Lynch was to direct *The Elephant Man*, however, Sanger would need the approval of Mel Brooks, who had not seen *Eraserhead*, and was keen to approach British director Alan Parker (*Midnight Express*, 1978). Sanger set up a screening of *Eraserhead*, which Lynch was too nervous to attend. 'As soon as the lights went down and the movie started, I thought to myself that this was a horrendous mistake,' Sanger recalls. 'Mel Brooks is gonna think I'm an idiot! So when the lights came on, I think I had my eyes shut. I thought he was gonna hit me! But he looked at me and said, "Yes, it's an adolescent's nightmare about responsibility – I get it. I'd love to meet this guy."'

Brooks remembers his first meeting with Lynch. 'When he came in, I looked beyond him,' he told Toby Keeler. 'I thought that maybe this kid was a messenger or something because he wore a little under-jacket and, I'll never forget, his shirt was always buttoned . . . It was kind of weird. No tie. Just a shirt.' He recalls Lynch's confidence: 'He said, "We just have to move things because I have to think about directing it, not, you know, not the screenplay, but the movie."' Brooks hired him there and then.

Next, Lynch sat down with Eric Bergren and Christopher De Vore and began to restructure and rewrite the script, in which process Sanger and Brooks had a great deal of involvement. According to Sanger, Brooks's ideas ranged from the sublime to the ridiculous, 'so my function was to pick through the ideas and say, "This one is a great idea, this one is not so good, and this one we don't even wanna talk about again!" Because if we said in the room, "Mel, that's a terrible idea," he would defend it forever.'

With the script in good shape, Brooksfilms began shopping the project around various studios, looking for a financing deal in exchange for US distribution rights. Two studios were interested: Universal and Paramount, where film critic Pauline Kael – an early proponent of *Eraserhead* – had crossed 'enemy lines' to work, briefly, as a production executive. Kael read, liked and recommended the new script, but it was ultimately Paramount president Michael Eisner's decision to back the film. 'I told [Brooks] we were prepared to make the film, depending on who he had in mind to direct,' Eisner wrote later. '"David Lynch," he replied. "You've never heard of him, but I think he'd be great." Mel then sent me over *Eraserhead*.' Impressed, Eisner asked Brooks to set up a meeting with the young director. 'I envisioned Lynch as a gnomish man – unkempt, unbathed and uncontrollable,' Eisner recalled. At the meeting, however, 'Mel introduced me to the best-dressed, most lawyerly looking person in the group. Naturally it was Lynch. The meeting went well,' he added. 'Afterward, I accused Mel of reaching out to central casting for an actor to play the role of Lynch.'

Brooks and Sanger were given complete control over the film, which had the knock-on effect that Lynch, whom they trusted, had a relatively free rein. This *laissez-faire* style of production soon backfired, however. As Paramount began mobilising its forces and cast and crew lists began filling out, Lynch moved to a rented house in Wembley, Middlesex, where he made his first serious error since the film on his follow-up to *Six Figures* came out blank: he tried to build Merrick's make-up.

'I worked [on it] for two months,' Lynch told *Rolling Stone*, 'and what I built was a complete and total disaster . . . For four days, I had nightmares at night, but when I woke up, being awake was worse than the nightmares.' Much to Lynch's relief, Mel Brooks rescued him by quickly hiring special-effects expert Chris Tucker (*Star Wars*, 1977) to start again. 'We had no idea when we were creating it whether or not it would be a successful image,' actor John Hurt told the *Guardian*. 'Chris Tucker had endeavoured to do in six weeks what it would normally take six months to do.' The first make-up application took twelve hours, and throughout Hurt was terrified that the crew were going to laugh when they saw him. Yet Jonathan Sanger recalls how stunned everyone was when Hurt made his first appearance in front of the cast and crew, 'I've been on a lot of movie sets but this was the quietest. And then Anthony Hopkins came over to me and shook my hand. "It's going to work," he said. "We've got a great movie." And at that time, I knew it, too.'

The scheduling problems early in the production resulting from the make-up problems did not endear the unknown director to his cast and crew. Dexter Fletcher (*Lock, Stock and Two Smoking Barrels*, 1998), the thirteen-year-old actor who played Bytes's young apprentice, recalls Lynch's initially frosty relationship with Anthony Hopkins. 'Lynch would turn up in a huge Crombie coat and a big hat, and he would wander around with one of those camera viewfinders, setting up shots with Freddie [Francis] and mumbling, "Peachy keen! Peachy keen!" – he always used to say that all the time, so we used to call him "Peachy Keen". And suddenly Hopkins went, "WILL YOU COME OUT FROM BEHIND THAT FUCKING COAT AND HAT, FOR FUCK'S SAKE! WE CAN'T HEAR A *WORD* YOU'RE SAYING!" And then he did,' Fletcher says, 'and he was there, bright and spiky-haired, and full of life and light. After that, they got on great, as far as I remember. I just think David was obviously a bit intimidated at the beginning.'

'I used to attack directors,' Hopkins later admitted to Lawrence Grobel. 'David Lynch was . . . very unsure of himself, and I always went for the jugular with people like that; in those days I was too tightly wrapped up . . . The funny thing is,' he added, 'I can look now and see somebody like James Ivory, who is like David Lynch, doesn't seem to direct you at all, but now I enjoy that.' Lynch refuses to comment on his relationship with Hopkins during the filming of *The Elephant Man*. 'I would never say anything about those kind of things,' he states firmly.

Lynch had spent more than four years making *Eraserhead*; now he was forced to adhere to a rigid 54-day shooting schedule, and although he knew that Brooks and Sanger were behind him one hundred per cent, he would later admit to having been in 'the worst, darkest hell' for most of the shoot. Thankfully, he was unaware of the fact that most of the British crew were not confident about his methods. After shooting was completed, Lynch did find out. Terry Clegg, the production manager, expressed his disappointment with the film and the crew wrote Lynch a letter telling him all the things they thought were wrong with it. Happily, Lynch recalls how, about two months later, he received a call from Clegg. 'He said the film had just opened in London, and he had seen it, and he said it was one of the most beautiful films he'd ever seen in his life, and he was sorry about that incident earlier. So it was a happy ending.'

CASTING: Even before Lynch was involved in *The Elephant Man*, Mel Brooks and producer Jonathan Sanger had discussed the idea of casting John Hurt, who had won a BAFTA award playing Quentin Crisp in John Hodge's *The Naked Civil Servant* (1975), and an Oscar nomination for Alan Parker's *Midnight Express* (1978). 'Very early on, David was thinking of Jack Nance to play Merrick,' Sanger reveals, 'but once he saw John Hurt in *The Naked Civil Servant*, he was convinced.' Brooks set up a meeting with Hurt when the actor was in Los Angeles for the 1979 Academy Awards. 'We blew up these huge mural-sized photographs of Merrick,' Sanger recalls, 'and we put them on the wall. John came in and sat down, and we never referred to [the photographs], but John kept looking up at the pictures, and eventually we had to tell him this was the character we wanted him to play. By the time the meeting was over, he wanted to do it.'

Surprisingly, Hurt did not throw himself into research for the role, preferring to get a feel for the character from the screenplay. 'I find that if the script doesn't tell you enough then I think there's something wrong with the script,' he explained. If Hurt truly set out to capture Merrick's personality without research, he mastered the voice perfectly by pure intuition for, after meeting Merrick, the actor W. H. Kendal told his wife, Madge, that 'out of [his] distorted frame came the most musical voice'.

With Hurt and Oscar-winning actress Anne Bancroft (*The Graduate*, 1967) on board early, the remarkable script soon began to attract other respected actors, including John Gielgud, Michael Elphick and Anthony Hopkins, a theatrical stalwart whose bright future in films was only just beginning, and whose agents were not convinced that *The Elephant Man* was the right project for him. Lynch was considering his second choice, Alan Bates, who had just appeared with John Hurt in *The Shout* (1979), when Christopher De Vore managed to get a copy of *The Elephant Man* script directly to Hopkins, who told his agent he wanted to do it. 'Treves was a remarkable man who stuck his professional neck out for John Merrick,' Hopkins said admiringly. 'He was genuinely concerned about him and felt a real love for this other human being who was in a terrible predicament. I think that makes Treves a very full and rich man. A bit eccentric, a bit blinkered, perhaps, but a lovely man.'

Now only Freddie Jones remained to be convinced, turning down the script because he felt the role of Bytes was under-written. 'He asked David to reread the script with his character in mind, and David did,' Sanger says. 'He agreed that he could do more with the character. So he and the writers did a polish just for that character, and once David convinced him that, regardless of how brutal he may be, Bytes really loved Merrick, that was a connection that Freddie understood, and that brought him around to the point where he said he'd like to do it.' According to Dexter Fletcher – who, as Bytes's boy, shared many scenes with Jones – the actor continued to make suggestions even during production. 'There's a scene in Belgium where Freddie Jones is getting ready to give his speech about Merrick – "His mother was raped by elephants" or whatever,' Fletcher says. 'We're standing there ready to shoot it, and Freddie suddenly says to Lynch, "You know, David, we're in Belgium – I should do it in French!" And David says, "Wow, yeah, that would be great!" So Freddie shouts, "READY!?" And he just launched into this speech and did it all in French. It was phenomenal.' Fletcher – who would later audition, unsuccessfully, for *Ronnie Rocket*, *Dune* and *Mulholland Drive* – remembers that his fourteenth birthday fell on the last day of filming – 31 January 1980. 'They brought me a cake on the set, a big square iced cake with a cherubic elephant on it – not this horrific Elephant Man, but this sweet smiley elephant, like Dumbo! They probably don't remember [that], but I do.'

One of the more sensitive areas of the film's casting was highlighted by a report which claimed that human freaks were being recruited for the film. Jonathan Sanger recalls how he felt annoyed that he was being portrayed as an exploiter. However, he understood how people couldn't tell how the film treated its subject until it was made. Although characters such as the bearded lady and the lion-faced man were contrived through make-up, figures such as the giant (7′9″-tall accountant Chris Greener) and dwarf (Kenny Baker, best known as the man inside R2-D2's casing in the *Star Wars* films) were recruited, along with diminutive pantomime veterans Marcus Powel and Gilda Cohen.

Perhaps the film's greatest casting coup came with the appointment of Frederick Treves, the veteran surgeon's real-life great-nephew, in the role of an alderman. Treves, a former National Theatre actor, proudly recalled how the producers consulted him before the film went into production. Not that they had to obtain his family's permission to film his great-uncle's story, which was safely out of copyright and in the public domain. Nevertheless, they offered him a role and he was delighted to be involved.

THE LYNCH MOB: Although none of Lynch's *Eraserhead* cast made it to England for *The Elephant Man*, the director's encounter with British actor Freddie Jones would yield many future collaborations, including *Dune*, *Wild at Heart* and *Hotel Room*. Cinematographer Freddie Francis would photograph *Dune* and *The Straight Story*. Costume designer Patricia Norris has worked on virtually every Lynch production since, often combining the duties of production and costume design. Finally, sound designer Alan R. Splet (*The Grandmother*, *Eraserhead*) did not make the trip to London, but was present during *The Elephant Man*'s post-production.

MEMORABLE QUOTES
Bytes: 'Life is full of surprises. Consider the fate of this creature's poor mother. Struck down in the fourth month of her maternal condition by an elephant, a wild elephant, struck down on an uncharted African

isle. The result is plain to see. Ladies and gentlemen, the terrible Elephant Man!'

Frederick Treves: 'It seems that I've made Mr Merrick into a curiosity all over again, doesn't it? Only this time in a hospital, rather than a carnival.'

Merrick: 'I am not an animal! I am not an animal! I am a human being!'

SOUND AND MUSIC: The influence of the fairground was strong on the music of *The Elephant Man*, which was the work of Mel Brooks's chosen composer John Morris. Lynch was delighted with Brooks's choice; only on the issue of the music for Merrick's death scene did Lynch and Morris disagree, screening for Mel Brooks two versions of the scene; one with Morris's original composition, the other with Lynch's favoured piece, Samuel Barber's 'Adagio for Strings'. Brooks liked Lynch's choice, a decision Morris accepted with good grace.

Lynch blended the gentle melodies and occasional phantasmagorical excesses of Morris's music with his own brand of *Eraserhead*-style sound, the steam engines and factories of post-Industrial Revolution London giving him all the excuse he needed. 'An image with the right sound and what it can do is what cinema is all about,' Lynch told Joy Kuhn, adding that he felt that sound was an area often overlooked by film-makers. 'Certain lighting can create feeling; sound can alter mood even more. I really like the idea of sound effects being used as music.' In post-production, Lynch once again turned to sound engineer Alan Splet, who, since working with Lynch on *Eraserhead*, had won an Academy Award for his sound work on *The Black Stallion* (1979). 'He's a great engineer,' Lynch added, 'and someone who has real feeling for sound.'

Around thirty minutes of Morris's original score appears on Milan's CD reissue of the soundtrack album (74321 19986-2), which also features all nine and a half minutes of 'Adagio for Strings'.

INFLUENCES: Not only did Lynch, Sanger and Brooks – who had filmed *Young Frankenstein* (1974) in monochrome – agree early on that *The Elephant Man* should be filmed in black and white, in the widescreen format, they even shared an enthusiasm for the same black-and-white film: Jack Cardiff's *Sons and Lovers* (1960), which won an Academy Award for British cinematographer Freddie Francis. By 1979, however, Francis was better known as a director of numerous Hammer horror movies, but Lynch was delighted to discover that he was eager to return to cinematography. Now Francis was one of two names on the shortlist; the other was Chris Challis, whose evocative photography had brought Victorian London to life in Arthur Lubin's black-and-white Cinemascope thriller *Footsteps in the Fog* (1955). 'Jonathan and I couldn't decide, so we decided we'd flip a coin,' Lynch told Richard Blanshard. 'We gave each of the two heads or tails, and flipped the coin, and Freddie lost the toss, [but] we both looked at each other and said, "No, no, no, it's got to be Freddie!"'

Lynch was never less than delighted with his choice. 'One of the great stars on this picture is Freddie's lighting,' he told Joy Kuhn. 'You have to light what you want to see and just the amount you want to see it, and keep light off everything else,' explains Lynch. 'You don't have the benefits of colours separating themselves from each other. Things can look pretty boring in black and white if you, for instance, flat-light something all over, whereas it might pass all right in colour. Freddie knows his way around black and white very well.'

For Francis, returning to the black-and-white photography of his earlier films, such as *Room at the Top* (1959), *Saturday Night and Sunday Morning* (1960) and *The Innocents* (1961), presented certain challenges. 'Going back to an old-fashioned medium was actually presenting a new one to modern-day people,' he explained. There was very little black-and-white stock being made any more, despite the fact that black-and-white film was enjoying a brief renaissance at the time, with both Woody Allen's *Manhattan* (1979) and Martin Scorsese's *Raging Bull* (1980) being filmed at the same time. Ultimately, Francis's return to cinematography after a fifteen-year absence revived his career; he won his second Oscar for *Glory* (1989), and went on to photograph such films as *The French Lieutenant's Woman* (1981) and Martin Scorsese's *Cape Fear* (1991).

There is no mention in any of the literature on the subject of John Merrick that he would have been disturbed by the ringing of bells at the London Hospital; therefore, it must be assumed that this scene was included to remind audiences of Victor Hugo's *The Hunchback of Notre Dame*, in which a similarly afflicted (though fictional) individual meets a tragic fate at the hands of an uncaring society. In addition, as *Monthly Film Bulletin*'s Richard Combs pointed out, the idea of 'the solidarity of the malformed in the face of the oppression of the healthy' suggested by Merrick's return to, and escape from, the fairground is strongly reminiscent of Tod Browning's *Freaks* (1932).

LEGACY: Almost overnight, *The Elephant Man* brought Lynch both recognition and respect; yet it also helped to change Hollywood's perception of Mel Brooks as someone who could only work in comedy, and signified his production company, Brooksfilms, as a key independent. One of its subsequent productions was David

Cronenberg's 1986 remake of *The Fly*, in which Jeff Goldblum's performance as a man whose DNA is fused with that of an insect bears more than a passing resemblance to John Hurt's in *The Elephant Man*. Both films were produced for Brooksfilms by Stuart Cornfeld, and both introduced avant-garde directors to mainstream audiences.

Goldblum went on to star in the British comedy *The Tall Guy* (1989), in which he plays an American actor who takes the starring role in *Elephant!*, an Andrew Lloyd Webber-style musical based on the life of John Merrick. This was not the only occasion on which the story of the Elephant Man was played for laughs. Indeed, Merrick's famous cry of 'I am not an animal, I am a human being' is much quoted and often parodied: in an episode of the short-lived comedy series *Police Squad!*, the hapless Lieutenant Frank Drebin (Leslie Nielsen) delivers the line in a John Hurt style while his mouth is full of dental equipment; and in an episode of *The Rugrats* entitled 'The Slide', two-year-old Chuckie Fenster also has a Merrick moment, insisting that he is 'not an am-in-al, I am a human bean!' A more famous variation on the same line appears in Tim Burton's *Batman Returns* (1992), in which the Penguin (Danny De Vito) begs for understanding of a different kind: 'I am not a human being,' he cries, 'I am an animal!'

Merrick re-emerged briefly into the public spotlight in the early 1990s, when pop singer Michael Jackson – for whom Lynch had made a 30-second promo in 1991 – announced his desire to buy Merrick's skeleton from the London Hospital (unaware that it had been destroyed during the Second World War). This typically bizarre publicity stunt was later immortalised in a song called 'If I Had $1,000,000' by Canadian rock group Barenaked Ladies: 'If I had a million dollars/(If I had a million dollars)/I'd buy John Merrick's remains/(All those crazy elephant bones).'

Finally, deadpan British stand-up comic Jack Dee once included this joke in his act: 'Whatever happened to the Elephant Man? He made that one film, never heard from him again . . .'

DÉJÀ VU: *The Elephant Man* contains many echoes of *Eraserhead*, a connection made more tangible by the black-and-white cinematography and the oppressive use of sound. The Victorian cityscapes, with their strange industrial noises and threatening shadows, strongly resemble Henry's world, cementing each protagonist's status as a fearful misfit and outsider.

THEMES AND MOTIFS: To De Vore and Bergren, there was little doubt that Treves was a character no less interesting than Merrick himself, and that the story should be told from his perspective, beginning with his discovery of the Elephant Man and ending just before he finds Merrick dead. 'As a scientist, Treves felt obliged to examine Merrick's body, and then, as a man, compelled to explore his soul,' the writers explained. This perspective led to one of the film's more interesting themes: the way in which Treves questions his own motives for procuring, photographing and ultimately presenting Merrick to fellow members of the Pathological Society of London. This self-questioning arises when Mrs Mothershead asks Treves if the steady procession of society figures visiting Merrick might not be merely a higher-class version of the audience at the carnival freak show. Nevertheless, the authors of *The True History of The Elephant Man* doubted that Treves could have 'seen the accident of his own intervention as carrying Joseph's career as a freak on to a new, unimaginable level of success; or himself as the alter ego to Mr Tom Norman, the showman he so consistently depised.'

CUT SCENES: According to Jonathan Sanger, the first cut of *The Elephant Man*, effectively a rough assembly, came in at three hours long. He and Lynch knew that cuts would need to be made, but Brooks generously allowed them to decide for themselves what to cut. Sanger recalls, 'He was extremely supportive of David's vision, and for David, it was like having final cut on your first film.' The resulting cuts were extensive, as Lynch had shot everything that was in the script. A brief outline of the more substantial cuts follows:

• A major scene in which Treves briefs Mrs Mothershead on Merrick's appearance, and asks her to give Merrick a bath, which she does, as Treves considers Merrick's background. The physician wonders where Merrick might have received the care that would have kept him alive after his (presumed) abandonment as a child. Mothershead suggests the workhouse, at which Merrick begins to babble wildly and thrashes about, until he is subdued, weeping.

• Immediately following this is a scene in which the night porter first learns of Merrick's existence from a young porter. That night, the night porter molests a beautiful young female patient in her bed. 'Hush, love,' he says. 'I told you before – one word from me, they'll toss you back on the street, and then those pretty little arms of yours will never grow straight. Now close your eyes.' The next morning, Treves and Mothershead find Merrick cowering, terrified, under his bed, as though the night porter has already paid him a nocturnal visit.

• A scene in which Mothershead chides Nora (surnamed Ireland in the script) for referring to Merrick as an 'it' instead of a 'he'.

• A scene in which Merrick impresses Mothershead with his pronunciation of 'Hello, my name is John Merrick,' although she says dismissively, 'Parrots can do as much', and warns Treves that the hospital committee will eventually evict Merrick.

- A scene in which Carr-Gomm admonishes Treves for not checking with other hospitals to see if they can accommodate Merrick.
- A scene in which Treves discusses Merrick's predicament with his wife, Anne. 'Is he simple?' he wonders. 'Or is that just something I've wished upon him to make things simpler for myself?' Anne asks why he is taking such an interest in Merrick's case, and Treves explains that he is fascinated with what lies beneath Merrick's exterior and has to know whether he is an imbecile or an intelligent man whom he would feel compelled to help.
- A subsequent scene has the night porter visit Merrick again, this time after learning that he can speak, to warn him not to breathe a word about his nocturnal visits.
- Immediately following this scene is one in which Carr-Gomm warns Treves that it will be difficult to convince the committee – in particular, a man named Broadneck – to allow Merrick to stay. This proves to be the case, as a triumphant Broadneck convinces the committee that a hospital is no place for an incurably deformed urchin.
- After Mrs Kendal reads about Merrick in the newspaper, Treves attends a dinner party at which several eminent physicians are present. They mock him for his unusual charge ('Makes you sound rather more like a zookeeper than a surgeon, Frederick') and he leaves. Treves's friend Fox stands up for him.
- Immediately after this scene is another in which two cleaning women complain about having to clear up the rooms in Bedstead Square, so that a 'circus animal' can take up residency there.
- This is followed by a scene in which Merrick reads about the Eddystone Lighthouse in the London *Evening News*, and considers that this lonely beacon might be the perfect home for him. Treves interrupts his reverie by bringing him a copy of Lewis Carroll's *Alice in Wonderland*. Treves tells him about his new home in Bedstead Square, but Merrick is fascinated by a picture of the Mock Turtle, weeping, as Alice and the Gryphon look on with intense sympathy.
- After being moved to Bedstead Square, Merrick asks if, when he is next moved, 'May I go to a lighthouse? Or to a blind-asylum?' Outside, Carr-Gomm bemoans the sluggish response to his letter to *The Times*.
- Just before Merrick's meeting with Mrs Kendal, there is a touching scene in which Nora is impressed by Merrick's cardboard model of St Phillip's Cathedral, and implies that she will find him more cardboard. This she does, later, delivering a box containing paste, paint and other modelling materials.

- After Mothershead suggests to Treves that London society's interest in Merrick has left him 'being stared at all over again', there is a scene in which Treves and Merrick read the Robert Browning poem 'Pippa Passes', from which the film's final speech ('Nothing will die,' etc.) is taken. According to Jonathan Sanger, the scene was cut after the film was mixed and finished, for reasons of time.
- The scenes showing Merrick's trip from Belgium to London – little more than a montage in the final film – were originally far more detailed. On the train, the other passengers in the third-class compartment move away from Merrick, 'forming almost a moat of space around him.' Merrick stares at his reflection in a window. At Ostend, Merrick is refused permission to board the steamship bound for England, despite having a ticket. Merrick is forced to wait for nightfall, dashing aboard the ship at the last moment and crouching beneath a stairway for the entire trip to Dover. There was also an interior scene of Merrick aboard the train to Liverpool Street, where a starving Merrick observes an elderly man eating an apple.
- After Merrick's safe return to Bedstead Square, Treves discusses Merrick's worsening health with Mrs Kendal. 'There is nothing more frustrating,' he says, 'nothing that makes a physician feel more useless, than standing by watching his patient deteriorate. And when that patient is a friend . . .'
- On the morning of Merrick's theatre visit, he surveys the smiling ladies in his collection of photographs. 'You women are such strange and wonderful creatures,' he says to them. 'Alas, it seems to be my fate to fall in love with each and every one of you. I especially wish you could all be with me tonight . . . I'm finally going to the theatre.'
- The script includes several speeches from the production of William Shakespeare's *Henry V* that Merrick attended; in the final film, of course, Merrick's visit is to a lavishly staged pantomime. 'Initially, we had shot the whole pantomime,' says Sanger, 'but ultimately it was long and protracted and it didn't seem to quite work. David started working on this montage idea, and the editor, Anne Coates, told me privately that she didn't think it would work. But it did.'

In addition to the cuts outlined above, the script also highlights the alteration of certain scenes, most significantly:

- In the screenplay, Merrick is totally revealed to Treves, and thus to the audience, during their very first meeting. At Mel Brooks's suggestion, and John Hurt's gentle cajoling, the revelation of his appearance was held back some thirty minutes for dramatic effect.
- The scene in which the nurses read the account of Mrs Kendal's visit to see Merrick originally took place in the home of a society woman

having tea with her friends, their gossiping interrupted by her daughter Jennifer (a name she shares with Lynch's own daughter), who reads the story to them.

TRAILER: A nurse reluctantly enters Merrick's room at the London Hospital, as an off-screen Treves tells her not to be afraid. Over fairground scenes, a voice-over begins: 'You will feel the chill of horror, yet this is not a horror story. You will feel the warmth of love, yet this is not a love story. It is the shocking true story of a very real monster, who was also a very real human being.' 'Ladies and gentlemen,' says Bytes, 'the terrible Elephant Man!' There follow a few clips of various characters discussing Merrick, before his cry is heard: 'I am not an animal, I am a human being!' A standard cast list concludes with a tantalising shot of Merrick, hidden in shadow behind a curtain. Other than this fleeting image, the Elephant Man is not glimpsed in the trailer. 'A shattering experience,' the voice-over continues over the title, following which we cut to Michael Elphick as the Night Porter: 'For the right price, you will see something you will never ever see again in your life.'

POSTER: The most commonly used poster image was that of the Elephant Man dressed in his famous disguise: a large shapeless overcoat, with an oversized hat from which is draped a piece of sacking with a single eyehole stitched into it. Occasionally, this image was used against a blank or fogbound background; in some cases, however, the figure was placed in context, on the prow of the steamship featured in the film.

TAG-LINES: 'I AM NOT AN ANIMAL! I AM A HUMAN BEING! I . . . AM . . . A MAN!' 'An incredible but true story . . . probably the year's best film.' 'A true story of courage and human dignity.'

WHAT THE PAPERS SAID: Contrary to popular myth, *The Elephant Man* was not universally acclaimed upon its release, although *Variety* bucked the trend towards mixed reactions by describing it as 'eerily compelling', adding that 'Hopkins is splendid in a subtly nuanced portrayal of a man torn between humanitarianism and qualms that his motives in introducing the Elephant Man to society are no better than those of the brutish carny. The centrepiece of the film, however, is the virtuoso performance by the almost unrecognisable John Hurt.'

Perhaps understandably, given the prominence of Bernard Pomerance's Broadway play at the time of *The Elephant Man*'s US opening, several critics compared Lynch's film to the stage version, many of them unfavourably. As *New York*'s David Denby wrote,

'We're no longer required, as we were at the play, to imagine the extremity of Merrick's condition, thereby projecting ourselves emotionally into the material; nor do we come to terms with the plain visceral loathsomeness of his appearance. Indeed, he's so easy to look at, and so nice a man (not like Pomerance's prickly, ironic Merrick), that the working-class slobs who shriek at him seem both hysterical and inhuman . . . I don't know what Lynch intended, but the movie expresses a boundless loathing for ordinary people and a rather pathetic worship of the wealthy and well-connected.' 'The sheer narrative is less successful than Pomerance's play,' wrote *Newsweek*'s Jack Kroll, 'which puts the story of history's most celebrated freak in a much fuller social and philosophical context,' whereas Lynch's film 'lacks dramatic punch and repeats its effects rather than developing a truly complex texture.'

In the UK, *Time Out*'s Tom Milne described *The Elephant Man* as 'a marvellous movie,' but one with 'much the same limpidly moving humanism as Truffaut's *L'Enfant Sauvage*', the celebrated French director's 1969 film about a late-eighteenth-century behavioural scientist's attempts to socially condition a boy found in a forest far from civilisation. *Monthly Film Bulletin*'s Richard Combs made the same comparison, but added that Lynch's treatise on the same subject was only partially successful: '[A]t the very least Lynch brings off inspired opening and closing sequences, uses the black-and-white Panavision format to intermittently unsettling effect in between, and only once goes badly wrong when he tries to identify the Elephant Man's social predicament with melodramatic personal cruelty.'

BOX OFFICE: *The Elephant Man* was released in the US in October 1980, proving a modest success for Paramount. In the UK, the film debuted on 25 October, remaining at the top of the box-office chart for two weeks, before being deposed – by the Penthouse production of *Caligula* (1980).

AWARDS: Lynch proved that he had truly arrived in Hollywood when *The Elephant Man* scooped eight Academy Award nominations, in the categories of best picture, best director, best actor (John Hurt), best screenplay adaptation, best music, best film editing, best costume design and best art direction. (Like many, Lynch was surprised that the film failed to achieve nominations for cinematography or sound. *Los Angeles Times* critic Charles Champlin even shortlisted *The Elephant Man* and *Tess* for the best cinematography Oscar, not realising that Lynch's film had not been nominated in that category.) Had 1980 not been such a watershed year for quality pictures, it is likely that *The*

Elephant Man would have converted at least a few of its nominations into awards; as it turned out, Robert Redford's *Ordinary People* took most of the year's top prizes, while John Hurt was beaten by Robert De Niro's equally visceral performance in the other monochrome masterpiece of 1980, Martin Scorsese's *Raging Bull*.

Hurt fared better in his native country, winning a second Best Actor prize at the British Academy of Film and Television Arts (BAFTA) awards, while *The Elephant Man* won Best Film, and Stuart Craig won top honours for production design and art direction. In addition to its three BAFTA wins, *The Elephant Man* was nominated in the categories of direction, writing, cinematography and editing. *The Elephant Man* was also nominated for four Golden Globe awards: best motion picture, best director, best actor (drama) for John Hurt and best screenplay. At the César Awards, the French equivalent of the Oscars, *The Elephant Man* won the prize for Best Foreign Film; Freddie Francis also won the British Society of Cinematographers' award for best cinematography; finally, the three screenwriters were nominated by the Writers Guild of America in the category of Best Drama Adapted from Another Medium.

CONTROVERSY: In February 1979, Bernard Pomerance's stage play *The Elephant Man*, also based on Merrick's life, made its debut at the Booth Theatre on Broadway. By this time, Brooksfilms had been in development with its own Elephant Man project for almost six months, but when the play became a huge success, the film-makers knew that they might have a legal problem on their hands. 'They didn't want us to use the title, because they said they had made it famous,' recalls Jonathan Sanger. 'And so they sued us.' Legal opinion suggested that the play's producers could not win, since the concept of the Elephant Man existed long before the play, but the film-makers preferred not to take the chance, and settled the matter out of court. Among the terms of the settlement were that a caption should be placed at the end of the film, giving a clear distinction between the film and the stage play. It read, 'Based on the life of John Merrick, the Elephant Man, and not upon the Broadway play or any other fictional account.'

Pomerance's play went on to win the prestigious Tony and New York Drama Critics' Circle awards for Best Play, and ran for a prosperous 916 performances. In 1982, the play was adapted by John Hofsiss into a made-for-television movie starring Phillip Anglim, one of the actors to portray John Merrick on Broadway, in the title role – again, as in the play, without make-up – and co-starring Kevin Conway, Penny Fuller and Glenn Close. 'And at that point, *we* could have sued *them*,' suggests Sanger, 'because by the time they made the film, they had added a lot of dream sequences very reminiscent of David's!'

TRIVIA: British viewers should watch out for *Birds of a Feather* actress Pauline Quirke and *Doctor Who* actor Peter Davidson in minor roles, as '2nd Whore' and 'Second Policeman' respectively.

Anyone wishing to learn more about Merrick's disease, neurofibromatosis, or make a donation to one of the charities that supports research into its causes, treatments and cures, should contact the National Neurofibromatosis Foundation at 141 Fifth Avenue, New York, NY 10010. The Carr-Gomm Society, a charitable housing trust set up by F. C. Carr-Gomm's grandson, Richard, and providing shelter for the homeless, also accepts donations: its head office is at Duke House, 6–12 Tabard Street, London SE1 4JU.

APOCRYPHA: Since *The Elephant Man* is ostensibly based on a true story, perhaps the opportunity should be taken to explore the numerous areas in which Lynch's film diverges from reality. The first and most obvious divergence is the use of the name John, instead of Joseph, as Merrick's first name, a misnomer that has been repeated ever since Frederick Treves mysteriously crossed out the name 'Joseph' in the handwritten manuscript of his memoir and wrote in the name 'John' over the top – despite the fact that Treves's volume reprinted two letters by Carr-Gomm that gave Merrick's name correctly. Why Treves did this has puzzled researchers into Merrick's story ever since the 'deliberate mistake' was made. 'We didn't find out about [the name] until after we had started shooting,' says Sanger, 'because Michael Howell's book came out after the movie. We probably would have made that adjustment had we known, but it was pretty late in the process that we discovered that, because we were relying on Treves, who called him *John* Merrick.'

Christopher De Vore and Eric Bergren's original script stuck closely to the facts of Merrick's life as they were known in the late 70s: Treves meets Merrick, displays him before his colleagues and returns him to his 'owner'; later, abandoned in Belgium after an ill-fated tour of the continent, Merrick finds his way back to England, and thence to the London Hospital, whereupon Treves takes him in; Carr-Gomm writes to *The Times*; its readers' charity allows Merrick to remain at the London Hospital, where he becomes a friend of many society figures, including the Prince and Princess of Wales, before dying peacefully in his sleep at the age of 29. Unfortunately, transposed to film, in sequence, the drama would evaporate at the end of the first act, resulting in something of a narrative 'plateau' around the mid-point of the story, after Merrick finds sanctuary in Treves's care. 'For me, the essence of *The Elephant Man* was in that script,' Lynch explains, 'but it was pretty flat. And Mel Brooks was the one who always said, "It needs something bad happening here; it needs this or this or this," and would send us back in the other room to cook stuff up.' As Sanger says, 'In biographical movies, you almost have to do that, because a life doesn't always fall into the neat dramatic structure required by a movie.' In other words, it was more important to stay true to the essence of the story than the facts of the story itself.

Undoubtedly, the most dramatic of the invented scenes were those involving the night porter's nocturnal visits, perhaps inspired by an intriguing – not to mention troubling – paragraph in Treves's account which suggests that not everyone who visited Merrick in hospital had good intentions. Could these unfortunate incidents account for Treves's description of Merrick's 'curiously uneasy' attitude during his first few weeks at the hospital?

The film-makers also chose their own path when it came to Merrick's early life. Treves's memoir erroneously assumes that Merrick's mother abandoned her deformed son to a life in the workhouse; he never considers the possibility that Merrick's gentle, kindly nature was as a direct result of the love and care his mother, Mary Jane, bestowed upon him until her death when Joseph was aged just ten. Lynch's film redresses the balance, just as Ashley Montagu's book vindicated Mary Jane, describing her almost as a paradigm of motherhood, and shifting the blame for the mistreatment Joseph suffered after her death to his father and stepmother. Montagu's theories were borne out by the exhaustive research carried out by Michael Howell and Peter Ford for their book *The True History of The Elephant Man*, first published in 1980. Now, thanks to the extensively revised third edition of this book, it is possible to compare the actual events of Merrick's life with those of the film, and point out the following discrepancies:

- Treves did not come upon the Elephant Man by accident during a visit to a fairground, but was alerted to his presence in a disused shop across the road from the London Hospital by a junior colleague, Dr Reginald Tuckett.
- It may be inferred that Merrick fell in with the freak-show crowd against his will; in reality, he wrote to showman Sam Torr from the Leicester Union Workhouse, in the hopes that Torr might accept him as a showpiece and thereby give him a means of earning a living.
- The screenwriters named Merrick's 'keeper' 'Bytes'; in reality, the showman who exhibited Merrick as the Elephant Man was named Tom Norman, the self-styled 'Silver King'.
- Merrick's maltreatment by Bytes, suggested by Treves's account (in

which the showman is not named), adds drama and pathos to the story, yet Norman objected vociferously to suggestions that his charges suffered in any way; indeed, his claim that his 'star artists' received 'princely salaries' that allowed them to enjoy 'every reasonable luxury of life' may be no great exaggeration, since by the time Norman and Merrick parted company, the latter had savings amounting to fifty pounds – enough to subsist for a year in Victorian London. Besides, as Norman himself noted, 'Had I attempted to be harsh with him . . . I would very soon have had the show wrecked, and me with it.' Michael Howell and Peter Ford tend to accept Norman's version of events, suggesting that Treves's description of Norman was deliberately coloured by his own attitude towards the man.

- In reality Merrick was perfectly well, aside from his deformities, when he came into Treves's care; he had not been beaten by his 'keeper', nor was he suffering from bronchitis.
- Norman did try to see Merrick after his admittance to the London Hospital, but not to reclaim him, as Bytes does.
- Treves did take Merrick to his home, but it is likely that his wife, Anne, was safely out of the way before his visit.
- The actress Madge Kendal did not learn about Merrick through Carr-Gomm's letter to *The Times*, nor did she personally meet Merrick; in truth, her husband W. H. Kendal, an actor and former doctor, met Merrick and later told his wife of Merrick and his uncertain future, and it is quite possible that it was, as she later claimed, Madge Kendal who anonymously launched the appeal fund that led to Merrick's permanent residence at the London Hospital. She certainly sent him an autographed picture, which he treasured; it was to her that he gave his completed cardboard model of the church; and she was, indirectly, responsible for making possible his visit to see *Puss in Boots* at the theatre. Thus, the artistic licence taken with the character seems entirely commensurate with the effect she had on Merrick's life.
- The scene in which, thanks to timely royal intervention, the committee of the London Hospital vote to keep Merrick in their care, was invented for dramatic purposes; in reality, the motion was carried unanimously and without argument on 7 December 1886, while HRH Alexandra, Princess of Wales, did not visit the hospital until the following May. On that occasion, accompanied by the Prince of Wales (the future King Edward VII) and the Duke of Cambridge, she met Merrick, with whom she would later correspond on several occasions.
- As has been noted earlier, Merrick was not abducted from the London Hospital and returned to a life as a freak-show exhibit on

the continent; these events occurred between Treves's first and subsequent encounters with Merrick, approximately two years apart.
- Merrick did indeed visit the theatre, in 1887, to see a lavish production of the pantomime *Puss in Boots*; he did so incognito, however, and certainly not in the company of the Princess of Wales, nor the presence of Madge Kendal.

All of the other events of the film may be said to be relatively true to the facts of Merrick's years in the care of the London Hospital – except, perhaps, for the extraordinary manner by which Merrick was said to have come by his affliction. It is clear from his own brief autobiography, published in pamphlet form during his years on tour with Tom Norman, that he believed his deformity to have been caused by the shock his pregnant mother suffered after being frightened by an elephant. 'My mother was going along the street when a procession of Animals was passing by, there was a terrible crush of people to see them, and unfortunately she was pushed under the Elephant's feet, which frightened her very much; this occuring during a time of pregnancy was the cause of my deformity.'

Although it may be expected that science does not support such a fanciful theory, researchers at Denmark's John F. Kennedy Institute recently suggested that minor deformities such as cleft palates might be caused by hormones such as cortisone, triggered by severe emotional stress during pregnancy. In Merrick's case, however, the discovery that both his mother and younger sister were crippled in some way tends to support the argument for a hereditary genetic defect, common in cases of multiple neurofibromatosis.

One area in which the film-makers were able to ensure absolute accuracy was in the depiction of Merrick's deformities. After meeting Lynch and Sanger, the London Hospital archivist Percy G. Nunn overcame his initial reservations about the project and allowed Chris Tucker access to Merrick's life cast (his actual remains having been destroyed during the Blitz). Nunn even visited Shepperton Studios during filming. 'There, I was confronted with John Hurt in full make-up,' he told Joy Kuhn. 'He was, quite simply, the epitome of the Elephant Man. It was as if John Merrick had come to life.'

AVAILABILITY: A letterboxed (2.35:1 ratio) transfer of *The Elephant Man* is currently available in the UK from Warner Home Video as a PAL VHS (S038357), digitally remastered and featuring the original cinema trailer. A full-screen (4:3) budget-priced PAL VHS (079 9043) is also available from 4Front Video.

Although the film is currently unavailable on DVD in the US,

Region 2 is well served: a letterboxed DVD was released in the UK in April 2001 as part of Momentum Pictures' 'Director's Chair' series; the French DVD (27334) features a widescreen transfer, optional French subtitles, and the French theatrical trailer; a Japanese DVD (PIBF-1119) is also available.

FINAL ANALYSIS: It is hard to believe what was going through Mel Brooks's mind when he entrusted the sensitive portrayal of one of history's most tragic figures to a young director whose only feature was one of the most startling and disturbing horror films of all time. Nevertheless, Brooks's faith, or prescience, paid off handsomely, as Lynch delivered an extraordinarily moving true story that, like *The Straight Story* two decades later, manages real sentiment without sentimentality, and wrenches deep emotional responses from the audience without manipulation. *The Elephant Man* is set against an emergent industrial background whose aural and visual resonances are as powerful as the story itself, which is filmed in glorious black and white, the print shining like silver engravings, and is packed with striking performances, not limited to John Hurt's astonishing portrayal of Merrick himself.

Like Victor Hugo's hunchback, Merrick is a true romantic hero, a beauty trapped in the body of a beast, a monster who teaches those he meets how to be human. Justly rewarded with eight Oscar nominations and comfortable box-office receipts, *The Elephant Man* should have secured Lynch's future as one of Hollywood's true visionaries, whose masterful handling of such sensitive material would seemingly allow him to take on any project with complete confidence. Alas, Lynch's next film was *Dune*.

EXPERT WITNESS: 'Lynch was utterly in control, and he did a brilliant job on *The Elephant Man*, which became both a critical and a commercial success. It taught me what an extraordinary combination it can be to marry a highly experimental director to a strong script with a conventional narrative.' – former Paramount Pictures president Michael Eisner

LYNCH ON *THE ELEPHANT MAN*: 'This was a major commercial picture with heavyweight actors. And all those considerations are *between* the idea and the film. You have to cut through the money and the cast and the Hollywood glamour, and remember that the idea, on a little piece of film, is what it's all about. *That's* what takes courage.'

Dune (1984)

35mm feature film / 137 mins (theatrical version), 189 mins (TV version) / colour / live action

Directed by David Lynch (theatrical version), 'Alan Smithee' (TV version)
Produced by Raffaella De Laurentiis
Screenplay by David Lynch
Based on the Novel by Frank Herbert
Photographed by Freddie Francis
Production Designed by Anthony Masters
Costumes Designed by Bob Ringwood
Film Editor Antony Gibbs
Prophecy Theme by Brian Eno
Music Composed and Performed by Toto
Additional Visual Special Effects by Albert Whitlock
Special Photographic Effects by Barry Nolan
Creatures Created by Carlo Rambaldi
Mechanical Special Effects by Kit West
Associate Producer José Lopez Rodero

CAST: Francesca Annis (*Lady Jessica*), Leonard Cimino (*The Baron's Doctor*), Brad Dourif (*Piter De Vries*), José Ferrer (*Padisha Emperor Shaddam IV*), Linda Hunt (*Shadout Mapes*), Freddie Jones (*Thufir Hawat*), Richard Jordan (*Duncan Idaho*), Kyle MacLachlan (*Paul Atreides*), Virgina Madsen (*Princess Irulan*), Silvana Mangano (*Reverend Mother Ramallo*), Everett McGill (*Stilgar*), Kenneth McMillan (*Baron Vladimir Harkonnen*), Jack Nance (*Nefud*), Siân Phillips (*Reverend Mother Gaius Helen Mohiam*), Jürgen Prochnow (*Duke Leto Atreides*), Paul Smith (*The Beast Rabban*), Patrick Stewart (*Gurney Halleck*), Sting (*Feyd-Rautha*), Dean Stockwell (*Doctor Wellington Yueh*), Max von Sydow (*Doctor Liet Kynes*), Alicia Roanne Witt (*Alia*), Sean Young (*Chani*), Danny Corkill, Honorata Magalone (*Otheym*), Judd Omen (*Jamis*), Molly Wryn (*Harah*)

UNCREDITED CAST: David Lynch (*Spice Worker*)

UNCREDITED CREW: Michael Douglas Middleton (Visual Effects Still Photographer)

TITLE SEQUENCE: After the pre-title prologue, read by Princess Irulan (Virginia Madsen), the titles play over images of sand dunes.

SUMMARY: The year is 10,191. The universe's most precious substance is the spice mélange, which extends life, expands consciousness, is vital to space travel – and is found on only one planet: the desert world Arrakis (Dune), home to gigantic worms and a mysterious race, the Fremen. Yet the Emperor, Shaddam IV, seeing a potential rival to the throne, hands spice mining over from House Harkonnen, led by a diseased Baron and his idiot nephews, to House Atreides, ruled by Duke Leto and his concubine, Lady Jessica, a member of the telepathic sisterhood known as the Bene Gesserit. His gesture is a trap, designed to bring down House Atreides. Prophecy foretells the coming of the Kwisatz Haderach, a messianic figure that the Bene Gesserit have been manipulating bloodlines to produce, without success. But Leto's and Lady Jessica's son, Paul, may hold the key to the prophecy: his premonitory dreams and precocious skills suggest that he is more than human. While the Harkonnens plot to bring down their enemies with the help of a traitor, the Atreides arrive on Arrakis, visiting the spice miners just as a giant worm attacks. Back at the palace, the duplicitous Dr Yueh disables the protective shields and betrays his Duke (Atreides), blackmailing him into killing the Baron (who killed Yueh's wife), in return for sparing Jessica and Paul. The Harkonnens overrun the defenceless palace, killing Yueh and sending Paul and Jessica to their deaths in the desert. Using Paul's growing powers, they escape to safety among the Fremen, where they discover huge underground water reservoirs. The Duke dies in his unsuccessful attempt on the Baron's life, but Jessica becomes the Fremen's new spiritual leader, and gives birth to a daughter, Alia, who has formidable power. Meanwhile, Paul's own powers increase, and he leads the Fremen to victory over the Baron's troops, eventually bringing down the evil Emperor, restoring peace to the universe and fulfilling the messianic prophecy: he is the Kwisatz Haderach, destined to change the face of Arrakis forever . . . with rain.

SOURCE: *Dune* is based on one of the biggest-selling science fiction novels of all time, originally published as two three-part stories, 'Dune World' and 'Prophet of Dune', written by Frank Herbert for *Analog* magazine in 1963–4 and 1965, and collected in book form in 1965. A complex sociological, ecological, political and theological saga spanning thousands of years, *Dune* has remained in print ever since, spawning five sequels by Herbert himself – *Dune Messiah* (1969), *Children of Dune* (1976), *God Emperor of Dune* (1981), *Heretics of Dune* (1984) and *Chapter House Dune* (1985) – a trilogy of official prequels by Herbert's son Brian and a collaborator (the *Prelude to Dune* series), and two screen productions: Lynch's, and an epic Sci-Fi Channel miniseries (2000). Literary fads have come and gone; Frank Herbert's reputation endures as the Tolkien of his genre, architect of the greatest science fiction saga ever written.

PRODUCTION HISTORY: 'A beginning is always a difficult time,' Princess Irulan tells us, and the gestation of the movie adaptation of *Dune* was no exception. The book was first optioned in 1969 by Arthur P. Jacobs (*Planet of the Apes*, 1968), whose death left the project in limbo, until Chilean-born director Alexandro Jodorowsky (*El Topo*, 1971) secured the rights seven years later, and set to work with illustrators-turned-conceptual-artists Jean 'Moebius' Giraud, H. R. Giger and Chris Foss, all of whom would later collaborate on *Alien* (1979). Storyboards were drawn up based on Jodorowsky's script, Salvador Dali was cast (as the Emperor) and vast sums were spent – until there was no money, and no film. The success of *Star Wars* – heavily influenced by Herbert's novel, with its desert planet, quasi-religious sect, young hero with mystical powers, and many other similarities – ironically led to a resurgence of interest in science fiction, and veteran producer Dino De Laurentiis (*Flash Gordon*, 1980) spent $2 million acquiring the film rights to the book. 'To make *Dune*, you must be crazy,' the producer claimed, 'and I believe I'm crazy enough, and have the courage enough, to do [it].' Herbert himself was contracted to write the script, but when his 176-page draft proved unworkable, De Laurentiis hired novelist Rudolph Wurlitzer (*Pat Garrett and Billy the Kid*, 1973) to start again, and a post-*Alien* Ridley Scott to direct, with Giger back on board as conceptual artist. Scott and De Laurentiis, however, did not see eye to eye over budget – 'over budget' being the operative phrase – and when Scott left the project to begin *Blade Runner* (1982), the producer's daughter, Raffaella, suggested David Lynch, director of *The Elephant Man*, as a possible replacement.

Having turned down *Return of the Jedi*, and failed to find a home at Francis Ford Coppola's Zoetrope for *Ronnie Rocket* [see 'In Dreams,' page 248], Lynch accepted their offer to direct. 'I like to go into weird worlds,' he declared, 'and *Dune* has four of them.' Lynch began adapting the script with his *Elephant Man* co-writers Eric Bergren and Christopher De Vore, producing a first draft which, at two hundred pages, was even longer than Herbert's. By the third draft, Bergren and De Vore had left the project at De Laurentiis's request, and it was another year before Lynch's sixth draft was finally given the go-ahead. A remarkably faithful distillation of Herbert's grandiose themes and ideas, his 135-page script would continue to evolve throughout production, the seventh and final draft being dated 9 December 1983.

Pre-production had begun much earlier, in May 1981, with one of Lynch's first decisions being to reject Giger's designs. Only when he and De Laurentiis visited Italy together did Lynch find inspiration for the film's look. 'I was inspired by Venice,' he says, 'not the whole of Venice, but a certain part of it.' Perhaps Lynch's first impression of the historical city gave him the key to representing the book's feudal society on screen, by suggesting it through Renaissance-influenced architecture, rather than making the politics explicit. '[Dino] wanted to make a science fiction film that was about people and not about ray guns and spaceships,' Lynch told *American Film*. 'We wanted to make everything very real and believable. It's not high-tech sci-fi like most of the space stuff you see. Everything looks old, like it's been around for a while.' To bring his vision to life, Lynch selected Tony Masters and Ron Miller – both veterans of *2001: A Space Odyssey* (1968) – as conceptual artists, and Bob Underwood (*Excalibur*, 1981) as costume designer, all of whom would be crucial to the creation of a science fiction film unlike any other. Masters's often breathtaking set designs would range from the rich, red wood textures of the Atreides family home on Caladan, through the subterranean world of the Fremen and the industrialised dystopia of House Harkonnen, to the harsh, desolate wasteland of Arrakis itself; each one a distinctly separate environment, giving a sense that the Houses of Atreides and Harkonnen live literally worlds apart, their destiny entangled in the mining of the universe's most precious substance. 'I can't say enough good things about Tony Masters, bless his heart,' says Lynch. 'He was so great to work with, and like a child. We had so much fun. A lot of people did great work on *Dune*.'

Filming began at Estudios Churubusco in Mexico on 30 March 1983, with Herbert himself present to clap the first slate. 'Frank was a very gracious person,' Lynch recalls, 'and he was just pumped up that something was finally going to happen to his book. He stayed very enthusiastic. And it's a little bit like Barry Gifford, who said, "There's my version of *Wild at Heart* and there's your version of *Wild at Heart* – just take the ball and run with it." And that's a little bit like Frank was.' Indeed, Herbert later wrote of his experience watching *Dune* unfold before his eyes as a happy one. 'My first visit to Churubusco Studios in Mexico City put a different stamp on what it means to adapt a novel to the screen. The snaking lines of electrical cables, the big yellow buses with "DUNE" on the front, the mobs of people in and around the sound stages, the shops turning out props, costumes and special effects, the pulsing sounds of machinery, the glaring lights, the shouted orders – all said "industry."'

Herbert also spoke of the problems that plagued the film: 'the necessity to bribe Mexican officials before you could work or ship your film; shoddy equipment; some of the worst air in the world.' But there were other problems, such as the sudden departure of special-effects expert John Dykstra, who left half way through the production, citing 'creative differences'; this pushed the film back by several months, leading, in turn, to Freddie Francis's departure to work on

Return to Oz (1985), replaced for the rest of the shoot by James Devis.

Having worked with far more immediate kinds of special effects in *Eraserhead* and *The Elephant Man*, Lynch found the processes required to render the incredible visual aspects of *Dune* ironically limiting, since they called for a more rigid directorial style. 'I'd be directing the actors in front of a blue screen, but I'd have to have storyboarded the sequence for the special-effects guys working on the backgrounds. I'd want to change something, and they'd come and say, "David, you did your storyboards and we've got these things going, you can't change that." I hate getting locked in because magical things can happen on the set.'

Production finally wrapped in Mexico City in early February 1984, following which Lynch returned to Los Angeles to supervise the extensive post-production. The biggest problem was honing the material down to a manageable, *releasable* length – the first rough assembly ran almost four hours, whereas Dino De Laurentiis insisted the film be no longer than two hours and seventeen minutes. 'A mound of stuff had to go,' Lynch complained. 'And the rest of the stuff had to go into a garbage compactor to push it together. You'd have a line instead of a scene and the line would be in voice-over. It's not a way to go.'

Herbert noted that, as early as 1985, Dino and Raffaella De Laurentiis had discussed the idea of restoring the out-takes and making a miniseries, adding, mysteriously, 'because Dino wanted a longer film all along'. Many of the cut scenes *were* restored in the 1988 TV version but, although Lynch had his name taken off this half-hearted re-edit, he was never happy with the theatrical version either. As Lynch's daughter Jennifer told Jonathan Ross, 'After *Dune* was released and the cut was what it was, he died a thousand deaths. A thousand deaths.' Indeed, after three and a half years from pre-production to release, the critical and commercial failure of the $52 million film almost caused Lynch to turn his back on film-making for good. 'I was beaten down badly after *Dune*,' he told Ross, 'and I had nowhere further to fall.'

CASTING: Lynch initially considered Dexter Fletcher, who had played Bytes's boy in *The Elephant Man*, for the role of Paul Atreides. Fletcher was rehearsing a Royal Shakespeare Company production of Shakespeare's *Henry IV* when Lynch and Raffaella De Laurentiis paid him a visit. 'We sat down and chatted about the whole project,' Fletcher recalls, 'and he said he wanted to make Paul as young as he could, because in the book he's, like, fourteen years old.' While they chatted, actor Patrick Stewart – who was playing Henry IV – sat in the corner learning his lines, and Lynch eventually asked Fletcher who he was. 'I said, "Oh, that's Patrick Stewart," and David wrote down his name. And when I finally saw *Dune*, Patrick was in it, but David had obviously gone for a Paul who was a bit older than fourteen.' Lynch denies that the casting of Kyle MacLachlan had anything to do with his age. 'We looked at people who were older, younger, big, small, dark-haired, blonds,' he says. 'Probably two hundred people for the role of Paul Atreides, and Kyle was the one that got it.'

Kyle MacLachlan was in his early twenties, and still enrolled in the Professional Actor Training Program at the University of Washington, when he read for Lynch. 'We just hit it off,' Lynch told the *Los Angeles Times*. 'We're both from the Northwest and we had a lot to talk about, like we had both been to the same lake . . .' For MacLachlan, it was a boyhood fantasy come true. 'I read a lot when I was a kid,' he explained. 'I had read *Dune* and I *was* Paul Atreides. I wanted to be able to say those words and do that stuff. The first time I stepped in front of the camera, it was kind of a special moment.'

The casting of nine-year-old Alicia Roanne Witt as Alia was particularly apposite, given that Alia is a precociously talented child born with the mental ability of an adult – not unlike Witt herself. 'She was a member of the genius club, the MENSA society,' Lynch says, 'and she memorised the whole script. She'd give people their lines.' In addition, Witt's great-grandfather was gored to death by a bull, the same fate shared by Alia's grandfather in Herbert's *Dune*. 'When I first read *Dune*, I got goosebumps,' Alicia's mother, Diane, told *Starlog*. 'Alia did things based on experiences she has never encountered; Alicia has always done that. There were so many similarities, right down to her hair colour. It was simply uncanny.' Lynch has since worked with Alicia on *Twin Peaks* and *Hotel Room*.

The remainder of the multinational cast included British singer Sting, and thespians Francesca Annis, Siân Phillips and Patrick Stewart; German actor Jürgen Prochnow (*Das Boot*, 1981), Swedish actor Max von Sydow (Ming the Merciless in De Laurentiis's *Flash Gordon*, 1980), the Mexican José Ferrer (father of *Twin Peaks* actor Miguel), Italian Silvana Mangano, Americans Paul Smith (Bluto in *Popeye*, 1980), Linda Hunt (*The Year of Living Dangerously*, 1982) and Sean Young (*Blade Runner*, 1982), and future Lynch Mob members Brad Dourif (*Blue Velvet*), Everett McGill (*Twin Peaks*, *The Straight Story*) and Dean Stockwell (*Blue Velvet*).

THE LYNCH MOB: Jack Nance and Freddie Jones had previously appeared in *Eraserhead* and *The Elephant Man* respectively. Behind the scenes were cinematographer Freddie Francis (*The Elephant Man*), additional unit supervisor and cinematographer Frederick Elmes

(*Eraserhead*) and sound designer Alan Splet (*The Grandmother*, *Eraserhead*), all of whom had previously worked with Lynch.

MEMORABLE QUOTES

Baron: 'He who controls the spice controls the universe!'

Idaho: 'I suspect an incredible secret has been kept on this planet – that the Fremen exist in vast numbers, vast, and it is they who control Arrakis.'

Dr Kynes (V.O.): 'He shall know your ways as if born to them.'

Paul: 'He who can destroy a thing, controls a thing.'

Paul: 'We Fremen have a saying: "God created Arrakis to train the faithful. One cannot go against the word of God."'

SOUND AND MUSIC: US soft-rock group Toto had just sold three million copies of their fourth album, *Toto IV*, when the film-makers invited them to compose *Dune*'s original score. The soundtrack album (823 770-2) features a modest selection of music by Toto and the Vienna Symphony Orchestra, and the Brian Eno/Daniel Lanois/Roger Eno 'Prophecy Theme'.

INFLUENCED BY: 'One of the first things we started out with was a commitment not to make just another science fiction picture,' production designer Tony Masters told *Cinefantastique*. 'In other words, we didn't want the background to outshine the foreground. Our first principle on *Dune* has always been: "If it's been done or seen before, throw it out!"' Indeed, *Dune*'s influences date back far beyond cinema itself. 'There's a distinct Victorian influence on Geidi Prime,' Masters explained. 'We wanted to suggest a similarity to, and awareness of, the past. You'll also see some Assyrian, even Mayan influences in *Dune* . . . There's also a little bit of Venetian influence in Arrakeen.'

LEGACY: The failure of *Dune* led Dino De Laurentiis to cancel Lynch's contract for the next two films in the trilogy, the first of which – based on Herbert's own sequel, *Dune Messiah* – would have entered production immediately after *Blue Velvet*.

Nevertheless, the spirit of *Dune* refused to die. Herbert's books remained in print, finding their way into new media such as computer and trading-card games, before a brand new trilogy, authorised by the estate of Frank Herbert and co-written by his son, Brian, was launched – along with new hardcover editions of all five original *Dune* novels – in 1999. A year later, the Sci-Fi Channel produced a lavish television miniseries adaptation of *Dune* by John M. Harrison, approved by the estate of Frank Herbert. Earning high ratings but mixed reviews, the six-hour version ironically reopened discussion about Lynch's version, and even led to a cautious reappraisal of the theatrical *Dune*. Asked about the show a few weeks after its widely publicised broadcast, Lynch responded, 'What miniseries?'

CUT SCENES / ALTERNATIVE VERSION: In May 1988, an extended, extensively re-edited version of *Dune* debuted on network television in the US, divided into two parts and running 189 minutes in duration. Although appearing to be some fifty minutes longer than the theatrical version, the restored footage comprised barely forty minutes of extra material – indeed, some theatrical material was cut, a result of stricter censorship on television. The remaining ten minutes are taken up by the repetition of credits, establishing shots, a recap of the story at the beginning of part two and a lengthy introduction.

This 'Special TV Edition' – broadcast, save for the opening titles, in the full-screen (4:3) format – was assembled by MCA Television's special projects vice-president Harry Tapelman, apparently using the original editor's script as a guideline. 'We added some of David Lynch's original footage not in the theatrical movie to give the picture a straight-line continuity,' Tapelman explained. 'In the theatrical version, Lynch tried to pour a quart of milk into a pint [pot]. We did lots of recutting within the picture, shortened the long walks and long exits, and reconstituted some of the battle scenes to make them more abrasive. Lynch couldn't see the forest for the trees.'

Lynch, who had no role in the re-editing process and did not authorise the new version, successfully lobbied to have his name replaced by the pseudonym 'Alan Smithee', the credit commonly used by the Directors' Guild of America when a director wishes his name to be removed from the credits of a film. The shoddiness of the television version was highlighted as early as the title sequence, as the credit 'A DAVID LYNCH FILM' is altered to read 'A [*sic*] ALAN SMITHEE FILM'. Lynch's screenplay credit was similarly changed, replaced by the name 'Judas Booth' – perhaps a combination of Judas Iscariot (who betrayed Christ) and either John Wilkes Booth (who assassinated Abraham Lincoln) or *Blue Velvet*'s Frank Booth.

Despite Lynch's disowning of the TV edition, the revised cut does have several advantages over the theatrical version in that it restores scenes that greatly enhance either the narrative sense or characterisation or both. The fact that the reinstated material was of vastly inferior quality to the theatrical footage, and that MCA did not bother to provide the 'blue-within-blue' eye colour to the relevant characters in the restored scenes, makes the TV version both fascinating and frustrating. For the fans who craved a 'director's cut' of *Dune*, with many of the scenes restored, the 'Special TV Edition' is halfway there – and most definitely halfway not.

The following is an attempt to sift through the *Dune*s and highlight the most substantial additions, subtractions and alterations of the TV version:

- Only the opening titles are letterboxed; the rest is 4:3.
- Princess Irulan's prologue is removed; instead, after a 'PROLOGUE' caption and a shot of Herbert's book (the latter perhaps designed to suggest that this version is more faithful), a painted starfield gives way to numerous other paintings, over which an unidentified male narrator (accompanied by often bizarre sound effects) begins reading a condensed history of the events before the film, spanning nearly five thousand years and lasting six minutes. After erroneously changing the year to 10,192, the prologue ends with the 'secret report within the Guild', originally read by a Guild member but annexed here by the narrator. (In the last draft of Lynch's script, dated 9 December 1983, Reverend Mother Ramallo is the narrator.)
- After Princess Irulan leaves, there is additional dialogue in which Shaddam dismisses his court, and insists on 'no eavesdropping'.
- After Shaddam requests telepathy and a report from the Reverend Mother, she says that Navigators' minds 'move in strange directions' and insists on sitting close to the Navigator. Shaddam refuses, knowing that only he will be allowed an audience.
- The scene between Shaddam and the Navigator is extended as it reminds the Emperor of the spice's importance in several things, including space travel. 'Without us your empire would be lost on isolated scattered planets.' During the previous exchange, references to '*House* Atreides' are changed to '*Duke* Atreides', and 'the Harkonnens' to 'Baron Harkonnen'.
- After the Navigator leaves, Shaddam and the Reverend Mother discuss the implications of the visit. When she leaves, Shaddam asks a guard to watch her because '[her] loyalty to the sisterhood is stronger than her loyalty to me'.
- Between the scenes on Kaitain and Caladan, an additional scene was constructed from stock footage and out-takes, to give the impression that the Reverend Mother was travelling to Caladan. (Nonsensically, Paul and Jessica can be glimpsed in one of the ship's interiors.)
- Information about the ducal ring in Paul's filmbook is replaced with images and narration about the flora and fauna of Kaitain.
- After Paul's consultation of the filmbook, the narrator introduces Gurney Halleck, Dr Wellington Yueh, Thufir Hwat and Duncan Idaho, describing their roles as Paul's mentors.
- Paul's discussion with Yueh about Arrakis is extended to cover the

seven-hundred-kilometres-per-hour sandstorms on Arrakis, and why the body shields do not work on the surface of the dry world. (Its surface is charged with static electricity.)

- There is more commentary from Gurney during Paul's fight with the robot.
- The scene between the Duke and Paul is modified, extended and even rescored!
- The scene in which the Reverend Mother admonishes Jessica for siring a son is extended, making the Reverend Mother more sympathetic.
- As Paul prepares to be tested with the box, Jessica tells him, 'Remember you are a Duke's son.'
- The scene in which Paul is tested with the box is extended, although his vision of Chani is removed. Paul tells the Reverend Mother he knows when people speak the truth, and that not all of his dreams come true. 'I know which ones will.' She wonders if he is the Kwisatz Haderach, 'the person who can be in many places at once. The one who bridges time and space. He will look where we cannot.'
- The scene showing Leto at his desk is explained in narration, as he writes a letter rejecting the Baron's peace gesture.
- Several shots of characters with sewn-up ears and mouths are deleted.
- All dialogue regarding the doctor's loving care of the Baron's diseases is deleted.
- The scene in which the Baron kills a handsome male servant, by removing his heart plug and bathing in his blood, is removed.
- The flashback scene in which Jessica says, 'Oh, I'll miss Caladan so much,' is removed; instead, a touching scene showing the Duke and Lady Jessica in bed together (conceiving Alia) is added earlier.
- The beginning of the Atreides' trip to Arrakis is slightly altered and re-scored.
- Over shots of the Fremen, the narrator introduces them and their prophecy. The added shots, deleted from the theatrical version before post-production, do not show the 'blue-within-blue eyes' we have been told to expect of them, and have just seen sported by the Reverend Mother Ramallo.
- Additional dialogue is added to the scene between the Duke and Duncan Idaho, in which they discuss the contents of a Fremen message: 'column of smoke by day, pillar of fire by night' – a warning.
- A nonsensical shot of a marching army is added.
- The scene in which Dr Yueh performs an autopsy is extended, so that we see him removing the message from the body.
- An additional filmbook sequence shows Paul researching the operations of the spice harvesters and carry-alls, accompanied by the narrator's description of their operation and number.

- During the ornithopter's flight over the spice harvester, Kynes gives some additional explanation about the spotters and seismic probes.
- After Paul survives the hunter-seeker, Leto questions Thufir about the breach of security, and thinks: 'And a traitor. God help us.'
- A narrator notes the significance of the ducal ring.
- Duke Leto and Paul have a nocturnal discussion in which the Duke fears for the future, until they are interrupted by the arrival of the Harkonnen ships. (This scene adds poignancy to the one in which Leto does not wake his sleeping son, and is captured.)
- The conference, in which the possible traitor is discussed, is extended considerably. Duke Leto rejects Thufir's resignation over the breach of security, observing that it was Thufir's training that saved Paul. After Thufir's explanation of the shielding, he talks of Dr Kynes, who 'may or may not be sympathetic to the cause'. He advises against Leto leaving the palace, but Leto calms him, telling Gurney to recruit more spice miners. 'They shall come all for violence,' Gurney responds stiffly. 'Their faces shall sup up as the east wind. They will gather the captivity of the sand.' Leto sends him on his way. 'Behold as a wild ass in the desert go I forth in my work,' Gurney says, and leaves. Leto smiles at Paul, who laughs, lightening the mood.
- In one of the other major additions, the Shadout Mapes visits Jessica, referring to her as 'noble born' and asking for orders. Jessica tells her that she is not 'noble born', explains her true status and asks about Mapes's name. 'You know the ancient tongue?' Mapes responds, startled. 'I know many things. I know you came prepared for violence with a weapon in your bodice.' Mapes explains that the weapon was sent as a gift, should Jessica prove to be the one. 'And the means of my death, should I prove otherwise.' Mapes screams and, unsheathed knife in her hand, throws herself at Jessica's feet, and her mercy. 'My Lady,' she says, 'when one has lived with prophecy for so long, the moment of revelation is a shock.' (This scene is a nonsensically truncated version of the scripted scene, in which, before Mapes falls at Jessica's feet, she unsheathes the knife, which Jessica deduces must be a crysknife and tells Mapes so. 'Say it not lightly,' Mapes responds. 'Do you know its meaning?' Jessica ponders the answer, and, deducing further that the correct response is 'maker of death,' begins 'It's a maker . . .' At *this* point, Mapes screams and falls to the floor, shocked (as she explains in the TV version) by the revelation of the prophecy. As scripted, the scene continues as Mapes offers Jessica her life. Jessica scratches a line across Mapes's breast with the blade, to which an awestruck Mapes responds, 'You are ours. You are the one.')

- The TV version deletes a scene in which a Harkonnen message is translated.
- An additional scene occurs between Dr Kynes, Yueh, the Duke, Paul and Thufir, in which Dr Kynes allies himself with the Duke, sealing the bond between the Atreides and the Fremen. Gurney plays the baliset he was seen holding earlier in both versions, and Kynes signals his approval by clicking his tongue in the manner of applause.
- Before the Duke is hit by a poison dart, some additional footage of Mapes's death is included, though it is not clear that she has committed suicide.
- The scene in which Feyd toys with the Duke is extended as Feyd feeds the traitor Yueh the Duke's insignia.
- The Baron shows his weakness when faced with Yueh.
- The scene in which the Baron spits on Jessica is removed, although the Baron's dialogue is extended, as is Piter's.
- After Jessica overcomes Stilgar, Jamis challenges Paul to a duel, in which Chani advises Paul on Jamis's fighting style. The scene in which Paul kills Jamis in a shieldless knife fight, and then honours him by shedding tears, is reinstated. (This explains why, in the theatrical version, Stilgar says 'You have strength' after Paul has run and hidden!)
- At Jamis's funeral, Paul meets his wife and sons, and the water of Jamis's life is given to Paul in a sacred ceremony involving the Water Masters.
- Paul is told of Dr Kynes's death, and realises that Kynes was Chani's father. 'Both of us have lost our fathers,' Paul says.
- Stilgar's explanation of the procedure for conquering and riding a sand worm is extended.
- The battle scenes on Arrakis are embellished.
- Stilgar allows Paul to witness the 'mystery of mysteries, the end and the beginning' – the way in which the Water of Life is 'milked' from a baby worm.
- During his meeting with the Baron, the Emperor asks why he was not told of the fighting ability of the Fremen, and introduces their only hostage – Alia.

TRAILER: The trailer for the theatrical version begins with Princess Irulan's opening narration, over images from the film. After a white-on-black title, the following voice-over is intercut with more images and dialogue from the film: 'You are about to enter a world where the unexpected, the unknown, and the unbelievable meet. Where kingdoms are built on earth that moves, and skies are filled with fire. Where a warrior is called on to free his people. A world that holds creation's greatest treasure – and greatest terrors. A world where the mighty, the mad, and the magical will have their final battle. *Dune*. A spectacular journey through the wonders of space and the mysteries of time, from the boundaries of the incredible, to the borders of the impossible. Now, Frank Herbert's widely read, talked about, and cherished masterpiece comes to the screen. Dino De Laurentiis presents *Dune*. A world beyond your experience, beyond your imagination.'

POSTER: Various different posters were prepared to promote *Dune*. One depicted the planet's two moons over a desert landscape, with no cast members in view. A better-known image was that of Paul carrying a thumper, with Chani in the background, an army behind them and the sky full of Harkonnen spaceships. (The UK turned this into a landscape-format 'quad' by blacking out the right-hand side of the poster and stretching the title and tag-line across it.) A further design was a composite featuring the Arrakis desertscape, with Paul and Chani about to kiss, and a knife-wielding Feyd in the foreground. Yet another featured Reverend Mother Ramallo, Paul, Feyd and the Baron above the desert, with the entrance to the Grand Hall on Caladan above them. One spectacular image was of a worm emerging, gaping-mawed, from the sand. Another showed the figures of Paul, Chani and most of the other principal characters in a complicated montage, which perhaps combined too many elements to be truly effective.

TAG-LINES: 'A place beyond your dreams. A movie beyond your imagination' ran the (rather patronising) tag-line on most *Dune* posters. UIP's British quad altered the line slightly, to 'A WORLD BEYOND YOUR EXPERIENCE, BEYOND YOUR IMAGINATION,' and reproduced a quote from *Newsweek*: 'Spellbinding saga of the future . . . towers over most futuristic epics. It is richer and stranger than just about anything the commercial cinema now has to offer.'

WHAT THE PAPERS SAID: After months of negative press and an absence of critics' screenings, *Dune* debuted in US cinemas in December 1984. '*Dune* is a huge, hollow, imaginative and cold sci-fi epic,' announced *Variety*. 'Visually unique and teeming with incident, David Lynch's film holds the interest due to its abundant surface attractions.' 'No science fiction film has ever been so inspired by the past, or so audaciously eclectic,' suggested *Newsweek*'s David Ansen. 'For all its quirks and confusions, *Dune* towers over most futuristic epics. It's richer and stranger than just about anything the commercial cinema now has to offer.' Others were not so sure. 'Those critics (admittedly not many) who managed to make *Dune* sound like a marvellous goof must have got high on mélange,' *New York*'s David Denby suggested. 'The worst thing about *Dune* is that director David

Lynch has inadvertently demonstrated in about a dozen ways how originality can be tedious.' The *New York Post*'s Rex Reed agreed. 'You only think you've seen rotten,' he said. 'Wait until you see *Dune*. This pretentious exercise in pointless insanity is so bad it's in a class by itself. It's diabolically bad.'

In the UK, *Dune* fared little better, with *Time Out*'s Anne Billson describing 'a first half of bewildering exposition . . . mish-mash of characters and feuding, feudal empires, which is only ironed out for a second half of *Flash Gordon*-style action.' Billson did, however, notice 'globs of pure Lynch, notably some of the most impressive sci-fi set design since *Blade Runner*' – faint praise, given that *Blade Runner* was released a mere two years earlier! *Empire* magazine was less kind, claiming that *Dune* 'looks like a million dollars. Unfortunately, it cost fifty.'

Perhaps the most important review of all was Herbert's own: 'What reached the screen is a visual feast that begins as *Dune* begins and you hear my dialogue all through it,' he wrote in 1985. 'What [you] saw was true to my book, even though most of it stayed on the cutting-room floor,' he added. 'The fact that David was able to translate the written words into screen language speaks of his visual genius. If you were disappointed or wanted more, chalk it up to "That's show biz."' Nevertheless, even Herbert had his quibbles, particularly with Lynch's own quasi-religious take on the ascension of Paul to literal godhood. 'Paul was a man *playing* god,' he chided, 'not a god who could make it rain.'

BOX OFFICE: Despite earning $6 million in its opening week, *Dune*, which had reportedly cost around $52 million to make, grossed barely more than half that figure in the US: $27.4 million – enough to make it the sixth-biggest earner of 1984. Although the De Laurentiis Entertainment Group stayed solvent for a further couple of years, the calamitous failure of *Dune* was probably instrumental in the eventual collapse of the company, which left the Lynch projects *Ronnie Rocket* and *One Saliva Bubble* [see 'In Dreams,' page 247] not only unrealised but mired in litigation.

AWARDS: By 1984, sound designer Alan Splet already had two Academy Awards under his belt, for *The Black Stallion* (1979) and *The Right Stuff* (1983), yet was not among the four names shortlisted for the Academy Award for Best Sound. (It was *Dune*'s only nomination: its breathtaking production design, inspired costumes, stunning cinematography and the extraordinary performance by Kenneth McMillan would all go unrecognised.) The film was also nominated for a 1985 Hugo Award, for Best Dramatic Presentation.

TRIVIA: Production designer Tony Masters makes a cameo appearance, of sorts – in a portrait hanging on a wall on Caladan!

Jürgen Prochnow's face was badly burned by the chemical used to simulate smoke pouring from his cheek.

AVAILABILITY: In the UK, the theatrical version of *Dune* is available as a full-screen (4:3) budget-priced PAL VHS (051 8063); all previously available letterboxed editions are deleted. In the US, both full-screen (80161) and letterboxed (A8-31353) versions are available on NTSC VHS, along with a letterboxed (2.35:1) Region 1 DVD (20184) which includes production notes, cast and crew biographies, 'film highlights' and the theatrical trailer.

Seldom seen in the UK, and unavailable on video or DVD in the US, the full-screen (4:3) 'Special TV Edition' was finally released as a Region 2 DVD (CHV 5008) on 18 September 2000 – the first time British fans were officially able to see it. This edition is an edited version of both parts of the TV version, runs 177 minutes, since it edits out the duplicated opening and end titles and the recap at the start of the second show. The DVD includes the theatrical trailer (a somewhat ironic inclusion) and an eighteen-page booklet, with many production stills and new liner notes by Alan Robinson, folding out into an A2 reproduction of the British quad.

The only available version of the two-part TV version, 189 minutes in duration, is a Japanese Region 2 DVD entitled *Dune Special Edition* (BBBF-1258).

FINAL ANALYSIS: 'Travelling without moving,' Paul's description of 'folding space,' is as good a description as any of sitting in a darkened cinema and being transported to a far-off galaxy in the eleventh millennium, courtesy of David Lynch. My own experience of *Dune* was a strange one: never having read the novel, my first encounter with the whole enterprise was a cinema screening of the film. I was stunned. By the power of the visuals; by the depth of the socio-political background; even by the lucidity of the storytelling. Next, I read the novel, which I found to be as remarkable and profound as I had hoped, but shorter and less dense than I had been told. I then watched the Alan Smithee cut, which made a great deal more narrative sense (to a *Dune* virgin such as myself) than the theatrical version, but was unsatisfying in other ways. Later, reading Lynch's various drafts of the script gave me what may be the purest form of the film in existence, allowing visual imagination and a recollection of the filmed version(s) to combine into an immensely satisfying experience. (Finally, I even conducted an experiment, watching the theatrical version on DVD, killing the sound every time one of the ridiculous 'inner thoughts' cropped up, and found that not *one* of these whispered expository voice-over lines enhances the viewer's understanding of events. *Do* try this at home, kids.) Having endlessly compared and contrasted all of these different versions – including the much-maligned 'TV' version that Lynch supposedly hates, yet may never have seen – I feel now that a true 'director's cut' restoring *some* of the excised material in the letterboxed format but removing a lot of extraneous exposition and the spoken 'thought-balloons' is clearly the way forward for *Dune*. This, of course, will never happen, because the compromises Lynch feels he made during production could not have produced a cut that would have satisfied him.

'The first step in avoiding a trap is knowing of its existence,' Thufir Hawat tells Paul; Lynch would have done well to take his advice before making the leap from a $5 million black-and-white biopic to a $50 million space opera. On the set of *Dune*, Lynch wore protective headgear to shield himself from the dirt thrown up by fans. Nothing, however, could protect him from the dirt thrown up by the millions of *Dune* fans, who – despite Frank Herbert's approval of Lynch's adaptation – either dismissed the film out of hand or grudgingly accepted that even this *Dune* was better than no *Dune* at all. Taking a cue from the House Atreides, Lynch set out to have his own 'weirding way' with *Dune*, and was probably fifty per cent successful, artistically speaking. (Of course, I speak as one who came to the book about thirty years late.) With even the director's compromises being compromised, it is astonishing to think that Lynch's own 'filmbook' came even *that* close.

If you remain unconvinced, remember this: Lynch's spice odyssey may have been swallowed up in the sand but, without it, *Blue Velvet* might never have got a green light.

EXPERT WITNESS: 'I was clueless; a lamb; and that saved me, I think. I didn't know how much was riding on it; how much I had to lose or gain . . . I was like, bring on the rubber suit! Bring on the worms! There were gigantic sets and men with giant boils and women wearing weird contact lenses, and we were running around shouting all this dialogue we didn't understand, and it didn't work at all. [But] if you go back to it, it's an amazing visual experience. And it's kind of responsible for everything that's happened to me since.' – actor Kyle MacLachlan (Paul Atreides)

LYNCH ON *DUNE*: 'I started selling out on *Dune*. Looking back, it's no one's fault but my own. I probably shouldn't have done that picture, but I saw tons and tons of possibilities for things I loved, and this was the structure to do them in. There was so much room to create a world. But I got strong indications from Raffaella and Dino De Laurentiis of what kind of film they expected, and I knew I didn't have final cut . . . Every decision was always made with them in mind and their sort of film. Things I felt I could get away with in their framework. So it was destined to be a failure, to me.'

Blue Velvet (1986)

35mm feature / 120 mins / colour / live action

Directed by David Lynch
Produced by Fred Caruso
Screenplay by David Lynch
Director of Photography Frederick Elmes
Sound Designer Alan Splet
Edited by Duwayne Dunham
Music Composed and Conducted by Angelo Badalamenti
Production Designer Patricia Norris
Executive Producer Richard Roth
Casting by Johanna Ray and Pat Golden

CAST: Kyle MacLachlan (*Jeffrey Beaumont*), Isabella Rossellini (*Dorothy Vallens*), Dennis Hopper (*Frank Booth*), Laura Dern (*Sandy Williams*), Hope Lange (*Pam Williams*), Priscilla Pointer (*Frances Beaumont*), George Dickerson (*Detective John Williams*), Frances Bay (*Aunt Barbara*), Ken Stovitz (*Mike Shaw*), Brad Dourif (*Raymond*), Jack Nance (*Paul*), Dean Stockwell (*Ben*), J. Michael Hunter (*Hunter*), Jack Harvey (*Tom Beaumont*), Dick Green (*Don Vallens*), Fred Pickler (*Detective Tom R. Gordon / The Yellow Man*), Philip Market (*Dr Gynde*), Leonard Watkins (*Double Ed #1*), Moses Gibson (*Double Ed #2*), Selden Smith (*Nurse Cindy*), Peter Carew (*Coroner*), Jon Jon Snipes (*Little Donny*), Andy Badale (*Piano Player*), John Pierre Viale (*Master of Ceremonies*), Donald Moore (*Desk Sergeant*), A. Michelle Depland, Michelle Sasser, Katie Reid (*Party Girls*), Sparky (*The Dog*)

UNCREDITED CAST: Even the dog is credited in the *Blue Velvet* cast list; Lynch, however, is not: the voice on the police radio is his, foreshadowing his vocal contributions to *Twin Peaks* (Gordon Cole makes his first 'appearance' over a speaker phone), *Hotel Room* (opening credits), and his PlayStation 2 commercial. Composer Angelo Badalamenti appears as the Slow Club's piano player, but is credited as 'Andy Badale', the Anglicised name he used on his earlier films as composer, *Across the Great Divide* (1976), *Gordon's War* (1978) and *Law and Disorder* (1974).

TITLE SEQUENCE: As Angelo Badalamenti's main title theme plays, the titles appear in a florid white text, over a background of blue velvet curtains.

SUMMARY: When his father has a seizure, Jeffrey Beaumont returns to his home town, Lumberton, and finds a severed ear in the grass, which he takes to Detective Williams. When Williams's daughter, Sandy, tells him she heard her father talking about a nightclub singer named Dorothy Vallens, Jeffrey devises a plan to break into her apartment, hide and observe. He does so, but is discovered by Dorothy, who strips and threatens him, and then seduces him. When they, in turn, are interrupted by the arrival of Frank Booth, Jeffrey hides in and watches from the closet while Frank abuses and assaults Dorothy, before leaving. Jeffrey emerges, and their own sexual tryst continues until Dorothy asks him to hurt her. Assembling the pieces of the puzzle, Jeffrey surmises that Frank has kidnapped Dorothy's husband and son to force her into fulfilling his desires. After spying on Frank, Jeffrey visits Dorothy and continues their affair, but is discovered by Frank, who takes him on a perverse joyride into his world, ultimately beating him unconscious and leaving him on waste ground. Jeffrey and Sandy are falling in love, but Jeffrey has suspicions that her father and another detective may be involved with Frank's drug deals. One night, a naked Dorothy visits Jeffrey at home, revealing, to Sandy's horror, their illicit affair. Unable to trust the police, Jeffrey returns to Dorothy's apartment, where he finds Dorothy's husband and the other detective dead. He hides in the closet as Frank comes looking for him, and shoots Frank dead. With the horror behind them, Jeffrey and Sandy get together, Jeffrey's father recovers and the arrival of a robin signifies love – even though it has a live bug in its beak, indicating that this is not a 'happy' ending. Dorothy recovers, and is reunited with her son. But she can still see blue velvet through her tears.

PRODUCTION HISTORY: Actor Jack Nance liked to tell the story of how, during the lengthy post-production of *Eraserhead*, he first learned about Lynch's plan to make a film called *Blue Velvet*. 'He had this three-by-five drawing that he'd done of this rustic roadhouse or saloon, out in the countryside,' he told *Wrapped in Plastic*. 'It was just by the side of the road with this big neon sign on top of the place that said "Blue Velvet". He showed it to me and said, "How do you like it, Jack?" I said, "It's beautiful." He said, "We're going to do that someday." I said, "Do what?" And he said, "We're going to do *Blue Velvet*. It's a movie."'

This may well be true; certainly, Lynch had spoken of making a contemporary thriller with teenage heroes prior to the release of *The*

Elephant Man, and completed the first drafts of *Blue Velvet* before production began on *Dune*. Nevertheless, it took many years for the ideas that would eventually comprise *Blue Velvet* to coalesce. 'I got three ideas that were like magnets for all the rest,' he told the *Village Voice*. 'The first was Bobby Vinton's song and the mood that came with that song – a mood, a time, and things that were of that time. The next idea I got was that I always wanted to sneak into a girl's room at night just to watch her. The idea was that I would be watching her and I would see a clue, whether I knew it then or later, an important clue to a mystery, like a murder. Then the third idea was the ear in the field, because it would be like finding a ticket to another world – you know, it would change your life.'

In early 1985, Lynch showed the script of what he described as 'a story of love and mystery . . . about a guy who lives in two worlds at the same time, one of which is pleasant and the other dark and terrifying' to producer Dino De Laurentiis. Despite the failure of *Dune*, De Laurentiis agreed to bankroll *Blue Velvet* – and, indeed, give Lynch final cut – on the condition that the budget would not exceed $5 million, and that Lynch accept half pay as writer and director. The other half would be payable if the film was a success, which it was.

Filming began in the summer of that year, in a small town – Wilmington, North Carolina – where Dino De Laurentiis had just constructed a new studio. 'He had nine or ten pictures going in Wilmington,' Lynch explains, 'and we were the underdog. We had the littlest budget, and he didn't pay any attention to us except the first day, [when] he came in and saw dailies.' It was not, it turned out, a good day for him to do so, as they had been having problems with the camera during filming in Dorothy Vallens' apartment block. Lynch recalls, 'I like things dark, but they were, like, *real* dark.' De Laurentiis, of course, demanded to know why. 'And I said, "The lens is broken, Dino." And he said, "Oh," and then he left. So we shot everything again the next day.'

One of the major advantages of Wilmington was that it was located only seventy miles from a real town called Lumberton, which enabled the inexpensive use of police cars carrying the town's insignia. Another advantage was that it allowed Lynch to capture the 50s feel he was looking for. '[Jeffrey] is an idealist,' he stated. 'He behaves like young people in the 50s, and the little town where I filmed is a good reflection of the naïve climate there was back then. The local people tended to think the way people did thirty years ago.' Although *Blue Velvet* was principally a location shoot, using a bare minimum of constructed sets, costume and production designer Patricia Norris was nonetheless able to realise Lynch's vision of a daylight world saturated with colour, counterbalanced by the muted hues of the interiors. 'All rooms come out of people,' Norris explained, referring to Dorothy Vallens's apartment, in which forlorn, washed-out colours reflect the emotional state of its only tenant. 'If you understand who the characters are, you understand how they live. Most decorating conveys what's not written, and gives you a sense of the people.'

Both Lynch and Kyle MacLachlan headed for North Carolina eager to begin *Blue Velvet*, each having suffered a career setback after the failure of *Dune*. Indeed, MacLachlan was so anxious, he arrived on location two weeks early, despite the often disturbing nature of the scenes he was to perform. 'It was sickly erotic, the stuff I did with Isabella [Rossellini],' he told the *Los Angeles Times*. 'It made your heart beat fast.' Yet, he added, 'I trusted David that he would do it in such a way that those scenes would be truly offensive and not erotic; that it would be horrific. That was my only concern – that it would not come across like cruel treatment [of women] is good.'

Understandably, Rossellini – whom Lynch reportedly asked to gain thirty-five pounds for the role – had similar concerns. One scene that proved particularly gruelling for the actress was the one in which she is discovered, stark naked, arms outstretched, outside Jeffrey's house. According to Lynch, it was inspired by a real-life incident in which he and his younger brother had seen a naked woman walking along the street. 'It was so strange,' he told the *Village Voice*, 'but it was also strange that my brother started crying. Because she was crazed, something bad had happened – we both knew she didn't even know where she was or that she was naked. The same as Dorothy.' Rossellini's own inspiration for the scene came from an even more unexpected source. 'My "model-trained" brain flashed me an image: the photo by Nick Ut of the girl in Vietnam walking in the street naked, skin hanging from her arms after a napalm-bomb attack. That devastated, helpless, obscene, frightening look seemed to me what David wanted,' she wrote in her autobiography, *Some of Me*, 'and I adopted it for my scene.'

When the time came to shoot the scene, several passers-by gathered to watch, resisting pleas for them to disperse. 'People came with blankets and picnic baskets, with their grandmothers and small children,' Rossellini recalled. 'I begged the assistant director to warn them that it was going to be a tough scene, that I was going to be totally naked, but they stayed anyway.' Just before the scene was shot, Rossellini apologised to them and concentrated on the scene. 'Once David called, "Cut – we have it," someone came with a robe for me to wear and my attention returned to our surroundings. Everybody had left,' she recalled. The next day, the police informed the crew that no further permits would be issued for shooting in the streets of Wilmington.

After some experimentation in this direction, Lynch and Elmes decided to deepen the black areas of the image in order to create a greater contrast with the colours. 'By not explaining everything with light,' Elmes told *American Cinematographer*, 'darkness gives my imagination an opening. So sometimes I choose to hold back light in areas of the frame, because I don't want to explain the image that clearly. I want to make the audience imagine, and fish for what's out there.' This combination of light and shade was crucial to the film's exploration of two worlds, the surface, with its almost unnatural blue skies, red roses and white picket fences, and the twilight world of horror, disease and decay. Lynch explained, 'I see it all as one world. That's the weird part of it. There's the surface and things you discover hiding. There's light and varying degrees of darkness.' Does he even give Jeffrey and Sandy a future? 'Yeah, absolutely. But in a way, an uneasy sort of future. It wouldn't be euphoric.' For Lynch, however, making *Blue Velvet* after the failure of *Dune* was most certainly a happy ending.

CASTING: Kyle MacLachlan had made his feature-film debut in Lynch's *Dune*, and when Val Kilmer (*The Doors*, 1991) passed on the role of Jeffrey Beaumont, Lynch offered it to MacLachlan – who also turned it down. 'I read the script,' he told the *Guardian*, 'and I said, "I understand everything that goes on. I understand how you could be drawn into a woman like this."' MacLachlan, however, sought parental approval before agreeing to take the role, not least because his mother had just been diagnosed with ovarian cancer. 'My mom objected to the film's treatment of women,' he told the *Los Angeles Times*. 'At the time I said her reaction was valid because she had cancer and I didn't want to do anything more to disrupt her life. So I turned it down.' Months went by, and whilst MacLachlan was unable to find work, Lynch was unable to find a replacement for him. 'And David called again, and partly because I needed to work and partly because the script had never left my head, I said yes. And David said, "I knew you'd come back."'

Laura Dern, the daughter of actors Bruce Dern and Diane Ladd (who would later play Dern's screen mother in *Wild at Heart*), was cast as Sandy Williams after Lynch saw her in Peter Bogdanovich's *Mask* (1985), a kind of contemporary retelling of *The Elephant Man*, in which Dern played a blind girl who falls in love with a boy (Eric Stoltz) with a monstrously deformed face.

According to legend, Dennis Hopper snagged the role of Frank Booth with the immortal words, 'I've got to play Frank, because I *am* Frank.' Hopper explained his reasoning: 'It wasn't so much that I *was* Frank Booth as that I'd seen [people like] Frank. I'd been with them, known them, they'd been friends. It was something I really understood.' Perhaps it was just as well that Hopper's enthusiasm won out, since Lynch had initially encountered difficulties casting the role. 'Frank was a character that actors, when they really started thinking about doing those things, had some problems with,' Lynch recalled. One actor who had no such qualms was Robert Loggia, the gravel-voiced Italian-American best known for his supporting role in *Prizzi's Honor* (1985). 'I wanted to do *Blue Velvet* the moment I read that script,' Loggia remembered. 'I was dying to play that role Dennis Hopper played. I thought I would test for it or whatever or try to convince [Lynch].' Loggia came in to read with stand-ins for Dorothy and Jeffrey, and time got away from Lynch. 'Three hours or so went by on this very hot afternoon in the Valley,' Loggia continued, 'and I got meaner than a junkyard dog. I mean, I was really pissed. And when David got there . . . I blew my fuse.' Evidently, Lynch bore Loggia no grudge, later casting him as Mr Eddy in *Lost Highway*.

Lynch encountered more difficulties with the casting of Dorothy Vallens, testing numerous actresses – including Helen Mirren (*Caligula*, 1980) – before finding Isabella Rossellini, who would become his leading lady, both on and off screen. Lynch recounted, 'I met her in a restaurant . . . then a week later I saw her picture in *Screen World* . . . I said, "Holy jumpin' George, she's an actress!"' Rossellini, the daughter of actress Ingrid Bergman and director Roberto Rossellini, immediately connected with the character. 'Something just seemed right about it for her,' Lynch added. 'She just had to do it. She just loved the script and wanted to do it.'

The only reservation that actor Dean Stockwell (*Quantum Leap*) had about the *Blue Velvet* script was the character Lynch wanted him to play, Ben. Having learned that Dennis Hopper had been cast as Frank Booth, Stockwell knew that his approach to the character was going to make Frank 'an all-time film antagonist', and his interpretation of the script suggested that Ben appeared to be 'the one individual that this Frank seems to gravitate toward and look up to, and even be in awe of him, in some respect. So it just seemed to add up – two and two is four – that Ben had to be weirder than Frank, and further out if possible. So I put on my further-out cap and came up with the character that I did.'

THE LYNCH MOB: In addition to Kyle MacLachlan, three other *Dune* alumni appeared in *Blue Velvet*: Dean Stockwell, Jack Nance and Brad Dourif. Nance had, of course, previously appeared in *Eraserhead*. *Blue Velvet* also reunited Lynch with *Eraserhead* cinematographer Frederick Elmes, production designer Patricia Norris and sound designer Alan Splet, and marked the beginning of his long associations with composer Angelo Badalamenti and editor Duwayne Dunham. Also among the crew was apprentice editor Mary Sweeney, who had assisted Dunham on *The Mean Season* (1985), and would become not only a regular collaborator with Lynch (*Twin Peaks, Wild at Heart, Fire Walk with Me, Lost Highway, The Straight Story, Mulholland Drive*) but also his long-term partner and mother to his youngest son, Riley.

MEMORABLE QUOTES
Jeffrey: 'It's a strange world, isn't it?'

Jeffrey: 'There are opportunities in life for gaining knowledge and experience. Sometimes it's necessary to take a risk.'

Sandy: 'I don't know if you're a detective or a pervert.'
Jeffrey: 'Well, that's for me to know and you to find out.'

Sandy: 'I had a dream. In fact, it was the night I met you. In the dream, there was our world, and the world was dark, because there weren't any robins. And the robins represented love. And for the longest time there was just this darkness, and all of a sudden, thousands of robins were set free, and they flew down and brought this blinding light of love. And it seemed like that love would be the only thing that would make any difference. And it did. So I guess it means there is trouble till the robins come.'

Dorothy: 'Hold me! I'm falling! I'm falling!'

SOUND AND MUSIC: The extraordinary (and often overlooked) soundscapes of *Blue Velvet* were once again the work of Alan Splet, who had begun his long association with Lynch as early as *The Grandmother*, and had since won an Academy Award for *The Black Stallion* (1979). Among the most startling effects were the sounds of Frank striking Dorothy (an effect obtained by hitting a dried-out pumpkin with a cork-backed steel ruler), and ants crawling over the severed ear (the sound of cockroaches scurrying across stretched latex).

Composer Angelo Badalamenti's own long working relationship with Lynch began when producer Fred Caruso suggested to Lynch that the Brooklyn-born Italian-American composer work with Isabella Rossellini as a vocal coach to help her sing the title song. At Caruso's suggestion, Lynch and Badalamenti worked together on an original song for *Blue Velvet*, 'Mysteries of Love', used in place of This Mortal Coil's recording of Tim Buckley's 'Song to a Siren', which Lynch was unable to afford to license for the film. With lyrics by Lynch and music by Badalamenti, 'Mysteries of Love' was sung by Badalamenti's friend Julee Cruise, who would go on to record an entire album of Lynch-Badalamenti songs, perform one of them in a roadhouse in the *Twin Peaks* pilot and later turn up as the centrepiece of the Lynch-Badalamenti performance piece, *Industrial Symphony No. 1*.

So successful was the Lynch/Badalamenti/Cruise collaboration that Lynch invited Badalamenti to compose the entire orchestral score for *Blue Velvet*. 'When we were talking about the main title theme,' Badalamenti told the *Los Angeles Times*, 'David said, "It's gotta be like Shostakovich, be very Russian, but make it the most beautiful thing, but make it dark and a little bit scary."' Indeed, according to the screenplay, Lynch had originally intended to use Dmitri Shostakovich's final work, Symphony No. 15 in A major, as a recurring leitmotif.

One famous song, now as synonymous with *Blue Velvet* as the title tune, is Roy Orbison's 'In Dreams'. Surprisingly, Lynch did not conceive of using this until he and Kyle MacLachlan were on their way to Wilmington, North Carolina, to begin filming, and Orbison's 'Crying' began playing on a cab radio. Lynch immediately knew he wanted it for the film. Having listened to more Orbison recordings, however, Lynch decided on 'In Dreams', whose lyric – 'In dreams I walk with you/In dreams I talk to you/In dreams you're mine, all of the time/We're together in dreams, in dreams . . .' – he felt explained some of the themes of the film, and could more easily be twisted by the character Lynch conceived of singing the song: Frank Booth. As Lynch recalled, 'All of a sudden Dennis stops singing and looks at Dean – who's continuing to sing. Dennis is solidly in character and he is moved by Dean's (Ben's) singing. There was the scene in front of me. It was so perfect.' Although Orbison originally expressed discomfort at Lynch's contextual use of the song, he changed his mind after a second viewing of the film, which ultimately gave him something of an autumnal career revival: on 21 January 1987, he was inducted into the Rock and Roll Hall of Fame, an event that was followed by the re-recording of nineteen of his songs for an album entitled *In Dreams: The Greatest Hits* (VGDCD3514), which featured a new version of the title song, recorded in Los Angeles in April 1987, and co-produced by Orbison, T-Bone Burnett and . . . David Lynch.

Blue Velvet's soundtrack album, still widely available (VCD47277 and CDTER1127), features almost 42 minutes of Badalamenti's music, including three versions of 'Mysteries of Love,' one of which is sung by Julee Cruise. The album also contains 'Honky Tonk Part 1' performed by Bill Doggett, Roy Orbison's 'In Dreams', Ketty Lester's 'Love Letters' and the version of 'Blue Velvet' sung by Isabella Rossellini. It omits Rossellini's performance of the Lynch/Badalamenti song 'Blue Star' and the Chris Isaak songs 'Livin' for your Lover' and 'Gone Ridin'' (both from his 1985 album *Silvertone*) and, as a consequence of copyright problems, Bobby Vinton's original recording of 'Blue Velvet'.

INFLUENCED BY: Jennifer Lynch has stated, 'I know that *Blue Velvet* came out of the light and dark extreme that are so much David, his whole world as a child which was very white picket fence and lovely woods . . . I don't think David bought it, that there was only peace going on inside those doors – I think he knew better, number one; and because he didn't think anybody believed him, he exaggerated what might be going on inside those homes, and I'm sure that segued into *Blue Velvet*.'

Lynch has often spoken of his admiration for American painter Edward Hopper, whose portraits of American (and, just as often, European) landscapes offer a subtle and intriguingly dysfunctional view of familiar locations – diners, gas stations, clapboard houses with white picket fences – whose dark-eyed inhabitants suggest a disquieting demeanour beneath the surface polish. This is Lynch's outlook, and especially *Blue Velvet*'s, in a nutshell.

If Lynch is 'Jimmy Stewart from Mars', as Mel Brooks once famously described him, *Blue Velvet* might be seen a kind of Martian version of *It's A Wonderful Life*. The central characters of Capra's film (George Bailey) and Lynch's (Jeffrey Beaumont) are not dissimilar: each is a good-hearted young man who sacrifices dreams of college to stay at home and look after the family business, after his father has a stroke. In any other discussion, Capra's and Lynch's cinematic world-views would seem to be diametrically opposed – in Capra's town, Bedford Falls, good and evil are mutually exclusive; in Lumberton, they co-exist – but in *Blue Velvet*, Lynch not only sets out to subvert *It's A Wonderful Life*, but attempts a similar feat with that other staple of cinema Americana, *The Wizard of Oz* (1939). Certain references are there for the taking – Dorothy (a singer, like Judy Garland), her red shoes (ruby slippers), Frank (as impotent as the Wizard, hidden inside his *booth*, played by *Frank* Morgan in the film based on a novel by *Frank* Baum), and, in earlier drafts of *Blue Velvet*, the subversive use of the song 'Somewhere Over the Rainbow' as Dorothy contemplates suicide. Lynch also liked the fact that Dennis Hopper was from Kansas. 'It's perfect that Frank would be from Kansas,' Lynch told the *Village Voice*, 'because Kansas has something to do with *The Wizard of Oz* and Dorothy.' Lynch would incorporate more overt themes from *The Wizard of Oz* in his next film, *Wild at Heart*.

Another obvious influence on *Blue Velvet* is Alfred Hitchcock's *Rear Window* (1954), with which it shares not only its pervading theme of voyeurism – both films making the audience complicit in the voyeuristic tendencies of their leading characters, who discover wrongdoing while spying into a woman's apartment – but also the names of their protagonists: in *Rear Window*, James Stewart's character is named L. B. Jefferies, but referred to as 'Jeff'. As Charles Drazin noted in his 1998 study of *Blue Velvet*, the female protagonists of both films are not dissimilar: 'Lisa and Sandy share a "feminine intuition" and both overcome their cautious natures to risk extreme danger . . . There's even a visual resemblance,' he added. If *Rear Window* gave Jeffrey his name, Sandy's may have come from that 70s slice of 50s nostalgia, *Grease* (1978), in which Olivia Newton-John plays an all-American girl named, appropriately, Sandy.

Finally, there is something about a toddler playing near a man struck down in his garden that recalls Don Corleone's death in Francis Ford Coppola's *The Godfather* (1972).

LEGACY: *Blue Velvet* ushered in a new era for cinema, in which the veneer of American suburban life was stripped away, revealing the dark beneath. It is impossible to list the vast number of films that *Blue Velvet* beneath; certainly, Hollywood seemed to take the film as a signal to allow such films to be made, even in the context of mainstream cinema. One of the most *Blue Velvet*-like films was Jonathan Demme's *Something Wild*, in which a strait-laced yuppie (Jeff Daniels) with a penchant for running out on restaurant bills enters a disturbed and cracked underworld, courtesy of a mysterious woman (Melanie Griffith) with dangerous associates (Ray Liotta, Lynch's friend Tracey Walter). Nevertheless, *Something Wild* was filmed at the same time as *Blue Velvet*, and released in the same watershed year: 1986.

Director Michael Almereyda – whose third film, *Nadja* (1995), was produced by Lynch – has said that Kyle MacLachlan's performance in *Blue Velvet* led him to cast the actor, against type, in his contemporary version of *Hamlet* (2000). 'In MacLachlan's face you could read the essence of Lynch's psychic universe: the spectacle of all-American "wholesomeness" flirting with multiple inner demons,' Almereyda stated. 'When we were casting about for an actor to play Claudius, Shakespeare's murderous, lecherous, treacherous, double-talking "smiling villain" in *Hamlet*,' he continued, 'it didn't really take much of an imaginative leap to consider Kyle.'

In an article in which he placed *Blue Velvet* among his own choice of '100 greatest movies', former *Guardian* film critic Derek Malcolm acknowledged the debt owed by Sam Mendes's Oscar-winner *American Beauty* (2000) to Lynch's 1986 film. 'Those celebrating the success of . . . *American Beauty* as a scorching exposure of

American suburbia,' he wrote, 'might benefit from taking another look at David Lynch's *Blue Velvet*, a much more radical fable on the same subject.'

DÉJÀ VU: In the scene where Jeffrey first meets Sandy, she appears out of the darkness in a manner that recalls the first appearance of Henry's neighbour in *Eraserhead*; later, Jeffrey sits on his bed in a style reminiscent of Henry. Dorothy's reverence of the photograph of her husband and son recalls two other cherished photographs: Henry's torn portrait of Mary X (*Eraserhead*) and John Merrick's picture of his mother (*The Elephant Man*). The fact that Brad Dourif and Jack Nance play Baron Harkonnen's lackeys in *Dune* and Frank Booth's goons in *Blue Velvet,* is also no coincidence; the Baron takes as much delight in humiliating Jessica Atreides (by spitting on her face) as Frank does in humiliating Dorothy.

THEMES AND MOTIFS: Many critics have talked of the themes of family contained within *Blue Velvet*. Cut off from his father by circumstance, and unable to communicate with his mother, Jeffrey finds a perverse substitute for parents in Dorothy and Frank. If Dorothy is the surrogate mother (or, more accurately, Jeffrey the surrogate son – her own son, Donny, has been kidnapped, and she often calls Jeffrey 'Don', the name of both her husband and her son) and Frank the substitute father (frequently calling Dorothy 'mommy,' and referring to himself as 'daddy'), then *Blue Velvet* unfolds according to an Oedipal logic, in that Jeffrey usurps his 'father', has sex with his 'mother', suffers an attack of conscience and finally kills his 'father'. As author and critic J. G. Ballard – who once described *Blue Velvet* as '*The Wizard of Oz* reshot with a script by Kafka and décor by Francis Bacon' – noted, 'It's interesting that the parents of the two youngsters in the film have very shadowy roles; they play almost no part in the film at all. The real parents – whether Lynch intended this or not – are the gangster and the nightclub singer.'

The Oedipus theme is something that Lynch had already explored, and would revisit repeatedly: in *The Grandmother*, the boy's mother's affection is more lascivious than motherly; in *Eraserhead*, Mary X's mother attempts to seduce Henry, just as Lula's mother does with Sailor in *Wild at Heart*; an early draft of *Dune* also added an incestuous relationship between Paul Atreides and his mother, Jessica, while an incestuous father-daughter relationship was a prominent element of *Twin Peaks*, and especially of *Fire Walk With Me*.

Blue Velvet also has strong echoes of fairy tales, the 'babes in the wood' theme prevalent in many such stories, as J. G. Ballard noted:

'Two innocent youngsters who are scarcely more than children enter the dark wood and find a strange haunted castle, in this case the nightclub singer's apartment.'

CUT SCENES: 'I never really asked David what it meant,' Kyle MacLachlan once told the *Los Angeles Times*, referring to *Blue Velvet*. 'It was pretty obvious.' Many fans of *Blue Velvet* might disagree with this view, given that the film has many mysteries, ambiguities and even discontinuities. However, many of the questions that remain about *Blue Velvet* can be answered by comparing the shooting script (dated 24 July 1985) with the release version, as a great many scenes were either never filmed or deleted from the film prior to release. According to Mary Sweeney, who was editor Duwayne Dunham's assistant, the original cut of *Blue Velvet* was four and a half hours long. The omissions, whether filmed or not, are detailed below:

• After Jeffrey's father, Tom Beaumont, collapses in his garden, a woman calls to her little boy (seen in the release version) from the window: 'Gregg! Billy's waiting for his teddy!' Seeing Tom's stricken form, she calls inside the house: 'TOM!' Cut to a college dance, later that night, where 60s music plays as a student rushes about, looking for someone. He asks a girl (Louise Wertham) where Jeffrey is. 'His mother's on the phone – it's an emergency.' Louise tells him that Jeffrey 'disappeared to the men's room' some time ago, and suggests that they go and look for him. In fact, Jeffrey is in the janitor's quarters, hiding behind a furnace, and watching, 'fascinated', as a male student tries to rape his girlfriend. Jeffrey hears his name being called, but continues to watch as the boy forces the girl to the ground, trying to remove her clothes. Before leaving the room, he calls out: 'Hey, shithead. Leave her alone. Don't force girls!' (Clearly, this scene foreshadows the one in which Jeffrey spies on Dorothy Vallens.) Outside the furnace room, the boy with the message tells Jeffrey his mother is on the phone, while Louise scolds him 'for keeping me waiting for so long'. He apologises and picks up the phone, and learns about his father's illness. His mother, now looking very tired and in poor health, tells him to come home from college – for good. Jeffrey starts crying; Louise turns away. As Mrs Beaumont hangs up, a winged termite next to her phone crawls into a shadow. (As well as including another early appearance of the insect leitmotif, this short exchange gives credence to Jeffrey's willingness to take chances in Lumberton, since his future as a student is in doubt. It also plants the seeds of Louise's subsequent betrayal, absent from the release version.) The following night, Louise tells Jeffrey that she cannot accompany him to the airport because she has a class (somewhat improbable given the hour). She says that she loves him;

he promises to call and tells her that he loves her, too. They kiss. A plane takes off. A plane lands. Jeffrey's mother and Aunt Barbara meet him at the airport, and drive him to the Beaumont family home. Mrs Beaumont tells Jeffrey that his father had a cerebral haemorrhage, and that he may have a clot or a tumour. He'll be in hospital for two weeks. Aunt Barbara points out the 'A & P' that was torn down. 'Aunt Barbara, that was five years ago,' he replies. At home, Jeffrey goes to his room, and looks out onto the dark, deserted street. The next morning, Jeffrey and his mother discuss his plan to visit his father in hospital. She tells him he'll have to walk as she needs the car, and asks him not to say that he has dropped out of school. 'Thanks a lot, Mom,' he says sarcastically. 'Jeffrey! Nobody wanted you to leave school and go to work in the store. Maybe going back to school will be an option one day. I hope so.' Aunt Barbara tells him not to get depressed – 'They say it can bring on illness.' At the hospital, Nurse Cindy asks Jeffrey to wait while Dr Gynde prepares Jeffrey's father for his son's visit. 'Prepares him?' Jeffrey says, as the doctor comes out to talk to him. 'He's fighting hard, Jeffrey. It's very important that your father doesn't try to move. He's been immobilised. It would be very painful for him. Sit close. You do the talking and moving. He knows you're here. He became very emotional. I don't think he likes the idea of you seeing him like this.'

- At the hospital, a brief exchange of small talk between Jeffrey and his father was cut (making the scene more effective).
- Back home, Jeffrey's mother and Aunt Barbara are in the kitchen watching the TV news, which reports on the mounting crime wave. Murders are being discussed, and a police drawing of a suspect appears on the screen. In his bedroom, Jeffrey calls Louise, and learns that she has been asked on a date by another boy. He tells her to go ahead, since he may never return to college. He tells her he still loves her.
- At the Williamses' home, Jeffrey and Pam, Detective Williams's wife, drink coffee and eat cake – 'Duncan Hones' devil's food. Real good.' – as they await the return of Pam's husband. Sandy and her sweetheart, Mike Shaw, appear from upstairs, prompting Sandy's mother to remark that they have been studying together. 'Yeah,' Jeffrey says, with a knowing smile.
- As Sandy and Jeffrey stroll, talking about the ear, Sandy tells him that 'a businessman over by the Franklin factory district' and 'a musician, and some others' were questioned about the ear. About six months ago, some body parts were found in the river, from people who were reported missing. 'They never found one complete body. Only parts.' Maybe the ear is from a missing person?
- As they watch Dorothy Vallens's apartment building, Sandy warns

Jeffrey not to stop to look too long, because 'the police are watching'. Jeffrey asks where they are. 'I don't know. You're not supposed to see them. They're supposed to see you.'

- During their walk back, Sandy tells Jeffrey that the businessman is also being watched, and that he had a partner who disappeared, or was murdered.

- As they part, Sandy repeats Jeffrey's line about it being 'a strange world.'

- Arriving at Dorothy Vallens's apartment building disguised as a bug exterminator, Jeffrey is greeted in the entrance lobby by an old lady who, seeing his rig, says, 'Well, it's about time you came.' As she leaves, Jeffrey says to himself, 'That's a good sign.' (Lynch cut this additional insect reference – evidently the apartments really *do* have a bug problem – but replaced it with another: the insect-like buzzing of the lobby's neon light.)

- Returning home after spraying Dorothy's apartment, Jeffrey finds Dr Gynde giving his mother (named as Frances) an injection to relieve her anxiety over her husband's condition, while Aunt Barbara looks on. 'Dr Gynde,' Jeffrey says. 'my whole family's sick. What's going on?' Jeffrey's aunt says 'I'm not sick,' to which Jeffrey makes the *lingua franca* gesture for 'crazy', making everyone laugh except her. 'We'll see who stays in my will,' she says. (This exchange would have added to the extant references to disease and sickness. Its removal, along with other scenes featuring Jeffrey's mother, also gives her the appearance of apathy over her husband's condition.)

- As Jeffrey and Sandy arrive at the Slow Club, there is a brief exchange of dialogue between Jeffrey, a sleazy French maitre d' and a waiter, the performance of a fat stand-up comic and a toast to 'an interesting experience'.

- Outside Dorothy's apartment building, Jeffrey asks Sandy to wait in case the key doesn't fit.

- After sexually assaulting Dorothy, Frank goes to the bathroom, where Jeffrey hears him talking to himself and laughing. Before leaving, he adds the line 'See you next Christmas' to his parting words to Dorothy.

- After Jeffrey and Dorothy begin making love, and she rejects him, she goes into the bathroom and screams. Jeffrey rushes in to find out what is wrong, and sees her watching water circle in the lavatory. 'I made it go down the toilet,' she says, as Jeffrey sees an ear circle the toilet bowl and disappear. Looking up, he sees the words 'LOOK DOWN' written on the mirror with soap, and bloodstains in the sink – evidently, Frank left Don's other ear there earlier. Jeffrey recalls Frank's parting words – 'See you next Christmas,' prompting him to think (i.e., speak internal thoughts as voice-over, à la *Dune*),

'"Next Christmas." Is he Santa Claus who has left a present for Dorothy? What was it? An ear? Another ear?!!' Now speaking aloud, he asks Dorothy what it was, making her wonder for a moment if *he*, not Frank, left the ear. 'Do you know?' she asks, breathing heavily, strangely. He says no, and asks her what is happening. 'Maybe you don't know,' she says. 'I know you, though. You're Jeffrey Beaumont and I know where you live and I know ways to get you and I know ways to kill you.' Jeffrey tells her not to talk like that, and apologises again for sneaking in. She tells him to go, adding, 'I can't let you put it in me now, but I want you. I like you.' 'Then don't talk about killing,' he says. 'Did I say that? I didn't mean it. Or did I?' She laughs. 'Sometimes I think it would be fun.' Smiling strangely, she asks him to leave – 'I can't open myself to you now' – but before he does, she tells him a secret – that she wants to die. Jeffrey is shocked. 'Someday I'll show you where,' she adds, conspiratorially, then: 'I've gotta go to sleep now.' Jeffrey, frightened by her craziness, says 'Okay.' (This explains Jeffrey's suggestion to Sandy, in the next scene, that Dorothy may be suicidal. Without this scene, his only rationale for that assumption is Frank's parting line to Dorothy: 'Stay alive, baby!') Jeffrey returns home to find his mother waiting up for him, annoyed that it is now too late to call his father. 'You can't stay out half the night and carry on, Jeffrey. There's got to be some order,' she says. The next day, Jeffrey calls Louise from his bedroom, only to be told that she has got married! Obviously flabbergasted, he wishes her luck, and sarcastically suggests that if things don't work out, 'I think you should go into comedy!' (Whether this unconvincing exchange was intended to illustrate the passage of time or bring closure to Jeffrey's relationship with Louise is unclear.)

- At the hardware store, before calling Sandy, Jeffrey speaks aloud to himself. 'How can I help her?' he wonders. 'I can't tell her to go to Detective Williams. She'll think I'm a policeman. She has my address. She can go there. If she has to. I'll tell her. And her. And she thinks I'm Don. Her husband? Where the hell is Don? Maybe he died.'

- After his phone call from the hardware store, Jeffrey is seen with Dr Gynde, looking at blood samples under a microscope. 'This is what my father's disease looks like?' he says, as the images fill the screen until they are so big, we can hear them moving. (Another lost reference to sickness and disease.)

- Jeffrey visits Dorothy at her apartment a second time, and they are again interrupted by a knock at the door. Jeffrey hides in the closet as the man in the yellow sports coat (the Yellow Man, now wearing a purple sports coat) arrives, high on drugs. Dorothy lies that Frank is due back, and remarks upon the man's drugged state. He gets upset. 'Frank's got me – and you – and really, it's all thanks to Don, isn't it? Remember that. Your husband was the one who started fucking my mind with drugs!' 'Oh, he forced you, huh?' she responds, prompting the Yellow Man to remind her (and explain to us) that Don, her husband, is 'the reformed dealer who wanted to turn himself in', and that it was he who involved Frank in the first place. The Yellow Man then renews his sexual advances towards Dorothy. 'I'm supposed to be here watching you, why can't I be here *fucking* you? Listen, I know his cock's the size of a pin; let me give you the real thing. Let me wet my whistle, baby.' She tells him to get out, promising to tell Frank what he said. 'Okay, I'm goin',' he says. 'You'll see. I'll get you.' As he leaves, Jeffrey steps out of the closet, and asks who it was. She starts to shake and sob. 'Oh God. Don!!! Why can't I just die,' she says. He comforts her, and she leads him up to the roof of her apartment building, making good on her promise (cut from the release version) to show him where she intends to kill herself. On the roof, the wind whips about them, bringing with it (according to the script) the sound of a very sad, forlorn version of 'Somewhere Over the Rainbow'. Despite her suicidal tendencies, Dorothy tells him of her fear of accidentally falling. (This explains Dorothy's later reference to falling, when she is loaded into the ambulance.) Jeffrey tells her that she should come to his house if she should ever need help. As an electrical storm crackles, they have sex under the stars, Dorothy banging her head on the roof, over and over. 'I have to make it hurt,' she says. The sex scene becomes a montage of images: Jeffrey's father speaking his name, a robin in a tree, and a red high-heeled shoe (a ruby slipper, also from *The Wizard of Oz*) falling from the roof and mutating into Dorothy's red lips. (The robin, mentioned in Sandy's dream about love, makes another appearance here, and the image of Jeffrey's father may have been intended to create another link between sex and disease, made explicit in Dorothy's line about having disease put in her.)

- The next day, Jeffrey tells Aunt Barbara of his plans to dine at the Williamses. She tells him there are termites in the house, and after he leaves, pulls one from the carpet, examines it and looks at the walls. Later, Jeffrey sits down to dinner with the Williams family and Mike Shaw, discussing football. Mike, conscious of Sandy's attraction to Jeffrey, remarks that Jeffrey doesn't really have a football player's build. 'No offence,' he adds. Mike talks about his vitamins. 'The body is like a machine,' he says. '*Everything* has got to stay in perfect tune for perfect health.' After dinner, Jeffrey, Sandy and Mike sit in the basement watching TV. Sandy watches Jeffrey eat a blueberry pie (a foreshadowing of Kyle MacLachlan's fondness for pie in *Twin Peaks*). Mike leaves the room, but spies on Jeffrey and Sandy as they discuss the mystery: 'There are some strange people involved,' he says. Sandy's mother catches Mike eavesdropping, and he asks to speak to Sandy alone, outside. Detective Williams calls Jeffrey into his study to look at some 8 x 10 black-and-white pictures of the vacant lot where Jeffrey found the ear. Mostly they are pictures of weeds, but they look quite beautiful in an abstract way. Jeffrey asks about the case, but all Detective Williams will say is that 'the criminals are winning'. He has seen some bad things, he says, 'so bad I wouldn't poison your mind by telling you' and remarks that he sees detective work as 'an act of defiance'. Jeffrey sees a piece of cloth in one of the photos, and asks what it is; what colour it is. 'Blue. It's blue velvet,' Detective Williams replies. Sandy comes into the study looking upset, asking to borrow the car so that she can take Jeffrey out for dessert. In the car, Sandy dismisses Mike's attitude as jealousy.

- Seeing Sandy home after her speech about robins, Jeffrey asks her for a goodnight kiss. 'You better not, Jeffrey.' Returning home, Jeffrey finds a note left out for him – 'Jeffrey, hope you enjoyed yourself. See you at breakfast. Love, Mom.' A postscript is added from Aunt Barbara: 'Jeffrey, honey, I found these.' On the table are two dead termites. In his room, Jeffrey picks up the phone and calls Dorothy. Hearing nothing but a click at the other end, he says, 'Hello?' and hears Frank's voice: 'Speak to me, fucker,' Frank says, and Jeffrey quickly hangs up, scared. 'Stupid!!' he says to himself. 'So stupid. Now she might be in even more trouble with Frank. I hope not. I hope not. Tomorrow I have to find out more about Frank.' (These scenes were all to have taken place *before* Jeffrey secretly photographs Frank and the Yellow Man, and before Frank catches Jeffrey at Dorothy's place.)

- After tailing the Yellow Man and the Well-Dressed Man, Jeffrey comes across a crime scene, at which a man has been shot in the head and a woman has had her legs broken. Jeffrey discusses it with two black onlookers. (In the release version, these scenes are removed, but elements of them are used as cutaways to Jeffrey's explanation of the plot to Sandy in the diner.)

- When Jeffrey and Dorothy make love at her apartment, Dorothy explains her dialogue line, 'I have your disease in me now.' She says, 'You put your disease in me. Your semen. It's hot and full of disease.' Jeffrey assures her that he has no disease. 'Men are crazy,' she says. 'Then they put their craziness into me. Then it makes me crazy. Then they aren't so crazy for a while. Then they put their craziness in me again.' She starts to cry. 'It's burning me. But I love you.' She tells him that she feels darkness entering her, in every hole, 'opening me to death.' Jeffrey recoils. 'If I die, then they'll be free,' she tells him, and calls him Jeffrey for the first time, then repeats his name over and over.

- On the way into Ben's place, Frank confronts a strung-out acquaintance, 'Winky' Willard, playing pool in a back room, with four naked girls. 'Hey shithead!' Frank says. 'That's the last time I get you high and watch you freak out. Motherfucker, you tore my coat and I lost my lucky piece of blue velvet, man!' (This refers to the scrap of velvet cloth, cut from Dorothy's robe, which turns up in the photographs of the vacant lot, as described above.) Frank roughs Willard up a little, says 'Come here and take a look at a dead man' to one of the girls, then leaves, at which point, one of the naked women strikes a match, sets her nipples on fire, and says to a terrified Willard, 'You're really going up in flames this time, motherfucker!' Lynch says that the actress could really do the flaming nipple trick. 'That's the one scene in *Blue Velvet* that I'd like to put back,' he says, referring to the possibility of the three-or four-minute scene's inclusion on a future *Blue Velvet* DVD. 'Not put into the film, but have it play on its own.'
- At Ben's apartment, Frank refers to Dorothy as 'this little tid-bit,' and Jeffrey as 'a neighbour', adding: 'What the shit we're doin' with a neighbour, I don't know.'
- Dorothy's son, Donny, is seen and heard in the bedroom, crying and clinging to her 'like a small monkey would grip its mother.' Suddenly, he breaks away, screaming, 'Mommy. You left me. You stopped loving me.' (The release version retains only Dorothy's reaction to this.)
- When Jeffrey comes to in the vacant lot after being beaten unconscious by Frank, he finds his pants around his ankles, and 'FUCK YOU' written in lipstick on his legs, implying that he has been raped by one or more of Frank's gang. He pulls up his pants, limps along the dirt road, and calls a cab from a phone booth. (In the release version, Frank's rape of Jeffrey is suggested by Frank's kisses prior to the assault, and the phrase 'pretty, pretty', which Frank also uses while molesting Dorothy in her apartment. It is subsequently alluded to when Mike rear-ends Jeffrey's car – Jeffrey's involuntary reaction is 'It's Frank!' – and when Frank, in disguise, refers to Jeffrey's 'cute little butt'.)
- The day after leaving the Williams home, Jeffrey visits his father in hospital, accompanied by his mother and Aunt Barbara. We see more microscope-style close-ups of dark cells overcoming healthy cells.
- As Dorothy clings to Jeffrey, naked and confused, at the Williams

house, she tells him that Don is being tortured at her apartment. (This explains why Jeffrey is anxious to go there – an apparently illogical act in the release version.)

- After Jeffrey is startled by the Yellow Man's police radio, there is a siege at Frank's apartment, as the police storm the building. They burst into Frank's apartment, where a dog with a gunshot wound growls and limps about on bloody legs. (Elements of the siege appear in montage in the release version, minus the interior of Frank's apartment and the wounded dog.)
- Hearing the radio reports, Jeffrey says to himself, 'So. Frank escaped.'
- As the Well-Dressed Man approaches the building, Jeffrey externalises his thoughts as he puts together the fact that the man approaching is Frank in disguise.
- Following his shooting of Frank, Jeffrey is questioned by several FBI agents and policemen, including Detective Williams, at the police station. Afterwards, Jeffrey asks what will happen to him, and the agent says that it's up to Detective Williams. 'I'll tell you, though. You're okay. You shot a real son of a bitch.' Jeffrey replies, 'Yeah, but how many more are out there?'

TRAILER: A caption appears, a deep voice reading it aloud: 'From the Mind of David Lynch Comes a Modern Day Masterpiece So Startling, So Provocative, So Mysterious, That It Will Open Your Eyes to A World You Have Never Seen Before.' From this opening, Bobby Vinton's 'Blue Velvet' is played over various mute scenes from the film, all intercut with Jeffrey looking through the slats in Dorothy's closet door. Frank's voice is heard – 'Hey neighbour! Here I come. You've got about one second to live, buddy!' – before the trailer cuts to a title, and press quotes from *California Magazine*'s David Thompson ('*Blue Velvet* is a mystery . . . A masterpiece . . . a visionary story, of sexual awakening, of good and evil, a trip to the underworld.'), *GQ*'s Ken Turan ('A nightmarish, intensely disturbing exploration of the hidden side of the soul. It is sure to cause a sensation') and *Vanity Fair*'s Stephen Schiff ('Brilliant and unsettling . . . this is the work of an all-American visionary – and a master film stylist.')

POSTER: Most poster designs featured one of two images: either a production still of Dorothy with a knife poised over Jeffrey, or Dorothy in Jeffrey's arms. Some later versions added an inset picture of Frank. The most bizarre alternative designs were the Polish and German posters, the former a crudely drawn image of Dorothy singing, the latter a broken white picket fence, with Frank pictured hitting Dorothy – ironic, given that this shot was cut from the German release prints – with Jeffrey, wide-eyed, in the foreground.

WHAT THE PAPERS SAID: In the US, the *New Yorker*'s Pauline Kael led the army of critics who quickly understood that *Blue Velvet* was something special. Announcing the film as 'the work of a genius naïf,' she prophetically suggested that 'Lynch might turn out to be the first populist surrealist – a Frank Capra of dream logic.' *Variety* cautiously lauded the film as 'a disturbing and at times devastating look at the ugly underside of Middle American life', and singled out Isabella Rossellini ('throws herself into this mad role with complete abandon') and Dennis Hopper ('creates a flabbergasting portrait of unrepentant, irredeemable evil') for individual praise.

Blue Velvet arrived in the UK in early 1987, borne on a tide of strong US reviews, and was greeted with similar acclaim. '*Blue Velvet* is revving up to become one of that choice cluster of movies that anyone who is anyone will *have* to go and see,' *Time Out* proclaimed. 'If you've seen it, you're triple hip. If you haven't seen it, you're *dead*.' In the same publication, Geoff Andrew applauded Lynch's film as 'a visually stunning, convincingly coherent portrait of a nightmarish substratum to conventional respectable society. The seamless blending of beauty and horror is remarkable . . . the sheer wealth of imagination [is] virtually unequalled in recent cinema.' Summing up the sense that Lynch had truly arrived in the mainstream with his subversive sensibilities laudably intact, *Sight and Sound*'s Sean French declared *Blue Velvet* 'the film that David Lynch's career so far had been preparing him to make . . . Lynch has wittily heeded the advice of his sternest critics, to deal with "real life", and shown that it is as surreal as the ménage of Mr and Mrs X in *Eraserhead*.'

One of the most surprising reviews of *Blue Velvet* was a scathing commentary by author Barry Gifford, whose subsequent collaborations with Lynch would include *Wild at Heart*, *Hotel Room* and *Lost Highway*. 'This is an ugly, brutal, naïve movie,' he wrote. 'One cut above a snuff film. A kind of academic porn.' 'I didn't immediately adore it,' he admitted later. 'I thought it was powerful and strange, but not necessarily my cup of tea. Upon revisiting it, I saw more in it.'

BOX OFFICE: Released in the US on 19 September 1986, *Blue Velvet* enjoyed a strong opening weekend, and went on to gross $8,551,228 during its domestic run, a modest return on its declared budget of $6 million. In the UK, the film took just £521,872 in eight weeks.

AWARDS: *Blue Velvet* scored Lynch a second nomination as Best Director at the Academy Awards; he was beaten by Oliver Stone for

Platoon (1986). Lynch's screenplay and Dennis Hopper were also nominated for Golden Globe awards. Lynch and Hopper were more successful at the Los Angeles Film Critics Association awards, in which they won Best Director and Best Supporting Actor (also for *Hoosiers*) respectively. Hopper also received a Best Actor award at the 1986 Montréal World Film Festival, and a Best Supporting Actor award from the National Society of Film Critics, which also awarded *Blue Velvet* Best Film, Best Director and Best Cinematography. Isabella Rossellini won Best Female Lead at the Independent Spirit Awards, at which the film was also nominated for Best Feature, Best Director, Best Male Lead (Dennis Hopper), Best Female Lead (Laura Dern), Best Screenplay and Best Cinematography. Lynch also received a nomination for Best Screenplay Written Directly for the Screen from the Writers Guild of America.

CONTROVERSY: In order to secure an 'R' rating, the Motion Picture Association of America (MPAA), the US ratings board, asked that the scene in which Frank Booth slaps Dorothy be edited so that his hand connects with her face offscreen. 'One hit from Frank onto Dorothy was taken out,' Lynch confirms. '[The MPAA] told me if I didn't want an "X", I had to take it out. And now you see the beginning of it, and you see Jeffrey in the closet looking out, and you hear it, and it's way worse than it was, because your mind kicks in.'

This cut notwithstanding, the disturbing relationship between Frank and Dorothy caused outrage among many critics, who accused the director of misogyny at best; at worst, the glorification of violence against women. Isabella Rossellini, who was as much the focus of these accusations as Lynch, felt that such charges were predictable and narrow-minded. 'David had a phrase for me to help me conjure up Dorothy Vallens's mood swings, tormented mind, and anguish: "The clouds are coming",' she wrote in her autobiography, *Some of Me*. 'When we created Dorothy, I already knew about battered women, and I gathered more information before playing the role.' She also researched sadomasochism, and even drew on her own experience of date rape, as well as 'a mysterious firmament that had appeared to me once when I had been brutally beaten. I had felt no pain, just total surprise,' she added, remembering the sensation of 'seeing stars' when she felt the first blows. 'When I played Dorothy, asking to be beaten, I recalled those stars. The way of stopping the anguished thoughts – "the clouds" – was to be hit and be bewildered in front of this firmament.'

Lynch explained that he is generally dismissive of the accusations of misogyny 'because people have an idea that Dorothy was Everywoman, instead of just being Dorothy. That's where the problem starts. If it's just Dorothy, and it's her story – which it is to me – then everything is fine. If Dorothy is Everywoman, it doesn't make any sense. It just doesn't add up. It's completely false, and they'd be right to be upset.'

TRIVIA: During the filming of *Blue Velvet*, Lynch and Rossellini became involved in an off-screen relationship that would last five years. They even starred in a film together: *Twin Peaks* director Tina Rathborne's *Zelly and Me* (1988).

When *Blue Velvet* wrapped, reformed alcoholic Dennis Hopper helped Jack Nance kick the booze, and later cast him in *Colors* (1988) and *The Hot Spot* (1990). The emphasis on Frank's preferred brand of beer ('Heineken? Fuck that shit! Pabst Blue Ribbon!') may even have been an inside joke about Hopper's preference for a particular brand of non-alcoholic beer, with which the *Blue Velvet* craft services table was always to be stocked.

That pin-up on Sandy's bedroom wall is of actor Montgomery Clift, the all-American hunk who kept a secret side – his homosexuality.

APOCRYPHA: According to author Barry Gifford, who later collaborated with Lynch, editor Duwayne Dunham suggested that Lynch alter an important dialogue line in post-production, which had the effect of changing the nature of Dorothy Vallens's plight. The change supposedly occurred at the point where Dorothy is at the sink while Jeffrey, offended by Dorothy begging him to hit her, gets dressed. Now, instead of saying 'Hit me' again, she says 'Help me.' 'For Duwayne, this changed the whole context of the film,' Gifford says, 'because if she says, "Help me" she's no longer a victim of herself.' 'That's absolutely not true,' Lynch demurs. 'Some lines were changed, but they weren't those.'

At the end of *Blue Velvet*, Sandy, Jeffrey and his aunt Barbara watch a robin on the kitchen windowsill, symbolising – according to Sandy's dream – the return of love and light to the world. Although the bug in its beak is a clear signifier that there will always be a darkness to balance the light, much has been made of the fact that the robin Lynch used was clearly artificial. And yet, Lynch claims, 'It wasn't an artificial bird. That was a real bird. It's playing a role, and this is what came out.'

AVAILABILITY: *Blue Velvet* is currently available on video in the UK as a PAL VHS (0618553), and in the US as an NTSC VHS (M206863), both in the full-screen (4:3) ratio. A letterboxed (2.35:1) PAL VHS (0478843) was previously available in the UK but is now deleted.

A letterboxed (2.35:1) Region 2 DVD (CHV 5009) is available in the UK, featuring a new 45-minute interview with Dennis Hopper – of which almost fifteen minutes are spent discussing *Blue Velvet* – and extensive liner notes. A letterboxed Region 1 DVD (908059) is available in the US, featuring the original theatrical trailer and an informative booklet.

The most recent NTSC laserdisc edition, Warner Home Video's 1991 letterbox version (692 A/B), is out of print and can be difficult to find.

FINAL ANALYSIS: The first time I saw *Blue Velvet*, on its first UK cinema run in early 1987, I disliked it immensely. (I even wrote a scathing review of it, for an office newsletter, now thankfully lost to obscurity.) With hindsight, I can see why. I was eighteen at the time, and knew no more of the dark underside of the peaceful suburban world in which I grew up than Jeffrey knows of Lumberton's. (An additional problem was undoubtedly that the poster led me to believe that *Blue Velvet* would be the perfect sexy date movie for myself and my sixteen-year-old sweetheart.)

With subsequent viewings, I was able to be less terrified by Dennis Hopper's combination of creature from the id and superego, a mass of contradictions whose confused sexual desires cause him to vacillate wildly from father ('It's daddy, you shithead!') to child ('Baby wants to fuck!') in a single breath. (In Lynch's early drafts, this dichotomy was reflected in the high-pitched 'baby' voice Frank adopted after inhaling helium from his own personal gas supply, while lines like 'Get ready to fuck!' were intoned like an army officer (authority figure, father) giving orders.) I was also reconciled to the masochistic tendencies of Dorothy, ironically through my developing relationship with the same young lady whose presence at that first viewing of *Blue Velvet* had caused me to cringe throughout the film, and for most of the journey home. But coming to understand, as Jeffrey and Sandy do, why there is 'so much trouble in the world' is an important step on the journey to adulthood, just as *Blue Velvet* was fundamental to proving Lynch's maturity and providing a foundation for his own development as an artist. Today, my own sentiments echo those of the anonymous cinemagoer overheard at a *Blue Velvet* screening attended by critic Pauline Kael: 'Maybe I'm sick, but I want to see that again.'

EXPERT WITNESS: 'I can describe working with David as: one, two, three – leap into the void. One, two, three is what's earthbound, and it had to be totally real and plausible. Like a good runway, it allows a leap into a mysterious world that may hold deeper truths. It's not a love of the strange and unusual that dictates David's surrealistic style;

it's as if our rational minds can go only so far, and then intuition is needed in order to float further into the mysterious, transcendental, inexplicable.' – actress Isabella Rossellini (Dorothy Vallens)

LYNCH ON *BLUE VELVET*: 'Surrealism . . . deals with things that are hidden beneath the surface, and in most of the cases the subconscious. *Blue Velvet* is a film that deals with things that are hidden within a small town called Lumberton, and things that are hidden within people.'

The Cowboy and the Frenchman (1988)

Video short / 24 mins / colour / live action

Written and Directed by David Lynch
Executive Producers Paul Cameron, Pierre-Olivier Barbet
Associate Producer David Warfield
Music by Offenbach, Radio Ranch Straight Shooters, Eddie Dixon, Jean-Jacques Perrey
Produced by Daniel Toscan du Plantier
Director of Photography Fred Elmes
Camera Assistant Catherine Coulson
Edited by Scott Chestnut
Production Design & Costumes by Patricia Norris, Nancy Martinelli, Frank Silva (Associate)
Sound Jon Huck
Choreography Sarah Elgart

CAST: Harry Dean Stanton (*Slim*), Frederic Golchan (*Pierre*), Jack Nance (*Pete*), Michael Horse (*Broken Feather*), Rick Guillory (*Howdy*), Tracey Walter (*Dusty*), Marie Lauren, Patrick Hauser, Eddie Dixon, Magali Alvarado, Ann Sophie, Robin Summers, Kathy Dean, Leslie Cook, Manette Lachance, Kelly Redusch, Michelle Rudy, Debra Seitz, Dominique Rojas, Audrey Tom, Amanda Hull, Talisa Soto, Jackie Old Coyote

UNCREDITED CAST: Monty Montgomery (*voice of Howdy*)

ALTERNATIVE TITLE(S): *Le Cowboy et le Frenchman* (original French title).

TITLE SEQUENCE: After a simple title – white letters across the image of a lasso – a caption card reads as follows: 'Slim, the foreman of the ranch – almost stone cold deaf on account of two rounds of 30.06 going off a little too close when he was thirteen-and-a-half – along with Pete and Dusty – sees something unusual coming down the mountain.'

SUMMARY: On a ranch in the American west, a rancher named Slim and his two ranch hands, Pete and Dusty, see something strange in the distance. Slim sends Pete and Dusty to investigate on horseback, and they return having lassoed a moustached Frenchman wearing a beret and carrying a large suitcase. The Frenchman, Pierre, tries to tell the group that he is a tourist who has lost his way, but since he only speaks French – and Slim is mostly deaf – communication proves difficult. Slim orders Pete and Dusty to open the man's suitcase, which contains wine, *Gauloises* cigarettes, a ripe Camembert cheese, baguettes, a model of the Eiffel Tower, two photographs, a plate of *escargots* and a letter written in French. When Pete notices French fries in the suitcase, the group suddenly realises that Pierre is French, and they quickly untie him. Slim orders Pete and another ranch hand, Howdy, to bring some beer for a celebration. Pierre offers Slim some Camembert cheese – which he refuses, thinking it has gone bad – and nervously regards a native American named Broken Feather, who previously mistook Pierre for a spy. That night, there is a bi-cultural party, at which girls dance the cancan while Slim and a country singer play country and western songs. Pierre displays a cake modelled on the Statue of Liberty, a symbol of the Franco-American relations, and everyone shouts 'Vive la France!' The next morning, Broken Feather admires Pierre's suitcase, and Slim finds a snail in his clothing.

PRODUCTION HISTORY: In 1988, the magazine section of the French newspaper *Le Figaro* chose to mark the bicentenary of the French Revolution (1789–1989) by commissioning, through associate Daniel Toscan du Plantier's Erato Films, five international directors to each make a short film, under the collective title *Les Français vus par . . . (The French, as seen by . . .)*. Lynch represented America; the other contributors were Werner Herzog (Germany), Andrzej Wajda (Poland), Luigi Comencini (Italy) and Jean-Luc Godard (France). Lynch was approached while in Paris with girlfriend Isabella Rossellini, but declined on the grounds that he was busy, and did not have an idea that would fit comfortably into the chosen format. But, as Lynch told *Rolling Stone*, 'That night I got an idea. I called him,' he added, giving a rough outline of the story. 'He said, "That's great, two clichés in one!" I said, "You got it!" So I made it.' Although the shoot did not go over budget, Lynch admitted it did go over schedule, 'because I was having so much fun.'

CASTING: The cast of *The Cowboy and the Frenchman* marked Lynch's first association with three actors who would return to work with him on numerous occasions. *Paris, Texas* star Harry Dean Stanton's future collaborations with Lynch encompassed *Wild at Heart* (Johnny Farragut), *Twin Peaks – Fire Walk with Me* (Carl Rodd), *Hotel Room* (Boca) and *The Straight Story* (Lyle Straight); Tracey Walter (*Repo Man*, 1984) had his scenes cut from *Wild at Heart*, but returned to portray Blinky Watts in *On the Air*; finally, native American actor Michael Horse, who would subsequently portray Deputy Tommy 'Hawk' Hill in *Twin Peaks* and deleted scenes from *Twin Peaks – Fire Walk With Me*. In fact, it was during the filming of *The Cowboy and the Frenchman* that Horse first learned of *Twin Peaks*: 'I asked David what he was doing next, [and] he said a TV series . . .'

THE LYNCH MOB: *The Cowboy and the Frenchman* reunited Lynch with actor Jack Nance (*Eraserhead, Dune, Blue Velvet*), cinematographer Frederick Elmes (*Eraserhead, Dune, Blue Velvet*) and production designer Patricia Norris (costume designer for *The Elephant Man*, production designer for *Blue Velvet*).

MEMORABLE QUOTE(S)
Slim: 'You and Dusty get on up there and see about that thing!'
Pete: 'Yes, sir, Slim, and I'll take Dusty with me!'
Slim: 'What?'
Pete: 'I said, "Yes, sir, Slim, and I'll take Dusty with me!"'
Slim: 'That's just what I said!'
Dusty: 'And I'll go with him, Slim!'

SOUND & MUSIC: *The Cowboy and the Frenchman* gave Harry Dean Stanton, who has his own band, a chance to sing, and also showcased the music of the Radio Ranch Straight Shooters, featuring Eddie Dixon.

INFLUENCED BY: The idea for the *Les Français vus par . . .* series came from the 1964 portmanteau film *Paris vus par . . .*, a collection of six sketches by directors of the French avant-garde film movement, *la nouvelle vague*. Interestingly, one of the six contributors to the 1964 film, Jean-Luc Godard, also contributed a segment to *Les Français vus par . . .*

Lynch's own inspiration for *The Cowboy and the Frenchman* is more difficult to imagine, since parallels with the work of one of his most commonly cited European influences, French comedian Jacques Tati, are tenuous at best; only the fixed-camera style, common to most comedies of the silent era, strikes a chord, but this approach was more likely a result of budgetary concerns rather than stylistic ones. Although Lynch has called *The Cowboy and the Frenchman* a Western, he claims to have 'zero interest' in the genre. 'Actually, *The Straight Story* is close to a Western,' he adds. 'I grew up in the West, and I got my fill of it. I mean, I could relate to cowboys, but that's not where I wanna go.' As for cowboy films by other directors, 'I don't think there's one Western that lights my fire. Zip.'

LEGACY: Although *The Cowboy and the Frenchman* was not widely seen outside France, and would probably not have influenced anyone in any case, one idea – that of Slim's almost total deafness – would recur in *Twin Peaks*, as a character trait of Gordon Cole, played by Lynch himself. Also in *Twin Peaks* (episode 1001), Jerry Horne returns home from a trip to Paris carrying souvenirs of his own – baguettes stuffed with Camembert!

DÉJÀ VU: Inexplicably, one of Pierre's photographs is of José Ferrer, who played the Emperor of the Known Universe in Lynch's *Dune*! 'Looks like a midget to me,' says Slim, examining the picture.

THEMES AND MOTIFS: Communication problems, represented here by Slim's hearing loss and the language barrier between the American and French, played a more significant part in *The Alphabet* and *The Grandmother*. Lynch's playfulness with language, not to mention American stereotypes of the French, is given added irony by the fact that Slim and his boys eventually realise that Pierre is French by the French fries – the American name for chipped potatoes – he carries in his *valise*. Even more ironically, this exchange is rendered almost meaningless by the French subtitling of the English language dialogue, in which 'french fries' is translated simply as '*frites*,' the French word for chips!

AVAILABILITY: Much to Lynch's regret, *The Cowboy and the Frenchman* is currently unavailable – officially, at least – on any format. 'I tried to get it from [the producers], but they want a lot of money, so I don't know if I'm gonna get it,' he complains.

FINAL ANALYSIS: Lynch's first comedy is as broad as the story is thin, although it is stretched to breaking point in a 24-minute film whose pace is so slack it feels like an hour. The set-up has comedy potential, and there are undeniably funny moments – two, in my view – but the overall feel is flat, uninspired and a waste of first-class talent like Stanton, Walter and Nance. Mercifully unavailable in any home video format, *The Cowboy and the Frenchman* is, at best, a curiosity;

at worst, an attempt at comedy whose gags fall, like most things said to Slim, on deaf ears. As Slim might say, 'What the Hell?'

EXPERT WITNESS: 'I think it was a two-day shoot for what was supposed to be a five-minute film, but David, of course, couldn't get it down to five minutes.' – production and costume associate Frank Silva

LYNCH ON *THE COWBOY AND THE FRENCHMAN*: 'It's my only Western. It's not a Western, really; it's got some Western elements. I feel so good about parts of it. Jack Nance, Tracey Walter, Michael Horse, and Harry Dean . . . That was the first time I'd worked with him. I'd work anywhere any time with Harry Dean – he's the best there is.'

Industrial Symphony No.1 The Dream of the Broken-Hearted (1990)

Video production of live theatrical performance / 49 mins / colour

Theatre Crew
Conceived and Directed by David Lynch
Musical Director Angelo Badalamenti
Produced by John Wentworth
Production Designer Franne lee
Lighting Designer Anne Militello
Choreographer Martha Clark

Video Production Crew
Produced by David Lynch, Angelo Badalamenti, Rob Jason
Executive Producers Monty Montgomery, Steve Golin, Sigurjon Sighvatsson
Editor Bob Jenkins
Head of Production Tim Clawson
Production Manager Bruce Roberts

CAST: Laura Dern (*Heartbroken Woman*), Nicolas Cage (*Heartbreaker*), Julee Cruise (*Dreamself of the Heartbroken Woman*), Lisa Giobbi (*Female Dancer*), Felix Blaska (*Male Dancer*), Michael J. Anderson (*Woodsman / Twin A*), Andre Badalamenti (*Clarinet Soloist/Twin B*), John Bell (*The Tall Skinned Deer*)

TITLE SEQUENCE: The title is the simplest part of the video production: white letters (some in the style of high-school jackets, like the one worn by Bobby in *Twin Peaks*) on a black background, reading as follows: 'INDUSTRIAL SYMPHONY NO.1 *the dream of the brokenhearted by* DAVID LYNCH AND ANGELO BADALAMENTI *featuring* JULEE CRUISE.'

SUMMARY: In a filmed prologue, a young man calls his lover to break off their affair. What follows is a visual and aural representation of the broken-hearted woman's emotional torment. Her 'dreamself' stands on a stage in a diaphanous chiffon dress, singing mournfully while surrounded by gantries, pipes, machinery and the rusted hulk of a 50s automobile. There are searchlights, sirens and smoke in the air. A man floats in the air while a half-naked young woman negotiates the latticework gantry and climbs in through the missing rear window of a car. Chainsaws whirr, bodies on hospital gurneys are brought on stage, and while the topless woman writhes on top of the car, the singer reappears, floating above the stage. A Lilliputian woodsman begins sawing a log, while figures search with flashlights. As the next song builds to a crescendo, it breaks into a discordant cacophony and chaos breaks out on stage, climaxing with the rise of a tall skinned deer, standing on its hind legs. The topless woman runs across the stage, while dark figures place the singer in the trunk of the car. The little woodsman reappears to recite the phone conversation, while another young woman writhes in ecstasy. The singer is released, her image captured on a video monitor, and sings as girls dance in prom dresses and Las Vegas-style costumes, until a wind blows across the stage. Sirens, gunfire and explosions can be heard as images of bombers, searchlights, fire and smoke fill the air, and a hundred tiny dolls are suspended above the stage. All but one of the dolls (seen on a video monitor) disappear, and as the woman finishes her final song, bathed in stardust, she rises to the heavens and the curtain falls.

PRODUCTION HISTORY: In autumn 1989, Angelo Badalamenti's involvement with the Brooklyn Academy of Music led to them to commission a unique performance piece for the opening of their annual New Wave music festival, scheduled to begin in November of the same year. Badalamenti approached Lynch, with whom he had collaborated on the soundtracks for *Blue Velvet*, the as-yet-unbroadcast *Twin Peaks* pilot, and the feature film *Wild at Heart*, and an album of songs for sultry singer Julee Cruise. 'We told them about this thing we were working on called *Industrial Symphony No.1*,' Lynch said, borrowing the title from the collective name he had once given to the series of paintings, drawings, animations and sculptures he had produced in his formative years at the Pennsylvania Academy of Fine Arts. 'I guess just the name and the idea of it got them going, and they said, "We want that thing!" Then we got off the phone, and Angelo and I looked at each other, and all we really had was the name, *Industrial Symphony No.1*. So we had to get to work!'

Lynch and Badalamenti pulled together numerous elements from their previous collaborations, most notably the songs they had written for Julee Cruise, and fused them into a baroque operatic event combined from a multitude of different media. 'It starts with a film clip,' Lynch said of the prologue, which was projected onto a screen in the auditorium, '[and then] it's one great, big, long mood.' 'Each piece is one great mood thing,' Badalamenti agreed, 'but those moods are interrupted at times. We would get into this kind of heavy violence [with] fire and sound effects, heavy winds and stuff like that. And musically we would get into that, and all of that [would] underscore what was going on on stage – baby dolls being dropped, burned from war and fire and all of those sick, sad things. Out of all this catastrophe we would suddenly fade and cross-fade into a beautiful thing from Julee's album: she would come down floating. And it all worked as one piece.'

With *Wild at Heart* in post-production and the first season of *Twin Peaks* being filmed around the same time, Lynch found the logistical demands of *two* live shows in front of 2,000 people especially demanding. 'There's many, many, many things that have to happen at certain times within it, even though a lot of it is pre-recorded,' he said. 'We only had a day and a half to install the entire set, rehearse everything, and get it all worked out to this precise way that it has to be before you go before the public.'

Despite the pressure, Cruise found the live performance aspect particularly exhilarating, and even found herself lost in her own dream-state as she hung, suspended from the auditorium ceiling, lip-synching to her own pre-recorded voice. 'They had me floating the whole time,' she recalled. 'I forgot where I was when I was up there. It was all dark, and I was up in the air, and I was singing, and there was fog all around me, and all I could see was this one real bright light way out there. And I just thought, "Am I dead?"'

For Lynch, the feeling *Industrial Symphony No.1* was designed to convey was not intellectual but emotional; connecting on a subconscious level rather than a conscious one. As he put it, 'The music's going along, and it's making pictures form in your mind . . . To make just an interpretation or intellectually try to understand them – it's sort of not what it's about.'

THE LYNCH MOB: In addition to Badalamenti, several collaborators from recent (and, in some cases, current) Lynch projects joined the director for the *Industrial Symphony No.1* event. Julee Cruise had sung the Lynch/Badalamenti composition 'Mysteries of Love' for the *Blue Velvet* soundtrack, and performed nine of their songs on an album entitled *Floating into the Night*; Michael J. Anderson had long been promised the title role in the unproduced *Ronnie Rocket* [see **'In Dreams,' page 248**], and had recently played the Man from Another Place in the European version of *Twin Peaks*; Laura Dern had played Sandy in *Blue Velvet*, and co-starred with Nicolas Cage in *Wild at Heart*, which had been filmed earlier, in the summer of 1989.

MEMORABLE QUOTES
Heartbreaker: 'I guess I'm sayin' goodbye, is what I'm doing.'

Heartbreaker: 'It ain't nothin' wrong with you. It's just us I can't handle.'

Voice: 'In the faraway world, Pinky's Bubble Egg, things change.'

SOUND AND MUSIC: As implied by the title, the music was the key to *Industrial Symphony No.1*. 'What comes out on the surface is very intimate and romantic and beautiful and ethereal,' Julee Cruise said of Lynch's lyrical style. 'What's going on underneath is depression and paranoia and fetishes and obsessions. That's why it's not "white-wine muzak." That's why there's a lot more to the music than just the beautiful melody or the beautiful voice.'

Badalamenti recalled how he and Lynch worked, 'David would come in, and I would be sitting at the keyboards, [and he] would say, "Just noodle around at the piano." I would noodle, and David would hear a few notes, a little motif, and say, "That's great. Now develop it, and kind of move it in this direction or that direction." And David would just create this verbal mood.' Sometimes, Lynch was unable to articulate his intentions in musical terms; yet, as Cruise explained, his message would always get through. 'One of David's famous things that he told the sax player is, "You know, Al, big chunks of plastic! Can't you play that?" And Al knew what he was talking about. That's when it gets kind of scary.'

Industrial Symphony No.1 features the following Lynch/Badalamenti songs, sung by Julee Cruise: 'Up in Flames', 'I Float Alone', 'Into the Night', 'Pinky's Bubble Egg (The Twins Spoke)', 'Rockin' Back Inside My Heart' and 'The World Spins.' Four Lynch/Badalamenti instrumentals are also featured – 'The Black Sea', 'I'm Hurt Bad', 'The Dream Conversation' and 'The Final Battle'. Sadly, no soundtrack album was ever released.

DÉJÀ VU: Although *Industrial Symphony No.1* was performed before the audience had been given the chance to see *Twin Peaks* or *Wild at Heart*, by the time the video version was released, many elements of the project would be hauntingly familiar. After seeing Cage and Dern in *Wild at Heart*, many felt that the filmed opening sequence of *Industrial Symphony No.1* – in which a young man (Nicolas Cage, using Sailor Ripley's voice) breaks off his love affair with a young woman (Laura Dern, physically and vocally resembling Lula Pace Fortune, but without the cigarette or chewing gum) – was Lynch's way of closing the Sailor-and-Lula relationship, something he had been unwilling to do in *Wild at Heart*. Absolutely not, says Lynch. 'It wasn't from *Wild at Heart*,' he insists, 'it's part of *Industrial Symphony*. I just happened to have them with me and I asked them if they would do that. It never had anything to do with *Wild at Heart*.'

Comparisons with *Twin Peaks* are even harder to resist, not least because much of the music is from the television series, in which both Julee Cruise and Michael J. Anderson appeared. The 'broken heart' of the title recalls Laura Palmer's necklace, a heart broken into two pieces, while the woodsman sawing wood, and the other representations of nature and industry on display, suggest the town of Twin Peaks. Cruise, floating in her chiffon wrap, is part homecoming queen, part angel, and the fact that she finds herself trapped in the trunk of a car recalls Laura's final journey – to the river in the trunk of her father's car.

THEMES AND MOTIFS: Dreams, the overriding theme of *Industrial Symphony No.1*, play an integral role in almost all of Lynch's films. In *Eraserhead*, Henry has nightmares borne out of his guilt and anguish; in *The Elephant Man*, dream sequences show Merrick's gestation; in *Dune*, the dreams of Paul Atreides hold the key to his destiny; in *Blue Velvet*, Jeffrey has tormented dreams, while Sandy dreams of robins; in *Twin Peaks*, Cooper believes that his dreams will help him solve the mystery of Laura Palmer's murder; in *Wild at Heart*, an unconscious Sailor dreams of the Good Witch; in *Fire Walk With Me*, Cooper reminds Cole of a premonitory dream.

WHAT THE PAPERS SAID: In 1990, *Time*'s Richard Corliss had this to say about the video version of the project: 'A fifty-minute video, *Industrial Symphony No.1*, featuring a dwarf, prom teens, a floating topless lady, a skinned deer and ethereal warbler Julee Cruise singing from a car trunk; it's Lynch's most brazenly avant-garde work.'

Although further press coverage of either the live event or the video version was scarce, film critic and *Art Papers* contributor Bret Wood describes *Industrial Symphony No.1* as 'a collision of idyllic love and the horrors of war, technology and medicine, [which] provided a profound synthesis of the themes and images that have haunted Lynch's films for years and which are also addressed in his paintings, photographs and sculpture, serving as a fascinating bridge between the two fields of artistic endeavour . . . *Industrial Symphony No.1* was an orchestration of Lynch's romantic id in all its sensory, absurd glory, and left the half-empty New Music America audience in stunned confusion.'

AVAILABILITY: The video version of *Industrial Symphony No.1* was released in the UK and US (7599–38179–3) in August 1990, the same month that *Wild at Heart* first appeared in cinemas, and a little over a month before the second series of *Twin Peaks* debuted in the US. Both the PAL and NTSC versions are technically still in circulation, but since only one pressing was ever done, they are increasingly difficult to find.

FINAL ANALYSIS: Lynch had begun making films because he wanted his paintings to move. With *Industrial Symphony No.1*, Lynch was able to take the concept of the moving painting a stage further, unveiling a living, breathing work of avant-garde art before a captive audience, who, it has to be said, were left in as much darkness and confusion as the broken-hearted girl dangling a few feet above the stage.

While its impact and immediacy are much diminished on the small screen, the video version allows for the repeat viewings that the stage show did not and, with the passing of time and the increasing surrealism of music promos, this rarest of fruits of the collaboration between Lynch and Badalamenti looks less like the self-indulgent fantasies of a pretentious and frighteningly untethered artist and more like what Lynch always intended it to be: a dream. A dream of the broken-hearted.

EXPERT WITNESS: 'It's this little strange doll floating around in the darkness, and just a glimmer of light shines through, and then it goes back into darkness.' – Julee Cruise

LYNCH ON *INDUSTRIAL SYMPHONY No.1*: 'A triple-exposure dream. A dream of the broken-hearted. A dream about floating and falling and rising upwards.'

Twin Peaks (1990–1991)

35mm pilot & 29-episode television series (+ direct-to-video feature) / 1532 mins (+ 18 mins) / colour / live action

Directed by David Lynch (1000, 1002, 2001, 2002, 2007, 2022), Duwayne Dunham (1001, 2011, 2018), Tina Rathborne (1003, 2010), Tim Hunter (1004, 2009, 2021), Lesli Linka Glatter (1005, 2003, 2006, 2016), Caleb Deschanel (1006, 2008, 2012), Mark Frost (1007), Todd Holland (2004, 2013), Graeme Clifford (2005), Uli Edel (2014), Diane Keaton (2015), James Foley (2017), Jonathan Sanger (2019), Stephen Gyllenhaal (2020)

Written by Mark Frost & David Lynch (1000, 1001, 1002), Harley Peyton (1003, 2002, 2013), Robert Engels (1004, 1006, 2003), Mark Frost (1005, 1007, 2001, 2007), Jerry Stahl, Mark Frost, Harley Peyton & Robert Engels (2004), Barry Pullman (2005, 2011, 2017, 2021), Harley Peyton & Robert Engels (2006, 2012, 2015, 2018, 2020), Scott Frost (2008, 2014), Mark Frost, Harley Peyton & Robert Engels (2009, 2022), Tricia Brock or Block (2010, 2016), Mark Frost & Harley Peyton (2019)

Created by Mark Frost & David Lynch

Associate Producers Philip Neel, Frank Byers

Produced by Gregg Fienberg (1000–1007), Harley Peyton (2001–2022), David J. Latt (European version)

Supervising Producer Gregg Fienberg (2001–2022)

Music Composed & Orchestrated by Angelo Badalamenti

Edited by Duwayne R. Dunham (1000, 2001), Jonathan P. Shaw (1001, 1002, 1005, 2002, 2005, 2008, 2011, 2014, 2017, 2020), Toni Morgan (1003, 1006, 2004, 2010, 2013, 2016, 2019, 2022), Paul Trejo (1004, 1007, 2003, 2006, 2009, 2012, 2015, 2018, 2021), Mary Sweeney (2007)

Director of Photography Ronald Victor Garcia (1000), Frank Byers (1001–2022)

Production Designer Patricia Norris (1000), Richard Hoover (1001–2022)

REGULAR CAST: KMacL, MO, MA, DA, RB, LFB, SF, WF, PL, JM, EMcG, JN, RW, JC, PLau (See key to *Twin Peaks* cast at end of section.)

UNCREDITED CAST: Mark Frost (reporter at sawmill, episode 2001), Hank Worden (episode 2007), David Lynch (voice only, episodes 2004 and 2011), James Marshall (voice only, episode 2018)

UNCREDITED CREW: Dan Kneece (Steadicam operator, 1000)

ALTERNATIVE TITLE: *Twin Peaks* was originally conceived under the title *Northwest Passage*, a reference to the passage between the Northwest Territories of North America and Canada and, perhaps, to the metaphorical passage of Laura Palmer to the other side.

TITLE SEQUENCE: A majestic, sweeping theme plays over picturesque images from the town of Twin Peaks: a robin perched on a bough, smokestacks, a sawmill's machinery cutting wood into intricate shapes. A green-brown title appears over an empty highway and a sign: 'WELCOME TO TWIN PEAKS – *Population, 51,200.*' Credits continue over a dramatic sweeping slow-motion waterfall, the water appearing to defy gravity itself, dissolving through to the red-hued surface of a lake, where the reflection of trees shimmers in the water, its stillness belying the tragedy about to unfold there.

SUMMARY: In the north-western logging town of *Twin Peaks*, located five miles south of the Canadian border and twelve miles west of the state line, the brutal murder of seventeen-year-old homecoming queen Laura Palmer sparks an investigation from the local sheriff's department and, because the murder took place across the state line, the FBI. Clean-cut special agent Dale Cooper arrives in town, later joined by his no-nonsense colleague Albert Rosenfeld, to assist Sheriff Harry S. Truman with the case, which throws up a catalogue of local suspects, ultimately leading to the conclusion that Laura's own father, Leland Palmer, committed the murder while under the influence of a psychotic duplicate personality known as 'BOB'. With the murder mystery solved, Cooper finds a new reason to remain in Twin Peaks: the arrival of his deranged former partner, Windom Earle, with whom he becomes involved in a deadly game of chess, in which the residents of the town are the pawns.

PRODUCTION HISTORY: In the period following the release of *Blue Velvet*, Lynch had been working with Mark Frost on the aborted feature film projects *Venus Descending* and *One Saliva Bubble* [see 'In Dreams,' pages 252 and 247], and on several other unmade projects of his own devising. It was early in 1988 that the idea of creating a television series for ABC was first tabled by Creative Artists Agency's Tony Krantz, who approached Lynch and Frost with the idea, and refused to take 'no' for an answer.

Unlike Frost, who had worked on numerous successful television series, including *The Six Million Dollar Man* and *Hill Street Blues*, Lynch had no background in the medium, nor any interest in it. Nevertheless, when the opportunity arose, he saw it as a way of avoiding the need to have the narrative arc of a story begin to descend at the halfway point: 'I really like the idea of a continuing story,' he told the *Los Angeles Times*. 'Movies have time limits. To really linger over the details of a crust of cherry pie, and really get into the saucer and the cup of coffee just as someone is talking about an affair – those are the things you can do in a soap opera. I think there are certain kinds of moods, especially in getting at the mood of a murder mystery, that take time to conjure up.'

Frost was equally clear about their intentions for the proposed show, hoping to re-imagine the night-time soap opera in the same way that *Hill Street Blues* had reinvented the police drama a decade earlier. 'I spent every summer when I was growing up in a small town,' he told the *Los Angeles Times*, 'and there were relationships and hidden agendas going back thirty, forty, even fifty years . . . the hidden power that secrets hold over lives is a fascinating part of human behaviour.'

Frost has claimed that the small-town setting – originally located in North Dakota – came before the murder mystery. 'We had worked on what was in Twin Peaks, what the town was like, for some months. But it wasn't until we said "a body washes up on shore" that we had a starting point not just for our first image, but for the whole mystery.' Lynch, however, says that the entire idea was sparked by the image of a body washing up on the shore of a lake. Whichever is true, the pair set to work on a pilot script, the first draft of which was completed on 7 December 1988, and pitched the idea to ABC (sometimes called 'the alphabet network', which augured well for Lynch) with the help of an important visual aid: a map of the town and its environs, featuring evocative place names such as Black Lake, Ghostwood National Forest, Lucky Highway and the Sparkwood Mountains. A rough story arc was established, more to satisfy network executives than for the scriptwriters' own benefit, and eventually ABC gave the newly-formed Lynch/Frost Productions the go-ahead to produce the pilot.

While casting got under way in Los Angeles, locations were scouted in the Pacific Northwest, and the production headed up to Snoqualmie, Washington State, to begin filming in February 1989. The cast and crew spent twenty-four days in freezing conditions before returning to the warmer climes of Los Angeles, where many of the interiors would be filmed. From the outset of filming, Lynch had a definite idea of the kind of effects he was looking for, as lighting cameraman Ron Garcia told *American Cinematographer*. 'On the pilot, I was doing a long-lens shot all the way down a river, through some logs and up into the smokestack of a sawmill,' he recalled, referring to a shot that would eventually form part of the title sequence. 'I was rushing through it, because this was television and you've got to have commercials and so on. But David just played the music he was thinking about using and said, "No, no, no – *reeeaaal slooow*." When I redid it, I felt like I had concrete on my hands!' Garcia soon got the hang of Lynch's laconic style, and even offered some suggestions of his own during second-unit photography in Seattle. 'I thought I'd do some really odd things with orange filters,' he said. 'But after David saw the dailies we talked about it on the phone, and he actually said to me, "RON – *too weird*."'

The network took its time making up its mind about *Twin Peaks*, and by the time it gave the go-ahead for a further seven episodes – a hedged bet, since the normal order for a mid-season show was thirteen – Lynch's commitment to *Wild at Heart* forced him to leave the town of Twin Peaks during the summer of 1990 to work on the feature. This evidently led to a souring of his relationship with Frost, who found himself taking all of the pressure, but none of the credit. 'There were times, when David was making *Wild at Heart*, when I was doing almost *all* the work on *Twin Peaks*,' he told *Empire*. 'But everybody wants to believe in the *auteur* theory, that it all somehow springs from one person, and David had a much higher profile.'

Nevertheless, after winning the Palme D'Or in Cannes, Lynch returned to *Twin Peaks* to direct the second season premiere and the episode in which Leland kills Madeleine, effectively revealing him to be Laura's killer. Lynch had finally bowed to pressure to resolve the mystery that had haunted the series since Laura's body washed up on the river bank, wrapped in plastic. 'Our disagreements would mostly revolve around the fact that I wished for more clarity and David wanted to draw things out a little bit more,' continues Frost. 'I mean, I think if David had had his way, we might *still* not know who killed Laura Palmer . . .'

Despite his recurring role as Gordon Cole, Lynch was absent for much of the remainder of the crucial second series, returning only to direct the dying show's swansong. 'David left in the second season,' Kimmy Robertson (Lucy Moran) told guests at the 1996 *Twin Peaks* fan festival. 'He never set foot at the office or anywhere. And Catherine [Coulson] was calling him all the time, saying, "You have to get down here. You have to get down here." Then, when he finally came, he went, "Oh my God!" And then he went on [Johnny] Carson, and he went on [David] Letterman, and begged everybody to watch and write letters. But it was too late.'

CASTING: With Kyle MacLachlan anchoring the series as FBI special agent Dale Cooper, casting director Johanna Ray assembled a combination of well-known actors (Piper Laurie, Peggy Lipton, Jack Nance, Richard Beymer, Ray Wise, Russ Tamblyn, Joan Chen) to play the senior residents of *Twin Peaks*, and young unknowns (Lara Flynn Boyle, Sherilyn Fenn, Mädchen Amick, Dana Ashbrook, James Hurley) to fill the high-school roles. Each audition was carried out in the presence of Lynch and Frost, the former eschewing traditional methods of script-reading in favour of his own *modus operandi*: casual chatter. 'I started asking David a million questions about *Eraserhead* and *Blue*

Velvet,' says Kimmy Robertson (Lucy Moran), 'because I wasn't gonna let that opportunity go by, and I could give a shit about actually auditioning! I started rambling on about my theories, and that was it.' 'It was fairly unorthodox,' Don Davis (Major Briggs) agreed. '[David and I] spent most of the time talking about trout fishing.'

The part of Jocelyn Packard was originally written for *Blue Velvet* actress Isabella Rossellini, with whom Lynch was romantically involved. In the event, her modelling commitments for Lancôme made it impossible for her to play a recurring role in the series, though the original character's name, Giovanna Pasqualini Packard, makes it clear for whom the part was intended, and would have given *Blue Velvet* fans reason to laugh when Cooper (Kyle MacLachlan) sees Giovanna (Rossellini) and asks, 'Who's the babe?'

Several *Twin Peaks* cast members originally auditioned for different roles on the show: Grace Zabriskie (Sarah Palmer) came in to read for Lucy Moran, while Ray Wise (Leland Palmer) originally read for Sheriff Truman.

THE LYNCH MOB: 'A lot of directors have tried to form some kind of ensemble,' Jack Nance (Pete Martell) told *Wrapped in Plastic* in 1995. 'By the time *Twin Peaks* came along, a lot of us from in front and behind the camera . . . had already worked together and knew each other.' Indeed, many cast members had appeared in one or more of Lynch's earlier productions: Kyle MacLachlan (*Dune, Blue Velvet*), Jack Nance (*Eraserhead, Dune, Blue Velvet, The Cowboy and the Frenchman*), Michael Horse (*The Cowboy and the Frenchman*), Charlotte Stewart (*Eraserhead*), Catherine Coulson (*The Amputee*), Julee Cruise (sang on the *Blue Velvet* soundtrack), Alicia Witt (*Dune*), Heather Graham (Lynch's commercial for Calvin Klein's *Obsession*) and Everett McGill (*Dune*). 'I think David created the part for me because his nickname for me is "Big E",' McGill told *Wrapped in Plastic*. 'He's called me that from day one [on *Dune*]. I think he always envisioned the character in *Twin Peaks*. We shared an interest in hot cars.' While Miguel Ferrer himself had never previously worked with Lynch, his father, José Ferrer, co-starred in *Dune* – and also appeared, somewhat mysteriously, in a photograph in *The Cowboy and the Frenchman*!

There were as many familiar faces behind the camera, including composer Angelo Badalamenti (*Blue Velvet, The Cowboy and the Frenchman*), costume/production designer Patricia Norris (*The Elephant Man, Blue Velvet, The Cowboy and the Frenchman*), casting director Johanna Ray (*Blue Velvet*), editor Duwayne R. Dunham (*Blue Velvet*) and director Jonathan Sanger (producer of *The Elephant Man*).

MEMORABLE QUOTES
Pete Martell: 'She's dead. Wrapped in plastic.'

Pete Martell: 'Fellas, don't drink the coffee! You'd never guess – there was a *fish – in* the percolator! Sorry.'

Man From Another Place: 'I've got good news. That gum you like is going to come back in style. She's my cousin. But doesn't she look almost exactly like Laura Palmer?'
Cooper: 'But it *is* Laura Palmer. Are you Laura Palmer?'
Girl: 'I feel like I know her, but sometimes my arms bend back.'
Man From Another Place: 'She's filled with secrets. Where we're from, the birds sing a pretty song and there's always music in the air.'

Gerard: 'One chants out between two worlds: Fire, walk with me.'

Lucy: 'Leo Johnson was shot, Jacques Renault was strangled, the mill burned, Shelly and Pete got smoke inhalation, Catherine and Josie are missing, Nadine is in a coma from taking sleeping pills.'
Cooper: 'How long have I been out?'

Jerry: 'Is this real, Ben? Or some strange and twisted dream?'

Cooper: 'I have no idea where this will lead us, but I have a definite feeling it will be a place both wonderful and strange.'

SOUND AND MUSIC: 'God, I love this music. Isn't it just too dreamy?' Audrey Horne says in episode 1001. She's talking about Angelo Badalamenti's compositions, of course; the Brooklyn-born musician provided the title theme and incidental music for the entire series, largely composed of languorous melodies laid over disturbing, abstract underlying themes. 'That's the darker side, I guess, of me,' Badalamenti told the *Los Angeles Times*. 'It's just very low, dark, sustained things that are so beautiful to me. Maybe a little strange to others, but it's transcendent, to me . . . And I love putting those things as a bed against something maybe a little more palatable.' Badalamenti confessed surprise that the music became the focus of so much attention: 'All the people are calling and saying, "The music is setting up so many of these moods, and the music makes you want to watch." I really don't take the credit for that. I think it's totally by accident.'

Almost fifty minutes of music from *Twin Peaks* was released in September 1990 on a soundtrack album (9 26316–2), produced by Lynch and Badalamenti, and containing eleven tracks: eight instrumentals, and three songs with lyrics by David Lynch and sung by Julee Cruise: 'The Nightingale', 'Into the Night' and 'Falling'. These last three appear on Julee Cruise's 1989 album *Floating into the Night* (9 25859–2), along with 'Floating', 'I Remember', 'Rockin' Back Inside My Heart', 'Mysteries of Love' (heard in *Blue Velvet*), 'I Float Alone', 'The Swan' and 'The World Spins'.

In October 1991, New York dance musician Moby stormed the British charts with 'Go', an improbably artful and irresistibly danceable instrumental based on the repetitive chords of 'Laura Palmer's Theme'. For Moby, the smash-hit single – credited to 'Moby/D. Lynch/A. Badalamenti', and appearing on Moby's debut album *I Like to Score* – marked the beginning of a decade of dance-music success.

In early 2001, The Autumns released an EP entitled 'Le Carillon', featuring a cover of the song James Hurley sang for Madeleine and Donna in episode 2002.

INFLUENCED BY: The co-creators of *Twin Peaks* were undoubtedly influenced by Otto Preminger's murder mystery *Laura* (1944), adapted from Vera Caspary's classic detective novel of the same name, in which a beautiful woman named Laura Hunt is murdered before the story begins, and a by-the-book detective investigates. A cherished portrait of the dead woman, and her secret diary, are central to the story. Lynch and Frost acknowledged the debt not only by naming their own murder victim after Laura, but also by taking the film's chief suspect, gossip columnist Waldo Lydecker, and dividing his name between the mynah bird who witnesses Laura Palmer's murder and the veterinarian who treated him (both references appear in episode 1004).

Cooper may take his name from an equally intriguing source. In 1932, NBC radio ran a series, *The Phantom of Crestwood*, which centred on the investigation of a prostitute named Jenny Wren, killed after attempting to blackmail several wealthy clients. For several months, the question 'Who killed Jenny Wren?' was a national obsession, culminating in the release of J. Walter Ruben's *Phantom of Crestwood* feature film (also 1932), which promised to solve the mystery. The film's producer was one Merian C. Cooper.

Many of the other character names have more obvious influences: Sheriff Harry S. Truman shares his name with a president; Leland Palmer, whose fondness for show tunes is demonstrated early, was named after an actor in Bob Fosse's *All That Jazz* (1979); actor James Marshall has confirmed that the James Hurley character was inspired by James Dean; Piper Laurie played a character named Sarah Packard in *The Hustler* (1961); the names of sheriff's office lovers Lucy and Andy may be references to two popular TV shows of the early 1950s: *I Love Lucy* and *The Andy Griffith Show*; similarly, Donna may have been named after the star of *The Donna Reed Show*, her sister Harriet after one of the characters in *The Adventures of Ozzie and Harriet*. Finally, the One-Armed Man is an obvious reference to television's most famous amputee, the killer in the long-running ABC-TV series *The Fugitive*; he takes his name (Gerard) from the detective in pursuit of Richard Kimball in the same show.

Many other references appeared as the series progressed.

- Cooper's reference to 'Marilyn Monroe and the Kennedys' in episode 1001 arguably acknowledges Lynch and Frost's debt to their abortive adaptation of Anthony Summers' biography *Goddess: The Secret Lives of Marilyn Monroe* [see '**In Dreams,**' page 245].

- Madeleine Ferguson (1003 onwards) is a fairly obvious reference to Alfred Hitchcock's *Vertigo* (1958), in which Judy (Kim Novak) dyes her hair blonde to resemble that of Scottie Ferguson (James Stewart)'s dead lover, Madeleine (Novak again), just as *Twin Peaks*'s Madeleine Ferguson dons a blonde wig to try and trap Laura's killer.

- Blackie's line 'She's ready for her close-up now' (2003) paraphrases Gloria Swanson's famous line from *Sunset Boulevard* (1950), in which Gordon Cole (1004 onwards) is a minor character. Although, as Lynch says, 'I realised, driving to Paramount, that if you go from east to west, you'll hit Gordon [Street] and then Cole. I think it's in that order and in that direction, but anyway, they're right next to each other.'

In addition to these influences, *Twin Peaks* also contains strong echoes of Tim Hunter's *River's Edge* (1987), in which a group of high-school kids (among them Crispin Glover, who would later turn up in *Wild at Heart* and *Hotel Room*) conspire to conceal their discovery of the body of a girl by a riverside, despite knowing that one of their number committed the crime. The bleak, bleached-out autumnal photography – by *Eraserhead* and *Blue Velvet* cinematographer Frederick Elmes – clearly set the tone for *Twin Peaks*'s pilot episode, as surely as Dennis Hopper's performance in *Blue Velvet* inspired, in turn, his casting in *River's Edge*. The circle was complete when Tim Hunter was invited to direct three episodes of *Twin Peaks*.

Rolling Stone writer David Breskin once suggested to Lynch that the inspiration for *Twin Peaks* might have come from a piece by Marcel Duchamp, dated 1946–66 and cryptically entitled *Given 1) The Waterfall 2) The Illuminating Gas*, which is displayed in the Philadelphia Museum of Art, the building next door to Lynch's former home. Breskin described the piece as follows: 'It's a dark, empty room. Along one wall are dark wood boards, nailed up. In the boards, at eye level, are two peepholes, and through them you can see a constructed scene. And in the scene is a naked, sort of dead woman, lying on her back, and off to the right pulses this amazing waterfall.' Lynch thought that maybe he had seen the piece, but pointed out, truthfully, that the waterfall had never appeared in the pilot script. 'We didn't know there was a waterfall up there.' Besides, he added wryly, 'The girl wouldn't have been naked. It was on television – you can't do that!'

The continuing use of 'cherry pie' as some kind of sexual innuendo (not to mention Audrey Horne's highly sexualised trick with the cherry stem) probably stems from Stanley Kubrick's *Lolita* (1962), in which Humbert Humbert gazes at Lolita for the first time, half-lying to her mother that it was her 'cherry pies' that led him to change his mind about staying at her home. Lynch also looked to *Lolita* for the inspiration of a scene in which Cooper and Truman struggle with folding chairs at Ronette Pulaski's bedside. 'One of my favourite films is *Lolita*,' Lynch stated, 'and one of the greatest scenes features this folding bed. The bell hop and James Mason put this bed in the room when Sue Lyon is asleep, and they don't wanna wake her up . . .'

LEGACY: When it was broadcast, *Twin Peaks* caught the public imagination and collective consciousness like few other television shows that had preceded it, a phenomenon that led to a plethora of imitations and *hommages* during the following decade. Chief among these were *Northern Exposure*, which attempted a similar level of supernatural strangeness and warped humour in a small-town setting; *Due South*, in which a straight-laced Canadian cop investigated sometimes supernatural crimes in small-town America; *Picket Fences*, a sophisticated small-town soap opera which often played like a serious spin on *Twin Peaks*; *The X Files*, which boasted *Twin Peaks*'s own David Duchovny as one of a pair of offbeat FBI agents investigating strange phenomena (mostly in small towns) and included several *Twin Peaks* alumni among its guest cast; *American Gothic*, an offbeat exploration of weird goings-on in – you guessed it – a small-town setting; and others.

The first *hommage* to *Twin Peaks* appeared even before the series hit the air, since the pilot had already been widely screened in the industry. (A version was also available in Europe.) A 1990 story arc in the US television series *Wiseguy* – significantly, co-written by *Twin Peaks* story editor Robert Engels – revolved around a murder in a small lumber town knowingly named 'Lynchboro'. The arc featured a detective who cried upon discovery of the body (*à la* Andy Brennan) and later turned out to be the killer.

On 29 September 1990, the night before the Lynch-directed second-season premiere was broadcast, Kyle MacLachlan was guest host on an edition of *Saturday Night Live*. The storyline of the inevitable *Twin Peaks* parody suggested that agent Cooper was deliberately stalling his investigation in order to remain in the town of Twin Peaks.

Five months later, on 26 February 1991, muppet-minded children's series *Sesame Street* managed its own parody, in which 'Special Agent Cookie' attempts to discover why the town he is visiting is called Twin Beaks. He meets several strange birds – including one named Laura, another known as The Log Bird, and another called David Finch – all of whom have two beaks. 'And that concludes Twin Beaks,' he says, stuffing his face with pie. 'Darn fine story, darn fine actor, and darn fine pie!'

In addition to the Georgia Coffee commercials Lynch directed in 1993 [see 'Industry,' page 266], *Twin Peaks* had a direct influence on two popular advertising campaigns in the UK. In the first, for Raffles potato crisps, Kyle MacLachlan plays a Cooper-like character investigating the mysterious 'peaks' on the surface of the crisps. In the second, for Vodafone telecommunications, MacLachlan appears as a trenchcoat-wearing FBI agent (as much a parody of *The X Files* as *Twin Peaks*), investigating various strange phenomena – the Loch Ness monster, the Yeti *et al.* – as part of Vodafone's 'You are not alone' campaign strategy.

The second half of a 1995 two-part episode of *The Simpsons* entitled 'Who Shot Mr Burns?' featured a well-observed *hommage* to the Red Room sequence. In the *Simpsons* version, Chief Wiggum dreams that he is in the Red Room, sitting in Cooper's chair, eating a doughnut. Lisa Simpson appears, speaking in a strange voice, her words subtitled on screen. She tells Wiggum not to eat the clues, and burns two different suits of playing cards as an obscure reference to Mr Burns's suit, while a dark shadow passes briefly across the red drapes. When he frustrates all of her attempts to make him understand, she reverts, frustrated, to her normal voice: 'Look at Burns's suit! Yeesh!' Wiggum wakes, one side of his hair standing on end. (A further *Simpsons* parody appeared in the 1997 episode 'Lisa's Sax', in which a flashback to 1990 reveals Homer watching The Giant dance with a white horse under a traffic light, while a voice says, 'That's damn' fine coffee you got here in Twin Peaks, and damn' good cherry pie.' A wide-eyed Homer says, 'Brilliant! Heh, heh, heh. I have absolutely no idea what's going on.')

The Red Room sequence was also parodied in writer-director Tom DiCillo's 1995 comedy *Living in Oblivion*, in which Tito (Peter Dinklage), a dwarf hired to appear in a Lynchian dream, questions its conception: 'Have you ever had a dream with a dwarf in it?!' Tito asks the director (Steve Buscemi). 'Do you know *anyone* who's had a dream with a dwarf in it? NO! *I* don't even have dreams with dwarves in them! The only place I've seen dreams is in stupid movies like this! Make it weird; put a dwarf in it. Everyone will go "Whoa whoa whoa, must be a dream, there's a fucking dwarf in it!" Well, I'm sick of it.

You can take this Dream Sequence and shove it up your ass!' DiCillo says the idea came to his partner Jane Gil when he became stuck on how to write the third act of his three-act screenplay, in which the first two acts are dreams. 'I immediately thought of a smoke machine and a dwarf,' he wrote later. 'The smoke machine will blow up and the dwarf will ridicule the director in front of the entire crew for casting a dwarf in a dream sequence.'

In 1998, acclaimed author Jonathan Carroll published his ninth novel, *Kissing the Beehive*, the tale of a writer who returns to the small town of his youth to research the story behind a murdered homecoming queen he pulled from the river when he was a young boy. 'I can honestly say when I wrote the book the thought of its parallels to *Twin Peaks* never once crossed my mind,' says Carroll, who does not describe himself as a David Lynch fan. 'But naturally, as soon as someone pointed them out, I grinned large and said, "Of course, you're right."'

The discovery of a murdered girl, wrapped in plastic, in Tarsem Singh's *The Cell* (2000) is shot identically to the revelation of Laura Palmer's face in the *Twin Peaks* pilot. (The body is crawling with ants, like the ear in *Blue Velvet*.) A few minutes later, the killer is heard singing 'Mairzy doats and dozy doats and liddle lamzy divey' – just like Leland Palmer.

DÉJÀ VU: Several observers have suggested that Kyle MacLachlan's *Twin Peaks* character felt like a grown-up version of his *Blue Velvet* persona, Jeffrey Beaumont. In *Blue Velvet*, Sandy (Laura Dern) tells Jeffrey that she is unsure whether he is 'a detective or a pervert' and the ending of the film is entirely consistent with the idea that Jeffrey, having discovered that there is more going on behind the white picket fences of America than meets the eye, decides to follow his propensity for voyeurism and amateur detective work into a career with the FBI. Aside from the general feeling that *Twin Peaks* inhabits the same 'strange world' as *Blue Velvet*, there are numerous references and resemblances to Lynch's earlier film: the robin which opens *Twin Peaks* recalls the closing image of *Blue Velvet*; Ronette Pulaski's shell-shocked walk across the railway bridge recalls Dorothy's after her own attack; close-ups of blown-out candles after Mike shoots BOB (in the European version) recall the one extinguished in Dorothy's apartment; the red drapes, in both the Red Room/Black Lodge and the roadhouse, suggest the backdrop to Dorothy's performance in the earlier film. Furthermore, in episode 1001, Cooper's rock-throwing episode recalls Jeffrey trying to hit an oil drum with a rock; in episode 1004, Shelly Johnson watches an episode of 'Invitation to Love' in which 'Jared' is seen tied up with a blue sash in his mouth, à la *Blue Velvet*. Audrey spying on Emory Battis through the slats of a louvre door recalls Jeffrey in the same film.

There are numerous connections to other, earlier, Lynch works. The song played on the jukebox is 'I'm Hurt Bad' from the Lynch/Badalamenti collaboration *Industrial Symphony No.1*; Lynch used flickering lights in *Blue Velvet* and *Eraserhead*; the zigzag design on the floor of the red room is identical to that of the lobby of Henry's apartment building in *Eraserhead*; the Venus statue may be a reference to *Goddess/Venus Descending*.

THEMES AND MOTIFS: Embarking on *Twin Peaks*, Lynch and Mark Frost were fresh from their abortive attempt to bring Anthony Summers's bestselling biography *Goddess: The Secret Lives of Marilyn Monroe* to the screen, in the guise of the fictionalised biopic *Venus Descending* [see 'In Dreams,' page 252]. It is clear from the central theme of *Twin Peaks*, however – a beautiful and popular blonde whose tragic and untimely death leads to the exposure of her troubled private life, involving deviant sex, hard drugs and powerful men, causing pain and sorrow to those who loved her – that Lynch and Frost were able to steal from *Venus Descending*. Indeed, Summers's portrait of Marilyn Monroe can be seen as a blueprint for Laura Palmer: the all-American girl whose smile is frozen in a portrait, yet whose eyes reveal a tortured soul, which she sells, piece by piece, in a desperate effort to be loved. Laura Palmer's image haunts her home town just as Monroe's haunts a generation, along with the mystery surrounding her death – which, unlike Laura's murder, may never be solved. Monroe's mother, like Laura's, was mentally unstable. Both Laura and Marilyn kept secret journals in which they recorded details of their affairs. Laura posed in front of red velvet drapes for a photograph published in *Flesh World* magazine. Significantly, Monroe once famously described herself as 'Jekyll and Hyde: two in one', echoing the theme of duality ('one and the same') that pervades *Twin Peaks*.

Beyond these obvious similarities between Laura Palmer and Marilyn Monroe, there are other striking parallels between *Twin Peaks* and *Venus Descending*. The investigating agents in both stories (Dale Cooper in *Twin Peaks*, Simon Campbell in *Venus Descending*) record their findings on miniature tape recorders. In *Twin Peaks*, Laura Palmer is involved with the politically-minded brothers Benjamin and Jerry Horne, a more provincial representation of brothers Bobby and Jack Kennedy (note the initials of their forenames), their juvenile behaviour recalling Jeanne Martin's description of the Kennedy brothers, described in *Goddess*, as 'sophomoric'. It is even possible that the name Norma Jennings (a baker) was a version of Norma Jean

Baker, and that Albert Rosenfield's name was borrowed from Monroe's friend and confidant Henry Rosenfeld. Finally, although the suggested identification of Bobby Kennedy as Monroe's killer was deemed too sensitive for inclusion in *Venus Descending*, Lynch and Frost had no qualms about naming him in *Twin Peaks*, both as Robert (from the letters under the victims' fingernails) and BOB.

Although Lynch falls short of admitting that *Twin Peaks* was inspired by the tragic life and mysterious death of Marilyn Monroe, he admits that the parallels exist. 'It's a phenomenon that's not just [limited to] Marilyn Monroe,' he notes. 'There's a lot of girls like that. It's human nature. But I think that whatever it was about Laura Palmer and Marilyn Monroe, that was a thing, you know, that . . . I'm not speaking for [Mark Frost], but for me, I was real interested in that.'

ALTERNATIVE VERSION: In November 1989, five months before *Twin Peaks* debuted on America's ABC network in April 1990 – and almost a full year before its UK television debut – an extended version of the pilot episode was released in the UK, directly to video, as a stand-alone David Lynch feature film. For this 'European' version, Lynch added an eighteen-minute coda to the pilot, in which the identity of Laura Palmer's killer was revealed to be a demented drifter named BOB, possibly the personification of the Devil tattooed on the severed arm of a local man named Mike. 'We needed a resolution, so I made a resolution,' Lynch told the *Los Angeles Times*. 'I just sort of took off and got into a very strange world. I was free to do whatever I wanted for the alternate ending, so I, uh, got into something that was very strange indeed.'

The point of departure of the *Twin Peaks* feature from the US pilot comes 89 minutes into the story, as Sarah Palmer has a vision not of the necklace being unearthed (as in the pilot), but of a long-haired man crouching at the foot of Laura's bed. Leland calls Lucy, then Lucy tells Truman that Sarah thinks she saw the killer. Truman and Hawk, the police sketch artist, head for the Palmers' house. Coop is awoken by a mystery caller from the hospital, who says he has information about the killer. Lucy tells Cooper of Sarah's vision; Coop says Truman and Hawk should bring the sketch to the hospital. Truman is already there when Coop arrives. A one-armed man insists on seeing Coop, who remembers him from the elevator. He calls himself 'Mike', recites a poem, and talks of 'BOB', whom he identifies from the sketch, and who, he says, is downstairs. BOB is in the basement as Cooper and Truman enter. He says the letters under the fingernails would have spelled 'R-O-B-E-R-T'. Mike rushes in, and shoots BOB. Twenty-five years later, an aged Agent Cooper sits in a red room with Laura and a dwarf who claims to be her cousin, and talks in riddles. Laura kisses Coop, and whispers in his ear. The dwarf dances.

Several elements of this 'closed' ending subsequently turned up in the series – most notably Cooper's dream, which closes the Lynch-directed episode 1002 – but the ideas put forward in it would become fundamental to the future development of the *Twin Peaks* series, as well as the feature-film spin-off, *Fire Walk With Me*. 'Fifty per cent of *Twin Peaks* was born because of being forced to do that closed ending,' Lynch says. 'And that's another perfect example of a restriction that isn't like a burden; it's like an opportunity. I just think it was something that was really beautiful, what it conjured up.'

TAG-LINE: 'Who killed Laura Palmer?' ran the inevitable copy on ABC's advertising campaign for *Twin Peaks*'s television debut, along with three other, less troubling questions: 'What's the FBI doing here?' 'Who videotaped Donna and Laura in the woods?' and 'Would you like a doughnut?' Bravo's ads for their *Twin Peaks* reruns were accompanied by the tag-line 'MURDER, GAMBLING, INCEST, PROSTITUTION AND DAMN FINE COFFEE'.

WHAT THE PAPERS SAID: 'If you pay any attention to *Time* magazine,' says Michael Ontkean (Sheriff Harry S. Truman), 'they opined it was the most hauntingly original work in the history of American television.' Indeed, even before *Twin Peaks* was broadcast, the press was championing the series as a television milestone. As early as September 1989, *Connoisseur* magazine published a TV special, describing *Twin Peaks* as 'The Series That Will Change TV.' The debut issue of *Entertainment Weekly*, published 16 February 1990, was the first to ask the question, 'Who killed Laura Palmer? Right now,' it went on, 'the question isn't on anyone's lips, but ABC hopes to change that with its hotly anticipated series *Twin Peaks*, David Lynch's prime time soap.' When *Twin Peaks* went on the air, the rave reviews were plentiful, with *Entertainment Weekly* giving it a rare 'A+' rating. 'How pleasurable it is to really care about a TV series,' wrote TV critic Ken Tucker, 'to the point of (national) obsession.' 'It is like nothing else on television,' enthused *Rolling Stone*. 'Or maybe it is like everything else on television, but with a twist that makes it seem completely new.'

By the end of the first series – which frustrated some, and infuriated others, by refusing to reveal who killed Laura Palmer – and the beginning of the second, a backlash began, with many critics damning the series they had once praised to the skies. In *Entertainment Weekly*,

Tucker rescinded his earlier praise and suggested that *Twin Peaks* was a faddish series whose fifteen minutes of fame had passed. By December 1990, a mere nine months after the series's debut, the *Los Angeles Times* proclaimed that *Twin Peaks* had 'degenerated into some poor, inferior imitation of *The Exorcist*' and that 'ABC should do the merciful thing and cancel this show before David Lynch's reputation is permanently tarnished.'

RATINGS: The television premiere of *Twin Peaks* garnered spectacular ratings on its US debut, on Sunday, 8 April 1990, winning an overall audience share of 33% – in other words, a third of all those watching television between nine and eleven p.m., or around thirty-five million viewers. Contrary to popular myth, which suggests that viewers tuned out as the commercial-free broadcast of the pilot progressed, audiences became increasingly hooked each half-hour, its audience share rising steadily from 29 per cent to 36 per cent by the cliffhanger ending. Ratings did begin to decline towards the end of 1990, however, as *Twin Peaks* audiences became increasingly frustrated by the series's refusal to reveal the answer to the mystery. By October, *Twin Peaks*'s market share had dwindled to seventeen per cent, and by February of the following year, Lynch and Mark Frost were calling upon loyal fans to call, write, fax and otherwise cajole ABC into continuing the series. But in May 1991, with the series's audience at an all-time low – though still attracting between nine and ten million viewers every week – ABC finally pulled the plug.

AWARDS: At the 1991 Emmy Awards, the television equivalent of the movie world's Oscars, *Twin Peaks* scored fourteen nominations – the highest number for any series – in such major categories as Outstanding Drama Series, Lead Actor (Kyle MacLachlan), Lead Actress (Piper Laurie) and Supporting Actress (Sherilyn Fenn). Lynch himself could conceivably have won in five categories: for direction, writing, musical lyrics, co-composition of the main title theme and as co-executive producer. In the event, *Twin Peaks* won only two technical awards, for editing and costume design.

The series fared rather better at the Golden Globe awards, winning three awards: Best TV Series, Best Actor (for Kyle MacLachlan) and Best Supporting Actress, Piper Laurie beating fellow nominee Sherilyn Fenn in the latter category. In addition, the Casting Society of America (CSA) gave its annual award for Best Casting for TV, Dramatic Episode, to Johanna Ray, while the American Society of Cinematographers nominated Ronald Victor Garcia for his photography of the series pilot.

EPISODE LOG

Pilot (1000) / 95 mins / 8 April 1990

Written by Mark Frost & David Lynch
Directed by David Lynch

Additional Cast RT, EDR, MJD, HG, GH, MH, GZ, THE, JB, RH, SL, RD, JDA, KR, JW, WR, DD, CS, PA, BV, DW, JJ, TPW, SH, DR, JC, ASten, AH, RT, MN, BDG, DC, CEC, AS. (See key to *Twin Peaks* cast at end of section.)

Synopsis 24 February 1989. In the north-western logging town of *Twin Peaks*, Pete Martell finds the naked body of seventeen-year-old homecoming queen Laura Palmer, wrapped in plastic, on the shore. He calls Sheriff Harry S. Truman, who arrives with deputy Andy Brennan and coroner Dr Hayward. Laura's parents, local attorney Leland Palmer and his wife Sarah, are devastated. At the Double RR diner, run by Norma Jennings (who is having an affair with gas station owner Ed Hurley, whose one-eyed wife is obsessed with drapes), waitress Shelly Johnson (wife of truck driver Leo Johnson) meets her lover, Bobby Briggs, who was also seeing Laura. Bobby is arrested for Laura's murder. Laura's friend, Donna Hayward, arrives at high school, where she, Audrey Horne and James Hurley, another of Laura's lovers, learn of Laura's death. Ronette Pulaski, missing since the previous night, turns up half-naked, having been raped and tortured. FBI special agent Dale Cooper arrives in town, meets Laura's psychiatrist, Dr Jacoby, and finds the letter 'R' under Laura's fingernail. A videotape of Laura and Donna, filmed by a third party (James), is found, along with Laura's diary, some cocaine and the key to a safety-deposit box containing $10,000 and a copy of *Flesh World* magazine marked with a pin-up picture of Ronette. At the murder scene, a railway carriage, Andy finds a bloody note ('FIRE WALK WITH ME') and half a gold-heart necklace (James had the other half, but buried it). Bobby is released. Johnny, Benjamin and Sylvia Horne's retarded son, is upset to learn that Laura, his tutor, isn't coming. At a town meeting, Cooper meets the Log Lady, a local spinster who cradles a log like a child, and tells the locals that a girl named Teresa Banks was murdered in the same manner as Laura almost one year ago to the day. Cooper gets a room at Benjamin Horne's hotel, the Great Northern, while Harry visits his secret girlfriend, Josie. Sarah Palmer has nightmarish visions, while black-gloved hands unearth the buried half of the necklace by torchlight.

Episode 1 (1001) / 48 mins / 12 April 1990
Written by Mark Frost & David Lynch
Directed by Duwayne Dunham

Additional Cast EDR, HG, MH, SL, RT, GZ, DD, MJD, CS, GH, WR, KR, CEC, AO, MM, JR, AS.

Significant Events Laura's pathology report. James, Bobby and Mike released without charge. Deputy Tommy 'The Hawk' Hill sees a one-armed man at morgue.

Comments Lynch's editor on *Blue Velvet* and the *Twin Peaks* pilot, Duwayne R. Dunham, directed this, the first episode of the series proper.

Episode 2 (1002) / 48 mins / 19 April 1990
Written by Mark Frost & David Lynch
Directed by David Lynch

Additional Cast EDR, HG, MH, SL, RT, GZ, DPK, MF, VC, WR, KR, JDA, MJD, GH, MJA, RBau, KL, FS, CSpr, AS.

Synopsis Ben's brother Jerry returns from Paris; together, they visit One-Eyed Jack's, a brothel across the border. Cooper gets an anonymous note ('JACK WITH ONE EYE') about the place. Bobby and Mike go to conclude their drug deal with Leo (and an unseen accomplice), explaining about the money being temporarily unavailable. Leo suspects Shelly is having an affair. Inspired by a dream about Tibet he had three years before, and Laura's final diary entry, Coop sets up a bizarre experiment in the woods: he chalks the names of all suspects with a 'J' in their name – James, Josie, Dr Jacoby, Johnny Horne, Norma Jennings, Shelly Johnson, 'Jack with One Eye' and Leo Johnson – on a blackboard, and asks Harry to read out the names, and their relationships to Laura, while he throws rocks at a bottle set on a log sixty feet and six inches away. He misses most of the time and finally smashes the bottle at the mention of Leo Johnson's name. Audrey falls for Cooper. FBI forensics expert Albert Rosenfield and his team arrive. Leland dances to 'Pennsylvania 6-5000', holding Laura's picture, which breaks when Sarah tries to stop him. Cooper dreams of being in a red room, twenty-five years in the future, with a dancing dwarf; in the same dream, he also sees a bearded, one-armed man ('Mike') recite poetry, tell how he cut off his arm after seeing the face of God in the devil tattoo on his shoulder, and talk of 'BOB', with whom he lived above a convenience store. Cooper also 'sees' BOB, who threatens to kill again. Back in the red room, Cooper 'sees' the dwarf's 'cousin', a Laura lookalike who speaks in riddles and whispers in his ear. The dwarf dances a strange dance. Cooper wakes and calls Harry: 'I know who killed Laura Palmer.'

Comments Nadine bends the arms of her rowing machine back (note the sound effect, straight out of Mark Frost's previous show, *The Six Million Dollar Man*!); later, Cooper dreams that a Laura lookalike tells him that 'sometimes my arms bend back', while Albert deduces that Laura's arms were bent back when she was tied up. Grace Zabriskie (Sarah Palmer) cut her hand when the glass in Laura's portrait broke. Cooper's dream sequence contains re-edited footage from the extended European version of the pilot.

Episode 3 (1003) / 48 mins / 26 April 1990
Written by Harley Peyton
Directed by Tina Rathborne

Additional Cast EDR, HG, MH, SL, RT, GZ, MF, WO, RDA, JMil, WR, KR, GH, DD, CS, RBau, CEC, JR, BV, CW, EA, LD, PMG.

Significant Events Cooper thinks dream was a coded message. Laura's lookalike cousin, Madeleine Ferguson, arrives for Laura's funeral. Laura was tied up, her arms bent back – a reference to Cooper's dream? Leland's breakdown.

Comments The episode of 'Invitation to Love' watched by Leland features a character called Montana (Lynch's birthplace), another called Gerard (like the one-armed man, and the detective who pursued Dr Kimble in *The Fugitive*) and two characters (Emerald and Jade, the former a *Wizard of Oz* reference), one blonde, one brunette, played by the same actress, a precursor of the Laura/Madeleine storyline that begins this episode. 'Maddy came along about six months after we had shot the pilot, when David flew me down to play the Good Witch in *Wild at Heart*,' Sheryl Lee told *Empire*. 'He said, "I want to bring you back." I said, "How, I'm dead?" and he just said, "We'll figure something out."' When Leland jumps onto Laura's coffin, Sarah hints at his complicity in her death by shouting, 'Don't ruin this, too!' At the Roadhouse, Leland says 'Home, home, home,' like Dorothy repeating 'There's no place like home' in *The Wizard of Oz*.

Episode 4 (1004) / 48 mins / 3 May 1990
Written by Robert Engels
Directed by Tim Hunter

Additional Cast EDR, HG, MH, SL, RT, GZ, CM, JM, KR, MBD, MC, JCra, AG, AS, EA, LD.

Significant Events Hawk draws the man in Sarah's vision (BOB) and catches one-armed man, Philip Michael Gerard, in a motel room (101).

Comments *River's Edge* (1987) director Tim Hunter made his *Twin Peaks* debut with this episode. Madeleine is said to be from Missoula, Montana, Lynch's birthplace.

Episode 5 (1005) / 48 mins / 10 May 1990
Written by Mark Frost
Directed by Lesli Linka Glatter

Additional Cast EDR, HG, MH, SL, RT, CM, DPK, DD, CS, DAmen, CEC, JR, BStr, MS, LD, RG, PMG.

Synopsis Cooper & Co. raid Jacques' cabin. Shelly shoots Leo.

Comments Madeleine says, 'I didn't really know Laura that well, but I feel like I do,' recalling Cooper's dream ('I feel like I know her'). Julee Cruise's recording of the Lynch-Badalamenti composition 'Into the Night' plays at Jacques' cabin, on repeat play ('There's always music in the air').

Episode 6 (1006) / 48 mins / 17 May 1990
Written by Harley Peyton
Directed by Caleb Deschanel

Additional Cast EDR, HG, MH, SL, RT, CM, DPK, WO, KR, WR, DAmen, VC, ML, EB, LAC, MS, BStr, EA, LD, RG.

Significant Events Cooper and Book House Boys visit One-Eyed Jack's incognito. Waldo the mynah bird speaks – 'Laura? Hurting me! Stop it! Leo, no!' – and Leo shoots the bird dead. Maddy dresses as Laura.

Comments Maddy leaves an unmarked videotape at Dr Jacoby's door, à la *Lost Highway*. Drugs hidden in James Hurley's motorcycle fuel tank recalls Dennis Hopper's *Easy Rider* (1969).

Episode 7 (1007) / 48 mins / 23 May 1990
Written and Directed by Mark Frost

Additional Cast EDR, HG, MH, SL, RT, CM, WO, VC, WR, KR, CH, BStr, LD, RG, PMG.

Significant Events Dr Jacoby has a heart attack. Cooper leads drug raid. Sawmill burns, with Catherine and Shelly trapped inside. Cooper is shot by a masked assassin.

Comments The first series ends with a sensational cliffhanger, a laudable but vain attempt to begin a new mystery ('Who shot Agent Cooper?') without resolving the issue of Laura Palmer's killer.

Episode 8 (2001) / 90 mins / 30 September 1990

Teleplay by Mark Frost
Story by Mark Frost & David Lynch
Directed by David Lynch

Additional Cast EDR, HG, MH, SL, RT, GZ, CM, MF, DPK, WR, DD, VC, MJD, CEC, GG, AS, CStruy, PA, SCM, CMil, MT, JW, SKW, AW, HW.

Synopsis Shot and bleeding, Cooper has visions of a giant who tells him three things – 'a man in a smiling bag', 'the owls are not what they seem' and 'without chemicals he points' – and takes Cooper's ring, promising to return it when they come true. Audrey narrowly avoids her sexual encounter with Ben. Catherine is missing, presumed dead. Nadine is in a coma. Cooper returns to duty. Ronette stirs. Maddy has visions of BOB. Leland returns to work, his hair turned white. Albert Rosenfield, FBI agent, returns. Leo has an alibi for the night Teresa Banks was murdered. James gives Cooper necklace he found at Jacoby's; tells Harry that Laura talked about 'playing with fire' and 'playing with BOB'. Donna plays sultry for James. Andy and Lucy check back issues of *Flesh World* for pictures of Teresa Banks. Jacoby tells Cooper & Co. Laura was living a double life, and that she wanted to die. Ed tells Cooper he shot out Nadine's eye in a hunting accident. Cooper sees a body bag hanging in a smiling shape. Bobby asks his father what he does for a living; it's classified. Cooper reviews case history. Leland collapses. Audrey sends telepathic message to Cooper from One-Eyed Jack's; Cooper dreams that the giant from his earlier dream reappears, and leaves another cryptic clue. Ronette has dream of Laura's murder; sees BOB kill her and then scream, either in anguish or victory.

Comments The elderly room service waiter asking a prone Cooper 'How you doing down there?' prefigures Alvin Straight's fall in *The Straight Story*.

Episode 9 (2002) / 48 mins / 6 October 1990

Written by Harley Peyton
Directed by David Lynch

Additional Cast EDR, HG, MH, SL, RT, CM, MF, DPK, WR, DD, VC, DAmen, FB, GZ, CEC, PA, AJL, JP, MT.

Synopsis Jacques Renault's autopsy reveals he was smothered, not strangled. Cooper learns that Audrey is missing, and that Windom Earle, his insane former partner, has escaped from a mental hospital. Donna delivers meals on wheels to Mrs Tremond, whose grandson performs magic, and whose agoraphobic neighbour, Harold Smith, knew Laura. Cooper and Harry visit Ronette in hospital, and show her sketches of Leo (no reaction) and BOB (she has a seizure). The Log Lady's log tells Major Briggs to 'deliver the message'; he responds by telling Cooper that a deep-space monitoring station received a message the night he was shot: 'THE OWLS ARE NOT WHAT THEY SEEM'. Leland sees BOB's picture in Ben's office and says he knows him – he lived next door to his grandfather's summer house when Leland was a little boy. Leo is in a coma, with probable brain damage. Audrey blackmails Emory into telling her that Ben owns One-Eyed Jack's, and that Laura came for a weekend, but was thrown out. Cooper dreams of BOB.

Episode 10 (2003) / 48 mins / 13 October 1990

Written by Robert Engels
Directed by Lesli Linka Glatter

Additional Cast MH, SL, RT, MF, IB, LVD, WR, DAmen, VC, MP, PA, MT.

Significant Events Letter 'B' found under Ronette's fingernail. Lucy is pregnant. Nadine's regression to adolescence begins. Leland is arrested.

Comments Richard Tremayne's physical appearance recalls Ben (Dean Stockwell) in *Blue Velvet*.

Episode 11 (2004) / 48 mins / 20 October 1990

Written by Jerry Stahl and Mark Frost & Harley Peyton & Robert Engels
Directed by Todd Holland

Additional Cast HG, SL, CM, IB, LVD, RDan, DAmen, FY, RBrin, MP, BL, CStan, MT, GG, MV, BA.

Significant Events Leland admits to killing Jacques.

Episode 12 (2005) / 48 mins / 27 October 1990

Written by Barry Pullman
Directed by Graeme Clifford

Additional Cast HG, MH, SL, GZ, CM, LVD, RDan, DLL, WR, VC, VDP, RBrin, FY, MP.

Significant Events Cooper rescues Audrey from One-Eyed Jack's.

Comments Director Graeme Clifford previously edited Nicolas Roeg's *Don't Look Now* (1973) and directed the Frances Farmer biopic *Frances* (1982), which Lynch had been offered.

Episode 13 (2006) / 48 mins / 3 November 1990

Written by Harley Peyton & Robert Engels
Directed by Lesli Linka Glatter

Additional Cast EDR, MH, SL, LVD, IA, DL, WR, FY, AS, JE, RK, LR, MT, BV.

Significant Events Gordon Cole visits Cooper. Windom Earle's deadly chess game begins.

Comments After a non-speaking role in *The Amputee* and a cameo in *Dune*, Lynch gave himself a plum role in *Twin Peaks*, beginning with this episode, as partially deaf FBI boss Gordon Cole who, like Slim (Harry Dean Stanton) in *The Cowboy and the Frenchman*, speaks loudly in order to hear his own voice. Lynch's reappearance seems to revive the mystery, the sense of the 'wonderful and strange' he brought to the show in its early days. Cole and Cooper look and dress alike – and take their coffee the same – confirming their status as unofficial alter egos. Audrey's delirious fear of sinking recalls Dorothy's fear of falling in *Blue Velvet*.

Episode 14 (2007) / 48 mins / 10 November 1990

Written by Mark Frost
Directed by David Lynch

Additional Cast EDR, HG, MH, SL, GZ, WR, AS, DL, FY, GH, PL, CEC, GG, AS, CStruy.

Synopsis Gerard accompanies Cooper & Co. to the Great Northern in search of BOB, clutching his missing arm and collapsing when Ben enters the room. Harold hangs himself, after mutilating Laura's diary, in which Cooper finds references to BOB – a disturbing presence in her life, and a friend of her father's – and to Ben, whom she threatens to expose. Maddy plans to return home. Shelly quits her job at the diner to look after Leo. Audrey forces Ben to confess about his affair with Laura, but denies killing her. Cooper arrests him anyway. The Log Lady tells Cooper there are owls at the Roadhouse. Sarah has a vision of a white horse, and collapses. Against the red drapes of the Roadhouse stage, The Giant appears to Cooper and tells him, 'It is happening again.' Leland sees himself as BOB in the mirror; Maddy smells burning, and sees BOB; Leland/BOB attacks Maddy, placing a letter under her fingernail. At the Roadhouse, the elderly room service waiter apologises to Cooper, and Donna and Bobby cry, all for no apparent reason.

Comments And thus Laura Palmer's murderer was revealed: at least, to series stars Sheryl Lee, Ray Wise and Richard Beymer. As Lee told *Empire*, 'David took [Ray] and [Richard] and me into his office, we sat on the floor in the dark with just this one small light on and he said, "Okay, now I'm going to tell you who did it, what you've all been waiting for." David said, "Ray Wise, Leland, *you* did it. And Sheryl Lee – *you're* gonna die *again* . . ."' Wise, who was assured that Lynch and Frost had always known the killer was Leland, was crushed by the revelation. 'I grew to love Leland Palmer and his strange ways,' he said, 'and I didn't want it to be him. It's like having a close friend turn out to be a killer and go to prison.' Yet, he added, 'Leland is a true innocent, in a sense, because he was totally possessed by this evil spirit, BOB.' The episode marked Mary Sweeney's transition from assistant editor on *Blue Velvet* and *Wild at Heart*, and 'swing editor' on *Twin Peaks*, to credited editor.

Episode 15 (2008) / 48 mins / 17 November 1990
Written by Scott Frost
Directed by Caleb Deschanel

Additional Cast HG, MH, SL, GZ, CM, DPK, JBoo, KW, JG, AS, EF.

Significant Events Leland sees BOB in his own reflection (again). Maddy's body is found, wrapped in plastic.

Comments With the discovery of Maddy's body, *Twin Peaks* comes full circle, in an episode written by Mark Frost's nephew, Scott, author of *The Autobiography of FBI Agent Dale Cooper: My Life, My Tapes*.

Episode 16 (2009) / 48 mins / 1 December 1990

Written by Mark Frost & Harley Peyton & Robert Engels
Directed by Tim Hunter

Additional Cast EDR, HG, MH, SL, MF, IB, JG, DD, AS, MJA, CR, FS, CStruy, MW, HW.

Significant Events Laura's killer was also Maddy's. Cooper's magic experiment to find Laura's killer. Cooper arrests Ben to trap Leland, who confesses to the murders of Laura and Maddy. BOB departs Leland, who dies in Cooper's arms.

Episode 17 (2010) / 48 mins / 8 December 1990

Written by Tricia Brock
Directed by Tina Rathborne

Additional Cast EDR, HG, MH, RTam, GZ, CM, IB, JBoo, JG, CWIII, GOH, WR, TJ, DD, MJD, DCal, MP, JB, LC, TMux, SS.

Significant Events Leland's funeral. Major Briggs disappears.

Episode 18 (2011) / 48 mins / 15 December 1990

Written by Barry Pullman
Directed by Duwayne Dunham

Additional Cast HG, MH, CM, IB, CWIII, JBoo, DDuc, WR, CS, GH, TJ, RL, AMcC, RDA, RTay, DOH, JB, CEC, JE, JK.

Significant Events Cooper learns of the White Lodge and its 'shadow self,' the Black Lodge. Cross-dressing DEA agent Dennis/Denise Bryson arrives in Twin Peaks.

Comments David Duchovny, who would later find fame as an FBI agent in the hit TV series *The X Files*, made his *Twin Peaks* debut with this episode (thanks to ex-girlfriend Kimmy Robertson's intervention). Clarence Williams III previously co-starred with Peggy Lipton (Norma Jennings) in the TV series *The Mod Squad*; his appearance here was almost certainly an in-joke.

Episode 19 (2012) / 48 mins / 12 January 1991

Written by Harley Peyton and Robert Engels
Directed by Caleb Deschanel

Additional Cast HG, MH, IB, DDuc, RL, TB, WR, DD, CS, TJ, GH, AMcC, NL, RTay, JA, JBoo, JH, GK, MShan.

Significant Events James begins an affair with Evelyn. Major Briggs returns.

Episode 20 (2013) / 48 mins / 19 January 1991

Written by Harley Peyton
Directed by Todd Holland

Additional Cast EDR, HG, MH, CM, IB, JBoo, DDuc, GOH, WR, DD, GH, AMcC, NL, MP, JMC, WS, CMacL.

Significant Events Major Briggs's disappearance may be linked to extraterrestrials. Ben's breakdown begins. Truman deputises Cooper during drug raid.

Episode 21 (2014) / 48 mins / 2 February 1991

Written by Scott Frost
Directed by Uli Edel

Additional Cast EDR, HG, MH, KW, RT, DPK, IB, RL, DD, AMcC, DW, DOH, BS, JA, JB, RBla, CMacL.

Significant Events Truman gives Cooper the Windom Earle case. Leo meets Windom Earle.

Episode 22 (2015) / 48 mins / 9 February 1991

Written by Harley Peyton & Robert Engels
Directed by Diane Keaton

Additional Cast EDR, KW, RT, DPK, MF, WR, AMcC, NL, DW, BS, RBau, MB, GLE.

Synopsis Windom keeps Leo prisoner. Pete plays chess.

Comments Miguel Ferrer's impression of Lynch's character, Gordon Cole, is a priceless moment.

Episode 23 (2016) / 48 mins / 16 February 1991

Written by Tricia Brock
Directed by Lesli Linka Glatter

Additional Cast EDR, MH, KW, BZ, MF, DPK, CM, WR, DW, DOH, MJA, RBla, FS.

Significant Events Josie's death.

Episode 24 (2017) / 48 mins / 28 March 1991

Written by Barry Pullman
Directed by James Foley

Additional Cast EDR, HG, MH, KW, RT, BZ, IB, HGra, DLL, WR, DD, GH, CEC, MJD, BS, RBla, JHay, BLG.

Significant Events Annie Blackburn, Norma Jennings's sister, arrives.

Comments Actress Heather Graham (*Drugstore Cowboy*, 1989), who had previously appeared in Lynch's commercial for Calvin Klein's *Obsession*, made her *Twin Peaks* debut with this episode, written in to replace Cooper's intended love interest, Audrey Horne, either because she was too young or – as was widely reported – because Kyle MacLachlan's off-screen love interest, Lara Flynn Boyle, did not want him doing love scenes with Fenn.

Episode 25 (2018) / 48 mins / 4 April 1991

Written by Harley Peyton & Robert Engels
Directed by Duwayne Dunham

Additional Cast EDR, HG, MH, KW, BZ, HGra, DL, WR, GH, MJD, CEC, BS, RBAu, RBla, JMcG.

Significant Events Cooper is vindicated. He falls for Annie, and visits Owl Cave.

Episode 26 (2019) / 48 mins / 11 April 1991

Written by Mark Frost & Harley Peyton
Directed by Jonathan Sanger

Additional Cast EDR, HG, MH, KW, BZ, IB, HGra, RL, DL, WR, DD, GH, MJD, JB, TR, JCS.

Synopsis Preparations for 'Miss Twin Peaks' pageant. Earle kills again.

Comments Jonathan Sanger, producer of *The Elephant Man*, directs. Sam Raimi's brother Ted (*The Evil Dead*) guests.

Episode 27 (2020) / 48 mins / 18 April 1991
Written by Harley Peyton & Robert Engels
Directed by Stephen Gyllenhaal

Additional Cast EDR, HG, MH, KW, BZ, HGra, RL, DD, MJD, DOH, JB, CStru, RBla, RK, TR, FS, LRR.

Signifiant Events The Giant gives Cooper a warning about Annie.

Comments When asked by Earle where he first encountered the petroglyph, Major Briggs answers, 'In dreams' – the Roy Orbison song to which Ben lip-synchs in *Blue Velvet*.

Episode 28 (2021) / 48 mins / 10 June 1991
Written by Barry Pullman
Directed by Tim Hunter

Additional Cast EDR, HG, MH, KW, RT, IB, HGra, DLL, RL, WR, DD, GH, MJD, CEC, DOH, JB, JE.

Signifiant Events Ben is Donna's father. Annie is crowned 'Miss Twin Peaks'. Earle kidnaps her.

Comments Originally broadcast as a two-hour 'movie' with Episode 29 (2022).

Episode 29 (2022) / 48 mins / 10 June 1991
Written by Mark Frost & Harley Peyton & Robert Engels
Directed by David Lynch

Additional Cast EDR, HG, MH, SL, KW, RT, HG, GZ, WR, DD, CS, GH, MJD, CEC, JVS, DOH, CStru, HW, EW, MJA, FS, PA, JDA, AH, AOK, BEM.

Synopsis Annie is missing; Cooper thinks the petroglyph/map is the only clue to her and Earle's whereabouts: Glastonbury Grove? Earle takes Annie there; Cooper and Truman are close behind. Nadine recovers. Cooper heads into the woods alone, and vanishes before Truman's eyes. He finds himself in the Red Room, with a mysterious singer, the dancing dwarf, Laura, the elderly room-service waiter, The Giant and Maddy. Audrey has chained herself to the vault of the bank in protest at the bank's involvement in Ghostwood. The bomb inside Thomas's safety deposit box goes off. In the Red Room, Maddy tells Cooper to watch out for her cousin. Laura screams. Cooper feels a stomach wound, and sees visions of Annie, Caroline, Windom Earle – and BOB. Earle asks for Coop's soul in return for Annie's life; BOB takes Earle's instead. Cooper sees Leland, and himself. Coop chases shadows, and finally reappears with Annie in the woods. He looks in the mirror – and sees BOB. He laughs, and asks, 'Where's Annie?'

TRIVIA: In the *Northwest Passage* pilot script, dated 7 December 1988, the sheriff's name is given as Dan Steadman (a reference to *Stead*icam operator *Dan* Kneece?), one of several slight alterations made to characters or names prior to filming: a black deputy named Bernie Hill became the Native American Hawk; Ronette Pulaski was named Sharon; the Book House was called Hemingway's; the fetish magazine *Flesh World* was called *Sex Toys: Swingers, Coast-to-Coast*.

The inspiration for the famous fish-in-the-percolator routine came from an incident in which Lynch's friend Bushnell Keeler investigated his brother's complaints about his coffee, and found a bar of soap in the percolator. The story stuck with Lynch until he and Frost were writing the *Twin Peaks* pilot, when 'that story crept in, and it became a fish, though, instead of a bar of lather soap.'

Much of the Red Room sequence was filmed in reverse, its dialogue recorded phonetically backwards, so that it is intelligible – well, almost – when the film and soundtrack are replayed in the normal way.

The Great Northern hotel is, in reality, the Salish Lodge hotel, perched on top of the Snoqualmie Falls in Snoqualmie, WA. Reservations can be made by calling 001 425 888 2556.

APOCRYPHA: Ever since a bug flew into one of Lynch's unfinished paintings and stuck to the still-wet paint, the 'artistic accident' has been an important phenomenon for him. This phenomenon is perhaps best expressed in film terms by the oft-told tale of how set decorator Frank Silva came to play 'Killer BOB' in the 'closed ending' version of *Twin Peaks*. As Deepak Nayar told Toby Keeler, it happened like this: '[Frank] was just a set decorator who was hiding behind the chair and, you know, we did our shot, and Sean Doyle was the [camera] operator and he said, "No, no, it's not good for me, David – I saw Frank Silva hiding behind the sofa!" And David said, "That's perfect – we got it."'

Lynch, however, challenges Nayar's simplified version of events. He claims that while they were filming in Laura Palmer's bedroom, Frank Silva was moving furniture around and someone shouted a warning to him not to trap himself in with a chest of drawers. According to Lynch, he wasn't even looking at Frank, but the image of him locked in that room jumped into his head. Lynch immediately asked if Silva had acted before, and he said that he had. Lynch concluded, 'And so I had Frank hide on one pan shot across Laura Palmer's bedroom, freeze down by the bar of the bed and just be looking right at the camera. And we shot that. And I didn't know what I was going to use it for. No idea at all.'

Lynch kept shooting more of the scenes in the Palmers' house, including the scene in which Sarah sees something in her mind's eye, sits bolt upright and screams. Lynch was happy with the shot, but Sean Doyle wasn't. Lynch recalls, 'I said, "Sean, what is the matter?" He said someone was reflected in the mirror. I said, "Who was reflected in the mirror?" And he said Frank Silva was reflected in the mirror. And that's when I knew that Frank was part of the scene.' Thus, although Sarah's scream appears in both versions, Frank Silva (as BOB) appears only in the 'closed ending' version.

Cinematographer Ron Garcia says of Lynch's gift for turning accidents into magic, 'Some directors try to force everything to fit their particular scheme, but David takes it with ease. Something will happen in the periphery of his vision and he'll take it as a sign.'

AVAILABILITY: Although the *Twin Peaks* pilot is unavailable in the UK, except as part of the European version (see below), episodes 1001–2022 are available across ten PAL VHS videocassettes (SE 9141–9150), confusingly labelled as 'Episode 001' through 'Episode 010' and divided as follows: '001' (SE 9141) contains episodes 1001–1003; '002' (SE 9142) episodes 1004–1006; '003' (SE 9143) features 1007 and the feature-length 2001; '004' (SE 9144) episodes 2002–2004; '005' (SE 9145) episodes 2005–2007; '006' (SE 9145) episodes 2008–2010; '007' (SE 9146) episodes 2011–2013; '008' (SE 9147) episodes 2014–2016; '009' (SE 9148) episodes 2017–2019; '010' episodes 2020–2022. The US releases follow the same format.

The extended European version of *Twin Peaks* is available on video in the UK as a full-screen PAL VHS (S035198), and in the US as an NTSC VHS (35198). It is also available on laserdisc from Warner Home Video (35198), and is even occasionally screened as a 35mm feature film.

In the absence of a DVD release of *Twin Peaks*, the best digital option would appear to be the boxed NTSC laserdiscs released in the US in 1993. Volume 1 (ID 2202 W) contains the seven first-series episodes (i.e. the entire first series, minus the pilot); Volume 2 (ID 2571 WV) contains the first seven episodes of the second series, including the two-hour series premiere; Volume 3 (ID 2570 WV) contains seven more episodes; Volume 4 (ID 2751 WV) concludes the series with the final seven episodes. The European version of the pilot is also available on an NTSC laserdisc (35198). A Japanese box set containing all 29 episodes of *Twin Peaks* (i.e. minus the pilot) is also available.

FINAL ANALYSIS: Baby boomers claim to remember precisely what they were doing when they learned about President Kennedy's death; the next generation probably remember where they were when J.R. Ewing was shot. But anyone watching television in the early 90s would have been much more interested in the killing of Laura Palmer, the girl who fulfilled the darkest of American dreams by living fast, dying young and leaving an exceptionally good-looking corpse. The residents of Twin Peaks literally loved Laura to death, blinded to her tragic fate by their resolute belief in her wholesomeness. 'You didn't know Laura Palmer,' Sheriff Truman tells Cooper in the extraordinarily accomplished pilot episode, aghast at the suggestion that Laura may have had a nose for nose-candy. As it turned out, *nobody*, least of all Truman, knew the *real* Laura Palmer – except, perhaps, for her killer: not Leland, but the possessing spirit BOB, who neatly sidesteps the righteous indignation of television standards and practices by taking possession of Laura's abusive father as he rapes and murders her. God forbid that anyone should bring a respectable middle-class father's rape and murder of his own daughter into American homes, without some kind of supernatural possession to explain it away!

Even the staunchest defender of *Twin Peaks* would admit that the identity of Laura's killer could not be teased out indefinitely; indeed, viewers were already screaming for the answer at the end of the seven-episode first season. Nevertheless, it must also be admitted that identifying the culprit killed the series as surely as Leland/BOB killed Laura. The sense of anticlimax that followed Leland's death was almost impossible for the writers to overcome, without a new and equally gripping mystery being exposed beforehand; even if another resident of *Twin Peaks* had been slain, as BOB took possession of a new host, it is hard to imagine any other character whose death would have the same profound effect on the collective unconscious as Laura's. Incredibly, this means that the audience mourned someone who was dead *before the opening credits of the very first show*, more than they would any other character in the series.

Such is the power of *Twin Peaks*, whose pilot is a relentless study of shared grief which Lynch depicts with raw, unflinching emotion. Remember Andy crying as he photographed Laura's body? Sarah and Leland breaking down at the news of their daughter's death? Donna and James realising with horror why there is an empty chair in the classroom? The anguished adolescent running screaming across the school field? This was storytelling rarely equalled in cinema, let alone on television, signalling *Twin Peaks* as a defining moment in the medium's relatively short history. *Twin Peaks* has since yielded many, many imitators but few, if any, equals. *Blue Velvet* mostly played to art-house crowds; *Twin Peaks* held the attention of millions, at least for a few months, the shining surface of the television screen reflecting the warped lives of middle-class Americans who could laugh, because it wasn't *them* that Lynch and Frost were talking about. The ignominy of *Twin Peaks*'s demise, just as it was getting to be as riveting and daring as it had ever been, left a void in the lives of the series' true fans that felt as real as Laura's loss to the residents of her little town. Like Laura herself, *Twin Peaks* was killed before its time, and will be mourned for many years.

EXPERT WITNESS: 'One of the more charming conflicts of *Twin Peaks* was when [David] came in to direct occasionally. He'd throw out whatever script had been devised to move the story on, and do what he felt like doing. And these amazing, mesmerising episodes that hardly related to anything that was going on around them would come out of that. The writers would be despairing.' – actor Kyle MacLachlan (Dale Cooper)

LYNCH ON *TWIN PEAKS*: 'I think that, finally, *Twin Peaks* was not for everyone. But it had a very strong following in television numbers. It wasn't big enough to keep going, but it was still a massive number of people who were digging every detail and understood what was happening.'

KEY TO *TWIN PEAKS* CAST
AG	Adele Gilbert (Midge Loomer)
AH	Andrea Hays (Heidi)
AJL	Austin Jack Lynch (Little Boy)
AMcC	Annette McCarthy (Evelyn Marsh)
AO	Alan Ogle (Janek Pulaski #2)
AOK	Arvo O. Katajisto (Security Guard)
AS	Al Strobel (Philip Michael Gerard, 'The One-Armed Man')
ASten	Arnie Stenseth (Sven Jorgenson)
AW	Alicia Witt (Gersten Hayward)
BA	Bob Apisa (Bodyguard on Stairs)
BDG	Ben DiGregorio (Max Hartman)
BEM	Brenda E. Mathers (Caroline Earle)
BL	Bellina Logan (Desk Clerk)
BLG	Betsy Lynn George (Teen Model)
BS	Brenda Strong (Ms Jones)
BStr	Brian Straub (Einar Thorson)

BV   Brett Vadset (Joey Paulson)
BZ   Billy Zane (John Justice 'Jack' Wheeler)
CEC   Catherine E. Coulson (Margaret Lanterman, 'The Log Lady')
CH   Charles Hoyes (Decker)
CL   Carol Lynley (Diane)
CM   Chris Mulkey (Hank Jennings)
CMacL Craig MacLachlan (Eric Powell, 'The Dead Man')
CMil   Charles Miller (Doctor)
CR   Clive Rosengren (Mr Zipper)
CS   Charlotte Stewart (Elizabeth 'Betty' Briggs)
CSpr   Charlie Spradling (Swabbie)
CStan Claire Stansfield (Sid)
CStruy Carel Struycken ('The Giant')
CW   Clay Wilcox (Bernard Renault)
CWIII Clarence Williams III (Special Agent Roger Hardy)
DA   Dana Ashbrook (Bobby Briggs)
DAmen Don Amendolia (Emory Battis)
DC   Diane Caldwell (Hotel Employee)
DCal   Don Calfa (Vice-Principal)
DD   Don Davis (Major Garland Briggs)
DDuc   David Duchovny (DEA Agent Dennis/Denise Bryson)
DL   David Lynch (FBI Regional Bureau Chief Gordon Cole)
DLL   David L. Lander (Tim Pinkle)
DOH   Dan O'Herlihy (Andrew Packard)
DPK   David Patrick Kelly (Jerry Horne)
DR   Dorothy Roberts (Mrs Jackson)
DWas   David Wasman (Gilman White)
DW   David Warner (Thomas Eckhardt)
EA   Erika Anderson ('Emerald'/'Jade' in 'Invitation to Love')
EB   Eve Brent (Theodora Ridgely)
EDR   Eric DaRe (Leo Johnson)
EF   Emily Fincher (Louise Dombrowski)
EMcG   Everett McGill ('Big' Ed Hurley)
EW   Ed Wright (Dell Mibbler)
FB   Frances Bay (Mrs Tremond)
FS   Frank Silva (Killer BOB)
FY   Fumio Yamaguchi (Hotel Girl)*
GG   Galyn Görg (Nancy O'Reilly)
GH   Gary Hershberger (Mike Nelson)
GK   Geraldine Keams (Irene Littlehorse)
GLE   Gerald L'Ecuyer (Bartender)
GOH   Gavan O'Herlihy (RCMP Sergeant Preston King)
GZ   Grace Zabriskie (Sarah Palmer)
HG   Harry Goaz (Deputy Andy Brennan)

HGra	Heather Graham (Annie Blackburn)
HW	Hank Worden (Elderly Room Service Waiter)
IA	Ian Abercrombie (Insurance Agent)
IB	Ian Buchanan (Richard 'Dick' Tremayne)
JA	John Apicella (Jeffery Marsh)
JAqu	Jennifer Aquino (Eolani Jacoby)
JB	John Boylan (Mayor Dwayne Milford)
JBoo	James Booth (Ernie 'The Professor' Niles)
JC	Joan Chen (Jocelyn Packard)
JCra	James Craven (Male Parole Board Officer)
JCru	Julee Cruise (Singer)
JCS	John Charles Sheehan (Bellman)
JDA	Jan D'Arcy (Sylvia Horne)
JE	Jill Engels (Trudy)
JG	Jane Greer (Vivian Smythe)
JH	Joshua Harris (Nicholas 'Little Nicky' Needleman)
JHay	Julie Hayek (Model)
JJ	Jane Jones (Margaret Honeycutt)
JM	James Marshall (James Hurley)
JMC	J. Marvin Campbell (MP #1)
JMcG	Jack McGee (Bartender)
JMil	Jed Mills (Wilson Mooney)
JN	Jack Nance (Pete Martell)
JP	Jill Pierce (Ice-Bucket Girl)
JR	Jill Rogosheske (Trudy)
JVS	James V. Scott (Black Lodge Figure)
JW	Jessica Wallenfels (Harriet Hayward)
KL	Kim Lentz (Bartender)
KMacL	Kyle MacLachlan (Special Agent Dale Cooper)
KR	Kimmy Robertson (Lucy Mogan)
KW	Kenneth Welsh (Windom Earle)
KWil	Kathleen Wilhoite (Gwen Morton)
LAC	Lisa Ann Cabasa (Jenny)
LC	Lisa Cloud (PE Teacher)
LD	Lance Davis ('Chet' in 'Invitation to Love')
LFB	Lara Flynn Boyle (Donna Hayward)
LR	Leonard Ray (Lounge Local)
LRR	Lane Robert Rico (Pilot)
LVD	Lenny von Dohlen (Harold Smith)
MA	Mädchen Amick (Shelly Johnson)
MB	Matt Battaglia (Cop)
MBD	Mary Bond Davis (Female Parole Board Member #1)
MC	Mary Chalon (Female Parole Board Member #2)
MF	Miguel Ferrer (Special Agent Albert Rosenfield)

MH	Michael Horse (Deputy Tommy 'Hawk' Hill)
MJA	Michael J. Anderson (Man From Another Place)
MJD	Mary Jo Deschanel (Eileen Hayward)
ML	Mark Lowenthal (Walter Neff)
MM	Michele Milantoni (Suburbis Pulaski)
MN	Marjorie Nelson (Janice Hogan)
MO	Michael Ontkean (Sheriff Harry S. Truman)
MP	Michael Parks (Jean Renault)
MS	Mary Stavin (Heba)
MShan	Molly Shannon (Judy Swain)
MT	Mak Takano (Jonathan Kumagai)
MV	Mike Vendrell (Outside Bodyguard)
MW	Mae Williams (Mrs Tremond #2)
NL	Nicholas Love (Malcolm Sloan)
PA	Phoebe Augustine (Ronette Pulaski)
PLau	Piper Laurie (Catherine Packard Martell / 'Mr Tojamura')
PLip	Peggy Lipton (Norma Jennings)
PMG	Peter Michael Goetz ('Jared')
RB	Richard Beymer (Benjamin Horne)
RBau	Robert Bauer (Johnny Horne #2)
RBla	Ron Blair (Randy St Croix)
RBrin	Ritch Brinkley (District Attorney Daryl Lodwick)
RD	Robert Davenport (Johnny Horne #1)
RDA	Royce D. Applegate (Minister)
RDan	Royal Dano (Judge Clinton Sternwood)
RG	Rick Giolito ('Montana' in 'Invitation to Love')
RH	Rodney Harvey (Biker Scotty)
RK	Ron Kirk (Cappy)
RL	Robyn Lively (Lana Budding Milford)
RT	Russ Tamblyn (Dr Lawrence Jacoby)
RTay	Ron Taylor (Coach Wingate)
RTut	Rick Tutor (Janek Pulaski #1)
RW	Ray Wise (Leland Palmer)
SCM	Stephen C. MacLaughlin (Pie Eater)
SF	Sherilyn Fenn (Audrey Horne)
SH	Shelly Henning (Alice Brady)
SKW	Sandra Kaye Wetzel (Nurse)
SL	Sheryl Lee (Laura Palmer / Madeleine 'Maddy' Ferguson)
SS	Susan Sundholm (Samantha)
TB	Tony Burton (Colonel Riley)
THE	Troy Evans (George Wolchezk)
TJ	Tony Jay (Douglas 'Dougie' Milford)
TM	Tiffany Muxlow (Cheerleader)
TPW	Tawnya Pettiford-Waites (Dr Shelvy)

TR   Ted Raimi (Rusty Tomasi / Heavy Metal Youth)
VC   Victoria Catlin ('Blackie' / 'Black Rose')
VDP   Van Dyke Parks (Mr Racine)
WF   Warren Frost (Dr William 'Bill' Hayward)
WO   Walter Olkewicz (Jacques Renault)
WR   Wendy Robie (Nadine Butler Hurley)
WS   Will Seltzer (Mr Brunston)

Wild at Heart (1990)

35mm feature film / 127 mins / colour / live action
Written for the Screen and Directed by David Lynch
Produced by Monty Montgomery, Steve Golin, Sigurjon Sighvatsson
Executive Producer Michael Kuhn
Director of Photography Frederick Elmes
Edited by Duwayne Dunham
Production Designer Patricia Norris
Music Composed by Angelo Badalamenti
Sound Designer Randy Thom
Based upon the Novel by Barry Gifford
Casting by Johanna Ray CSA

CAST: Nicolas Cage (*Sailor Ripley*), Laura Dern (*Lula Pace Fortune*), Willem Dafoe (*Bobby Peru*), J. E. Freeman (*Marcello Santos*), Crispin Glover (*Cousin Dell*), Diane Ladd (*Marietta Pace Fortune*), Calvin Lockhart (*Reggie*), Isabella Rossellini (*Perdita Durango*), Harry Dean Stanton (*Johnnie Farragut*), Grace Zabriskie (*Juana*), W. Morgan Sheppard (*Mr Reindeer*), David Patrick Kelly (*Dropshadow*), Sherilyn Fenn (*Girl in Accident, Julie Day*), Marvin Kaplan ('*Uncle Pooch*' *Puchinski*), Freddie Jones (*George Kovich*), John Lurie (*Sparky*), Jack Nance (*00 Spool*), Pruitt Taylor Vince (*Buddy*), Gregg Dandridge (*Bob Ray Lemon*), Glenn Walker Harris Jr (*Pace*), Frances Bay (*Madam*), Blair Bruce Bever (*Hotel Custodian*), Sally Boyle (*Aunt Rootie*), Peter Bromilow (*Hotel Manager*), Lisa Ann Cabasa (*Reindeer Dancer*), Frank A. Caruso (*Old Bum*), Frank Collison (*Timmy Thompson*), Eddy Dixon (*Rex*), Brent Fraser (*Idiot Punk*), Cage S. Johnson (*Man at Shell Station*), Sheryl Lee (*Glinda, the Good Witch*), Valli Leigh (*Mr Reindeer's Resident Valet #2*), Nick Love (*Man in Wheelchair*), Daniel Quinn (*Young Cowboy*), Mia M. Ruiz (*Mr Reindeer's Resident Valet #1)*, Charlie Spradling (*Irma*), Billy Swan (*Billy Swan*), Koko Taylor (*Singer at Zanzibar*), Ed Wright (*Desk Clerk*), Darrell Zwerling (*Singer's Manager*)

UNCREDITED CAST: Neil Summers, who plays the policeman who questions Perdita Durango before being knocked down by her car, is only credited among the stunt players, despite the fact that he has more dialogue than many of the credited cast. Several other actors had their scenes deleted: Zachery Berger (*Man in Gents' Room*), Scott Coffey (*Billy*), Jack Jozefson (*Chet*), Tommy G. Kendrick (*Red*), Belinda Logan (*Beany Thorn*), Albert Popwell (*Barkeeper at Zanzibar*), Shawne Rowe (*Waitress*), Michele Seipp (*Girl at Zanzibar*), Bob Terhune (*Earl Kovich*) and Tracey Walter ('*Roach' DeLoache*).

ALTERNATIVE TITLE: Lynch's shooting script added a subtitle: *A Love Story*. In France, one of the few territories where the book was released prior to the film (in fact, a month before the film was shown in Cannes), *Wild at Heart* retained the French title of the novel: *Sailor et Lula* (*Sailor and Lula*).

TITLE SEQUENCE: A match ignites in slow motion, sparking an inferno as an excerpt from Richard Strauss's 'Im Abendrot' plays and white titles are superimposed over the flames. The music changes to Glenn Miller's 'In the Mood' as the images dissolve through to the ceiling of an ornate building, as a further title is supered: "CAPE FEAR SOMEWHERE NEAR THE BORDER BETWEEN NORTH AND SOUTH CAROLINA".

SUMMARY: Sailor Ripley and his girlfriend Lula are attending a function with Lula's mother, Marietta Pace Fortune. When Sailor rejects Marietta's drunken sexual advances, she pays a man named Bob Ray Lemon to kill Sailor, but Sailor kills him instead, and is sent to prison. Almost two years later, Sailor is freed, and calls Lula, who defies her mother's wishes by collecting him from jail and hitting the road to California with him, which breaks his parole. Furious, Marietta tells her boyfriend, private eye Johnnie Farragut, to bring Lula home, but secretly hires her lowlife former lover Marcello Santos to kill Sailor. While the love-drunk Sailor and Lula drive through several states, narrowly avoiding Johnnie in New Orleans, Santos delegates Sailor's murder – and that of Farragut, his own idea – to his associate, Mr Reindeer. He, in turn, hires two men, Reggie and Dropshadow, to kill Johnnie in New Orleans, and arranges for ex-convict and Vietnam veteran Bobby Peru to kill Sailor in Big Tuna, Texas. Sailor and Lula wind up stranded in Big Tuna, where Lula's sickness alerts her to the fact that she is pregnant, and Sailor meets Bobby Peru, who offers to cut him in on a feed-store robbery for which a mutual associate, a Mexican woman named Perdita Durango, will act as driver. Thanks to Bobby, the hold-up goes disastrously –

and deliberately – wrong; Bobby shoots the proprietors before accidentally killing himself, and Sailor is arrested. Six years later, he is freed from jail, and Lula takes their son, Pace, to collect Sailor, but after an awkward initial encounter, Sailor decides that he will be bad for them, and ends the relationship. Walking away alone, he is beaten senseless by thugs, has a vision of the Good Witch from *The Wizard of Oz* telling him not to turn away from love, and runs back to Lula, whereupon he sings her a song signifying a marriage proposal, proving that he is truly wild at heart.

SOURCE: *Wild at Heart* is based on Barry Gifford's novel *Wild at Heart: The Story of Sailor and Lula*, the first of a series of books featuring the eponymous couple. The inspiration for the book came from an unexpected source. 'I was down in Cape Fear in the summer of 1988, writing a book on deep-sea fishing, and one morning I woke up in this little motel in Southport, North Carolina, and I heard these voices,' Gifford recalls. 'Not voices from another room, but the voices of Sailor and Lula talking in my head. And I immediately sat down and started writing down their conversation. And they just kept going.' Gifford soon realised that he would be unable to finish his fishing piece, and began writing the book that would become *Wild at Heart* instead. 'For the first time in my life, I felt that I was taking dictation. Basically I was letting them run, and I almost didn't publish *Wild at Heart* on its own. I was gonna see how it played out, because it was turning into a saga.'

Opinion on the novel, published in hardcover in June 1990 and in paperback barely two months later, was largely positive: *Booklist* declared it 'the sexiest, most tender-hearted and life-affirming love story of the year,' while *Details* recalled a frequent Lynch leitmotif when describing it to be a 'taut, electric tale where the writing not only comes in strobelight bursts but is as charged and potent'.

PRODUCTION HISTORY: In April 1989, producer-director Monty Montgomery (1984's *The Loveless*, also starring Willem Dafoe), a friend and aficionado of Gifford's, was given a draft manuscript of *Wild at Heart* while on his way to Washington, where the pilot of *Twin Peaks* was being shot. Montgomery took an option on the unpublished book the very next day, with a view to directing the adaptation himself, but when Lynch read it, his enthusiasm was such that Montgomery agreed to produce the film version if Lynch would direct. 'I just fell in love with them,' Lynch told the *Los Angeles Times*, referring to Sailor and Lula. 'I liked the way they talked and behaved and how in love they were and I liked the world surrounding them. It got my imagination going, and I wanted to go into the world.'

Thus, a few days after handing the manuscript to Montgomery, Gifford received a phone call telling him that Propaganda Films wanted to make the movie immediately. Gifford was largely ignorant of Lynch's work at the time, but on the evidence of the films he had seen (*The Elephant Man* and *Blue Velvet*) saw that Lynch was a director of great vision, and since he did not have time to work on the script adaptation himself, gave the director his blessing to make it his own. 'David undertook the screenplay,' Gifford says, 'wrote it in six days, and rested on the seventh, and checked with me in terms of a creative consultant. And it was perfect. I loved it all.' At the urging of Propaganda Films partners Steve Golin and Sigurjon Sighvatsson, casting and other pre-production duties happened at a similar pace, and shooting began on 9 August 1989, between the filming of the *Twin Peaks* pilot and *Industrial Symphony No.1*. Over the coming weeks, the production would encompass locations ranging from Los Angeles to New Orleans to El Paso.

Although Lynch's adaptation was mostly – sometimes *slavishly* – faithful to Gifford's novel, he made several departures and inventions, both in the plotting and in the characterisation. As Lynch told *Rolling Stone*, 'Barry said, "I don't care what you do with this. There will be Barry Gifford's *Wild at Heart* and David Lynch's *Wild at Heart*. Go with it. Go for it."' Gifford's *Wild at Heart* was essentially a series of linked encounters on the road to California, with most of the supporting characters having little or no relationship to each other. Lynch deftly interconnected Marietta, Santos, Johnnie, Lula's late father and Uncle Pooch, so that the reasons for Marietta's hatred of Sailor go far beyond those of an over-protective mother: in Lynch's version, Marietta believes that Sailor witnessed her involvement in the death of her husband, Lula's father, and is also incensed that Sailor rejected her sexual advances. Lynch added to this demonisation of Marietta by making her aware that Uncle Pooch raped Lula; indeed, she walks in on the two of them, and it can be inferred that she was the cause of Pooch's subsequent death in a car 'accident'.

Ingeniously, Lynch used the invented character of Mr Reindeer to knit the various plot threads together. In the novel, Marietta threatens to hire Marcello Santos to kill Sailor, but in the film she does so; Santos readily agrees, but – fearing that Johnnie Farragut (a budding writer) will sour his and Marietta's dealings with Reindeer – asks Reindeer to see that Sailor and Johnnie both end up dead. Reindeer, in turn, hires Bobby Peru to kill Sailor, which he attempts to do at the botched robbery, having saddled Sailor with an unloaded gun. Reindeer also hires the freakish figures of Reggie and Dropshadow – merely innocent bystanders in the book – to kill Johnnie, which they do with help from another of Reindeer's associates, a woman named

Juana. In the novel, the character of Santos is mentioned but never seen, there is no contract out on Johnnie, and it is he, not Santos, who accompanies Marietta to collect Lula from Texas.

Numerous other memorable scenes in *Wild at Heart* are also Lynch's own invention. Sailor and Lula witnessing the aftermath of a car accident, only alluded to in the novel, was born out of Lynch's impression of *Twin Peaks* actress Sherilyn Fenn as a porcelain doll, and the idea of what a girl who looked like a porcelain doll would look like if she was broken. Another wholly invented scene, in which Bobby Peru seduces and humiliates Lula in her motel room, seems to remain true to the spirit of the novel, since it implies the same kind of complicity from Lula that Gifford ascribes to her deflowerment at the hands of Uncle Pooch. Lynch says he wanted Peru to go to work on Sailor and Lula, offering the former an easy way out of his predicament, and reminding the latter of her earlier abuse.

No single aspect of Lynch's adaptation represented a more radical departure from the source material than the ending, however. The novel ends as Sailor and Lula part, shortly after she and their son collect Sailor upon his release from prison for the robbery in which Bobby Peru died. Lynch disliked this ending, which he felt betrayed the love which Sailor and Lula clearly felt for each other, but it was not until Samuel Goldwyn – whose eponymous company would distribute the film in the US – vocalised his own dissatisfaction with it that Lynch felt compelled to change it. 'I didn't buy the ending of the book,' Lynch told *Rolling Stone*, noting that his first draft of the screenplay retained it. 'But emotionally, it wasn't ringing true at all! I couldn't think of a reason when Samuel Goldwyn asked me, "Why is he leaving?"'

The decision to change the ending posed a moral dilemma for the director, who feared a critical backlash if he was seen to be eschewing Gifford's resolution in favour of a more commercial, upbeat dénouement of his own devising. 'So, I almost wanted to do a miserable ending just to show that I wasn't trying to be commercial,' Lynch explained. 'And that's wrong – doubly wrong. And so, like I said, it's got to feel honest, and if it does, that's what you have to do.' What may have swung Lynch in favour of the happy ending was the fact that he called Gifford to ask if, in the next Sailor and Lula novels, the couple got back together. 'And I said, "Absolutely",' Gifford recalls. '"They get back together, and they stay together, and they live to a ripe old age together." And he said, "Great!" And he went back and he rewrote it . . . It was justified,' he adds, 'because I figured we're only gonna have one movie, so it's better that the clear intention of the rest of the books is brought out in the movie.'

CASTING: Lynch knew exactly who he wanted to play Sailor and Lula, and he got his first choices. Nicolas Cage – nephew of Francis Ford Coppola, with whom Lynch once had a brief and unproductive movie deal – then best known for his performances in his uncle's *Peggy Sue Got Married* (1986), and Norman Jewison's *Moonstruck* (1987), had the right combination of reckless cool, wide-eyed innocence and vulnerability that Lynch felt Sailor needed. 'I knew that Nicolas was Sailor,' Lynch explained. 'A nice guy, very much in love with his gal, who finds himself in the wrong place at the wrong time too often.' The director felt equally strongly – 'with every fibre of my being', he said – that Laura Dern was perfect to play Lula. It was a decision that surprised many, not least because Gifford described his leading lady as having black hair, grey eyes and breasts that were slightly too large for her body.

Lynch introduced Cage and Dern to each other in a Los Angeles restaurant, close to a cinema on Beverly Boulevard that happened to be on fire ('It seemed like a sign,' he said, 'because fire is so important in the film'). Lynch was delighted when their on-screen sparks ignited a real-life romance, perhaps induced by his suggestion, prior to filming, that the pair spend the weekend in Las Vegas together, to see what effect it would have on them to become a unit, rather than being individuals. Laura Dern knew what he meant. 'Lula and Sailor are like one person walking through this journey,' she said. 'They are two people in love surrounded by a tortured world. No matter what else is out there, it's not going to affect them because they are following their hearts.' Despite his initial scepticism, shared by many, Gifford admits that Dern nailed the character. 'What Laura captured perfectly was the essence of Lula, and her fire, and being who she was – a middle-class girl from a bourgeois family, who is slightly downwardly mobile, who falls in love with a white-trash boy.'

Although several of the supporting cast were drawn from actors who, like Dern, had worked with Lynch before (see below), almost as many were new to the director's repertory company. Laura Dern's real-life mother, Diane Ladd, had not worked with her daughter for several years until Lynch cast her as Lula's mother, Marietta. 'We spent twenty years warming up for this,' she said. 'There was never a moment that we had to adjust to.' Crispin Glover, a former classmate of Cage's who had appeared in the *Back to the Future* series, and with Dennis Hopper in Tim (*Twin Peaks*) Hunter's very Lynchian *River's Edge* (1986), was cast as Cousin Dell; J. E. Freeman (*Hard Traveling*, 1984) as Marcello Santos; and Willem Dafoe (*Platoon*, 1986) in the role of Bobby Peru, for one simple reason: 'Clark Gable is dead.' As Dafoe said, 'What makes Bobby Peru so dangerous is that he's a bad egg who really has no problems. He's at peace with himself. His conscience is clean and that's a feat. He's a guy who has been around the block and there is no guilt.'

THE LYNCH MOB: *Wild at Heart* features an impressive ensemble of actors from Lynch's unofficial repertory company, including alumni from *Eraserhead* (Jack Nance), *The Elephant Man* (Freddie Jones, W. Morgan Sheppard), *Blue Velvet* (Nance, Laura Dern, Isabella Rossellini, Frances Bay), *The Cowboy and the Frenchman* (Nance, Harry Dean Stanton) and *Twin Peaks* (Nance, Sherilyn Fenn, Grace Zabriskie, Sheryl Lee, David Patrick Kelly), the pilot of which had finished filming by the time work on *Wild at Heart* began. Behind the camera, Lynch was reunited with a similar number of former collaborators, including cinematographer Frederick Elmes (*Eraserhead*, *The Cowboy and the Frenchman*), editor Duwayne Dunham (*Blue Velvet*, the *Twin Peaks* pilot), production designer Patricia Norris (*The Elephant Man*, *Blue Velvet*, the *Twin Peaks* pilot), composer Angelo Badalamenti (*Blue Velvet*, *Twin Peaks*), music consultant Jon Huck (*The Cowboy and the Frenchman*'s sound designer), casting director Johanna Ray (the *Twin Peaks* pilot), script supervisor/first assistant film editor Mary Sweeney (*Blue Velvet*), property master Frank Silva (Killer Bob in *Twin Peaks*), casting assistant Eric DaRe (Leo Johnson in *Twin Peaks*).

MEMORABLE QUOTES
Sailor: 'Hey-hey-hey-hey, my snakeskin jacket! Thanks, baby! Did I ever tell you that this here jacket represents a symbol of my individuality and my belief in personal freedom?'
Lula: 'About fifty thousand times!'

Sailor: 'The way your head works is God's own private mystery.'

Lula: 'You better run me back to the hotel. You got me hotter'n Georgia asphalt.'

00 Spool: 'My dog barks some. Mentally, you picture my dog, but, I have not told you the type of dog which I have! Perhaps you might even picture Toto, from *The Wizard of Oz*. But I can tell you my dog is always with me. *Arf!*'

Lula: 'This whole world's wild at heart and weird on top!'

Good Witch: 'If you're truly wild at heart, you'll fight for your dreams. Don't turn away from love, Sailor. Don't turn away from love.'

SOUND AND MUSIC: With *Wild at Heart*, Lynch once again turned to Angelo Badalamenti to compose the film's original music, which strongly recalls several of the themes used in their previous collaboration, *Twin Peaks*. Yet the vast majority of the music in the film is in the form of 'needle-drops', some of which act as ironic counterpoint to the scene, or to comment on and underline it, as in the case of Johnnie innocently singing along to Them's 'Baby Please Don't Go' as he drives to his doom in the same Louisiana town mentioned in the song ('Baby please don't go down to New Orleans . . .'), or in the use of 'Be-Bop A Lula' as a signature tune for Lula. With similar style, Sailor and Lula declare their delight at finding Powermad's 'Slaughterhouse' on the radio, commenting on the music in a manner which recalls Audrey putting Angelo Badalamenti's music on the jukebox, or Bobby changing the music on his car radio, both in *Twin Peaks*. Two of the tracks – 'Love Me' and 'Love Me Tender', both performed by Nicolas Cage – might even be described as musical interludes, of the kind found in an Elvis Presley movie, or any musical.

The soundtrack album for the film (845 098–2) features a good selection of music, in chronological order, with tracks sometimes blending together in a style adopted by producer Trent Reznor for his supervised soundtracks of Oliver Stone's *Natural Born Killers* and, later, Lynch's own *Lost Highway*. The full track listing is as follows: an excerpt from Richard Strauss's 'Im Abendrot', Powermad's 'Slaughterhouse', Badalamenti's 'Cool Cat Walk', 'Dark Lolita' and 'Dark Spanish Symphony' (two versions), Chris Isaak's 'Wicked Game' and 'Blue Spanish Sky', Nicolas Cage's own renditions of 'Love Me' and 'Love Me Tender', Rubber City's 'Perdita', Gene Vincent's 'Be-Bop A Lula', Koko Taylor's recording of the Lynch/Badalamenti composition 'Up in Flames', and Glen Gray and The Casa Loma Orchestra's 'Smoke Rings'.

Music featured in *Wild at Heart*, but absent from the soundtrack album, includes Glenn Miller's 'In the Mood', Duke Ellington's 'First Movement', Shony Alex Braun's 'Chrysanthemum' and 'Avant De Mourir', John Ewing and the Allstars' 'Streamline', Billy Swan's 'Buried Alive', African Head Charge's 'Far Away Chant', Les Baxter's 'Boomada' and Krzysztof Penderecki's 'Kosmoginia.'

By the time of *Wild at Heart*'s release, the Chris Isaak songs 'Wicked Game' and 'Blue Spanish Sky' had already appeared on his 1989 album *Heart-Shaped World*, but their use in Lynch's film gave them a new lease of life. In late 1990, assisted by a Lynch-directed video that incorporated images from the film in which it appeared – albeit in instrumental form – Chris Isaak's 'Wicked Game' (LONCD 279) became a top ten single in several countries, while the identically titled album (7599265132) hit number three in the UK charts. In addition to the title track, the album included 'Blue Spanish Sky' and the instrumental version of 'Wicked Game' heard in the film. Lynch evidently struck up a friendship with the 1950s-influenced singer-songwriter, subsequently casting him as FBI agent Chester Desmond in *Twin Peaks – Fire Walk With Me*.

INFLUENCED BY: There were countless road movies prior to *Wild at Heart*, but only one in which the road was made of yellow bricks. According to Lynch, the thinking behind his overt use of L. Frank Baum's classic slice of American myth – absent from the novel – was simple: Sailor and Lula, he figured, were just the kind of people to embrace the fantasy and make it cool. 'The world in the film was awful tough,' he pondered, 'so there was something beautiful about Sailor being a rebel but a rebel with a dream of *The Wizard of Oz*.' The more Lynch thought about his adaptation of Gifford's story, the more Baum's story infiltrated it, sneaking in and out throughout the picture. 'I remember writing a line for Jack Nance's character, 00 Spool, about the dog: "And you may even picture Toto from *The Wizard of Oz*." The idea that someone else was speaking about something that Sailor and Lula shared secretly was a double whammy. It fits in with the theme, but it's scary at the same time.' Gifford agrees. 'I thought it was a rather ingenious way for David to end up with a happy ending,' he says. The full list of references is as follows:

- At the Cape Fear motel, Lula says that the laughter of the woman in the next room reminds her of the Wicked Witch (of the West).
- Lula asks Sailor if he ever thinks something, hears a wind and sees the Wicked Witch of the East come flying in.
- 'Sometimes, Sail', when we're making love,' Lula says, 'you just about take me right over that rainbow.'
- Sailor says it's too bad that Lula's confused cousin, Dell, couldn't visit 'that ol' Wizard of Oz, and get some good advice.' 'Too bad we all can't, baby,' she replies.
- Driving at night, Lula sees an image of her mother on a broomstick.
- Entering Big Tuna, Texas, Sailor says 'It ain't exactly Emerald City.'
- 00 Spool wonders if the dog he describes reminds Sailor and Lula of Toto from *The Wizard of Oz*.
- Lula is sad that she and Sailor seem to have 'broken down on that yellow brick road.'
- After being psychologically 'raped' by Bobby Peru, Lula clicks her red shoes ('ruby slippers') together several times, Dorothy's escape route in *The Wizard of Oz* (cf. *Blue Velvet*).
- Bobby tells Sailor that his share of the robbery takings will get him and Lula 'a long way down that yellow brick road'.
- An omniscient observer watches events in a crystal ball.

- Lula tells Sailor she wishes she was 'somewhere over that rainbow', a reference to Dorothy's song from *The Wizard of Oz*.
- Glinda, the Good Witch of the North, appears to Sailor, telling him to fight for his dreams, and not to turn away from love.

If Lynch was influenced by *The Wizard of Oz*, the characterisation of Sailor Ripley was inspired by another great American institution and cultural touchstone, Elvis Presley. Not only does Nicolas Cage speak in a soft Memphis drawl and croon songs like 'Love Me' and 'Love Me Tender', his whole feverishly 50s cool, rock-and-roll rebel attitude and angular physical performance seems to take its inspiration from The King. '[Sailor] is like an old Corvette in a snakeskin jacket,' Cage has said. 'He breaks down, he starts up, he breaks down. When he's driving, he drives fast and he drives cool, but he needs a tune-up. And even though he would beg and steal – like in that Elvis song – even though he killed a man, he did it because of love. He felt he was doing the right thing, even though it was pretty screwed up. There's not a lot of rationality between his instincts and his actions.' The Elvis influence was deliberate, Cage said, because '*Wild at Heart* is the kind of movie I wish Elvis would have done.'

Isabella Rossellini used a more unusual inspiration for the distinctive look of her own character, Perdita Durango: Mexican artist Frida Kahlo, many of whose paintings were a series of obsessive self-portraits. 'Frida Kahlo portrayed herself as attractive and repulsive at the same time,' Rossellini explained. 'She is beautiful and feminine, but she is hairy, a bit like an ape, with a moustache and two eyebrows that are really one big one across her forehead. This combination of attractiveness/repulsiveness fascinated me, and I told David I'd love to play a character with these qualities.' To effect her Frida Kahlo look, Rossellini enhanced her eyebrows, donned a blonde wig under which thick black roots were visible, and wore a tight dress she described as 'sexy but vulgar', creating a memorable character despite the brevity of her appearance.

LEGACY: In 1990, the stylised violence of *Wild at Heart* seemed to be in direct contravention of the unwritten rules of independent film-making. Within a few short years – largely thanks to writer-director Quentin Tarantino and his imitators – those rules would have been rewritten in *Wild at Heart*'s own image: gratuitously violent, impossibly cool, and shot through with liberal doses of pop-culture references, record-collection soundtracks in preference to specially composed music, and characters who reflect their own idols, just as Sailor's playful Elvis impression recalled Martin Sheen's deference to James Dean in Terrence Malick's *Badlands* (1973). *Wild at Heart* begat a steady stream of such films from independent sources, most notably Tarantino's *Reservoir Dogs* (1992) and the Palme D'Or-winning *Pulp Fiction* (1994), which are often credited with creating the pop-culture style that Lynch borrowed from Barry Gifford. The 'road movie' did not thrive during the 80s, but *Wild at Heart* revived the genre for the new decade, bringing forth such films as *True Romance* (1993), *Natural Born Killers* (1994) and *The Doom Generation* (1995), all of which used *Wild at Heart*'s colourful widescreen style to tell their own tales of lovers united on the road in a world that's 'wild at heart and weird on top'. Some of the imagery in *My Own Private Idaho* (1991) also has strong recollections of Lynch's film.

One of the film's most obvious legacies was on writer-director John Dahl's *Red Rock West* (1992), which brought together Lynch alumni Nicolas Cage (*Wild at Heart*), Dennis Hopper (*Blue Velvet*) and Lara Flynn Boyle (*Twin Peaks*) for a noirish thriller in which a drifter named Michael Williams (Cage) is mistaken for the hit man (Hopper) hired to kill the wife (Boyle) of a local sheriff. Like Sailor Ripley, Williams is a good man in a bad situation, who finds trouble more through bad luck than through actually looking for it. And like *Wild at Heart*, the film was produced by Propaganda Films's Sigurjon Sighvatsson and Steve Golin.

Lynch's film version of *Wild at Heart* brought Barry Gifford from critical acclaim and obscurity to centre stage, and in 1991 the author published a continuation of the misadventures of *Wild at Heart*'s central characters (including Perdita Durango) in a book of linked novellas – *59% and Raining: The Story of Perdita Durango*, *Sultans of Africa*, *Consuelo's Kiss* and *Bad Day for the Leopard Man* – collected in the US under the title *Sailor's Holiday: The Wild Life of Sailor & Lula*. Although many critics noted how Gifford's writing had taken a turn for the weird following Lynch's fast, loose and bizarre adaptation, Gifford himself denied that he had been influenced by the director's style. 'The truth of it is that parts of *Sailor's Holiday* were written before I ever saw the film of *Wild at Heart*,' he demurred. Gifford's relationship with Lynch certainly endured *Wild at Heart*; they subsequently collaborated on *Hotel Room*, the feature-length television adaptation of Gifford's trilogy of plays, as well as the original screenplay for *Lost Highway*, inspired by the novel *Night People*.

One of the stories in *Sailor's Holiday* – *59% and Raining: The Story of Perdita Durango*, also published separately as *Perdita Durango* – gave the character played by Isabella Rossellini in Lynch's film centre stage. Originally to be directed by Bigas Luna (*Jamón Jamón*, 1992), then Pedro Almodóvar (*All About My Mother*, 1999), the film was finally made in 1999 by director Alex de la Iglesia (*Accion Mutante*,

1993), from a script co-written by Gifford, and with Rosie Perez (*Fearless*, 1993) as the anti-heroine.

In late 2000, discussions began between Gifford and various interested parties about the possibility of a stage musical based on *Wild at Heart*. 'It seems like a very natural idea,' Gifford says, 'because we have the love story [of] Sailor and Lula, and we have the demon Bobby Peru, so there are some good roles. I think it would stick fairly closely to the story. There's already one theatre that would like to sponsor this before it goes to Broadway, so now we have to find a director and a composer.'

DÉJÀ VU: The presence of *Blue Velvet*'s Laura Dern and Isabella Rossellini, and generous helping of *Twin Peaks* actors, perhaps gives a false impression of the number of echoes of Lynch's earlier films in *Wild at Heart*. Nevertheless, Lula's mother makes sexual advances to Sailor, just as the boy's mother does in *The Grandmother*, and Mrs X does to Henry in *Eraserhead*. Humans (Johnnie Farragut, 00 Spool) barking like dogs recalls *The Grandmother*, while Bobby Peru refers to his penis as One-Eyed Jack, confirming the true meaning of the name of the *Twin Peaks* brothel. 'Hello, pretty woman,' Bobby says to Lula: a reference to Roy Orbison? Night shots of the yellow lines down a two-line highway recall Jeffrey's 'joyride' in *Blue Velvet*, and there is something about Bobby's accidental decapitation, and the appearance of his fallen head, that recalls *Eraserhead*. The ending – in which the angelic Glinda, the good witch, appears to Sailor – also has echoes of *The Grandmother* (the grandmother's ghost appears to the boy at the end), *Eraserhead* (the Lady in the Radiator appearing to Henry), *The Elephant Man* (Merrick's mother) and *Industrial Symphony No.1* (the dreamself of the broken-hearted girl floating in space in a fairy dress). In addition, much of the music recalls Angelo Badalamenti's dreamy compositions for *Twin Peaks*, while the song 'Up in Flames' was performed (by Julee Cruise) during *Industrial Symphony No.1*.

THEMES AND MOTIFS: Fire has been a theme that Lynch has favoured since his first film experiment, *Six Figures Getting Sick* (1967), showed the six figures bursting into flame when ignited by birthday candles. Fire, as a symbol of destruction and a metaphor for burning passion, is a powerful leitmotif in *Wild at Heart*, both as an actual force (the supposed self-immolation that kills Lula's father and a young man burns his hand on a lit cigarette discarded by Sailor) and as a visual signature, most commonly extreme close-ups of lighted matches and burning cigarettes. With the burning of the sawmill in *Twin Peaks*, obvious connections to *Twin Peaks – Fire Walk With Me*, burning houses *and* burning homes in *Lost Highway* and *The Straight Story*, fire clearly remains a powerful force in Lynch's world.

CUT SCENES: Lynch's screenplay includes a number of scenes, many lifted wholesale from the novel, which do not appear in the finished film:

- The film opens with three short scenes of Lynch's own invention: a speeding motorcycle hits a speed bump and violently disgorges its rider; an old couple remark upon two rabid dogs fighting ferociously in a vacant lot; a group of 'hardened criminal nine-year-olds' attack a wasps' nest while making animal noises. Lynch did not shoot these scenes, and does not remember why, but their omission led to the suggestion, by editor Duwayne Dunham, that the killing of Bob Ray Lemon be moved to the front to provide a dramatic opening.
- As in the novel, Lula and her friend Beany Thorn (played by Belina Logan) discuss their men in a music bar while listening to a white blues band called The Bleach Boys. Lula arranges to borrow Beany's car to evade pursuit.
- After finding Lula missing, Marietta looks for Johnnie at the Southern Time bar.
- Lula's description of being raped by Uncle Pooch is more detailed, like the novel.
- When Marietta asks Marcello Santos to kill Sailor, the scene is longer, and contains a great deal of absurdist humour.
- In the restroom where Marietta tries to seduce Sailor, an old man (Zachery Berger) mistakes her for a man and mutters, 'Lousy fuckin' homosexuals . . .'
- In The Hurricane bar, Lula says 'Take a picture, bitch – it'll last longer!' to a girl eyeing up Sailor, before threatening her.
- During Sailor's story about leeches and skin grafts, Lynch included a shot of a man with his forearm sewn to his nose.
- The backstory of Johnnie's killers, named in the script as Reginald San Pedro Sula ('Reggie') and Drop Shadow ('Dropshadow'), is expanded in several scenes taken from the book, including one in which they join Johnnie at his table in the Round Room restaurant in New Orleans, claiming to work for the Honduras secret service.
- The scene in which George Kovich (*The Elephant Man*'s Freddie Jones) talks of pigeons and makes strange noises was originally scripted and shot much as it appeared in the novel, with Kovich's brother Earl (Bob Terhune) also making an appearance. In the longer version, Kovich tells Sailor and Lula of his former business venture, in which he and his brother acted as self-styled pest controllers, shooting pigeons that had become a nuisance or a health hazard. According to Lynch, Jones delivered the monologue so perfectly, he

Jack Nance as Henry in *Eraserhead*: 'We live inside a dream.' (© Catherine E Coulson/
David Lynch/AFI)

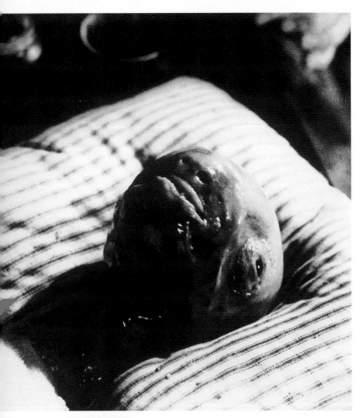

Left Baby 'Spike' in *Eraserhead* (© Catherine E Coulson/David Lynch/AFI)

Right top *Dune*: 'It's a strange world isn't it?' (© Dino De Laurentiis/ Universal Pictures)

Right bottom José Ferrer in *Dune*: 'This whole world's wild at heart and weird on top!' (© Dino De Laurentiis/Universal Pictures)

Below Anthony Hopkins and John Hurt in *The Elephant Man*: 'The man behind the mask is looking for the book with the pages torn out.' (© Brooksfilm)

Above *Blue Velvet*: 'He who can destroy a thing controls a thing.' (© Dino De Laurentiis Entertainment Co.)

Above *Blue Velvet*: 'She's filled with secrets.' (© Dino De Laurentiis Entertainment Co.)

Left Sheryl Lee in *Twin Peaks*: 'Are you talking about that little girl who got murdered?' (© Lynch/Frost Productions)

Below *Twin Peaks*: 'I don't know if you're a detective or a pervert.' (© Lynch/Frost Productions)

Above *Wild at Heart*: 'Did you ride that thing all the way out here to see me?' (© Polygram/ Propaganda)

Left *Twin Peaks – Fire Walk With Me*: 'Hold me! I'm falling! I'm falling!' (© CiBy 2000)

Right Patricia Arquette as Alice in *Lost Highway*: 'The way your head works is God's own private mystery.' (© CiBy 2000)

Below *Lost Highway*: 'Is this real? Or some strange and twisted dream?' (© CiBy 2000)

Bottom *Lost Highway*: 'You better run me back to the hotel. You got me hotter'n Georgia asphalt.' (© CiBy 2000)

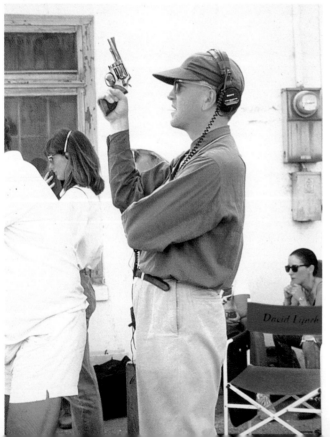

Above The late Richard Farnsworth in *The Straight Story*: 'Where we're from, the birds sing a pretty song.' (© The Straight Story Inc.)

Left David Lynch prepares his next shot on the set of *Wild at Heart*.
(© Polygram/Propaganda)

was forced to wear a handkerchief across his mouth to stop himself from laughing – and even if he did, either Jones, Cage or Dern would crack up instead. Even with the scene in the can, Lynch realised during editing that the monologue ran too long, and after experimenting with numerous ways to cut it down, finally realised that it had to be cut out. 'But one time Duwayne [Dunham] was running the scene on the Kem and he was going fast-forward, and I heard Freddie's voice speeded up,' Lynch told Chris Rodley. 'And I almost *passed out*! I said, "I'm gonna do that!"' Lynch called Jones in London, told him that most of the scene had been cut, but that he wanted to leave a little of it in, and change the pitch of his voice to a helium-fuelled squeak (cf. Lynch's original idea for Frank's voice in *Blue Velvet*). Much to Lynch's delight, Jones agreed to the change.

- As Lula tells Sailor she imagines being ripped apart by a gorilla, her hand opens and spreads wide in a gesture already established as orgasmic.
- As in the novel, Sailor and Lula pick up a filthy hitch-hiker named Marvin 'Roach' DeLoach, who is on his way to Alaska with some husky pups. Lula ejects him from the car when he tries to feed them with a piece of raw cow's liver. These scenes were filmed, with Tracey Walter (*The Cowboy and the Frenchman*) in the role of Roach.
- As in the novel, Sailor and Lula ask directions to a music bar from two boys, Buck and Billy (Scott Coffey), at a Red Devil gas station. They direct them to the Club Zanzibar (where Albert Popwell played the barkeeper), where Lula calls her mother and comes back to find Sailor dancing with a bleached-blonde woman (Michele Seipp). She throws a bottle at Sailor, which hits him, and scolds him for dancing with 'some oil-town tramp'.
- At Galatoire's, Johnnie remarks to Marietta that he keeps seeing Reggie and Drop Shadow. Lynch used this scene to compound the threat to Johnnie's life from the two men.
- The scene in which Johnnie is tortured and killed was originally much longer, as Juana, Reggie and Drop Shadow play a strange psychotic game in which she touches empty soda bottles, starts to masturbate, and shows him Santos's cufflink before Drop Shadow kills him. Lynch trimmed the scene following a mass walkout at an early test screening. As Lynch told *Rolling Stone*, 'It really taught me something: an audience can really be with you, but if you rub it in their face too much – which I didn't think I was doing – they say, "That's enough!" and out they go. And you can't blame them. I thought it was more powerful that way, but it reached a point where it was too much.' Lynch initially took the scene out entirely, but felt

that it removed the life-or-death threat hanging over the rest of the film; instead, he truncated it. Ironically, the portion of the scene which remains in the film contains the most violence: those of the test audience remaining in their seats would have realised that the scene's dénouement is no more or less disturbing than the build-up to it. Had the audience stayed, they would have realised that their own imaginings about where the scene were headed were probably more unpleasant than Lynch's.

- After Sailor tells Lula he was outside her house the night her father died, Lula admits to knowing that Marietta was with Santos that night and to suspecting that her mother was responsible for her father's death.
- Lula, alone at the Iguana Motel, listens to a piece of sad, nostalgic music as she remembers her good times with Sailor. The montage ends with an image she does not recognise: 'an abstract image of reflected light with two eyes looking through it at her'. As the script shows later, it is a premonition of an image of her son's eyes.

TRAILER: The trailer opens with Sailor's voice ('Can I talk to Lula?') followed by a quick cut of a telephone being slammed down. 'You are not going to see him ever,' Marietta tells Lula. 'Like Hell,' Lula replies, as the image cuts to a title – 'DAVID LYNCH'S Wild at Heart' – over flames. Marcello Santos asks Marietta if she wants him to shoot Sailor in the head, and Sailor is heard saying 'Uh-oh', kicking off a breakneck-paced montage of fast-cut images from the film, which ends as Sailor shouts 'Lula!' Credited cast shots follow, many of which are intercut with images of them making strange noises: Diane Ladd growls like a tiger, Willem Dafoe laughs idiotically, Harry Dean Stanton barks, Isabella Rossellini blows a kiss. A flaming caption announcing the film as 'WINNER BEST PICTURE CANNES FILM FESTIVAL' is followed by Lula's announcement that 'this whole world is wild at heart and weird on top', and a reprise of the flaming title.

POSTER: The US poster was a brightly coloured image of Sailor and Lula looking out of frame. Similar images were used in most European territories (but in far more muted colours in Germany and France), although in these images, Sailor and Lula are far more interested in each other than they are in 'us'. In the UK, the Creative Partnership's highly influential teaser campaign featured a symbol that was to become synonymous with Wild at Heart, and a key to the film's British success: weeks before the film opened, black posters appeared everywhere, with the title appearing as a sash across the painted image of a heart pierced vertically by a dagger. This iconic image was

followed by a one-sheet and landscape-format 'quad' in which Sailor
and Lula were pictured with their blue convertible, against a
background in which the highway and the surrounding countryside are
aflame.

WHAT THE PAPERS SAID: *Wild at Heart* may have won over the
jury at the Cannes Film Festival (see below), but it was unable to
inspire a similar level of critical fervour at home. 'Lynch works better
with constraints like network standards and practices that require him
to be sly and inventive,' said David Denby of *New York* magazine.
'Given complete freedom, he gives way to his obsessions. It becomes a
procession of freaks which is now getting grotesque.' Peter Rainer, in
the *Los Angeles Times*, agreed. 'For Lynch, wickedness is, in visual
terms, all goblins and demons, and there's something peculiarly child-
like and limiting about that vision.' Many, like *USA Today*'s Mike
Clark and *Time*'s Richard Corliss, felt that Lynch was repeating
himself, 'doing a David Lynch' like a guest director on *Twin Peaks*.
'He needs to find new toys to play with,' suggested the *Chicago Sun-
Times*'s Roger Ebert, who gave the film two-and-a-half stars out of
four. 'Things gross you out, but it's only fake-disturbing – not up to
Lynch's usual stuff,' commented *Newsweek*'s David Ansen, who
further described the film as 'very cartoonish and campy'.

The *Hollywood Reporter*'s Robert Osborne was one of the few to
disagree with this view. 'It smarts to think that David Lynch, who is so
young and has such a short catalogue of films, can already be accused
of copying himself,' he said, noting that John Ford was widely admired
for sticking to his own formula and suggesting that critics were
applying a double standard by 'encouraging [Lynch] to do his thing
and coming down hard on him when he does'. *Variety*'s Richard Gold
even ventured to suggest that *Wild at Heart* was better than *Blue
Velvet*, describing it as 'an American *Heart of Darkness*, an all-out
bombardment on the senses . . . extraordinarily cinematic . . .
mesmerising'.

In the UK, the feeling that Lynch was, at best, repeating himself or,
at worst, drifting dangerously into self-parody, was expressed by
numerous critics, though many agreed that *Wild at Heart* had enough
positive attributes to allow this to be overlooked. Geoff Andrew, in
Time Out, summed up this view by commenting that 'Lynch evokes a
surreal, sinister world a mite too reminiscent of his earlier work . . .
sometimes the weirdness seems so forced that Lynch appears merely to
be giving fans what they expect.' Nevertheless, Andrew felt it 'churlish'
to focus on flaws when so much of the film was 'exhilaratingly
unsettling' and concluded his review with the poster-friendly
soundbite: 'funny, scary and brilliantly cinematic'.

BOX OFFICE: Released in the US on 17 August 1990, almost one year to the day after it began filming, *Wild at Heart* went on to earn $14.56 million at the box office, a fair return on its budget of $9 million. *Wild at Heart* was also successful in Japan and much of Europe – especially the UK, where the now-defunct Palace Pictures turned the film into a modest hit, thanks to a highly evocative and iconographic advertising campaign.

AWARDS: *Wild at Heart*'s most famous award came early when, in May 1990, the film was awarded the Cannes Film Festival's prestigious Palme D'Or by a jury presided over by director Bernardo Bertolucci (*The Last Emperor*, 1987). 'I was very surprised that it won,' Lynch admitted to Jonathan Ross. 'Thrilled, but surprised.'

Diane Ladd's extraordinary performance as Marietta Pace Fortune earned her a second Academy Award nomination for Best Supporting Actress. (She would earn a third, again playing Laura Dern's mother, in 1991's *Rambling Rose*.) Ladd was also nominated in the same category at the Golden Globe awards. Frederick Elmes's cinematography won an Independent Spirit Award (Willem Dafoe was nominated, in the category of Best Supporting Male), while the British Academy of Film and Television Arts (BAFTA) nominated Jon Huck, Richard Hymns, David Parker and Randy Thom in the category of Best Sound.

CONTROVERSY: As if being awarded the Palme D'Or wasn't controversial enough for some – and it most certainly was – the award-winning film itself soon fell foul of the US classification board, the Motion Picture Association of America (MPAA), which threatened to give the film a potentially fatal 'X' rating – usually reserved only for pornographic and extreme horror films – unless the violence was toned down. 'This is the version that will be shown in Europe,' Lynch said after the film's first public screening at the Cannes Film Festival, 'but we're going to have a few problems in the US for sure. There will be some changes we have to make,' he added. 'We're upset about [it], but there's not a whole lot we can do about it.' Lynch's predictions proved correct: among several scenes which Lynch was forced to trim in order to secure an 'R' rating was Sailor's killing of Bob Ray Lemon, and the accidental suicide of Bobby Peru.

TRIVIA: Laura Dern passed out during the filming of a scene in which she was required to smoke four cigarettes at once, after having smoked around four thousand cigarettes in twelve weeks.

APOCRYPHA: Despite some theories, the title of Gifford's novel was not taken from the Tennessee Williams line, 'A prayer for the wild at heart kept in cages' (also one of the tattoos sported by actress Angelina Jolie). Gifford claims, 'It was just something Lula said in that hotel room in Cape Fear, and that's really where I got it.'

AVAILABILITY: In Britain, *Wild at Heart* is currently available on video only as a budget-priced, full-screen (4:3) PAL VHS (0566143). The film was previously available on video in a letterboxed (2.35:1) version, most notably in the Palace Classics range (PVC 2278S), an edition that also featured comprehensive sleeve notes, the theatrical trailer and the Lynch-directed promotional video for Chris Isaak's 'Wicked Game'.

In the US, the film is currently available only as a full-screen (4:3) extended-play (EP) NTSC VHS (MDC2756).

The only known DVD is the Japanese letterboxed (2.35:1) Region 2 edition (COBM-5010), in English with Japanese subtitles.

FINAL ANALYSIS: Although undeniably a lesser work than his previous feature, *Blue Velvet*, *Wild at Heart* is a wild, wickedly funny and extraordinarily erotic ride, which shows Lynch at the height of both his productivity and his creative powers. If anything, the extremes of beauty and horror in *Blue Velvet* are even more pronounced here, as the light of Sailor and Lula's love is all but eclipsed by the machinations of Lula's misguided mother and her evil underworld associates.

Wild at Heart is ripe with details that reward repeat viewing – the images that foreshadow Johnnie Farragut's imminent death (the mint on Johnnie's hotel pillow, like the silver-dollar contract out on him, and the television pictures of hyenas tearing a carcase to pieces), and the lipstick 'blood' on Marietta's hands (a connection made concrete by the bloodied and dying car-crash victim asking for her lipstick), to name but a few – and, while it is certainly not a work of maturity, Lynch's playful handling of the material is hard to resist – even when its darker moments are hard to stomach.

EXPERT WITNESS: 'David is like a criminal director. He's not concerned with Establishment laws and rules. He just does what he does – and it's honest. He's constantly sculpting and fishing. A scene can turn into a comedy or into heavy horror in a fraction of a second. He's very much a sculptor, a spontaneous sculptor . . . Sailor is a romantic, I wanted that. I wanted the love story aspect of *Wild at Heart* to be strong – to have a pure love in this hellish world that they're surrounded with. So did David.' – actor Nicolas Cage (Sailor Ripley)

LYNCH ON *WILD AT HEART*: 'Sailor could be very wild and like a rebel and be masculine, and Lula could be wild and a rebel and feminine, and they treated each other with respect, and they were totally in love, and they were kind of equals in the relationship. So I thought of it as kind of a modern romance.'

Twin Peaks – Fire Walk With Me (1992)

35mm feature / 134 mins / colour / live action

Directed by David Lynch
Produced by Gregg Fienberg
Written by David Lynch & Robert Engels
Executive Producers Mark Frost & David Lynch
Director of Photography Ron Garcia
Edited by Mary Sweeney
Production Design by Patricia Norris
Music Composed and Conducted by Angelo Badalamenti
Casting by Johanna Ray, CSA

CAST: Sheryl Lee (*Laura Palmer*), Ray Wise (*Leland Palmer*), Mädchen Amick (*Shelly Johnson*), Dana Ashbrook (*Bobby Briggs*), Phoebe Augustine (*Ronette Pulaski*), David Bowie (*Agent Phillip Jeffries*), Eric DaRe (*Leo Johnson*), Miguel Ferrer (*Albert Rosenfield*), Pamela Gidley (*Teresa Banks*), Heather Graham (*Annie Blackburn*), Chris Isaak (*Special Agent Chester 'Chet' Desmond*), Moira Kelly (*Donna Hayward*), Peggy Lipton (*Norma Jennings*), David Lynch (*Regional Bureau Chief Gordon Cole*), James Marshall (*James Hurley*), Jürgen Prochnow (*Woodsman*), Harry Dean Stanton (*Carl Rodd*), Kiefer Sutherland (*Agent Sam Stanley*), Lenny von Dohlen (*Harold Smith*), Grace Zabriskie (*Sarah Palmer*), Kyle MacLachlan (*Special Agent Dale Cooper*), Frances Bay (*Mrs Tremond / Mrs Chalfont*), Catherine E. Coulson (*The Log Lady*), Michael J. Anderson (*Man from Another Place*), Frank Silva (*BOB*), Walter Olkewicz (*Jacques Renault*), Al Strobel (*Philip Gerard, The One-Armed Man*), Gary Hershberger (*Mike Nelson*), Sandra Kinder (*Irene at Hap's*), Chris Pedersen (*Tommy*), Victor Rivers (*Buck*), Rick Aiello (*Deputy Cliff Howard*), Gary Bullock (*Sheriff Cable*), Jon Huck (*FBI Agent*), Mike Malone (*FBI Agent*), Joe Berman (*Bus Driver*), Yvonne Roberts (*First Prostitute*), Audra L. Cooper (*Second Prostitute*), John Hoobler (*Pilot*), Kimberly Ann Cole (*Lil the Dancer*), Elizabeth Ann McCarthy (*Giggling Secretary*), C.H. Evans (*Jack at Hap's*), Page Bennett (*French

Girl at Hap's), G. Kenneth Davidson (*Old Guy at Hap's*), Ingrid Brucato (*Curious Woman*), Chuck McQuarry (*Medic*), Margaret Adams (*Fat Trout Neighbour*), Carlton L. Russell (*Jumping Man*), Calvin Lockhart (*The Electrician*), Jonathan L. Leppell (*Mrs Tremond's Grandson*), David Brisbin (*Second Woodsman*), Andrea Hays (*Heidi*), Julee Cruise (*Roadhouse Singer*), Steven Hodges, William Underman, Joseph 'Simon' Szeibert, Gregory 'Smokey' Hormel, Joseph L. Altruda (*Band at Roadhouse*), James Parks (*Service Station Mechanic*), Jane Jones (*School Teacher*), Karin Robison (*Angel in Train Car*), Lorna MacMillan (*Angel in Red Room*)

ALTERNATIVE TITLES: Several international territories dropped the difficult-to-translate *Fire Walk With Me* subtitle, retitling the film *Twin Peaks – The Movie*. In Japan, distributor Nippon Herald Films chose a title that would capitalise on two 'brand names', releasing the film as *Twin Peaks – The Last Seven Days of Laura Palmer*.

TITLE SEQUENCE: White titles, in Lynch's preferred typeface, appear over the white noise of an untuned television set, the camera pulling back until the set is smashed by a blunt object, and a girl screams, signifying the murder of Teresa Banks.

SUMMARY: The murder of seventeen-year-old drifter Teresa Banks prompts FBI chief Gordon Cole to dispatch Special Agent Chester 'Chet' Desmond with Agent Sam Stanley to Deer Meadow to investigate. During the investigation, Desmond disappears after finding Teresa's missing ring. The news reaches Cole and Special Agent Dale Cooper in Philadelphia, where anomalies in the closed-circuit cameras coincide with the reappearance of long-lost agent Philip Jeffries, who raves incoherently before disappearing again. Cooper takes up the Teresa Banks case, fearing that the killer will strike again, and begins having premonitions about the next victim. One year later, in Twin Peaks, seventeen-year-old Laura Palmer is involved with two high-school boys – Bobby, a coke dealer, and James, her secret lover – and two men: Jacques Renault, proprietor of a Canadian brothel, and a mysterious stranger, BOB, who she believes comes in through her window at night to rape her. Laura begins to suspect that her own father, Leland, is BOB. After another nocturnal visitation, she wakes to find a ring (like Teresa's), also worn by a one-armed man who tries to warn her about her father. Indeed, the next time BOB rapes Laura, she sees that it is Leland. The following night, Leland/BOB kills Laura, leaving her friend Ronette Pulaski for dead. Laura, Leland, BOB, Cooper and a dwarf meet in the red room from Cooper's vision, and an angel smiles benignly down on Laura. She smiles back.

PRODUCTION HISTORY: The *Twin Peaks* series had been dead barely a month before the news emerged that Lynch was planning a big-screen version of the critically acclaimed but ultimately ratings-starved series. 'We think there is a good audience for the show,' Lynch/Frost chief executive officer Ken Scherer announced. 'Even at its lowest rating it represented nine to ten million viewers.' French financier CIBY-2000 would fund the film, as the first of a three-picture deal originally designed to comprise the long-gestating projects *Ronnie Rocket* and *One Saliva Bubble* [see 'In Dreams,' pages 247–8].

Yet, on 11 July 1991, Ken Scherer announced that the planned *Twin Peaks* film, already subtitled *Fire Walk With Me*, would not go ahead after all, due to series star Kyle MacLachlan's refusal to reprise his career-making role as Special Agent Dale Cooper. At the time, MacLachlan claimed that he preferred to move on to new challenges, rather than remain too closely associated with his most famous character – not to mention the director for whom he had become an on-screen alter ego. Lynch, for his part, seemed to sympathise. 'It is very tough for an actor, I think, to find a role that everyone loves them in and they want to break out and show they can do other things,' he said at a press conference for the film. 'In the very beginning, he was tired of doing the series, because we'd done 32 hours and he didn't know if he wanted to go in and do it again.' Nevertheless, as Scherer noted, 'The story as conceived relied heavily on the Cooper character, [and] Kyle no longer wants to do the role. That's unfortunate for *Twin Peaks*,' he added. 'We're all very sad.'

Then, a little more than a month later, Lynch/Frost announced that MacLachlan had changed his mind, and that the film would now go ahead as planned, albeit without either Lara Flynn Boyle (Donna Hayward) or Sherilyn Fenn (Audrey Horne), whose new-found popularity – due, ironically, to the success of *Twin Peaks* – reportedly led to scheduling conflicts that forced them to decline. At the time, Fenn was busy filming *Of Mice and Men* (1993), but in an America On-line interview in 1995, she gave her true reasons for turning down the role: 'I was extremely disappointed in the way the second season [of *Twin Peaks*] got off track. As far as *Fire Walk With Me* [is concerned], it was something that I chose not to be a part of.' In any event, Lynch decided to proceed without Boyle and Fenn, replacing the former with actress Moira Kelly (*Cutting Edge*, 1992), and dropping the latter from the script. 'I love restrictions,' Lynch says of the decision, 'and there's no such thing as a problem. There are only solutions, and you just go forward. No matter what, you go forward.' Indeed, as Lynch/Frost publicist Gaye Pope told the *Los Angeles Times*, 'We might even have gone on without Kyle, rewriting the script [accordingly].'

As it turned out, Lynch and co-writer Robert Engels *were* forced to rewrite the script, so that MacLachlan could take a smaller role. Thus, what would have been Cooper's investigation into the murder of Teresa Banks was reassigned to another FBI agent, Special Agent Chester 'Chet' Desmond, played by singer Chris Isaak. Speaking in late 2000, MacLachlan admitted the real reason he had declined to take a larger role in the big-screen prequel to *Twin Peaks*. 'Without getting too specific about it, David and Mark [Frost] were only around for the first series [of *Twin Peaks*],' he told the *Observer*. 'I fought and fought to try and get them back, but . . . I think we all felt a little abandoned. So I was fairly resentful when the film, *Fire Walk With Me*, came round. I wanted to have a meaningful discussion about some of [the early] scenes, and David was unwilling to do that, so I was not in those scenes; Chris Isaak was in them, instead of me.'

Fire Walk With Me began filming on 5 September 1991, returning to many of the locations that had served as backdrops for the series but now using a more cinematic ratio of 1:1.85, rather than the series's television standard of 1:1.33. 'We got a bit more unbalanced in the design of the film, using high and low angles,' cinematographer Ron Garcia told *American Cinematographer*. 'The high-angled shots reflect an angelic presence that continues throughout the film, with an unseen angel looking down on the evil events below.' Despite such stylistic changes, Lynch did not consider that filming *Fire Walk With Me* was significantly different from the series. 'There are obviously some things we couldn't do on television that we did in the film,' he said, 'but I was always amazed at how much we could do in television.'

The breakneck pace of the series evidently had an effect on the production of the film, however, as principal photography was completed in a little over three months, despite the fact that around half a million feet of film was shot – an extremely generous allowance for what would become a two hour, fifteen minute film. In fact, it was a mere nine months from the French financier's green light to the world premiere at the Cannes Film Festival in 1992. This, however, was where the film's – and Lynch's – problems began. At the same festival two years earlier, *Wild at Heart* had won the coveted Palme D'Or; now, the unveiling of Lynch's prequel to the television series – which had been wildly successful in France – was greeted with boos from the audience and derision from the press. 'The parade had gone by,' was how Lynch put it. 'During the year that it took to make the film, everything changed,' he recalled. 'The big news,' he added, 'was that I'd finally killed *Twin Peaks* with this picture.'

CASTING: Naturally, Lynch and casting director Johanna Ray did their best to reunite the cast of the television incarnation of *Twin*

Peaks for the feature-film prequel. Mostly, and despite Kyle MacLachlan's initial reluctance, they were successful – more successful than the final cut of the film suggests, in fact, since many other supporting characters (including Benjamin, Sylvia, Jerry and Johnny Horne; Pete Martell, Sheriff Truman, Deputy Hawk, Andy Brennan, Lucy Moran, Ed and Nadine Hurley, Major and Betty Briggs, Dr Bill Hayward and his wife Eileen) had their roles cut before the film's release. For her considerable labours in rounding up the cast from the four corners of the Earth, Ray received a credit as producer.

Joining the familiar faces from the series and other Lynch projects (see below) were actor Kiefer Sutherland, star of *The Lost Boys* (1987) and *Flatliners* (1990), as Agent Sam Stanley; and singer David Bowie, whose ventures into acting include such diverse films as Nicolas Roeg's *The Man Who Fell to Earth* (1976), Nagisa Oshima's *Merry Christmas, Mr Lawrence* and Tony Scott's *The Hunger* (both 1983).

If casting Bowie was a risk that was repaid with reviews lambasting his odd performance, an even bigger risk was the casting of Sheryl Lee as Laura Palmer, a character she had previously only played as dead, or in flashbacks; now, the actress would be the focus of an entire film. 'I felt really great about the decision because I never felt complete with Laura,' Lee told *Wrapped in Plastic*. 'I never got to be Laura *alive*, just in flashbacks, [so] it allowed me to come full circle with the character. [Laura] always had a tremendous amount of life, because everybody talked about her, yet I didn't get to do those things and *be* her.' Lynch was equally enthusiastic about Lee's performance. 'It turns out, at least in my opinion, she's an unbelievable actress and there are things that she's done in this movie that are truly incredible. I haven't seen too many people get into a role and give it as much. So, the big news for me was this person hired to be a dead girl turns out to be a great actress and a perfect Laura Palmer.'

THE LYNCH MOB: For obvious reasons, *Fire Walk With Me* featured numerous actors from the television incarnation of *Twin Peaks*. Yet among the cast were a few familiar faces from other Lynch projects: *Twin Peaks* actresses Sheryl Lee and Grace Zabriskie had both appeared in *Wild at Heart*; Chris Isaak had provided Lynch with songs for the soundtracks of *Blue Velvet* and *Wild at Heart*, and appeared in a Lynch-directed promotional video for 'Wicked Game'; Harry Dean Stanton had played Slim in Lynch's *The Cowboy and the Frenchman* and Johnnie Farragut in *Wild at Heart*; Frances Bay appeared in *Blue Velvet* and *Wild at Heart*; Calvin Lockhart played Reggie in *Wild at Heart*; Jürgen Prochnow, whose role was reduced to a cameo in the release version (see below), had previously appeared in *Dune*.

Behind the camera there were an equal number of familiar faces, including such *Twin Peaks* alumni as co-screenwriter Robert Engels, producer Gregg Fienberg, executive producer Mark Frost, editor Mary Sweeney and director of photography Ron Garcia. Collaborators from other Lynch projects included first assistant director Deepak Nayar (*Wild at Heart*'s second assistant director), production designer Patricia Norris (*The Elephant Man* onwards), casting director Johanna Ray (*Blue Velvet*, *Twin Peaks*, *Wild at Heart*) and composer Angelo Badalamenti (*Blue Velvet*, *Twin Peaks*, *Wild at Heart*).

Sadly, aside from commercials for Georgia Coffee, *Fire Walk With Me* would be the last time Lynch and his doppelgänger Kyle MacLachlan would work together, after an association spanning twenty years and encompassing *Dune*, *Blue Velvet* and the various incarnations of *Twin Peaks*. MacLachlan has said he blames himself for the souring of the partnership. 'I really abused the relationship,' he told the *Observer* in late 2000. 'I don't know if David and I will work together again. I hope so.' Lynch bears MacLachlan no ill will, however. 'Kyle is a good guy, and I wouldn't like to say anything about anything like that,' he says. 'Kyle's my neighbour; he's a really great person. But, you know, when you're in a TV show, the first year is golden, and the second year, things get strange, and so *Twin Peaks* was no exception.'

MEMORABLE QUOTES
Old Guy at Hap's: 'Are you talking about that little girl that got murdered?'
Desmond: 'Do you know anything about that?'
Old Guy at Hap's: 'I know shit from shinola!'

Cooper: 'Diane, it's four-twenty p.m. I'm standing here at Wind River, near the location where the body of Teresa Banks was found. Diane, this case gives me a strange feeling. Not only has Special Agent Chester Desmond disappeared without a trace, but this is one of Cole's "blue rose" cases. The clues that were found by Special Agent Desmond and Agent Stanley have led to dead ends. The letter that was extracted from beneath the fingernail of Teresa Banks gives me the feeling that the killer *will* strike again. But like the song goes, who knows where, or when?'

Donna: 'Do you think if you were falling in space, that you'd slow down after a while, or go faster and faster?'
Laura: 'Faster and faster, and for a long time you wouldn't feel anything, then you'd burst into fire, for ever. And the angels wouldn't help you because they've all gone away.'

Laura: 'Fire walk with me.'

Laura: 'Open your eyes, James. You don't even know me. There are things about me. Even Donna doesn't know me. Your Laura disappeared. It's just me now.'

SOUND AND MUSIC: 'Musically speaking, it might be a shade broader and just a little larger than the approach on the television series,' composer Angelo Badalamenti said of *Fire Walk With Me*, which marked the closest-yet collaboration between himself and Lynch on a film project. The soundtrack to the film itself includes numerous songs with a lyric by Lynch and music by Badalamenti: 'She Would Die for Love', 'Blue Frank', 'Falling' and 'The Pink Room', 'Questions in a World of Blue' (sung by Julee Cruise); 'A Real Indication' and 'The Black Dog Runs at Night' (Thought Gang, with a vocal by Badalamenti and percussion by Lynch); and 'Sycamore Trees' (vocal by Little Jimmy Scott). There are also three instrumentals with music by Lynch and David Slusser ('Double Swing', 'Best Friends' and 'Deer Meadow Shuffle'), three instrumentals by Badalamenti ('Moving Through Time', 'Love Theme' and 'The Voice of Love'), and Luigi Cherubini's Requiem in C minor, performed by the Ambrosian Singers and Philharmonic Orchestra.

The soundtrack album (9362–45019–2), produced by Lynch and Badalamenti, features some 57 minutes of music, including the aforementioned 'Sycamore Trees', 'A Real Indication', 'The Pink Room', 'Best Friends', 'Questions in a World of Blue', 'The Black Dog Runs at Night', 'Moving Through Time' and 'The Voice of Love', but also included are 'Theme from *Twin Peaks – Fire Walk With Me*', 'The Pine Float', 'Don't Do Anything (I Wouldn't Do)', and 'Montage from *Twin Peaks*', the latter a combination of 'Girl Talk', 'Birds in Hell', 'Laura Palmer's Theme' and 'Falling'.

Fire Walk With Me inspired a recording by Steve Hooker Rumble, which appeared on the 1999 album *Hell for Leather*, released on Crazy Love Records. The track, entitled '(Fire) Walk With Me', opens with two samples: the Log Lady's warning to Laura ('When this kind of fire starts, it is very hard to put out . . .') and Phillip Gerard's from the European version of the *Twin Peaks* pilot ('One chants out between two worlds . . .'), before reinterpreting numerous elements of *Twin Peaks* music – most notably *Fire Walk With Me*'s 'Pink Room' sequence – with a 50s sensibility.

INFLUENCED BY: During the height of the *Twin Peaks* series' success, Lynch's daughter Jennifer wrote a bestselling novel entitled *The Secret Diary of Laura Palmer*, which drew on the series' established lore, but expanded it into a first-person narrative detailing Laura's troubled life. Although the book is sketchy on details, actress Sheryl Lee told the *Twin Peaks* fanzine *Cooper's Dream* that the book was with her 'night and day' during *Fire Walk With Me*'s ten-week shooting schedule. 'I carried it everywhere and would constantly refer back to it,' she said.

Critic Tim Lucas has suggested that *Fire Walk With Me* may have also been inspired by Mario Bava's 1966 horror film *Kill Baby Kill*, a.k.a. *Operazione Paura* or *Operation: Fear*. 'The heroes of both films are jut-jawed, out-of-town officials who are summoned to small towns haunted by a recent death,' he wrote. 'Clues in the mystery are unearthed by autopsy: instead of finding letters inserted under fingernails, the hero of *Kill Baby Kill* (played by Giacomo Rossi-Stuart) finds coins implanted in the hearts of the dead.' In Bava's film, a series of murders is eventually traced to the ghost of a little girl, who is acting through the agency of her mother, a medium (physically resembling Grace Zabriskie's Sarah Palmer, who is also sensitive to occult forces), who refuses to let her daughter rest in peace. In one incredible scene, Rossi-Stuart becomes lost in a metaphysical annexe of the medium's villa, and chases an indistinct figure through a repeated cycle of corridors, eventually catching his own doppelgänger by the shoulder. Not only do these climactic scenes recall the chase through the Red Room in *Twin Peaks*'s final episode, Lucas noted in *Video Watchdog* that the idea of a ring acting as a conduit to evil forces was the subject of a more famous Bava film, *Black Sabbath* (a.k.a. *I tre volti della paura*, or *The Three Faces of Fear*, 1963), in which a nurse steals the ring from the finger of a dead woman, and is tormented to death as a result.

The more surreal sequences of *Fire Walk With Me* also have strong overtones of a film that Lynch has often cited as being highly influential: Jean Cocteau's self-absorbed surrealist tract *Le Sang d'Un Poete* (a.k.a. *The Blood of a Poet*, 1930), in which Cocteau, like Lynch in *Fire Walk With Me*, cast himself.

We already know that the name of Lynch's character, Gordon Cole, was lifted from *Sunset Boulevard* (1950); could Chester 'Chet' Desmond be named for the same film's leading lady, Norma Desmond (Gloria Swanson)?

Finally, *Fire Walk With Me* seems to have an obsession with the number 6. Not only does the telegraph pole linked to Desmond's disappearance bear this number but, in the script, Jeffries is in a hotel room numbered 612 (6 and its doubled sum), while Leland arranges to meet Teresa in room number 123, the sum total of the digits of which is 6. Could this, coupled with the fact that behind the mask worn by Mrs Tremond's grandson is the face of a monkey, suggest overtones of the classic sixties TV series *The Prisoner*?

LEGACY: After its critical and commercial failure, one would assume that *Fire Walk With Me* would have been the last nail in Laura Palmer's coffin. Although Lynch no longer considers returning to the town of Twin Peaks ('It's as dead as a doornail,' he says), this fact has not prevented *Twin Peaks* fans from converging on Snoqualmie, Washington, every August for the three-day Twin Peaks Lynch Fest which attracts fans from all over the world, together with many *Twin Peaks* actors. Nor has the absence of *Twin Peaks* hurt Craig Miller and John Thorne's long-running magazine *Wrapped in Plastic* (details www.wrappedinplastic.com), which celebrated its fiftieth issue in early 2001.

Fire Walk With Me itself had an enduring effect on painter-turned-film-maker James Gray (*The Yards*, 2000), who believes it not only to be Lynch's most underrated film, but his best. 'Sheryl Lee gives an incredible performance, [and] I cast Moira in *Little Odessa* [1994] because I'd seen that movie and thought she was great in it. And that ending,' he adds, 'where Laura's dying, and she's crying and laughing, and the angel comes down and Cherubini's Requiem in C minor is playing . . . It's truly a masterpiece. I think Lynch is a great artist, and *Fire Walk With Me* is just God.'

DÉJÀ VU: Aside from the obvious *Twin Peaks* references, the relationship between Mrs Tremond and her grandson echoes Lynch's short film *The Grandmother*. The mound of dirt on which Teresa's ring is found recalls Henry's private dirt-stash in *Eraserhead*, while the night-time shots of double yellow lines on a two-lane highway not only echo *Wild at Heart* but prefigure similar shots in *Lost Highway*. The angel who releases Ronette from her bonds and later greets Laura in the Red Room recalls the ending of two other Lynch films: *The Elephant Man* and *Wild at Heart*. Most bizarrely of all, the numb left arm that afflicted Teresa Banks and Laura Palmer – not to mention its connection to the One-Armed Man and the Man from Another Place (a.k.a. 'The Arm') – recall Mr X in *Eraserhead*, whose left arm was numb after an operation. 'Doctors said I wouldn't be able to use it, but what the hell do they know, I said? And I rubbed it for a half-hour every day, and then I got so's I could move it a little, and then it got so's I could turn a faucet, and pretty soon I had my arm back again. Now I can't feel a damn' thing in it. All numb! I'm afraid to cut it, you know?'

THEMES AND MOTIFS: While incest, child abuse and the inner torment of high-school beauty Laura Palmer are all important themes of *Fire Walk With Me*, there are far more obviously Lynchian themes beneath the surface of the film. Chief among these is Lynch's obsession with electricity, which has informed his work since *Eraserhead*, with its crackling lamps, shorting wires and sparking sockets signifying an apparent electronic empathy with Henry's (or is it the baby's?) plight. Electricity is also the major theme of the unproduced *Ronnie Rocket* [see 'In Dreams,' page 248], written after *Eraserhead*, while *Blue Velvet* has extinguished and faulty lights accompanying several appearances by Frank, and *Wild at Heart* features a character (Uncle Dell) who wears black gloves in order to avoid extraterrestrials who appear during thunderstorms, when there is literally electricity in the air. In the Lynch-directed *Twin Peaks*, the strip lighting in the autopsy room is faulty during Cooper's examination of Laura's body, and the series contains many other instances of electrical disturbance, not least the fizzing Lynch/Frost logo that closed every episode! Yet it was with *Fire Walk With Me* that Lynch was able to explore fully the possibilities of electricity as a malign force, suggesting that electrical disturbance occurs whenever BOB is present, or close.

While an extraordinary number of electrical phenomena appear in the shooting script, the release version of the film contains enough evidence to support the theory that electricity is as fundamental to the movement of malign spirits between worlds as the ring, inlaid by a mystical symbol, worn by each of BOB's victims.

- The film opens with the image of a television set tuned to a dead channel, like the white noise through which malevolent forces from the afterlife contact the little girl in *Poltergeist* (1982).
- Cole's obscure reference to a blue rose case is never explained, yet Desmond clearly understands it. Since a blue rose is an anomaly that cannot occur in nature, could this be a reference to the supernatural, the blue signifying something to do with electricity? Or is it somehow related to Project Blue Book, the government investigation of extraterrestrials, in which Major Briggs was involved? There are also scripted exchanges about Sarah Palmer's blue sweater, and the Blue Diamond City Motel room at which Leland arranges to meet Teresa and her two girlfriends (Laura and Ronette)?
- At Hap's Diner, a flickering blue light is attributed to an oxyacetylene torch trying to cut open a safe (although, in the script, Stanley asks Desmond if the blue light was aesthetic, or due to faulty wiring).
- At the trailer park, Desmond is more interested in the telegraph pole whose wires lead to Deputy Howard's trailer than in Teresa Banks's own residence.
- Agent Jeffries' reappearance occurs simultaneously with Desmond's *dis*appearance, and both events are accompanied by electrical phenomena, such as the faulty closed-circuit camera system. During Jeffries's scene, Lynch includes a close-up of a mouth whispering the

word 'electricity' and shots of power lines (In the script, Cole has trouble with static on his intercom.)
- As scripted, BOB refers to 'the light of new discoveries' during the convenience-store meeting. Is he referring to electricity?
- The lighting in both the Red Room and the sleazy club (identified in the closing credits as the Pink Room) flickers.

With *Fire Walk With Me*, Lynch continued to explore the theme of duality, of light and darkness, that had been prevalent in both *Blue Velvet* and *Twin Peaks*. Here, Lynch gave the town a shadow self in Deer Meadow, with its corrupt and belligerent police force (contrasting with the Twin Peaks sheriff and his deputies), a diner with an unpleasant hostess and no specials (a far cry from the 'Double R' diner), and a sleazy and unkempt trailer park (about as far from the luxurious Great Northern as you could get).

Fire Walk With Me also explores the notion of time as an abstract and violable concept, an idea first explored in the European version of the *Twin Peaks* pilot, set '25 years later', with an aged Dale Cooper and an ever-youthful Laura sharing the Red Room with the Man from Another Place. In *Fire Walk With Me*, Phillip Jeffries seems somehow 'out of phase' with time and space, reappearing after an absence of two years, after his visit to the convenience store in which various other-worldly entities meet. As well as being set in the past and containing numerous flashbacks that reverse the flow of time still further, *Fire Walk With Me* contains echoes of the *future* (the ending of *Twin Peaks*'s second series), as a bloodied Annie Blackburn appears to Laura in her dream, with a warning: 'My name is Annie. I've been with Dale and Laura. The good Dale is in the Lodge and he can't leave. Write it in your diary.' Will this cryptic message, if correctly decoded in the future, lead to 'the good' Dale's rescue? And if so, does that mean that time has 'bent back' so that the *prequel* to *Twin Peaks* actually gives the whole series a happy ending?

CUT SCENES: Although Lynch claims to have had final cut on every one of his films since *Dune*, the director almost certainly felt pressure from financier and international sales agent CIBY-2000 to deliver a cut of the film with a running time suitable for theatrical audiences. This mandate resulted in the excision of an extraordinary number of scenes and the deletion of numerous sequences that in total, add up to a considerable loss, both to *Twin Peaks* fans and to the film as a whole. 'It was five and a half hours, with everything they shot laid out,' confirms editor Mary Sweeney. 'Jack Nance had whole scenes that weren't in there, and [there were] so many characters from the TV show, and they were all in the feature. They're very stand-alone scenes,' she adds, 'because they're all individual characters with their own storylines.' As Michael Horse (Deputy Horse) says of his own deleted scenes, 'David called and said, "I'm so sorry I can't use your work, but there was four hours of film and I had to cut it to two,"' suggesting that Lynch did not, after all, make such cuts willingly.

Mary Sweeney says that Lynch would love *Twin Peaks* fans to be able to see the cut scenes, not re-edited back into the film but perhaps included as additional material on a DVD edition of the film. Unfortunately, they couldn't come to an agreement with Fine Line, who had the rights. 'We were ready to go, but they never got it together,' Lynch agrees. 'It costs money to find all those scenes; [to] finish cutting them, prep all the sound and music, and mix them; then go to the lab, colour-correct them, go through all the timing you do for anything, and get those things on high-def, clean and nice, all prepared; and then go on the DVD.'

Despite Lynch's assertion that there were 'only seventeen' deleted scenes, a comparison of the shooting script (dated 8 August 1991) with the finished film reveals the following deletions, in chronological order:

- The conversation in the car between Desmond and Stanley continues, as Stanley asks if Cole's tie was part of the code ('That's just Gordon's bad taste,' Desmond demurs), and Desmond explains Cole's reasons for using the code in the first place: 'He talks loud. And he loves his code.' (Surely a reference to the dispenser of the code, aptly played by Lynch himself.)
- At the morgue, Stanley takes out a 'special machine' that he claims to have used to solve the Whiteman case, and wonders what is in the mortuary drawers.
- Jack tells Desmond that the FBI visited Hap's diner 'back in the Fifties when Hap was running the place', but that Hap is 'good and dead'.
- Before Desmond questions Irene, she says, 'Take a look around. There's nobody in this place – you're meeting the reason why.' Asked why Jack lets her work there, Irene reveals that they are married.
- Irene mentions that Teresa 'came looking for a job with a friend of hers. Pretty girl. Could've been her sister.' (Possibly a reference to Laura; certainly, the fact that both girls were murdered by Leland Palmer gives them a morbid sisterhood.) Desmond asks what happened to her. 'There was only one job. Teresa took the job. Her friend took a hike. Never saw her again.' At the trailer park (named Canyon Trailer Park in the script), Carl also mentions a friend, who 'took off'. Desmond asks if there was an argument. 'Not that I know of,' Carl replies. 'But arguments do happen, don't they?' Carl refers to Sheriff Cable as 'Sheriff Not-Quite-Able.'
- Stanley privately estimates the value of the trailer park as $5,600.

- After the old woman with the ice pack leaves Teresa's trailer, the sheriff's deputy, Cliff Howard, appears in the doorway, and the agents learn that he lives in the trailer park. When Desmond asks Howard where he was the night Teresa was murdered, he says 'I was at a party and I got fifteen fuckin' witnesses.' To which Carl responds, 'Maybe if you did a little less partyin' that little girl would still be alive?' Howard claims not to have known Teresa, except from the diner, and then asks where Desmond gets off questioning a lawman. Cliff drives away, and Desmond finds a Titleist golf ball under Teresa's trailer, and asks Carl if there is a golf course nearby. 'Not a lot around here, no,' he replies. 'Got some clubs, but not very many fellas with balls.' As they leave, Desmond tells Stanley that Cliff is not the murderer, but that 'he is a bozo'.
- In the script, the confrontation between Desmond and Sheriff Cable over the body continues until both take their badges off, bend steel bars (as in the 'Cable Bends Steel' clipping in Cable's office) and fight bare-chested until Desmond lays out the sheriff.
- Before Stanley heads back to Portland, he asks Desmond about the shorting lamp at the diner.
- The script has no mention of the telegraph pole, nor the woman who wants her 'goddamn hot water', but just before Desmond knocks on the trailer door he sees a hand appear in the window, then disappear.
- After Desmond disappears (see below), two further scenes take place in the FBI office in Philadelphia. Cole is in his office, talking to Albert. 'Every syllable of every word is the sound of two hands clapping. Is that what you said, Albert?' 'Six to eight hands clapping,' Albert replies. 'I was referring to the possibility of a little silence.' Cole's phone rings. Across the hall, Cooper is playing a game with Diane, unseen and unheard in the next room, in which he practices his observational skills by trying to spot the object she has moved in his office. He does, and walks triumphantly over to join Cole, who tells him of Desmond's disappearance. (As in the series, Diane is never seen.)
- Immediately following this is a scene set in Stanley's apartment in Spokane, Washington, the central feature of which is a plastic pool hooked up to one of the many bizarre pieces of machinery in the room. Stanley seems more interested in telling Cooper about the 'Whiteman' machine than discussing Desmond's disappearance. Cooper examines the letter 'T' under a microscope, and asks about the ring.
- Between Cooper's surveillance-camera test and Agent Jeffries's appearance in Philadelphia, the script has a scene set in Buenos Aires as Jeffries checks into room 612 of the Palm Deluxe hotel, collecting a message that the head clerk says was left by a young lady. (Could

this be 'Judy', to whom Jeffries, and Major Briggs in *Twin Peaks,* refers?)

- In the script, the exchange between Cole, Jeffries and Albert and the convenience-store meeting are not intercut, but played separately. Thus, there are additional non-sequiturs from the First Woodsman ('We have descended from pure air'), the Man From Another Place (who talks of 'intercourse between the two worlds'), BOB ('light of new discoveries' – a possible reference to electricity), Mrs Tremond (who asks 'Why not be composed of materials and combinations of atoms?') and her grandson ('This is no accident'). Angered with 'the fury of [his] own momentum', BOB forms a circle of fire through which the Red Room is visible. Back in Philadelphia, Jeffries breaks down, talking about 'The ring . . . the ring . . .' As Albert leaves to get some water, an electrical disturbance makes static build on Cole's intercom. He punches buttons and says 'Mayday!' – a word that prompts Jeffries to look at a calendar on the wall, seeing that, somehow, the date is May 1989. The static build-up continues until Jeffries vanishes into thin air.

- After the realisation that Jeffries has disappeared, Cole tries word assocation with Cooper and Albert. Cooper is thinking about Teresa Banks ('It was a year ago today that Teresa Banks was killed. I'm wondering if the murderer will ever kill again'), Albert is thinking about Tylenol ('No offence, sir, but after a day with you it is mandatory').

- Immediately after this is a further scene set in Buenos Aires, as Jeffries stands in the second-storey hallway of the Palm Deluxe Hotel, the wall behind him seared black and smoking, the maid and bellhop terrified as Jeffries tries to stave off an epileptic fit.

- After Laura picks up Donna from her house, a dialogue exchange occurs in which Donna promises to help Laura with an upcoming maths test, says that James was looking for Laura the previous night and asks if Laura and Bobby are still fighting. Laura says 'No, and yes,' and tells Donna that Bobby is seeing someone else, just as she is.

- Arriving at school, five of the girls' admirers kneel, arms outstretched, chanting the names 'Laura' and 'Donna' over and over.

- James's line to Laura ('It *does* matter') is explained by the deleted exchange that precedes it, as Laura tells him that she loves him but that 'it doesn't really matter'.

- At Donna's house, her mother makes a brief appearance, during which Laura, Donna and Eileen Hayward refer to each other by their initials.

- Just before Laura finds the pages missing from her secret diary, she takes a packet full of cocaine from her 'public' diary and takes a snort.

- Leaving her house on the way to Harold's, Laura meets her mother outside, asks to borrow the car ('I forgot my books at school') and is warned about smoking.
- After Laura begs Harold to hide her diary, she asks him if *he* is BOB. 'If you are, you can kill me right now,' she says. He demurs, says that he wishes he could help her, and holds her. 'I hate him,' she says. 'I hate it. Sometimes I love it. But now I'm afraid. I am so afraid.'
- After Laura says goodbye to Harold, she drives home, and is confronted by her mother for lying about the forgotten school books, which Sarah found on her bed. Laura asks what Sarah was doing in her room; her mother replies that she was looking for a blue sweater Laura borrowed. Laura says she lied because she had to see Bobby, whom she knows Sarah doesn't like. 'Oh, honey,' Sarah responds, 'you don't have to lie to me. Ever. You can tell me anything. I'll understand.' In the next scene, in the dining room, Leland comes in pretending to be a giant, speaking in a big giant voice, and asking where his axe is. He says 'How are you? My name is Leland Palmer' in Norwegian and explains that the Norwegians are coming. As they practise Norwegian, 'an air of insanity seems to come over the Palmer dining room as they all begin to laugh hysterically and talk in broken Norwegian.' (This is the only instance in *Fire Walk With Me* in which the Palmer family seems like a happy household.)
- That night, Laura sneaks out of her room, climbs into a truck (the eager trucker says 'Friend of Leo's, right? Partyland?'), unbuttons her blouse and sneaks a toot of cocaine. 'Wait a minute,' the trucker says, 'Leo says this is my party.' Laura puts her hand between his legs. 'If you can fuck and drive, the party starts right now,' she says, putting his hand on the gearstick. 'You shift that one. This one's mine.' She climbs on top of him as the truck drives into the distance, its sound replaced by the hooting of an owl.
- As the action returns to Philadelphia, but before Albert quizzes Cooper about the killer's next victim, they discuss Cole's taste for word association.
- At the diner, after Norma asks Shelly to help Laura with the 'Meals on Wheels', Ed and Nadine Hurley come in for coffee, but Nadine changes her mind after seeing Norma.
- After Laura's encounter with Mrs Tremond and her grandson, Shelly returns to the diner, asking Norma to handle Leo while she delivers the meals. The cook, Toad, calls out from the kitchen that it is 'kind of quiet'. Norma, evidently thinking of Ed, starts to cry.

- After Laura sees Leland leave the house, a neighbour sees her sobbing. Laura pretends to have lost her gold half-heart necklace, then finds it around her neck. When the neighbour leaves, she searches the house for BOB, and sets off for Donna's house.
- At Donna's house, the scene between Laura and Donna continues as Donna says she doesn't mean to be 'so uptight' and that she is planning to sleep with Mike. Laura laughs, asks if that's Donna's way of proving she isn't uptight, and points out that Donna doesn't even like Mike. 'This is about sex, not like,' Donna responds. Bill Hayward comes in with a magician's handkerchief, fails to produce a red rose from it, but says that the trick worked by 'the light at Sparkwood and 21'. (In the series, this was the intersection with the traffic light leitmotif, and the last place where James saw Laura alive. Here it is used to convey not only the significance of the place but to provide a literal connection with roses, appearance and disappearance.) Instead, he scolds Laura good-naturedly for smoking in the house. Eileen brings huckleberry muffins, which they share. Bill complains that he cannot read his own handwriting. Leland calls, telling Laura it's time for dinner. Donna senses something is wrong, and tries to cheer Laura up by calling her Muffin. 'You're the muffin,' says Laura, then calls back, 'No, you're right. I am the muffin.' (This explains Laura's muffin reference in the Pink Room.)
- As Leland and Sarah get ready for bed, he tells her he cannot remember the last time he told Laura he loved her. Sarah says to tell Laura now.
- Before the Red Room sequence, Laura dreams that Mrs Tremond's grandson holds his hands above him, circling a ring of fire, through which the camera moves into the Red Room. (This makes the idea of the ring as the conduit to the other world more explicit.)
- A line is cut from the Red Room sequence, as the Man from Another Place asks Cooper, 'Is it future? Or is it past?'
- After Laura wakes from her dream about Annie, she puts Mrs Tremond's picture in the trash.
- After James asks Laura why they didn't get together the previous night, Laura replies, 'How can I be together if I'm not together?'
- After James roars away on his bike, Leland asks Laura if he is 'a special friend'.
- Back in the house, Laura hears BOB's voice calling to her and tells him to go away. 'I'm glad you let me talk to you,' the voice says. 'You used to not let me talk to you.' She tells him to go away. 'I want you,' the voice says, as Laura is interrupted by Sarah, looking for the blue sweater again. Laura points out that Sarah is wearing it. Sarah fears she is going to have another breakdown: 'This can't be happening.'

- Some dialogue about thorough cleaning was cut from the scene in which Leo scrubs the floor while Shelly smokes.
- After Laura asks Buck if he goes all the way, she adds ominously: 'All the way for me means all the way – dead.'
- After Laura, Donna, Tommy and Buck leave the roadhouse, Buck does an Indian whoop in Laura's face, recalling her dream and frightening her. Donna refuses Buck's offer of cocaine, telling Laura, 'I don't need to take this to be your friend.' 'Yes, you do, Donna,' Laura replies. 'What a downer you are!'
- After Laura is jolted by Jacques's revelation that Teresa asked after her father, Jacques continues: 'But it wasn't him – she was after a huge guy, six foot four with a broken nose. She said he looked just like a boxer.'
- Upon seeing Tommy kissing a topless Donna, Laura hears BOB's voice: 'See what we can do to Donna?'
- The next day (Sunday) begins at the Hurley household as Nadine, wielding a big butcher's knife, ferociously skins a deer, while Ed and his assistant, Sparky, watch good-humouredly.
- Immediately following this is a scene in which a guitar-strumming Sheriff Truman tells Josie Packard he would like to 'go public' with their affair, despite her fears that this would offend the customs of his country, since Andrew has only been dead a year.
- Immediately following this, Philip Gerard is seen in a motel room, kneeling before a circle of twelve lit candles, gasping for air and straining to hear something.
- The scene at Donna's house begins earlier, as Laura scolds Donna for trying to prove her friendship, and explains her anger at Donna for borrowing her blouse. 'All my things have me in them,' she says. At the end of this scene, when Donna says, 'Why do you do it, Laura?' Laura replies, ''Cause I like it.'
- Lynch's sound mix of the scene in which the One-Armed Man accosts Leland and Laura while they are out driving deliberately obscures Gerard's crucial dialogue. In the script, it reads as follows: 'You stole the corn! I had it canned about the store!' (Shouting at Laura:) 'Miss, the look on her face when it was opened! There was a closeness! Like the formica table top!' (To Leland:) 'The thread will be torn, Mr Palmer! The thread will be torn!' (To Laura:) 'It's him! It's your father!'
- During Leland's flashback to his encounter with Teresa Banks, he recalls phoning her to arrange a meeting at the Blue Diamond City Motel, room 123. As scripted, the scene has another flashback, in which Teresa calls Jacques to ask what Ronette's and Laura's fathers look like. Teresa is dissatisfied with his reply, in which he accurately describes them. 'No, this was a big huge guy. Six four . . . nose

broken . . . like he was a boxer.' Smiling, Teresa hangs up and calls Leland at his office. 'Hey, handsome, this is your little party girl.' His jaw tightens.

- After Laura recalls the One-Armed Man shouting about the ring, she remembers being with Ronette and Teresa at the Blue Diamond City Motel, and remembers seeing Teresa's ring. Her reverie is interrupted by BOB's voice: 'That's not important. I will tell you what is important. The fan will soon be starting.' Laura asks who he is, really. 'I am the One who wants to breathe through your nose and taste through your mouth.'

- The next morning, Leland cheerfully reminds Laura that today (Tuesday) is Johnny Horne's birthday.

- After Laura's meeting with Bobby about the 'big score', she runs into James, telling him she can't see him tonight.

- Immediately after this is a scene set at Johnny Horne's birthday party, which takes place in Benjamin Horne's office. Johnny acts with customary irrationality, ruining his birthday cake and saying 'Happy birthday, Johnny' to everyone in the room. Seeing a framed portrait of Laura on Ben's desk, Leland and Sylvia ask why he has no pictures of his family. When Ben defuses the confrontation, Jerry and Leland discuss playing the French against the Norwegians, and discussing the French love of wood. An exasperated Sylvia asks the three of them if they are crazy.

- Following this, the action moves to the Sheriff's office, where Truman, Tommy 'The Hawk' Hill and Andy Brennan discuss their observation of Jacques, and a trap they intend to set for 'Bernie, the mule.'

- Back at Ben's office, Laura arrives late for the party and gives Ben a kiss in exchange for a packet of coke. She remarks that Leland has always been jealous of Ben.

- That night, Laura climbs out of her window and is picked up by Bobby for 'Bobby and Laura's big score'. As they drive, Pete Martell passes their car and pulls into Big Ed's Gas Farm, where Pete and Ed exchange a few pleasantries, and moan about their respective spouses.

- When Laura returns home after Bobby shoots Deputy Howard, BOB's voice calls to Laura on the stairs, under the fan, saying: 'I want to kill through you.' She tells BOB he'll have to kill her instead. 'I want you to kill *for* me,' he replies.

- At school the next day, Bobby gives Laura the unused drug money – ten thousand dollars – to put in her safety deposit box. He is furious when she laughs and says, 'You killed Mike.' He drives away, stopping the car to sample the cocaine, and realises it is actually laxative. 'Sssshhhhiiiitttt!' he yells, angrily scattering the powder.

- The scene in Laura's bedroom continues as Dr Jacoby calls to admonish her for missing her appointment and to ask if she has made him a third tape. 'Laura, you have to deal with *all* of this,' he says. 'I'm dealing with it, Doc,' she replies. 'Big time. Maybe I'll make you a tape tomorrow. Good night.' He asks for a kiss, but she hangs up.
- Laura's last evening begins with her at dinner, telling her mother how she hates asparagus. (This is a reference to Laura's last 'public' diary entry, as per the *Twin Peaks* pilot.)
- In the script, Laura is met at Bobby's house by his parents, and finds him in the basement, churning at having killed a guy for baby laxative.
- As Laura leaves the Briggses' house, Major Garland Briggs is reading the Book of Revelations to his wife, Betty.
- Immediately after this is a scene set in Truman's office, as Lucy Moran buzzes to say that Josie thinks she heard a prowler at her house. Lucy continues talking about her aunt's racoons, and is surprised when Truman – who she thought was still listening – appears next to her. Andy hears her plight and goes to her, and Lucy is left talking to an empty room. She runs to find Andy, and they collide on the stairs. They both scream.
- As Laura sneaks out of the house, she sees Leland coming home and hides in the bushes. He senses something, and seems to stare right at her, until he hears James coming and goes inside.
- Riding on the back of James's Harley, Laura says 'The trees . . . the trees.'
- As Jacques tells Laura she is right on time, she says, 'Buy me a ticket to The Great Went.' 'We're on our way, baby,' he replies. 'Let's go *all* the way.'
- At the cabin, Jacques puts a thousand-dollar poker chip in the bound Laura's mouth, saying, 'Bite the bullet, baby.' Leo and Jacques fight over Laura before Jacques stumbles out to be attacked by Leland.
- In the cabin, Leland/BOB's smiling eyes are on the terrified Laura as he rapes Ronette. In the Log Lady's cabin nearby, the Log Lady holds her log and listens to the sound of distant screaming, while the tattoo on her leg (established in the series as two triangles, the same mystical symbol as on the ring worn by Teresa and Laura) glows 'beet red and burning'.
- The script makes more explicit reference to the fact that Laura taunts Leland/BOB into killing her because it is preferable to being possessed by BOB.
- Hearing the screams as he arrives, too late, at the cabin, Gerard says 'BOB, I can hear you singing.'

- Later, witnessing Leland/BOB's murder of Laura, Gerard cries out 'That's his own daughter you're killing.'
- After Laura's body is found, a further scene takes place, preceded by a caption that reads 'TWO MONTHS LATER'. Annie Blackburn is rushed into an emergency room as a paramedic tells a nurse that Sheriff Truman found her at Glastonbury Grove. Meanwhile, in the Red Room, The Man From Another Place repeats his earlier words to Cooper:

> MAN FROM ANOTHER PLACE
> Is it future? Or is it past? Do you know who I am? I am The Arm. And I sound like this.
>
> The Man From Another Place puts his hand in front of his lips and makes an Indian whooping sound.
>
> COOPER
> (looking at the table)
> Where is the ring?
> MAN FROM ANOTHER PLACE
> Someone else has it now.
> COOPER
> That would indicate that it's the future.
> MAN FROM ANOTHER PLACE
> The later events have never been kept a secret.
> COOPER
> Where am I? And how can I leave?
> MAN FROM ANOTHER PLACE
> You are here and there is no place to go . . . BUT HOME!

- Immediately after this, the script cuts back to Annie in hospital, as a nurse mops her forehead and Annie repeats her words from Laura's dream. The nurse takes Annie's ring and, in the next room, puts the ring on her own finger.
- From the hospital room, the script cuts to Cooper's room at the Great Northern hotel, as Doc Hayward and Truman stand outside the bathroom door, worried about Cooper. The Sheriff breaks down the door, finding Cooper lying prone on the floor in his pyjamas, bloodied from the broken mirror.

> COOPER
> (smiling strangely)
> I slipped and hit my head on the mirror. The

```
glass broke as it struck my head. (laughs) It
struck me as funny, Harry. Do you understand me,
Harry, it struck me as funny.
                    DOC
You are going right back to bed.
Doc and Truman help Cooper up.
                    COOPER
But I haven't brushed my teeth yet.
Cooper smiles at the uneasy pair.
```

The remainder of the script is a simplified version of the Red Room scenes that close the movie.

In addition to the missing scenes highlighted above, there was at least one other that Lynch has hinted at. 'There was one scene with Jack Nance and Mr Mibbler that someday has to be finished and seen,' he reveals, referring to a scene in which Dell Mibbler (Ed Wright) returns a piece of two-by-four timber to Pete Martell (Nance) because it does not measure two inches by four inches.

ALTERNATIVE VERSIONS: Although the running time and sequential scenes are identical in all versions of *Fire Walk With Me*, there are several slightly different versions of the film in circulation.

The first detectable differences are slight but significant, and involve the scene in which Chester Desmond finds the ring beneath Deputy Howard's trailer. In the script, Desmond disappears at the precise moment he touches Teresa's ring. In US theatrical prints, the image freezes and fades to white as Desmond reaches for the ring; in the home-video version, the shot fades to black *without* a freeze frame. UK versions freeze the frame for several moments, and then cut directly to the next scene, while Japanese versions have the image freeze and then fade to black.

The second, more fundamental alterations concern the subtitling of the scene at the sleazy club (named 'Partyland' in the script, but not identified in the film until the end credits reveal the title of the music: 'The Pink Room') where Laura meets Jacques and Ronette, and Donna succumbs to the effects of a cocktail of drugs and alcohol. Lynch shot the scene, as he often does, by playing loud music that cinematographer Ron Garcia described in *American Cinematographer*, as 'driving, repetitive stuff that just hits you like a hammer on an anvil, over and over . . . The actors had to scream over it, but David came up with the brilliant and economical idea of subtitling the scene instead of looping it!' In fact, Lynch was so unsure about whether to subtitle the low-level dialogue in the scene that there were no subtitles in territories such as France, Germany, the UK and Japan, where the film was released earlier than it was in the US.

The subtitles, as they appear in US prints, are as follows:

JACQUES:	Welcome to Canada.
LAURA:	Don't expect a turkey dog here.
JACQUES:	Hey, slowpokes. Guess what?
BUCK:	What?
JACQUES:	There's no tomorrow. Know why baby? 'Cause it will never get here.
LAURA:	Hey Jacques.
JACQUES:	I'm not Jacques. I am the great Went.
LAURA:	I am the muffin.
JACQUES:	And what a muffin you got . . . I'm as blank as a fart.
LAURA:	Chug-a-lug, Donna.
LAURA:	Ronette Pulaski . . . I haven't seen you since I was thrown out of One-Eyed Jack's.
RONETTE:	What else did we do together? I remember.
JACQUES:	Hey, the party twins. My high-school sandwich. Let's put some meat inside.
RONETTE:	She's been dead a year.
JACQUES:	Yeah, who?
RONETTE:	Teresa . . .
LAURA:	Teresa Banks. Yeah, a whole year.
RONETTE:	She was going to get rich. She was blackmailing somebody.
JACQUES:	Right. She called me. She even asked me what your fathers looked like.
LAURA:	What? She asked about my father?
JACQUES:	Hey . . . Why don't you two come up to the cabin this week? Thursday.
RONETTE:	Here we go again. Like we're back at One-Eyed Jack's.
LAURA:	My God, it sure is.
RONETTE:	Oh shit . . . Isn't that Donna Hayward?

Non-US versions also divide the narrative of the Twin Peaks portion of the film into days. After the 'TWIN PEAKS ONE YEAR LATER' caption retained by the US version, a further caption reads 'EXACTLY SEVEN DAYS BEFORE THE MURDER OF LAURA PALMER'. From here, each day's events are preceded by captions that read 'THURSDAY – SEVEN DAYS BEFORE', 'FRIDAY – SIX DAYS BEFORE', and so on until 'LAST MORNING' and 'LAST NIGHT'.

TRAILER: The US trailer is a small masterpiece. It begins with the sound of a ceiling fan played over the company logos, before opening with a shot of the fan, a shot of Laura Palmer's dead face and a caption in the film's standard typeface: 'THE LAST 7 DAYS OF LAURA PALMER'. From here, Angelo Badalamenti's music carries us through a delirious, dialogue-free (and, interestingly, Donna-free) montage of images both mundane and bizarre: from Laura's daytime meetings with James and Bobby, a car-screech sound effect carries us into Mrs Tremond's picture, through which we enter the Red Room and Laura's nightmare world, until Laura's laugh (from the film's closing scene) takes us into the title, which appears, as it does in the film, on a background of blue television static.

POSTER: The US poster image was a composition featuring a shot of Laura Palmer in black lingerie, smiling out from a burning half of the gold heart necklace she wore, looming large against a background image of the Red Room. Most European territories tended towards a simplified version of this, with the same shot of Laura Palmer, used without the necklace and patterned floor, but with Cooper glimpsed behind the drapes. In the UK, a somewhat unsuccessful collage featured Laura against the red drapes, with Cooper looking heavenwards and the image of BOB glaring from the background.

TAG-LINE: 'MEET LAURA PALMER', the US poster copy-line ran, in flagrant disregard of the millions of *Twin Peaks* fans who knew her intimately already, 'IN A TOWN WHERE NOTHING IS AS IT SEEMS . . . AND EVERYONE HAS SOMETHING TO HIDE.' Other tag-lines used: 'These are the last seven days of Laura Palmer' and 'In a town like Twin Peaks, no one is innocent.'

WHAT THE PAPERS SAID: The first press coverage of *Fire Walk With Me* came immediately following its world-premiere screening at the Cannes Film Festival, of which the *New York Times*'s Janet Maslin wrote, 'It was hard to say whether the film played worse to *Twin Peaks* fans, who already knew more than enough about the death of Laura Palmer, or to anyone happening onto this impenetrable material for the first time. Either way, Mr Lynch's taste for brain-dead grotesque has lost its novelty, and it now appears more pathologically unpleasant than cinematically bold.'

After this hostile reaction, US distributor New Line felt it prudent to release the film, on 28 August 1992, without further preview screenings, hoping to avoid further critical wounding. Of course, a lack of press screenings does not endear a film to the press, and the fact that the practice is usually reserved for the worst films tends to render it something of a self-fulfilling prophecy. Forced to pay for the privilege of seeing the film, many critics didn't bother; others did, however, sharpening their poison pens in the queue. The *Los Angeles Times*'s Michael Wilmington even commented on the critical reaction to the film, suggesting that, 'When movie artists with idiosyncratic sensibilities inject themselves into the mainstream, there are two dangers. The mainstream may swallow them up or spit them out. Lately, it's the critics who have been spitting. And perhaps, by *Wild at Heart*, Lynch lost some admirers because they felt that, instead of the genius movie rebel they originally took him for, he was just a cultural-political conservative with kinky tastes.'

Editor Mary Sweeney feels that there were two reasons for the mauling the film received from most critics. 'As soon as someone gets that high, everybody's looking for them to fall, or to help pull them down,' she says. She also feels that the film soured the taste left by the TV show. 'They so badly wanted it to be like the TV show, and it wasn't. It was a David Lynch *feature*. And people were very angry about it. They felt betrayed. I think that the enthusiasm with which it was mauled had to do with that sense of betrayal.' According to Sweeney, Lynch was stung by the critical response and took it personally. Nevertheless, she says, 'he feels very proud of *Fire Walk With Me*. He *loves* that film. And it only hurts him that people don't get what he's trying to communicate.'

'I felt this black cloud roll in,' Lynch told the *Guardian*. 'It lasted for over two years, and I knew the thing was there, and I watched, and sure enough . . . I thought I was being true to myself, but the reactions were coloured by this cloud . . . Now I don't know if the cloud was created by their opinions, or the cloud came and their opinions changed.'

For Sheryl Lee, the critical reaction to *Fire Walk With Me* was unsurprising, given its controversial subject matter. 'Laura Palmer is a victim of incest *and* she has turned to drugs,' she told *Empire*. 'In [America] we are still denying that incest is a *huge* problem, and so in that sense it can be very confrontational to certain people.' Nevertheless, she added, 'I have had many people, victims of incest, approach me since the film was released, so glad that it had been made because it helped them to release a lot. And so for me, it doesn't *matter* what the critics say – if one person walks away having released something, then it's worth seeing.'

BOX OFFICE: The first wide release of *Fire Walk With Me*, in Japan on 16 May 1992, appeared to augur well for the film's international box-office performance. Within a month, 450,000 avid fans had seen the film in a country where *Twin Peaks* fever had struck like nowhere else on earth, and the film continued to perform strongly throughout the summer. As Taku Ushiyama of Japanese distributor Nippon Herald Films told the *Los Angeles Times* in June, 'We're booked into more than one hundred theatres around Japan. That's the equivalent of a two-thousand-theatre release in the US. This is going to be one of the top ten films of the year.'

New Line Cinema, which paid $6 million for the North American distribution rights to *Fire Walk With Me* without seeing the film, did not fare so well; with the cost of prints and advertising, and a hefty cut for exhibitors, it would need to gross north of $15 million to break even. In the event, after a disastrous opening weekend ($1.8 million from 691 screens) and calamitous weekly drops (53 per cent the second week, on 692 screens), *Fire Walk With Me* grossed just $4.16 million overall. Despite stronger performances in the UK and France, the film did not perform well enough to warrant the sequel/spin-off that Lynch had promised if *Fire Walk With Me* proved successful.

AWARDS: *Premiere* magazine's assertion that 'Sheryl Lee deserves an Oscar just for showing up and trying' held no sway with the Academy of Motion Picture Arts and Sciences: with no major awards forthcoming, Ms Lee had to settle for a Best Female Lead nomination at the Independent Spirit Awards. The film's music fared rather better: at the same ceremony, Angelo Badalamenti won for Best Music, and the film won Best Soundtrack honours at the UK's Brit Awards.

TRIVIA: A licence plate in the film reads 'IS 432', possibly a coded reference to Isaiah 43:2, part of which reads: 'When you walk through the fire, you shall not be burned, nor shall the flame scorch you.'

Fire Walk With Me opened in the US on the same day that *Twin Peaks* co-creator Mark Frost's feature debut *Storyville* (co-starring Piper Laurie; photographed by Ron Garcia) was released.

In the UK, the promotional video sleeves sent to reviewers prior to the original Guild Home Video rental release (G 8692) were misprinted so that the title read *Twin Peaks – Fire Walk With Fire*. Although the error was quickly corrected, a few copies remain in circulation. Highly collectable they are, too.

Following *Fire Walk With Me*, Angelo Badalamenti arranged, orchestrated and conducted David Bowie's version of the George Gershwin song 'A Foggy Day in London Town' for the AIDS benefit album *Red, Hot and Rhapsody*.

APOCRYPHA: 'The plot of the film dovetails perfectly into the pilot,' cinematographer Ron Garcia told *American Cinematographer*. 'David was adamant about the details of the script and how they merged with the series.' In reality, there are numerous inconsistencies: there is no appearance by, nor even mention of, Dr Jacoby, to whom Laura was said to be close during her final days (although a scripted telephone conversation between the two was cut from the release version); there is also no mention of the picnic attended by Laura, Donna and James, the videotape of which is introduced as evidence in the pilot episode (in fact, on the evidence of Laura's emotional state in *Fire Walk With Me*, it is hard to imagine her looking as carefree and happy as she does at the picnic); nor is there an explanation for the scrawled note reading 'FIRE WALK WITH ME' found at the murder scene.

AVAILABILITY: Although previously available from Guild Home Video, *Fire Walk With Me* is not currently sold in any format in the UK. In the US, the film is available only as a full-screen (4:3) NTSC VHS (75843) which, although losing some of the image in the conversion of the theatrical 1:1.85 ratio to the small screen, counters this by revealing the full frame at the upper and lower portions of the screen. Not only does this provide additional vertical information not visible in theatres, it serves to restore *Twin Peaks* to its former and most natural state: the television-shaped image.

Since the only DVD currently available is a German edition (52018) with no English subtitles, the best home video version of *Fire Walk With Me* is probably the Japanese laserdisc (PILF-7192), which makes a compromise between the original aspect ratio (1:1.85) and the full image (4:3) described above, partially matting the frame at 1:1.70. This edition, presented on two discs in a gatefold sleeve, omits chapter stops, but includes the US theatrical trailer.

FINAL ANALYSIS: After a pilot and 29 episodes of *Twin Peaks*, we may not know Laura Palmer, but – to paraphrase a famous line from the series – we 'feel like we know her'. Yet the Laura Palmer depicted in *Fire Walk With Me* is not, despite appearances, the one we have come to 'know' through the memories of those who loved and mourned her: from the moment she appears on screen, the Laura Palmer of *Fire Walk With Me* is as *emotionally* dead as the body found in the *Twin Peaks* pilot. As Tim Lucas noted, 'We never really see the Laura who was, the charismatic teenager who held Twin Peaks in thrall . . . *Twin Peaks* was so dominated by the memory of Laura Palmer, and the reverberations of her murder, that most viewers came away from the series convinced that it had shown them, at some time or other, some form of her that wasn't refracted through the sorrow, guilt, and memories of her survivors. *Not so*. We're meeting Laura Palmer for the first time.'

Of course, for those who did not follow *Twin Peaks* on television, this was literally true, and avowed fans would perhaps be surprised to learn that the film – which plays, on its most basic level, as the decline and fall of an abused teenager with a double life – is mostly comprehensible to the uninitiated; remember, however, that even to the long-term fan, the film contains much that is seemingly impenetrable, obscure and unexplainable. In the light of the hostile response to the film by many *Twin Peaks* fans, a more interesting question is why it was a disappointment to them. Could it be that they secretly longed for a sequel, rather than a retread of old ground? That they mourned the virtual absence of Dale Cooper, and the very real absence of many of their other favourite characters? That the excised humour, so fundamental to the series, meant that Laura's downward spiral was unleavened by lighter moments? Or were those whom *Fire Walk With Me* disappointed the same disaffected fair-weather fans who lost interest in the series soon after the murder mystery at the centre of it was solved, despite the fact that this opened up a far greater puzzle where much more was at stake?

The customary nature of a cinema prequel, as established by the flashback scenes in Francis Ford Coppola's *The Godfather, Part II* (1974), is that it can be watched chronologically, so that its events precede those that follow it. *Fire Walk With Me* does not work like this, however, not only because it seems to be situated in a time warp (Cooper is already trapped in the Black Lodge, Annie Blackburn is dead), but also because it is as much an exercise in nostalgia as it is an explanation of some of the themes at work in *Twin Peaks*. (In this respect it is more like Arthur C. Clarke's novel *2010*, a sequel to the deliberately obscure movie version of *2001: A Space Odyssey*.) Yet it relies, to a degree, on prior knowledge of the series. Indeed, like *Titanic* (1997), the fact that the outcome is already known actually *enhances* the experience of watching the film, as the crushing sense of the inevitable – considerably enhanced in versions containing the captioned countdown to Laura's murder – eventually overwhelms the viewer until one can barely look as Leland finally puts Laura out of her misery. Ours, however, is only just beginning, as *Fire Walk With Me* shows us a living, breathing Laura Palmer who turned to drugs and prostitution as an escape from the habitual abuse she was suffering at home.

And there it is, ultimately: *Twin Peaks – Fire Walk With Me* is a tragedy as American as Marilyn Monroe, apple pie, damn' fine coffee – and overlooked cinema masterpieces.

EXPERT WITNESS: 'We were preparing for the [cabin] scene, and all of a sudden [David] would go off on this tangent telling us about how they were building this new addition to his house. Frank Lloyd Wright

Jr was designing this part of his house. Then the cinematographer came in and said, "David, we're ready." He said, "We're working on the scene, just a few more minutes." We weren't preparing for the scene at all. That's his way of preparing, because he's bonding with the actors and making them comfortable and making them feel the mood he wants them to be in.' – actor Walter Olkewicz (Jacques Renault)

LYNCH ON *TWIN PEAKS – FIRE WALK WITH ME*: 'I love that film. I say now that *The Straight Story* is my most experimental movie, but up till then, *Fire Walk With Me* was my most experimental film, and some of the things, the combos, you know, like, sequences . . . It was a dark film, but like Peggy Lipton said in an interview, it was just too much in people's faces, and it didn't have the humour of *Twin Peaks*. So it was what it was supposed to be, but it wasn't what people wanted. It was supposed to be stand-alone, but it was also supposed to be the last week of Laura Palmer's life. And all those things that had been established, they could be pleasant on one level to experience, but unpleasant on another level.'

On the Air (1992)

Television series / 7 x 23 mins / colour / live action

Directed by David Lynch (Episode 1), Lesli Linka Glatter (Episodes 2, 5), Jack Fisk (Episodes 3, 7), Jonathan Sanger (Episode 4), Betty Thomas (Episode 6)
Written by Mark Frost & David Lynch (Episode 1), Mark Frost (Episodes 2, 5), Robert Engels (Episodes 3, 6), Scott Frost (Episode 4), David Lynch & Robert Engels (Episode 7)
Produced by Gregg Fienberg (Episode 1), Deepak Nayar (Episodes 2–6)
Edited by Mary Sweeney (Episode 1), Paul Trejo (Episodes 2, 5), Toni Morgan (Episodes 3, 6), David Siegel (Episode 4)
Director of Photography Ron Garcia (Episode 1), Peter Deming (Episodes 2–6)
Production Designer Okowita
Co-Executive Producer Robert Engels (Episodes 2–6)
Music Composed & Conducted by Angelo Badalamenti
Casting by Johanna Ray, CSA
Created by Mark Frost and David Lynch

REGULAR CAST: Ian Buchanan (*Lester Guy*), Nancye Ferguson (*Ruthie*), Miguel Ferrer (*Buddy Budwaller*), Gary Grossman (*Bert Schein*), Mel Johnson Jr (*Mickey*), Marvin Kaplan (*Dwight McGonigle*), David L. Lander (*Vladja Gochktch*), Kim McGuire (*Nicole Thorn*), Marla Rubinoff (*Betty Hudson*), Tracey Walter (*Blinky Watts*), Irwin Keyes (*Shorty the Stagehand*), Everett

Greenbaum (*ZBC Announcer*), Buddy Douglas (*Buddy Morris*),
Raleigh Friend, Raymond Friend (*Hurry Up Twins*)

TITLE SEQUENCE: The strains of a saxophonist (with a blown-
raspberry effect mixed in for good measure) are heard over a sepia-
tinted still photograph of New York City, the Chrysler building
prominent in the foreground, with a large caption reading '1957'
superimposed over it. This fades through to a colour shot as a camera
moves up the side of another building before cutting to the title,
rendered in a neon semicircle around the fizzing mast on the top of
another building, placed against a star-filled background. This mixes
through to some colour footage of New York in the 50s as bubbly
yellow-and-red cast names appear. As the captions continue, we see the
headquarters of the Zoblotnick Broadcasting Corporation and its
zigzag ZBC logo before cutting to another sepia shot, this time an
animated graphic showing the Earth from space, with a single mast
fizzing away. There are more period shots of New York, then an
interior showing a family washing their brand new 1957 De Soto
automobile, its name and year of launch written on the wall behind, in
the style of an early television commercial. The daughter hula-hoops
against a white picket fence as we cut to the ZBC logo in close-up,
now surrounded by the neon 'on the air' sign we have already seen.
Finally, the image dissolves back to the model building against the
starry sky, the mast fizzing dramatically.

SUMMARY: New York, 1957. The production staff of the Zoblotnick
Broadcasting Corporation's cornerstone series, *The Lester Guy Show*,
suffer a series of disasters during the live broadcast of the very first
show. These problems – including the accidental incapacitation of the
eponymous star, washed-up matinee idol Lester Guy – are momentarily
alleviated by the sweet singing of supporting cast member Betty
Hudson, who steps into the breach and effectively saves the show.

As the weeks progress, Lester grows to resent Betty's new-found
popularity. However, his efforts to steal back the limelight are
thwarted by the numerous other catastrophes, calamities and technical
difficulties that befall the show, much to the chagrin of network
executive Buddy Budwaller and his linguistically challenged boss, Mr
Zoblotnick, whose equally incomprehensible nephew, Vladja
Gochktch, is the show's director.

PRODUCTION HISTORY: According to Lynch, the inspiration for
On the Air apparently came to him while he was mixing the sound for
an episode of *Twin Peaks*, just as the show was beginning to struggle in
the ratings following its ill-fated move to Saturday nights. 'It just came

into my head, the idea of people trying to do something successful and having it all go wrong,' he told the *Los Angeles Times*, perhaps echoing his own feelings about the imminent demise of *Twin Peaks*.

After their successful writing collaborations on *Twin Peaks* and several unproduced projects, in late 1990 Lynch and Frost set to work on the pilot script for *On the Air*, intended as a half-hour sitcom for ABC, the network that broadcast *Twin Peaks*. Despite the humour evident in that show, the failure of *One Saliva Bubble* and *The Lemurians* [see 'In Dreams,' pages 246–7] meant that the Lynch/Frost partnership had been denied an out-and-out absurdist comedy of the kind the pair admired. Says Lynch, 'I really have a respect for comedy. People have said that comedy is like mathematics: two and two is four, this and this – you gotta get a laugh. And it's really difficult, and yet comedies are throwaway things.'

The pilot script was completed in December 1990 and filmed in March of the following year, borrowing several of the *Twin Peaks* cast while the show was on a six-week hiatus, its future hanging in the balance. According to Lynch, the *On the Air* pilot tested well with audiences, and was liked well enough by the network. 'They were very, very happy with the show,' he told the *Los Angeles Times*. 'They ordered six more episodes after they saw the pilot – they *had* to be happy.' They were not happy. With *Twin Peaks*'s audience dwindling rapidly, ABC refused to take a chance on a further commitment and did not order any more episodes after the initial six.

Worse still, after cancelling *Twin Peaks* in April 1991 and holding back the final two episodes for broadcast in the manner of a made-for-TV movie in June, ABC shelved the completed episodes of *On the Air* for a whole *year*, finally scheduling them for broadcast in June 1992. Naturally, the network rebuffed accusations of sabotage, stating that review tapes had been dispatched to television critics across the country, and that promotions were being aired, as for any new series. Lynch was having none of it. 'I've heard that summertime is pretty much the worst time you can be on,' he told the *Los Angeles Times*, 'but we're going on in summer, [and] that Saturday night is the worst night of the week to be on, and we're going on Saturday night . . . When I love the show, and people seem to love the show, what's wrong when we're not given a primo spot?' Like Lynch, Miguel Ferrer felt that *On the Air* could have had a real shot. 'Because it's a half-hour comedy,' he said shortly before the first episode aired, 'this show is more self-contained than *Twin Peaks* and therefore accessible to a wider audience.'

THE LYNCH MOB: The regular cast of *On the Air* included three familiar faces from *Twin Peaks* (Ian Buchanan, Miguel Ferrer and David L. Lander), one from *Wild at Heart* (Marvin Kaplan), and one from *The Cowboy and the Frenchman* (Tracey Walter). Episode 4's guest star was Freddie Jones (*The Elephant Man, Dune, Wild at Heart*).

In addition to Mark Frost, other Lynch regulars cropped up behind the camera, including writer and co-executive producer Robert Engels (*Twin Peaks* story editor), composer Angelo Badalamenti (*Blue Velvet, Twin Peaks, Wild at Heart*), casting director Johanna Ray (*Blue Velvet, Twin Peaks, Wild at Heart*), writer Scott Frost (*Twin Peaks, My Life, My Tapes: The Autobiography of FBI Special Agent Dale Cooper*); directors Lesli Linka Glatter (four episodes of *Twin Peaks*), Jack Fisk (*Six Figures Getting Sick, Eraserhead*) and Jonathan Sanger (producer of *The Elephant Man*, director of *Twin Peaks* episode 2007); *Twin Peaks* editors Mary Sweeney, Paul Trejo and David Siegel.

Significantly, *On the Air* marked the first association between Lynch and cinematographer Peter Deming, although the fact that Deming did not photograph Lynch's episode meant that the two did not work together until their next collaboration, *Hotel Room*.

MEMORABLE QUOTES
Narrator: 'Blinky Watts is not blind. He suffers from Boazman's Simplex. He actually sees 25.62 times as much as we do. If we were to see what Blinky is seeing right now, it would look something like this.'

Lester Guy: 'What do they know in South Dakota?'
Budwaller: 'They know what they like.'
Lester Guy: 'If they knew what they liked, they wouldn't live in South Dakota.'

Lester Guy: 'The show must go on!'

Blinky: 'I had a fish this morning. You know how much that fish cost me? A fin. And it weighted itself, and had its own scales. A brave little fish. Boy, it had guts.'

SOUND AND MUSIC: 'So many different sounds in the universe,' says sound effects man Blinky Watts. 'Infinitesimal,' agrees his assistant, Mickey. 'Each combination meaning different things to different people.' That may be, but the comedy sound effects of *On the Air* – those used throughout the show, not the show *within* the show – rarely serve to increase the comic value of the accompanying visuals. Nevertheless, considerable comedy is derived from *The Lester Guy Show*'s sound effects department, especially in the pilot, when Blinky's precisely set levels are accidentally shifted, and in episode 7, when the effects of an avant-garde performance artist and a contraption called the 'voice disintegrator' are combined on stage.

INFLUENCED BY: Lynch once said that the character of blind sound engineer Blinky Watts was inspired by a sequence from the W.C. Fields comedy *It's a Gift* (1934), which included a comic sequence involving a blind man with a cane, a plate-glass window and a box of light bulbs, and which Lynch found hilarious. As it turned out, the network was uncomfortable with the idea of a blind person being used to comedy effect in the politically correct 1990s and Blinky therefore became a person who sees the world in a unique way – not unlike Lynch himself.

LEGACY: On the surface, *On the Air* might be seen as a fledgling version of HBO's *The Larry Sanders Show*, which intercut the backstage shenanigans of a 'live on tape' late-night talk show with the show itself, but to suggest a direct link between the slapstick silliness of *On the Air* and the sophisticated satire of *Larry Sanders* would be to make a tenuous, not to say generous, connection.

DÉJÀ VU: *On the Air* is rife with *Twin Peaks* references. The sweet little-girl voice of Marla Rubinoff as Betty Hudson recalls the dulcet tones of Kimmy Robertson as Lucy Moran; Miguel Ferrer's performance as network president Bud Budwaller recalls his equally irritable *Twin Peaks* persona, Albert Rosenfield; as Ruthie, Nancye Ferguson looks and dresses like a cross between Donna (Lara Flynn Boyle) and Audrey (Sherilyn Fenn); and as well as sharing his first name and initials with *On the Air* director David Lynch, David Lander's performance as *The Lester Guy Show*'s director is strangely reminiscent of Lynch's loudly spoken role on *Twin Peaks*. Blinky's talk of coffee and fish in episode 7 recalls the *Twin Peaks* pilot, while the subtitling of Gochtchk's and Zoblotnik's dialogue echoes the subtitled characters in *Twin Peaks*. After the Lynch/Badalamenti collaborations with sweet-voiced singer Julee Cruise, the song sung by Betty Hudson (Marla Rubinoff) in the pilot sounds familiar, even recalling Lynch's pre-Badalamenti composition 'In Heaven (Lady in the Radiator Song)' from *Eraserhead*.

THEMES AND MOTIFS: Communication problems and the difficulty of making oneself understood are constant aspects of *On the Air*, and are themes that have recurred in many of Lynch's works, from *The Alphabet* (the pressure of learning linguistic forms makes the girl sick), through *The Grandmother* (the boy's parents communicate only in strange barking sounds), *The Cowboy and the Frenchman* (Slim's deafness), *The Elephant Man* (Merrick's speech problems), *Twin Peaks* (many instances, such as the mortuary attendant who blurts out his name after mishearing Cooper, a device reused during Gordon Cole's appearances) and *Wild at Heart* (Sailor and Lula's bizarre conversation with George Kovich). In *On the Air*, Gochktch and his uncle's dialogue requires Ruthie's translation, and sometimes even subtitles, while McGonigle's dim brain and Betty Hudson's painful naivety lead to constant misunderstandings.

WHAT THE PAPERS SAID: Reviewing the Lynch-directed pilot episode, the *Los Angeles Times*'s Chris Willman wrote that, while Lynch clearly had a gift for staging bizarre comedy, 'it doesn't necessarily follow that he's able to sustain it through an entire show . . . For someone with such an avant-garde rep, Lynch offers up too much standard-brand character shtick here for comfort, at least in the dialogue-heavy first half.' Nevertheless, he added, 'Once the talk stops and the episode becomes a series of physical sight-gags, *On the Air* suddenly takes off and really does begin to look like a silent comedy directed by a modern absurdist painter.'

RATINGS: *On the Air* debuted on the ABC network at 9.30 p.m. on Saturday, 20 June 1992. The fact that only two more episodes were broadcast before *On the Air* went *off* the air suggests the level of ratings the show drew, said to be the lowest of any prime-time comedy in the network's history.

EPISODE LOG

Episode 1 / 23 mins / 20 June 1992
Written by Mark Frost & David Lynch
Directed by David Lynch

Additional Cast Dorsay Alavi, Vanessa Angel, Reo Danzelle, Carolyn Lowry (*Chorus Girls*), Bruce Grossberg (*Control Booth Technician*), Susan Russell (*Announcer's Assistant*), Angelo Badalamenti (*Piano Player*), Walt Robles (*Flying Stagehand*)

Synopsis New York, 1957. The production staff of the Zoblotnick Broadcasting Corporation's cornerstone series, *The Lester Guy Show*, suffer a series of disasters during the live broadcast of the very first show. These problems are momentarily alleviated by the sweet singing of supporting cast member Betty Hudson, who steps into the breach and effectively saves the show. Mr Zoblotnick himself calls to give the good news: the network has a hit on its hands.

Episode 2 / 23 mins / not broadcast

Written by Mark Frost
Directed by Lesli Linka Glatter

Additional Cast Sydney Lassik (*Ivan Zoblotnick*), Joseph Pecoraro (*Giuseppe*), Ben Kronen (*Waiter*)

Synopsis After her success on the first *Lester Guy Show*, Betty Hudson is invited out to dinner by ZBC boss Ivan Zoblotnick. Lester, Buddy Budwaller and Nicole conspire to ruin the evening, but Betty wins the old man over.

Episode 3 / 23 mins / 27 June 1992

Written by Robert Engels
Directed by Jack Fisk

Additional Cast Diana Bellamy (*Ethel Thissle*), Richard Riehle (*Dr Winky*), Charles Tyner (*Professor Right Answer*), Peter Pitofsky (*Worker #1*), Loren Janes (*Executive*)

Synopsis With Betty's fan mail coming in by the sackload, Lester plans to win back the spotlight by humiliating her on a rigged quiz show. Meanwhile, McGonigle has trouble with his new allergy medicine.

Episode 4 / 23 mins / not broadcast

Written by Scott Frost
Directed by Jonathan Sanger

Additional Cast Freddie Jones (*Stan Tailings*), Billy Zuckert (*Crusty Old Stagehand*)

Synopsis The cast of *The Lester Guy Show* is graced – and disgraced – by the presence of legendary English thespian Stan Tailings, some Mexican mariachis and a flock of ducks.

Episode 5 / 23 mins / 4 July 1992

Written by Mark Frost
Directed by Lesli Linka Glatter

Additional Cast Anne Bloom (*Sylvia Hudson*), Chuck McCann (*Wally Walters*)

Synopsis The week's guest star is Betty's famous – and famously mean – older sister, Sylvia, an old flame of Lester's. When disaster strikes, as usual, a ventriloquist's dummy is the unlikely saviour of the show.

Episode 6 / 23 mins / not broadcast
Written by Robert Engels
Directed by Betty Thomas

Additional Cast Robert Costanzo (*Mr Plumber*), I. M. Hobson (*The Great Presidio*)

Synopsis The new plumbing creates havoc in the studio as gypsy magician 'The Great Presidio' prepares for his debut on the show.

Episode 7 / 23 mins / not broadcast
Written by David Lynch & Robert Engels
Directed by Jack Fisk

Additional Cast John Quade (*Billy 'The Ear' Mulkahey*), Bellina Logan (*Woman With No Name*), Sydney Lassik (*Ivan Zoblotnick*), Gregory Sporleder (*Sax Player*)

Synopsis Lester wants to put avant-garde performance artist The Woman With No Name on the show. Gochktch and his uncle mistake the 'beatnik' for a 'bootmaker'. Betty cannot remember her mother's first name. Lester hires Billy 'The Ear' Mulkahey to ruin Betty's voice with a bizarre contraption, but she resists all efforts to record her voice. Instead, the machine breaks down, ruining Lester's voice.

Comments Lynch's characteristic use of sound is particularly keen in this episode, directed by his long-time friend Jack Fisk, with a great deal of reversed music and *Lost Highway*-style sax.

AVAILABILITY: In the US, all seven episodes (including the four not broadcast) were released by Worldvision as a single extended-play NTSC VHS video (5065), sadly long deleted and very difficult to find. In Japan, a two-disc CLV laserdisc set was released by Amuse Video (ASLF-5021), in English with Japanese subtitles.

FINAL ANALYSIS: Lynch co-created *On the Air* at a time when he must have thought he could do anything. The charmed artistic life he seemed to have led since *Blue Velvet* had culminated, between 1989 and 1991, with the success of *Twin Peaks*, the Palme D'Or-winning *Wild at Heart*, several hit albums, the live performance/video

Industrial Symphony No.1 and numerous other side projects, which put him on the cover of *Time* magazine whose critics proclaimed him 'The Czar of Bizarre'. By 1991, however, the tarnish was already beginning to show on the Renaissance Man's artistic reputation: the critical backlash against *Wild at Heart* was at full pelt, and *Twin Peaks* died in ignominy, no doubt forcing ABC to reconsider its other ongoing Lynch/Frost production, *On the Air*.

Being funny, without being forced, had not previously been a problem for Lynch: witness the bizarre humour of *Blue Velvet* and *Wild at Heart*, and the character-based comedy of *Twin Peaks* and absurdly amusing *One Saliva Bubble*, the latter two, like *On the Air*, co-written with Mark Frost. The problem with Lynch's first produced comedy was that, quite simply, it wasn't *funny* – or, at least, not funny *enough*. As the pilot shows, all the elements were there for a combination of character-based comedy and slapstick farce inspired by Murphy's Principle that if anything can go wrong, it will. But the limitations of the format were evident from the outset, and as the ensemble of highly irregular regular characters – among them the inspired but under-used Blinky Watts, and the humourless but hilarious Buddy Budwaller – were forced to find ever more ridiculous guest stars, so the comedy itself became forced.

Looking back at *On the Air* provokes a combination of wincing and cringing, and only the occasional laugh, and ABC's cancellation of the show, with more than half of the episodes unbroadcast, seems less like a murder and more like a mercy killing.

EXPERT WITNESS: 'Directing *On the Air* was one of the most bizarre, yet fun experiences I've had directing. It was a Hellzapoppin for the 90s. We had ducks, people speaking in completely incomprehensible accents, strange set pieces and stranger actors. It was episodic and yet, oddly, non-linear. For most of us, I think, it was an exercise of the id, and we were encouraged to let go and allow ourselves to get caught up in its impossible world. Unfortunately, I fear the audience was unable to get the joke. But for those of us who had the opportunity to work on *On the Air*, it was an unforgettable experience. I have often tried to imagine the network executives watching the dailies and evaluating them . . . that would have been a terrific episode of the show.' – director Jonathan Sanger (episode 4)

LYNCH ON *ON THE AIR*: 'I had a blast making the pilot, and everybody who did an episode had fun. And it was like the greatest cast, the greatest group of people – one of those casts that I could see being friends and liking each other, if that had been a success, for years. They were just happy being with each other. But there's another one with ABC: they hated it. And they didn't think it was one bit funny. So that bit the dust.'

Hotel Room (1993)

Three-act television play / 85 mins (TV version) 100 mins (video version) / colour / live action

Directed by David Lynch ('Tricks,' 'Blackout'), James Signorelli ('Getting Rid of Robert')
Written by Barry Gifford ('Tricks,' 'Blackout'), Jay McInerney ('Getting Rid of Robert')
Produced by Deepak Nayar
Executive Producers Monty Montgomery & David Lynch
Edited by Mary Sweeney ('Tricks'), David Siegel ('Getting Rid of Robert'), Toni Morgan ('Blackout')
Director of Photography Peter Deming
Production Designer Patricia Norris
Music Composed and Conducted by Angelo Badalamenti
Original and Series Casting by Johanna Ray, CSA
Created by Monty Montgomery & David Lynch

CAST: Clarke Heathcliffe Brolly (*Sean the Bellboy*), Griffin Dunne (*Robert*), Chelsea Field (*Tina*), Crispin Glover (*Danny*), Mariska Hargitay (*Diane*), Glenne Headly (*Darlene*), Freddie Jones (*Louis 'Lou' Holchak*), Camilla Overbye Roos (*Maid*), John Solari (*Cop #1*), Harry Dean Stanton (*Moe Boca*), Carl Sundstrom (*Cop #2*), Deborah Unger (*Sasha*), Alicia Witt (*Diane*)

TITLE SEQUENCE: Sinister music plays over black-and-white images of a lightning storm, time-lapse photography of a moon, and construction workers building a tall structure: a New York hotel. As they toil, a soft, slightly nasal voice begins a narration: 'For a millennium, the space for the hotel room existed, undefined. Mankind captured it, gave it shape and passed through.' Still in monochrome, the camera pans up the side of a high-rise hotel, dissolving through to an old-fashioned elevator indicator coming to rest on the sixth floor. This, in turn, dissolves through to the sign outside room 603, where the door opens into whiteness. Shadowy male and female figures, ill-defined but seemingly dressed in period clothes, enter the frame and walk through the doorway into whiteness. 'And sometimes, in passing through,' the voice continues, 'they found themselves brushing up against the secret names of truth.' The title appears, in red capital letters, flashing slightly like the neon sign of a hotel.

SUMMARY: Room 603 of New York's Railroad Hotel provides the setting for a series of human dramas, in which the bellboy and maid remain constant, but the story is never the same.

SOURCE: Two of the three original stories filmed as the pilot for *Hotel Room*, 'Tricks' and 'Blackout', were written by Barry Gifford, author of the novel on which *Wild at Heart* was based. The third story, 'Getting Rid of Robert', was written by New Yorker Jay McInerney, whose first novel – *Bright Lights, Big City* – catapulted him to literary stardom and led to comparisons with F. Scott Fitzgerald. McInerney's episode of *Hotel Room* was directed by James Signorelli, who previously helmed the Rodney Dangerfield comedy *Easy Money* (1983) and *Elvira, Mistress of the Dark* (1988).

PRODUCTION HISTORY: *Hotel Room* was conceived by *Wild at Heart* producer Monty Montgomery and Lynch as a series of short plays set in a single hotel room. 'The only rules regarding composition were that the action take place in specific years, and be set in a particular New York City hotel room (numbered 603), the corridor immediately outside the room, and/or the hotel lobby,' noted Barry Gifford, one of the writers commissioned to write original teleplays for the show. 'A bellboy and maid, the only continuing characters in the series, were to be included in the plays at [the writer's] option.'

Home Box Office (HBO), a newly launched cable channel specialising in adult-themed material, gave the green light to a feature-length pilot incorporating three stories: one by Barry Gifford ('Tricks'), another by Jay McInerney ('Getting Rid of Robert') and a third by playwright-turned-screenwriter and director David Mamet, whose recent work included *Homicide* (1991) and the screen adaptation of his own play, *Glengarry Glen Ross* (1992). 'If I recall correctly,' says Gifford, 'Monty Montgomery wasn't pleased with what Mamet gave him, so Monty and David came to me and said, "We have two days. Can you write us another play?"' Thus, he says, 'Blackout' was written in 48 hours, 'with the admonition . . . that it be "something our grandmothers could watch." I told Monty that would not be a problem; I'll write the play, I said, you guys gag and tie up the old ladies.'

Hotel Room was filmed in late 1992, with each of the three sets – the lobby, the hallway, and the room itself – being constructed on a sound stage. 'We shot all of it on a stage at what used to be called CBS Radford Studios, which was where we had shot *On the Air*,' recalls cinematographer Peter Deming. 'We had three days to shoot each one,' he adds, 'which is pretty quick. So "Tricks" was almost shot like a play, in that we had two cameras, and we would just begin the action and just keep rolling until we were out of film, and then pick it up from there, and then maybe turn around and do the same thing, because it was a pretty dialogue-heavy piece, and I think once the actors got in the flow, it worked much better.'

CASTING: Aside from British actress Glenne Headly (*Dick Tracy*, 1990), almost all of the leading players in Lynch's segments of *Hotel Room* were taken from Lynch's unofficial repertory company. However, according to Barry Gifford, Jack Palance was Lynch's first choice for the role of Lou Holchak in 'Tricks', but the fact that he had just won an Academy Award for *City Slickers* (1992) meant that his asking price was too high.

THE LYNCH MOB: Several of the actors in Lynch's segments of *Hotel Room* had worked with the director before: Harry Dean Stanton (*The Cowboy and the Frenchman, Wild at Heart, Fire Walk With Me*), Freddie Jones (*The Elephant Man, Dune, Wild at Heart, On the Air*), Alicia Witt (*Dune, Twin Peaks*) and Crispin Glover (*Wild at Heart*). Many of the crew had, too: writer Barry Gifford (*Wild at Heart*), producer Deepak Nayar (first assistant director on *Wild at Heart*, second assistant director on *Fire Walk With Me*, producer of *On the Air*), composer Angelo Badalamenti (*Blue Velvet* onwards), production designer Patricia Norris (*The Elephant Man* onwards), casting director Johanna Ray (*Blue Velvet* onwards), cinematographer Peter Deming (*On the Air*), editors Mary Sweeney (assistant editor on *Blue Velvet* and *Wild at Heart*, editor of *Twin Peaks* episode 2007 and *On the Air*) and Toni Morgan (episodes of *Twin Peaks*).

MEMORABLE QUOTES
Darlene: 'I've had some strange tricks, man, but you two guys are *weird*. You got a game goin' I ain't seen before.'

Diane: 'A fish by any other name is still a fish.'
Danny: 'Even if it's Chinese?'
Diane: 'Definitely if it's Chinese.'

Diane : 'Danny, you were always the sweetest child. You were one of 'em.'
Danny: 'One of who?'
Diane: 'Our six children. You were the first. The largest. With red hair and blue eyes. The rest were girls. Five perfect girls. Each one of them had brown hair, and brown eyes, and brown skin. They looked like fawns. *Danny, these are our children! Don't you recognise them?*'

SOUND AND MUSIC: The train noises that provide a constant aural leitmotif to Lynch's contributions to *Hotel Room* and the images of locomotives on the walls of the hotel room were there because the stories take place in the *Railroad* Hotel. For music, Lynch once again called upon Angelo Badalamenti to compose the score for his newest project; inevitably, the results were typical of both men's sensibilities and the music is as omnipresent as it was in *Twin Peaks*, though less intrusive.

INFLUENCED BY: The idea of a portmanteau piece presenting stories that take place in a single hotel arguably started with Neil Simon's comic stage farce *California Suite*, filmed by Herbert Ross in 1978. The resemblance between this and *Hotel Room* is superficial, despite David Foster Wallace's suggestion that *Hotel Room* was 'a hoary mainstream conceit ripped off from Neil Simon and sufficiently "Lynchianised" [*sic*] in *Hotel Room* to be then subsequently rip-offable by Tarantino *et posse* in 1995's *Four Rooms*.' Gifford agrees with the latter part of the statement, at least. '*Four Rooms* was stolen from our *Hotel Room*,' he says. 'But *Four Rooms* was shitty.'

Prior to *Hotel Room*, the anthology format had been tried and tested on HBO through its own successful production *Tales from the Crypt*, a series of short, self-contained horror stories adapted from, or inspired by, the EC comics of the 1950s. Gifford says that HBO was consciously looking to emulate the success of *Tales From the Crypt*, but that 'they wanted sexier or comedic pieces, not serious sex and not satire exactly, but something else.'

Actor Freddie Jones recognised the influence of Harold Pinter and Samuel Beckett on 'Tricks', but observed that the story offered an entirely American take on sexuality. Although Gifford says he was familiar with the work of Pinter and Beckett, he claims not to have been directly influenced by their sparse style, though a similarly pared-down style of his own is emphasised by Lynch's equally sparse direction.

Finally, the idea of hotel staff members whose age and appearance remain constant despite the passing of years recalls Stanley Kubrick's *The Shining* (1980), a film much admired by Lynch.

LEGACY: 'The nice thing about *Hotel Room* is that it got me writing plays, which I had never done before,' Gifford says, 'And they were immediately directed by Lynch and broadcast on cable, so that was a great thing.' Gifford ultimately wrote five 'hotel room' stories: 'Tricks', 'Blackout', 'Mrs Kashfi', 'Room 584, The Starr Hotel' and 'Do the Blind Dream?' 'I retained all literary and theatrical rights,' says Gifford, 'and the plays have subsequently been performed all over the country, from San Francisco to New York, Dallas, New Orleans and Los Angeles. Sometimes they perform one of the plays, sometimes two, three, or four. I've seen several of those productions, and some of them are even good. Even better than Lynch's versions!'

It is doubtful that Danish director Lars von Trier (*Breaking the Waves*, 1996) ever saw *Hotel Room*, yet the opening of his supernatural television series *The Kingdom* bears a strong resemblance to that of *Hotel Room*, complete with sepia-tinted opening images and a voice-over suggesting that the building where the action takes place – in the case of *The Kingdom*, a haunted hospital – has supernatural associations.

DÉJÀ VU: The room number, 603, is identical to the population of Big Tuna, Texas, in *Wild at Heart*. Boca's story about the seductive woman in the nightgown to whom he delivered Chinese food recalls Henry's seduction in *Eraserhead* and Jeffrey's relationship with Dorothy Vallens in *Blue Velvet*.

THEMES AND MOTIFS: 'Tricks' contains intriguing themes of dual identity, foreshadowed by Boca calling Darlene 'Arlene', and concluding with the realisation that the identities of Lou and Boca are interchangeable. 'Tricks' also explores the treachery of memory, the title itself referring both to the slang term for a prostitute's clients and the tricks that memory can play. Amnesia is a theme that also figures strongly in 'Blackout', which explores the way in which the mind shuts out traumatic events. It takes its title both from the literal blackout of the city and Diane's blocked memory. In this, both stories recall Lynch's version of Barry Gifford's *Wild at Heart* (Lula repressing the memory of her rape at the hands of Uncle Pooch), as well as prefiguring the next Lynch/Gifford collaboration, *Lost Highway* (Fred's psychogenic fugue). In 'Blackout', Diane's repressed guilt over the death of her child manifests itself as psychosis, her highly symbolic dreams, imaginings and false memories showing the cautious re-emergence of her recollection of their son Danny Junior's accidental drowning 'in a sea of red'. Some analysts took Diane's reference to this 'sea' as evidence that Diane had had an abortion (as Lula did); according to Gifford, this was not his intention. Diane's husband, Danny, also has an imperfect memory: he remembers the details of Danny Junior's death but his memory also plays tricks on him – he forgets whether New York or Paris is 'the city of lights' and whether New York or London has 'the great white way'. He also forgets certain details of the anecdotes he tells. Diane confuses the identities of her husband and son, both named Danny, and asks if, when they see the doctor, they can 'forget about Dan-bug'.

As well as echoing the reference to Chinese food in 'Tricks', the many Chinese references in 'Blackout' – a Chinese restaurant, the bellboy's discussion of the hotel's Chinese guests, a fortune-telling Chinese fish, the bellboy whom Diane mistakes for a Chinese doctor – are used as symbols of confusion, as someone might say that something illegible 'looks Chinese'.

CUT SCENES / ALTERNATIVE VERSION: Due to time constraints, minor adjustments were made to 'Tricks' during editing, none of which affect the story in any significant way. Some of these include:

• During Moe's story about Martine Mustique, after Moe says 'some state like that', the text originally described how she was married twice before she turned nineteen, had a couple abortions, ran off to Europe and ended up becoming a model and then making it in Hollywood.

• After Moe says that Martine Mustique was found dead in her bathtub, he explains that a guy she had dated and then dumped wrote a confession letter before committing suicide. Apparently, he said she was the only woman with whom he was able to achieve an erection. When she turned down his marriage proposal, he said she denied him his only chance for lifelong happiness. Rather than murder all of the psychiatrists who'd attended him since childhood, Edgard said, it was easier just to do away with the object of his affection. And, of course, himself.

There is a major edit after Moe says, 'Why doubt her, Lou? I don't, I don't believe she would lie about that.' In the original text, Darlene tells a story about snakes and their mating habits.

More significant edits were made to the other Lynch/Gifford segment, 'Blackout', the original version of which lasts approximately 47 minutes – extraordinary, given that the published form of the play runs to only seventeen pages. These cuts vary from Danny's description of the Chinese food, stage directions relating to the sequence in which Diane walks with the candle, to Danny's final line. His question to Diane about whether she'd like some Chinese food was replaced with Diane's joyous exclamation, 'Danny!'

WHAT THE PAPERS SAID: The three-episode 'omnibus' edition of *Hotel Room* debuted on HBO at eleven p.m. on Friday, 8 January 1993. *Los Angeles Times* television critic Chris Wellman described the show as 'definitely not for the tastes of typical travellers, but a marvellously absorbing stay for the Lynch true-faithful.' While admiring the McInerney-Signorelli contribution, which he described as 'a truly vicious romantic comedy', Wellman said that Lynch's episodes were 'considerably more gruelling, but rewarding in other ways', singling out Glenne Headly's 'stoned cheerleader routine' and the Crispin Glover-Alicia Witt two-hander for special praise. 'Her slipping in and out of sanity could be played for quirky laughs, but Lynch – working in super sloooow mode – actually makes their co-dependent passion poignant; though unsettling as ever, it may be the most moving work he's ever done.' Wellman also praised Angelo Badalamenti's 'powerful yet near-subliminal scoring . . . ominous in "Tricks", jazzy in "Robert" and just on the cusp of transcendence in "Blackout".' Noting that HBO had only agreed to order more episodes if the initial broadcast was a success, Wellman suggested that this was 'as likely as a Laura Palmer resuscitation', and that fans would therefore be wise to 'catch it before checkout time'.

RATINGS: On its first broadcast, *Hotel Room* rated first in its time slot on HBO. This success, however, did not encourage the cable channel to produce further episodes.

EPISODE LOG

'Tricks'

Directed by David Lynch
Written by Barry Gifford
Edited by Mary Sweeney

Synopsis September, 1969. Moe Boca brings Darlene, a prostitute from Des Moines, Iowa, to room 603 of a New York hotel. Before he can make love to her, however, his 'friend' Lou Holchak interrupts them. Lou talks about his wife, Felicia, and son, Arthur. Moe talks about murdered movie star Martin Mustique, who shared a birthday with Felicia. Lou cajoles Darlene into performing an impromptu cheerleader routine, then makes love to her while Moe sits dejectedly nearby. Afterwards, Darlene talks about herself, and Lou seems to know something about her: that she stabbed her ex-boyfriend after following him to New York from Des Moines. When Lou goes to the bathroom, Moe tells Darlene that Felicia was *his* wife, not Lou's; furthermore, he seems to suggest that the boy Darlene almost stabbed to death was Arthur, his son. She denies it, but things turn ugly – Moe and Lou seem about to do her harm when the maid knocks on the door, and Darlene escapes. After she leaves, Moe tells Lou about a woman he met while delivering Chinese food as a teenager; as he listens, Lou slips his wallet into Moe's jacket. Lou leaves, warning Moe not to wait too long, but Moe falls asleep. He is woken by police, who, believing him to be Louis Holchak – Lou's wallet is in his jacket, Moe's picture is on Lou's driver's licence – arrest him for the murder of Felicia Boca.

'Getting Rid of Robert'

Written by Jay McInerney
Directed by James Signorelli
Edited by David Siegel

Synopsis June, 1992. Sasha, a thirty-something socialite, comes to room 603 with two girlfriends, and tells them that she intends to break up with her boyfriend, Robert, later that evening. By the time he gets there, Sasha has discovered that one of her friends had a fling with Robert, and the other wants to; what is more, Robert tells her *he* wants to end the relationship, because she is 'not a nice person.' Insulted, she brains him with an antique poker, before they effect a kind of reconciliation while he bleeds.

'Blackout'

Directed by David Lynch
Written by Barry Gifford
Edited by Toni Morgan

Synopsis April, 1936. In the middle of a city-wide blackout and an electrical thunderstorm, Danny brings his wife Diane to New York, where she is to see a doctor about her psychiatric problems, apparently caused by the accidental drowning of their son, Danny Junior, a.k.a. 'Dan-bug.' Diane's repression of the tragic incident, and the fact that she believes she can have no more children, causes her memory to play tricks on her. Nevertheless, during the blackout, Danny and Diane confront the reality of Dan-bug's death, and when they kiss, the electricity miraculously comes back on, suggesting that Diane's own blackout has been overcome, and that the future will be brighter.

TRIVIA: Lynch not only wrote the opening narration to *Hotel Room*, it is his voice we hear reading it.

Freddie Jones improvised his feigning of a heart attack in 'Tricks'.

A third story written by Gifford for *Hotel Room*, but unfilmed, is entitled 'Mrs Kashfi', and is set in 1952. It tells of a young boy who receives a visitation from his dead grandmother while accompanying his mother on a visit to the eponymous clairvoyant. The grandmother tells him that she left the key to a safety deposit box containing his 'future' – presumably a large sum of money – taped to the bottom of his toybox, and gives him instructions on how to recover the money without his free-spending mother's knowledge. However, since it has already been established that Mr De Witt, the boy's contact at the bank, is suffering from amnesia (recalling the principal theme of 'Tricks' and 'Blackout'), the boy's future remains uncertain. The play joins 'Tricks' and 'Blackout' in the *Hotel Room Trilogy* collection, published by the University Press of Mississippi in 1995.

APOCRYPHA: It is often assumed that HBO somehow amalgamated the first three episodes into a single feature-length show, instead of showing them separately as part of a series. In fact, *Hotel Room* was always intended to be broadcast as a feature-length pilot incorporating three stories, followed by subsequent episodes in the half-hour format – which, of course, never materialised.

Despite the fact that, in 'Tricks', the police officers identify Moe as Lou from the picture on a driving licence, there were no pictures on driving licences in 1969. 'That was absolutely not a mistake,' is Gifford's dubious response to being caught out. 'You've got to understand that it's fiction, and it really could have taken place in any year.' To add to the deliberate confusion about Moe's and Lou's seemingly interchangeable identities, 'Tricks' features a brief filmed insert of Lou placing his wallet inside Moe's jacket. This does not exist in the text, but was added by Lynch at the request of HBO executives, who did not fully understand the 'mistaken identity' aspect of the story without it. 'David thought that if he included the switching of the wallets, it would satisfy them,' Gifford continues. 'I said, "No, we don't need it," but he did it, and now every time that sequence comes up I close my eyes. But it doesn't matter,' he adds, 'because the whole idea of the confusion of identity is still there, and this just further confuses the issue, rather than clearing anything up. At least, that's how I prefer to think about it.'

AVAILABILITY: In the US, the three stories comprising the feature-length pilot were released by WorldVision as a single NTSC VHS (4192), although this is now deleted and difficult to find. The tape includes the longer version of 'Blackout', which has never been broadcast on HBO. 'David prefers the longer version,' Gifford remarks, 'as do most people who've seen it. And by all rights I should.

But I have to say I like the shorter version, too. I like the snappiness of it.'

In Japan, *David Lynch's Hotel Room* was released as a CLV laserdisc by Pony Canyon (PCLP-00506), in English with Japanese subtitles.

FINAL ANALYSIS: Although undoubtedly lesser works than many of his features, Lynch's contributions to *Hotel Room* are thematically significant stories, their puzzles as intricate as anything in *Eraserhead* or *Lost Highway*, and the fact that they remain either unseen or overlooked is a great loss to Lynchdom. In the filming of the stories, Lynch shows uncharacteristic restraint, shooting in an uncomplicated and unobtrusive two-camera style that allows Gifford's writing and the uniformly excellent performances to shine through, despite the limitations of the setting.

It is intriguing to wonder, yet impossible to say, how much 'Tricks' and 'Blackout' might have benefited from *Wild at Heart*-style flashbacks during the stories told by their characters. Certainly, such an enterprise would have opened out the episodes beyond the realm of the hotel room – and beyond the confines of the budget. Nevertheless, it should be said that Gifford's writing is evocative enough to make viewers *imagine* they have seen the things in these stories, and the power of his images is undeniable.

Although written and directed in a lively fashion, 'Getting Rid of Robert' has a major flaw when compared with the Lynch-Gifford segments: it simply does not fit. Its black humour feels far better suited to a *Tales From the Crypt*-style series, and sits uncomfortably between the other two episodes. Nevertheless, 'Tricks' and 'Blackout' are more than enough to make *Hotel Room* worth checking into.

EXPERT WITNESS: 'I think it's a great lost directorial work of David's. It has some wonderful performances, especially the performance by Glenne Headly, and Harry Dean Stanton, and Crispin Glover . . . And, of course, we had the great Freddie Jones . . . It was the perfect format, too. David did a great job and I'm really sorry we couldn't continue, and I know he was too' – screenwriter Barry Gifford

LYNCH ON *HOTEL ROOM*: 'I loved *Hotel Room*. I loved working on them. I think one script Barry wrote was eleven pages and one was seven or nine or something. I just thought they were fantastic, and so away we went. I don't know how much more overlooked they could be.'

Premonitions Following an Evil Deed (1996)

35mm short film / 50 secs / black and white / live action

Directed by David Lynch
Produced by Neal Edelstein
Cinematography by Peter Deming
Edited by Mary Sweeney
Wardrobe by Patricia Norris
Casting by Central Casting
Music by David Lynch & Angelo Badalamenti

UNCREDITED CAST: Jeff Alperi, Mark Wood, Stan Lothridge (*Cops*), Russ Pearlman (*Dead Son*), Pam Pierrocish (*Mother*), Clyde Small (*Father*), Joan Rurdlestein, Michale Carlyle, Kathleen Raymond (*Women*), Dawn Salcedo (*Woman in Tank*)

SUMMARY: Three police officers approach the body of a dead boy lying in a field. A woman sits anxiously in her home. Three beautiful women in white dresses lounge in a garden; one of them rises, and sudden concern crosses each of their faces. A group of impassive beings with overalls and misshapen faces walk through a laboratory in which a naked woman struggles vainly to escape from the tank of water in which she is submerged. Flames burn the frame through to the anxious woman and her male companion, both getting up to admit a police officer who appears to bring bad news.

PRODUCTION HISTORY: In 1995, one hundred years after the Lumière brothers, Louis and Auguste, publicly demonstrated the use of the first motion picture camera, the Cinématographe, forty international film directors – including Lynch, Patrice Leconte, Wim Wenders, Peter Greenaway, Spike Lee, Claude Lelouch, Liv Ullmann, Zhang Yimou, Bigas Luna, John Boorman and Arthur Penn – were invited to make a short film using the same camera.

The project was the brainchild of Philippe Poulet, the researcher at the Musée du Cinéma in Lyon, who restored an original Cinématographe, a lightweight wooden box containing a combination camera/projector, through which film is hand-cranked at the rate of at least two turns (between sixteen and twenty frames) per second. The emulsion used on the 35mm film also followed the Lumière brothers' recipe, although it was made of acetate rather than the more volatile nitrate.

For the directors, the 'rules' were simple: the film should be a continuous shot with a duration of 52 seconds (the precise length of the film reels used by the camera); there was to be no artificial light, and no synchronised sound (though a soundtrack could be added in post-production); a maximum of three takes was permitted. There were two further caveats: directors would not be able to view what they were filming through the camera (a limitation of the Cinématographe), and none of them would be paid for their labours (a limitation of the production funding).

Lynch's contribution required the construction of six sets, and reportedly cost him around $6,000 to make. 'I thought it was an honour to be asked to make a film with the original motion picture camera,' Lynch said, setting to work on what would effectively be a filmed recording of a live event, not unlike *Industrial Symphony No.1*. In *Lumière et Compagnie* (*Lumière & Company*), the documentary-style feature that shows each of the films, and the directors working on them, Lynch is seen at work on his contribution, which manages to include five location changes (courtesy of two extended fades to black, accomplished by manipulating the shutter and moving the camera to a new set-up, a fade to white, and a burn-out) and a complex narrative – without breaking any of the rules. 'It's about premonition,' is all he will say about the subject matter. The title, however, reveals more.

'One of the things that strikes me is how exciting it must have been to have been a film-maker in the early days of cinema,' he once said, 'because not only was it so magical to see paintings begin to move, but they could start altering time.'

THE LYNCH MOB: For the brief but complex shoot, Lynch assembled a group of trusted long-term associates, including producer and business partner Neal Edelstein, composer Angelo Badalamenti (*Blue Velvet* onwards), cinematographer Peter Deming (*On the Air*, *Hotel Room*), costume designer Patricia Norris (*The Elephant Man* onwards) and *Fire Walk With Me* editor Mary Sweeney, also his long-term partner.

SOUND AND MUSIC: *Premonitions Following an Evil Deed* features two new Lynch/Badalamenti compositions, 'Mysterious Morning' and 'FRANCK 2000'.

DÉJÀ VU: Any Lynch project that begins with the discovery of a body cannot help but put one in mind of *Twin Peaks*.

WHAT THE PAPERS SAID: *Lumière et Compagnie* debuted at the AFI Film Festival in the spring of 1996, and was given a limited theatrical release in the US the same year. (It missed the anniversary year by several months.) 'David Lynch's ingenious showstopper plays like a cross between *Creature from the Black Lagoon . . .* and *Intolerance*,' *Variety* said of Lynch's contribution. 'An unsettling *tour de force* [which] defies literal interpretation,' commented the *Los Angeles Times*. 'Suffice to say he packs a lot into fifty seconds, including a dead body, what appear to be mutants flagellating a glass enclosure that contains a naked woman, a couple sitting in a living room, and the arrival of the police.'

TRIVIA: Although Lynch says that the films were supposed to be titled, the titles do not appear in *Lumière et Compagnie*.

AVAILABILITY: *Lumière et Compagnie* is available in subtitled/English-language editions in the US, as an NTSC VHS (6304287356) and a Region 1 DVD (FLV 5013). The DVD has a useful facility that allows viewers to jump directly to particular directors' contributions, beginning with the behind-the-scenes shots of them making the short films.

FINAL ANALYSIS: Lynch's first short film since the 70s – and, indeed, his shortest ever, if commercials are discounted – is almost as ambitious as any he had previously attempted, and certainly the most ambitious of the entire *Lumière et Compagnie* project. From its opening discovery of a dead body, through the disturbing SF/S&M imagery of the premonition itself, Lynch manages to convey a more complex narrative, and a greater intensity of feeling, than most two-hour Hollywood features.

EXPERT WITNESS: 'It was very interesting. Their parameters were that it be shot with their handcranked camera that was basically just a box, with no viewing system whatsoever, aside from opening the camera and looking through the lens. The ASA was about 20. No electric lights and no live sound. And no cuts. David designed an apparatus in front of the lens to black out between sets. The camera was put on a dolly and track and we dollied from set to set. The shot you see was done in real time (check out the actress in parts 2 and 5!) in one take. There was a limit of three takes. It took us about four hours to set and the temperature was over a hundred degrees.' – cinematographer Peter Deming

LYNCH ON *PREMONITIONS FOLLOWING AN EVIL DEED*: 'It was a great experience. Pure heaven. I love restrictions, and this had a bunch of restrictions! And the camera is super-cool, as an object. The first motion picture camera, supposedly. It was just a great experience.'

Lost Highway (1997)

35mm feature film / 135 mins / colour / live action

Directed by David Lynch
Written by David Lynch & Barry Gifford
Produced by Deepak Nayar, Tom Sternberg, Mary Sweeney
Director of Photography Peter Deming
Production Designer / Costume Designer Patricia Norris
Edited by Mary Sweeney
Music Composed and Conducted by Angelo Badalamenti
Casting by Johanna Ray, CSA and Elaine J. Huzzar

CAST: Bill Pullman (*Fred Madison*), Patricia Arquette (*Renee Madison/Alice Wakefield*), Balthazar Getty (*Peter Raymond Dayton*), Robert Blake (*Mystery Man*), Natasha Gregson Wagner (*Sheila*), Richard Pryor (*Arnie*), Lucy Butler (*Candace Dayton*), Michael Massee (*Andy*), Jack Nance (*Phil*), Jack Kehler (*Guard Johnny Mack*), Henry Rollins (*Guard Henry*), Giovanni Ribisi (*Steve 'V' Vincenzio*), Scott Coffey (*Teddy*), Gary Busey (*William 'Bill' Dayton*), Robert Loggia (*Mr Eddy / Dick Laurent*), John Roselius (*Al*), Lou Eppolito (*Ed*), Jenna Maitland (*Party Girl*), Michael Shamus Wiles (*Guard Mike*), Mink Stole (*Forewoman*), Leonard Termo (*Judge*), Ivory Ocean (*Guard Ivory*), David Byrd (*Doctor Smordin*), Gene Ross (*Warden Clements*), F. William Parker (*Captain Luneau*), Guy Siner (*Prison Official #1*), Alexander Folk (*Prison Official #2*), Carl Sundstrom (*Hank*), John Solari (*Lou*), Jack (*The Dog*), Al Garrett (*Carl Broling*), Heather Stephens (*Lanie*), Amanda Anka (*Girl #1*), Jennifer Syme (*Junkie Girl*), Matt Sigloch (*Assistant #1*), Gil Combs (*Assistant #2*), Greg Travis (*Tail Gate Driver*), Lisa Boyle (*Marian*), Leslie Bega (*Raquel*), Marilyn Manson (*Porno Star #1*), Twiggy Ramirez (*Porno Star #2*)

TITLE SEQUENCE: The driving drum-and-bass and haunting vocals of David Bowie's 'I'm Deranged' – which opens with the line 'Funny how secrets travel' – plays over clean-moving point-of-view shots, apparently taken at night from a moving vehicle, of a two-lane highway, with double yellow lines running down the middle. Each of the credits appears, in sequence, in large yellow italicised capitals, rushing towards us, holding for a moment on the screen, then continuing past our point of view. As the credits end, the song fades to a soft echo and the screen dims to blackness, as though the car headlights have been killed.

SUMMARY: Free-jazz saxophonist Fred Madison and his possibly adulterous wife Renee receive a series of anonymous videotapes, first of their house, but later of their sleeping forms. The police are called. At a party, Fred meets a Mystery Man whom no one else can see. When the next videotape shows a butchered Renee, Fred is arrested, convicted and put on death row. In prison, racked with remorse, Fred constructs an alternate reality for himself, disappearing into a psychogenic fugue – an amnesiac/schizoid state from which he may or may not return – and emerging as a young car mechanic named 'Pete Dayton'. In Fred's mind, this metamorphosis gets him released from prison, but no sooner is he free than the relics of his previous identity begin to haunt him: Renee reappears in the guise of the blonde Alice Wakefield, moll to a violent pornographer named Mr Eddy. The two begin a passionate affair. Alice convinces him to join her in a robbery – which, in turn, leads to murder – but after the crime, she rejects him. Faced with the disintegrating life of this alternative identity, 'Pete' reverts to Fred and kills Mr Eddy while the Mystery Man (the manifestation of Fred's psychosis) videotapes them. After this latest murder, Fred is pursued across a desert highway by police, returning the Möbius-strip narrative to its point of origin.

SOURCE: Although *Lost Highway* was an original screenplay by Lynch and *Wild at Heart* author Barry Gifford, the title had its origin in Gifford's 1992 novel *Night People*, a violent satire about two lesbian lovers who, after being released from the prison in which they met, set off across America on a kind of immoral crusade, kidnapping and killing random men in the name of their saviour, 'Miss Jesus'. Lynch read the novel shortly after publication and immediately expressed an interest in filming it, not least because his daughter Jennifer wanted to play one of the story's serial killers. Gifford says that Lynch optioned the book, 'but I think, at the time, he didn't want to do something that was so graphic.' Instead, Gifford proposed that they collaborate on something original.

PRODUCTION HISTORY: With the passage of time, Lynch realised that what he liked most about *Night People* was the concept of the 'lost highway', which Gifford had borrowed from a Hank Williams song of that title. The phrase comes from an exchange between Betty Salcrup and her partner in crime, Cutie Early. 'Cutie,' says Betty, 'we just a couple Apaches ridin' wild on the lost highway, the one Hank Williams sang about.' 'Don't know that I've ever heard of it,' says Cutie. 'Travellin' along the way we are, without no home or reason to be or stay anywhere, that's what it means bein' on the lost highway.' As Lynch elaborated, 'It's just a dreamy thing. It evokes all kinds of things in your head . . .' He was determined that he and Barry should write something together. Although Gifford was keen, nothing happened for a long while.

During that time, Lynch worked on numerous commercials and several stillborn projects, including *The Metamorphosis* and *The Dream of the Bovine* [see 'In Dreams,' pages 243, 246], before returning to the lost highway – much to Gifford's surprise. 'David called up and he said, "Barry, we've got to write a movie,"' the author recalled. 'So I said, "Okay, but, you know, I'm working on this new novel right now, I can't really do it now." He said, "No, Barry, we have to write a movie, and we have to do it *now!*"' In the meantime, Lynch had grown attached to an idea he had had in the car, while driving home with Mary Sweeney on the last night of shooting *Fire Walk with Me*. As Sweeney recalls, 'We were shooting somewhere out in the Valley, and he was meditating at a break. After we wrapped, I was driving him home, and he told me that he got this idea about somebody getting videotapes being dropped off at their door in an anonymous package; videotapes of them inside their home.' Gifford says that Lynch already had an idea about the character of Mr Eddy, 'so we had this one line from *Night People* – "You and me can really out-ugly the sumbitches" – which sounded like something Mr Eddy would have said, and the phrase "lost highway".' It was enough.

Although both Lynch and Gifford had previously collaborated with other writers, they had never written anything together: *Wild at Heart* was adapted by Lynch, while *Hotel Room* was written by Gifford. Both found it to be a rewarding experience. 'It was great,' Lynch told *Cinefantastique*. 'I trust Barry's instincts. We like similar things and had a great time.'

'We wrote it all in my studio in West Berkeley, over a period of a couple of months,' Gifford adds. 'We worked very intensively from nine in the morning – when David would call up and say, "I'll be there in seven minutes," and seven minutes later he'd come walking through the door – until six or seven that night.' Gifford suggests that it would be 'unseemly' to delineate who had written what; the process, he explains, was far more organic than that. 'We don't say, "He wrote this line and I wrote this line." We wrote the story together. We each came up with different aspects of the story that then were integrated and blended into the screenplay.'

After the failure of *Fire Walk With Me*, Lynch's production partner CIBY-2000 was understandably cautious about backing the next feature of its three-picture deal with Lynch. In order to convince them, he and Gifford wrote a treatment, which was presented to CIBY-2000 before they started working together on the actual script. But since neither of the writers knew what shape *Lost Highway* would ultimately take, it was difficult for CIBY-2000 to know what to make of it. Thus, although the second draft of the script was finished in March 1995, and the shooting script finalised in June, it was not until November of that year that principal photography began, winding up on 16 February of the following year.

Cinematographer Peter Deming says Lynch had definite ideas about what he wanted for *Lost Highway*, but mostly left the interpretation of those ideas to him. 'Being a painter, David has a very good eye for both light and composition,' Deming explains. 'When we talked about things, it would be more in terms of story and emotion, and he would leave it up to me to interpret that. I'm kind of on a similar wavelength to David in terms of things that I like in film, and a lot of times, particularly in *Lost Highway*, you might have an idea of how things are going to look. And then when you get to set, and the scene is rehearsed and played out in front of you, you have to completely change it because it doesn't fit the tone of how the scene is being played.'

Deming says that it was necessary to shoot pre-production tests on only two of the scenes: the desert love scene between Alice (Patricia Arquette) and Pete (Balthazar Getty), which would be deliberately over-exposed; and the scene in which Fred Madison (Bill Pullman) walks down a hallway and disappears into black. 'Normally you would try and separate people from the background by putting a little backlight on them,' he says. 'But we thought it was subtly creepy to have people coming in and out of black, or standing there and becoming part of the background, and to have the audience not really knowing what could come out of the black, so you're anticipating stuff.' Understandably, Deming needed to work closely with the laboratory which processed the film, so that film which had been deliberately over- or under-exposed would not be 'corrected'.

When production wrapped in early 1996, Lynch embarked on one of the longest post-production periods on any of his films since *Dune*. Ever mindful of his 'it's not finished till it's finished' philosophy, Lynch eventually deemed the film complete, delivering it to the distributor in time for a February 1997 release – too late for Academy Award consideration; too early for the international exposure provided by the Cannes Film Festival. Lynch was not about to bow to external pressures, whether from financiers, distributors, studio executives, release dates, festivals or award qualification periods. 'There's never any outside force that keeps you from making the film the way it wants to be,' says Lynch, who, along with Woody Allen, is probably the only director to enjoy final cut despite the fact that their films are mostly unprofitable. 'If there's a thing like that, then you should stop. You always think you're gonna get it into Cannes,' he adds, 'but if you're gonna get it into Cannes at the expense of the film, then you're stupid, and you'll hurt the film, and you'll kill yourself.'

CASTING: With Bill Pullman and Patricia Arquette in the lead roles, *Lost Highway* was clearly cast closer to the mainstream than any Lynch project save *Wild at Heart*. Pullman, like Nicolas Cage, remains one of the very few actors who has truly managed to combine commercial and critical success, thanks to a diversity of films ranging from blockbusters like *Independence Day* (1996) to low-key arthouse films like Wim Wenders's *End of Violence* (1997). Pullman was always Lynch's first choice for the role of Fred Madison, for reasons he made clear to the actor. 'David has said that he thought that it was important to have a guy who the audience wouldn't give up on,' Pullman recounted, 'because Fred gets accused of murdering his wife, and there's a lot of evidence that suggests he did. But, you see, he's wrestling with a demon, and you're concerned for him at the same time.'

Pullman was also instrumental in the casting of Robert Loggia (*Prizzi's Honor*, 1985) as Mr Eddy, having given the actor a copy of the *Lost Highway* script while the two were co-starring in *Independence Day* (1996), and suggesting that the role was perfect for him. Loggia, however, remembered how he had lost his temper with Lynch during a reading for the role of Frank Booth in *Blue Velvet*. 'I said, "Well, there's not a rat's ass chance that I'm going to be in that play",' Loggia said, '"because David Lynch has got to, you know, remember that happening and not want a damn thing to do with me." But paradoxically, I think, my berserk/meanness/junkyard dog/ferocious/rabid attitude [was] maybe what David had in mind for Mr Eddy.'

When it came to casting the Mystery Man, Lynch had only one actor in mind: Robert Blake, best known as one of the two stars of Richard Brooks's 1967 adaptation of Truman Capote's 'true novel' *In Cold Blood*. 'He just said, "Hey, I want you to play this",' Blake recalled. 'I have no idea why! I read the script like nine fuckin' times, and I didn't understand one fuckin' word of it!' The actor found Lynch less than forthcoming when quizzed about the specifics of the Mystery Man's character. 'I realised that he really is too much of an artist to be that specific about things,' Blake added, adding that he found Lynch's directorial style refreshingly different: liberating, but sometimes terrifying. '[Most directors] want the spine of the character, and the subtext, the conflict, the psycho-neurotic mumbo-jumbo, and all of that . . . He doesn't do anything that directors, as such, do. He really speaks an entirely different language.'

THE LYNCH MOB: Actor Scott Coffey would have appeared in *Wild at Heart*, had his scenes not been deleted; thus, *Lost Highway* features only one other actor who had actually been seen in a Lynch film before: Jack Nance, who had appeared in virtually every Lynch project since he agreed to take the lead role in *Eraserhead* back in 1971. Nance's appearance in *Lost Highway* was his last film project; he died from complications caused by a fall – outside a doughnut shop, of all places – on 30 December 1996. 'In *Lost Highway* there is only one scene (the mechanic who loves free-jazz on the radio) but it is memorable,' Lynch said of his friend's last performance. 'I'm not even sure that he had the chance to see *Lost Highway* [finished].'

Behind the camera, there were many more familiar faces. In addition to co-screenwriter Barry Gifford, the crew included producer and unit production manager Deepak Nayar (second assistant director on *Wild at Heart*, first assistant director on *Fire Walk With Me*, producer of *On the Air* and *Hotel Room*), *Fire Walk With Me* editor Mary Sweeney (now also producer, and Lynch's off-screen partner), cinematographer Peter Deming (*On the Air*, *Hotel Room*, *Premonitions Following an Evil Deed*), production and costume designer Patricia Norris (*The Elephant Man* onwards), casting director Johanna Ray (*Blue Velvet* onwards) and composer Angelo Badalamenti (*Blue Velvet* onwards). Eric DaRe, who had played Leo Johnson in *Twin Peaks* and *Fire Walk With Me*, is also credited, as 'Buyer/Swing.'

MEMORABLE QUOTES

Fred: 'There you were . . . lying in bed . . . but it wasn't you . . . It looked like you . . . but it wasn't.'

Mystery Man: 'We've met before, haven't we?'
Fred: 'I don't think so. Where was it you think we met?'
Mystery Man: 'At your house, don't you remember?
Fred: 'No, no, I don't. Are you sure?
Mystery Man: 'Of course. As a matter of fact, I'm there right now.'

Mr Eddy: 'I'm sorry about that, Pete. But tailgating is one thing I cannot tolerate.'

Pete Dayton: 'I want you . . . I want you . . . I want you . . .'
Alice: 'You'll never have me.'

Fred Madison: 'Where's Alice?'
Mystery Man: 'Alice who? Her name is Renee! If she told you her name was Alice, she was lying. And your name . . . *WHAT THE FUCK IS YOUR NAME?*'

Al: 'I think there's no such thing as a bad coincidence.'

SOUND AND MUSIC: Lynch has always said that sound is one of the key elements in his own style of film-making; certainly, there are precious few other directors who spend months of post-production working on sound elements alone. The results of this uncommon dedication can be seen – or rather *heard* – to great effect in *Lost Highway*, which was made at a time when the sound systems in cinemas were finally beginning to keep pace with Lynch's aspirations. (At the first preview screening in the UK, in the screening room of London's Planet Hollywood, Lynch had the projectionist set the volume a notch or two higher than normal, to emphasise the background drones and other almost subliminal effects.)

Yet again, David chose Angelo Badalamenti to compose music for the film, although in this case, a great many pre-existing songs were used, along with several instrumental tracks by Barry Adamson, who receives a credit for additional music. 'It's a very dark score,' Badalamenti said of his *Lost Highway* music, '[because] it's a kind of a dark movie. But even in its uneasiness and disturbing nature there's a beauty, and that's what we're looking for.' Badalamenti's music was recorded by the Film Symphony Orchestra of Prague, with whom Lynch and his composer had collaborated during post-production on *Blue Velvet* and to whom they would return in late 2000 to record music for *Mulholland Drive*. 'They're a great bunch,' Lynch enthuses. 'On *Lost Highway* I thought it was the same orchestra, but there was only one player that had been at the *Blue Velvet* session.' Nevertheless, he adds, 'there's something about the way they play Angelo's stuff.'

For Badalamenti, the atmosphere of the Czech studio perfectly captured the mood of the film. 'You come onto a very quiet street and you go into this place with these gigantic doors [which] must weigh a thousand pounds each,' he recounted. 'Everything was kind of muted tones and sepia colours.' Working closely with engineer John Ross, Lynch experimented with recording techniques, just as he had during his innovative sound work on *Eraserhead*, placing microphones inside bottles and lengths of plastic tubing to try to capture a unique sound. 'John Ross is the best digital thinker I've ever run across,' Lynch stated. 'He knows everything about every wire . . . plus his talents for music mixing, and he really has a total grasp of the whole digital world.'

The *Lost Highway* soundtrack album (IND-90090) was produced by Trent Reznor and executive produced by David Lynch, and includes two versions of David Bowie's 'I'm Deranged'; 'Videodrones: Questions' and 'Driver Down' by Trent Reznor; 'The Perfect Drug' by Nine Inch Nails; 'Eye' by The Smashing Pumpkins; 'Something Wicked this Way Comes,' 'Hollywood Sunset,' 'Mr Eddy's Theme 1' and 'Mr Eddy's Theme 2' by Barry Adamson; Lou Reed's 'This Magic Moment'; edited versions of Rammstein's 'Rammstein' and 'Hierate

Mich'; Marilyn Manson's 'I Put a Spell on You' and 'Apple of Sodom'; Antonio Carlos Jobim's 'Insensatez'; and the following tracks by Angelo Badalamenti: 'Red Bats with Teeth', 'Haunting & Heartbreaking', 'Dub Driving', 'Fred and Renee Make Love', 'Fats Revisited', 'Fred's World' and 'Police'. Only one track heard in the film is not included: 'Song to the Siren' by This Mortal Coil, originally planned for inclusion in *Blue Velvet*.

INFLUENCED BY: The influences of *film noir* on *Lost Highway* are obvious. It contains a number of elements – a jazz musician, a gangster with seedy connections, a Mystery Man, a 40s Cadillac, two *femmes fatales*, both with 40s hairstyles – common to the genre. As James Naremore noted, *Lost Highway* 'brims with allusions to three decades of noir, which it uses to create a dream narrative . . . Almost every image and every character in the film has an archetypal quality: a nocturnal road out of *Detour* [1945] and *Psycho* [1960]; a "Lost Highway Motel", where a woman may or may not be dead; an exploding house on stilts like the one in *Kiss Me Deadly* [1955]; an alienated jazz musician who might be a killer; a brooding rebel-without-a-cause who lusts after a gun moll; a sadistic gangster who is obsessed with porn movies and prostitutes; a woman's mutilated body, reminiscent of the Black Dahlia; and not one but two *femmes fatales*.' No single influence stands out, although Gifford is fond of describing *Lost Highway* as '*Double Indemnity* meets Orpheus and Eurydice,' referring to Billy Wilder's 1944 adaptation of James M. Cain's novel – in which a conniving woman, apparently unhappily married, contrives with an insurance salesman to have her husband murdered for the insurance money – and the Greek Orpheus myth, popularised in Jean Cocteau's *Orphée* (1949), in which a musician goes to Hades to reclaim his dead wife, only to be tricked into giving her back.

The dual-personality motif, elongated corridors, unseemly hotel rooms, even the overall colouring of the film might be said to have been influenced by Stanley Kubrick's 1980 adaptation of Stephen King's horror novel *The Shining,* which, significantly, features a black-and-white photograph that reveals the identity of one of the characters, and involves a supernaturally assisted escape from confinement (in *The Shining*, Jack's escape from a locked freezer; in *Lost Highway*, Fred's release from prison). 'I love *The Shining*,' Lynch admits, although he falls short of acknowledging its influence on *Lost Highway*. 'If I see it on TV, no matter what else is on, I have to watch it. And it just gets better and better. And yet when it came out, it didn't make that much of a noise. But that's the way it always was with Kubrick's stuff. It's pretty amazing how they grow. I like everything he's done.'

LEGACY: *Lost Highway* may not have been well received upon its initial release (see below), but it has already proved the subject of a great many analyses. In 1999, film theorist Slavoj Zizek, who teaches at the University of Ljubljana in his native Slovenia, published *The Art of the Ridiculous Sublime: On David Lynch's 'Lost Highway'*, an in-depth analysis of the film. 'There's also a course taught about *Lost Highway* at the University of Southern California in San Diego,' Barry Gifford reveals. 'A French professor, who wrote this huge exegesis on *Lost Highway* and sent it to me and to Lynch, has been teaching it there for some years. His essay is really as full of shit as anything I've ever seen in my life. But it's funny because one of my sons took the course, and he got an A.' Gifford sees this academic analysis as evidence that *Lost Highway* will continue to fascinate, and provoke debate, for years to come. 'In the long run,' he says, 'I think *Lost Highway* is going to continue to provoke a lot of thought and comment, as people see new things in it. The movie endures, it's taken very seriously, and it stands out in Lynch's oeuvre.'

DÉJÀ VU: Shots of yellow lines down a two-lane highway at night recall similar shots in *Blue Velvet* and *Wild at Heart*. The screen filled with white noise recalls the beginning of *Fire Walk With Me*, while the close-up of Alice's bright red lips recalls a similar shot of Dorothy's mouth in *Blue Velvet*. Fred Madison's appearance recalls the beatnik sax-player in the final episode of *On the Air*, while Andy's slicked-back hair and pencil-thin moustache make him a dead ringer for *Wild at Heart*'s own pornographer, Bobby Peru. The red curtains in the Madison house – and the shadow that passes across the inside of the house – recall the billowing curtains in Dorothy's apartment in *Blue Velvet*, and the Red Room sequences of *Twin Peaks*. The scene in which Fred and Renee look for each other in the apartment recalls Agent Cooper's hunt for Phillip Jeffries in *Fire Walk With Me*.

More thematically, Fred's killing of Renee while apparently gripped by psychosis recalls Leland Palmer's murder of his daughter, Laura. Pete Dayton's observation of the garden next door to his house recalls the opening scene of *Blue Velvet*; even the Jack Russell terrier looks familiar. Pete himself reminds us of Bobby Briggs and James Hurley in *Twin Peaks*; his name, like Hurley's, was also chosen to indicate his interests (Hurley = Harley, Dayton = Daytona). Obviously, the brunette and blonde played by the same actress (Patricia Arquette) recall the Laura Palmer/Madeleine Ferguson likeness in *Twin Peaks*. In addition, Alice's affair with Pete has striking parallels with auto mechanic James Hurley's dalliance with Evelyn Marsh, a blonde married to a wealthy thug, in later episodes of *Twin Peaks*.

Perhaps more intriguingly, given the fact that *Lost Highway* was co-written by Barry Gifford, are the undeniable similarities to the 'Tricks' strand of *Hotel Room*, a tale intended, according to Gifford's stage direction, to give the impression of being 'one or two steps removed from reality.' In the story, a man we believe to be named Moe Boca – but who may actually be named Louis Holchak, even though a man by this name appears in the same story – is arrested for the murder of Felicia Boca, whom we have come to believe is, or was, Moe's wife. The overall impression we are given is that after killing his wife, Moe Boca has taken refuge in another personality, that of Louis Holchak, even though the two men are actually one and the same. The echoes of this story in *Lost Highway* are undeniable, and it is fitting that Moe/Lou's final dialogue lines in 'Tricks' are 'I don't understand! I don't! I don't understand!'

THEMES AND MOTIFS: When *Lost Highway* was being readied for release, Lynch was characteristically tight-lipped about its meaning, limiting his description of the film to the phrase 'psychogenic fugue' – 'psychogenic' meaning 'having origin in the mind' and 'fugue' being a musical term in which one theme starts and is taken up by a second theme. 'Fugue' is also used as a medical term to describe a particular kind of schizoid amnesiac psychosis. 'It sounds like such a beautiful thing – "psychogenic fugue",' Lynch, who latched onto the phrase after a unit publicist discovered it in a medical journal, commented. 'It has music and it has a certain force and dreamlike quality. I think it's beautiful, even if it didn't mean anything . . . I think they call it a "psychogenic fugue" because it goes from one thing, segues to another, and then I think it comes back again,' he added. 'And so it *is Lost Highway*.'

Lynch's reliance on the phrase, as though it explained everything, did not win him favour from critics, many of whom found the film confusing at best; at worst, impenetrable. It also created problems for co-screenwriter Barry Gifford who, faced with Lynch's reluctance to explain the film, found himself under increasing pressure to do so. 'David and I pledged never to explain the movie,' he admits, 'and I don't think it needs explanation at all. It was never meant to confuse.' He adds, 'It's a very serious movie, and everything was very well thought out. The structure is complex. Everything had to add up.'

Nevertheless, Gifford *did* explain the film, to *Cinefantastique*: 'Fred Madison creates this counter world and goes into it, because the crime he has committed is so terrible that he can't face it. This fugue state allows him to create a fantasy world, but within this fantasy world, the same problems occur. In other words, he's no better at maintaining this relationship, dealing with or controlling this woman, than he was in his real life. The woman isn't who he thinks she is, really, so all the so-called facts of his known life with Renee pop up again in Alice Wakefield.' As for the Mystery Man, he added, 'he's a product of Fred's imagination, too.' Asked about this apparent betrayal of his and Lynch's conspiracy of silence, Gifford is evasive. 'What I meant to convey is that that's only one way to think about it,' he says. 'That's just one possible explanation. I'm not trying to cop out in any way,' he adds, 'but you can say, "Oh yes, it's a guy who goes crazy and has some kind of psychotic episode, and a schizophrenic split," but there are many things in there that don't fit easily into that category, including the ending.' He corrects himself. 'Or end*ings*.'

CUT SCENES: The first cut of *Lost Highway* – privately screened for a hand-picked audience of fifty demographically diverse people – ran at two and a half hours; Lynch and his editor, Mary Sweeney, knew that the running time had to be trimmed, but were less certain about what should be cut. 'We're like mesmerised chickens,' Mary Sweeney says of this stage of post-production. 'We're so loving the material, and have worked so long on it already, we have really lost any freshness, so it's time to get other people in.'

Thus, Sweeney arranged her own version of a Hollywood test screening, hand-picking an audience of fifty 'friends who are normal entertainment moviegoers, people preferably who've never read the script or seen anything and are not familiar with the project' to sit with herself and Lynch so that the film-makers could try to learn from the audience's reaction. 'It's always a hard thing to get David to do,' Sweeney admits, 'but I've gotten him into the very difficult habit of letting me show it to a group of people who we know, but who don't stack the deck. It's a very valuable part of the process, because . . . when you get out there with people and you feel these long silent gaps, and people shifting in their seats, you can feel slow areas in ways you don't otherwise.'

The scenes detailed here are those that appeared in the script dated 21 June 1995 but did not make it to the final cut. Since Barry Gifford, who was present for most of the shooting, confirms that almost all of these scenes were filmed, the following can be taken as a good guide to the additional material which appeared in the original 150-minute cut:

- After watching the first videotape, Fred questions Renee about the book she is reading, asking if it was the same one she was reading when she failed to make it to the club. (The subtext is that he suspects that she is having an affair.)
- After watching the second videotape, the two detectives discuss the camera angles, with some expertise. (This was probably a joke aimed squarely at the cine-literate Hollywood police.)
- In the script, Andy's party takes place before the third videotape

arrives, and it is this tape that reveals the murder. The screenplay inserts another tape between the second and third, which Fred and Renee watch together, and which contains a tormented image of Fred. The detectives return, asking more questions and promising to double the patrol of the house. Renee says she would feel safer in a hotel. Fred reveals that for the last two nights he forgot to set the alarm system and, anyway, he hates the idea of acting paranoid. Renee blows up at this, but the detectives promise to get to the bottom of the mystery.

- Shortly after entering the house after Andy's party, Renee tells Fred that when she was waiting outside in the car she had a feeling of déjà vu.
- A scripted scene set at the city morgue, placed just after Fred's brutal interrogation, was deleted in its entirety. George, the medical examiner, attends Renee's corpse while dressed in a tuxedo and accompanied by his girlfriend, Joyce. Individual parts of Renee's body are wrapped and identified. 'Just like Christmas,' George says grimly, examining the mutilated body while Joyce smokes and steps nervously in place, like a spooked horse. 'Easy, girl, easy,' George says. 'You talking to me or . . . her?' Joyce replies. 'A corpse can tell you plenty, Joyce.' (According to Barry Gifford, this was one scene that nobody wanted to lose. 'I thought it was a wonderful scene,' he says. 'But I wasn't there when they were shooting it – it was one of the few scenes that I missed – but David said that the corpse itself looked bad. There was some bad production value, and he just didn't like the way it all looked. So he cut it, and it's a shame, because it was really a sequence that should have been in the movie. But David is very exacting, and I trust him.')
- The script shows the jury's female foreman finding Fred guilty of murder in the first degree, and the judge's death sentence; in the film, portions of this dialogue play over Fred's walk to jail.
- Directly after this scene, the script includes another, in which two exquisite young women, Marian and Raquel, discuss the Madison murder as they try on lingerie in a store. After discussing in grisly detail the relative merits and disadvantages of death by firing squad or hanging, Andy arrives to collect Marian.
- After the montage of scenes showing Fred in prison, he listens in horror as a prisoner named Sammy G is led to the electric chair, ribbed good-naturedly by his fellow inmates. The script cuts back to Fred's cell just as the lever is thrown. The lights dim almost to nothing. There were some reaction shots of Fred imagining the execution, and although the execution was dropped, Lynch used the shots of Fred reacting for his transformation into Pete Dayton instead.
- The script shows several other instances of Fred's headaches.

- During one of Fred's fever dreams, the script cuts to a scene in which Marian and Raquel are dancing, 'as sexy and wild as it is possible for them to be,' in the lingerie they purchased earlier. Andy lies on the floor, strung out.
- Just after the discovery of Pete Dayton in Fred's cell, the guard named (in the script and end credits) as 'Johnny Mack' alerts a 'Captain Henderson' to the situation. (In the film, 'Henderson' is renamed 'Luneau'.)
- After Mack's 'spooky shit' line, the script cuts to the prison warden's office, where Henderson and warden Marshall R. Clements address the mystery of Fred's apparent escape. This scene is followed by another excised sequence, in which Dr Rogoff confirms that the man brought in by Henderson is not Fred Madison. The man is staring straight up as the warden asks him, 'Where the hell did you come from, mister?'
- The scene in which Pete Dayton is identified continues as Henderson, the warden and the two prison officials discuss Fred's disappearance, and learn that the story has been leaked to the press. After a brief examination of Fred's cell by Johnny Mack, the warden gives a press conference, assuring the reporters that Fred will be recaptured soon. Understandably, no mention is made of the manner of his disappearance, or of Pete Dayton.
- The script adds several pages of dialogue to the handover of Pete to his parents, a scene played silently in the film. Pete's father tells the warden that Pete was in good physical health when they last saw him two days earlier. Dr Mel Rogoff informs them that Pete has a hematoma on his forehead and blepharitis – 'redness and swelling around the eyes' – symptoms that do not suggest that he was in a fight. In addition, Rogoff tells them that Pete cannot talk, or *won't*, and that he has experienced some form of trauma. When Pete's parents fail to shed any light on the mystery, they are reunited with their son, whose first words are, understandably, 'Where am I?' He denies any knowledge of Fred Madison, and the prison officials reluctantly agree to release Pete into his parents' custody.
- As Pete relaxes on a chaise longue in his garden, the script includes an interior in which the camera moves through the Daytons' house as shadows play over the walls.
- Immediately following this, the script adds a scene in which Pete's parents question him further about the events of the night before he 'showed up in the slammer.' They seem to know something he doesn't.
- When Carl, 'V' and Lanie come to pick up Pete, the dialogue continues as Lanie relates the story of an ovarian cyst she had removed. She shows Pete the scar. V suggests that they go to 'Tops'

or the 'Ten Pen', and Pete seems bothered by the fact that Sheila will
be at 'Tops'.
- Between Pete's departure with his friends and the bowling alley
where he meets Sheila, the script includes a scene in which the group
cruise Van Nuys Boulevard in V's souped-up but beaten-up
automobile, while Pete (previously established in the script, but not
the film, as a mechanic) complains about the way the car is running.
They pull into the parking lot outside Tops, where Pete reluctantly
meets Sheila outside (not inside as in the film).
- The script adds a brief but important exchange between Pete and
Sheila, which follows Sheila asking what happened to his face:

<pre>
                   SHEILA
You've been acting strange lately . . .
Like the other night.
                   PETE
What night?
                   SHEILA
Last time I saw you.
                   PETE
I don't remember . . . What happened that
night?
                   SHEILA
You sure weren't acting like the Pete
Dayton I've always known.
                   PETE
Whatya mean?
                   SHEILA
You were acting like a different person.
Pete laughs, but Sheila doesn't.
                   PETE
Who else could I be?
Sheila stares seriously at Pete, but then
laughs too.
</pre>

- The script indicates that several of Arnie (Richard Pryor)'s dialogue
lines were improvised.
- In the script, Pete drives to Sheila's house, and later makes love to
her, after he meets Alice for the first time.
- As Pete and Alice drive from their first motel liaison, she spots a car
she thinks may be tailing them (Ed and Al). Pete manages to lose
them.
- Between the shots of Pete on his Harley and his next lovemaking
session with Sheila, the script includes another intriguing scene cut

from the finished film. At 'Tops', Pete meets Carl and V, but when Sheila looks Pete's way, she does not see him. Pete watches her dance. Suddenly, he can't see her. He thinks maybe she may be dancing on the other side of the building – out of view. As he moves to look, his head is struck by a violent pain. When 'V' asks him if he is OK, Pete doesn't seem to recognize him. Pete shakes his head to drive out the pain, and when he looks over again for Sheila, he sees her there dancing with her girlfriend. The scene continues as some drunk guys start molesting Sheila and her friend, and Pete (in a scene reminiscent of *Wild at Heart*) rescues them. When the fight is over, Sheila asks where Pete came from, and he tells her that he was here all along, and how she looked right through him.

- After Pete's father tells him about the man who was with him the night Sheila brought him home, Pete calls Sheila to quiz her. (Although she seems to give him some information, the audience hears only Pete's side of the conversation, and is therefore none the wiser.)

- When Mr Eddy calls Pete, the script does not reveal that the voice of Mr Eddy's friend belongs to the Mystery Man (though we can infer it from the repeated dialogue). In the same exchange, after Pete claims not to remember meeting the mystery caller, the voice says, 'We just killed a couple of people,' adding: 'We thought we'd come over and tell you about it.' Pete then asks what is going on, to which the caller replies, 'Good question!!'

- In the script, after the mystery caller describes the execution method favoured in the far east, he continues: 'It could be days . . . weeks . . . or even years after the death sentence has been pronounced . . . This uncertainty adds an exquisite element of torture to the situation, don't you think?'

'While I regret having to lose things that are really fantastic,' Mary Sweeney says, 'I don't miss them *per se*, because by the time we lock picture, we feel like the film is working in the best way we could make it work.'

POSTER: Several striking posters were used for *Lost Highway*. The US and French one-sheets featured an image of Alice in Mr Eddy's Cadillac, with images of a highway and of Fred at the wheel of his car superimposed in the black areas of the car, the road continuing through the lower half of the poster. The second US one-sheet was a laterally bisected design featuring a dark shot of the lower half of Fred's face, below which was a lighter shot of the lower half of Alice's face. In the German poster, Fred and two other faces peered out from blackness, while Alice in Mr Eddy's Cadillac occupied the bottom of the image; in Italy, a large image of Pete and Alice making love was overlaid with repeated shots of Fred at the wheel (which, oddly, give the impression of a cinema audience made up of Freds, or of a bug's multi-faceted eye). The UK was the most daring of all, the 'quad' (landscape format) poster featuring only a blurred image of the highway at night.

TRAILER: The *Lost Highway* trailer was brief and to the point, using images from the film intercut with the cast, director and title captions from the opening of the movie, cut to David Bowie's 'I'm Deranged'.

WHAT THE PAPERS SAID: For the most part, mainstream critics were not kind to *Lost Highway*. The *Los Angeles Times*'s Kenneth Turan found it 'beautifully made' but ultimately 'troublesome' and 'emotionally empty'. *Newsweek*'s Jack Kroll mentioned Lynch's 'dazzling style', but suggested that Lynch had 'forgotten how boring it is listening to someone else's dream . . . [The] mysteries becoming not fascinating but maddening . . . It's a dead end.' Mixed reviews appeared in *Variety* ('Lynch's visionary, impressionistic approach [is] boldly on display . . . uneven and too deliberately obscure in meaning to be entirely satisfying'), *Time* ('*Lost Highway* isn't refuse. But it ain't revelation either. What's missing is the shock of the new') and *Entertainment Weekly* ('has scattered moments of Lynch's poetry . . . [but] the film's ultimate shock is that it isn't shocking at all').

Outside of the mainstream, there were some positive reviews. *Rolling Stone*'s Peter Travers declared the film 'low on logic,' but added that it was 'stunningly shot . . . hilarious, hypnotic and sizzlingly erotic'; *Film Threat* called it 'a staggering *tour de force*'; *Cinefantastique* hailed it as 'a brilliant new film that forges [Lynch's] signature elements, film noir stylings, and hard-boiled plot motifs'; *Spin* rated it 'the most breathless work Lynch has produced since *Blue Velvet* . . . *Lost Highway*'s first half is an astonishingly chilling exploration of marital anxiety'; and *Interview* reckoned it was 'the best kind of bad dream . . . darker, kinkier, nastier, and more thoughtfully disturbing than anything [Lynch]'s done in years.' None of these remarks, however, would prove as influential on the public's perception of the film as the negative press.

In fact, so convinced was US distributor October Films that the critical response did not reflect the quality of the film itself that they attempted to use the negative reviews to its advantage. In late March, with the film already on general US release for more than a month, October launched a new advertising campaign, trumpeting the 'two thumbs down!' given by Gene Siskel and Roger Ebert, accompanied by the tag-line 'two more great reasons to see [*Lost Highway*].' As Lynch later told *Entertainment Weekly*, 'My rule of thumb is, what Siskel and Ebert like, I don't – and vice versa. They're getting too warm in those sweaters. It's affecting their thinking.'

BOX OFFICE: *Lost Highway* opened in the US on 21 February 1997, three days after its star-studded Los Angeles premiere, which raised $20,000 for the restoration of the Egyptian Cinema in Hollywood. Despite a strong screen average from its platform release in just twelve cinemas – $24,784 per screen, a first-week gross of almost $300,000 – the film's per-screen performance dropped sharply when it hit 200 more cinemas the following week, and by April it had dropped off the radar with a final US gross of $3.57 million. Given that October Films reportedly paid $10 million for North American distribution rights, this was devastatingly disappointing, even compared to the paltry $4.15 million performance of Lynch's last film, *Fire Walk With Me*.

CONTROVERSY: Numerous reviewers echoed the accusations of exploitation levelled at Lynch for Dorothy Vallens in *Blue Velvet*, suggesting that Patricia Arquette's numerous scenes played naked or semi-naked were gratuitous. The *New York Times* suggested that 'the movie exploits Ms Arquette as frankly as [Mr Eddy] does', the *Los Angeles Times* agreed that it was 'sexually exploitative', while *Vogue* described Renee/Alice as 'a particularly unsavoury creation'.

Actress Patricia Arquette responded thus to such criticism: 'Part of the reason I did this movie was that I have a serious phobia about nudity, just in my general everyday life,' she told Toby Keeler, adding that she found Lynch to be sensitive to her fears. Whenever other men had to be present during her nude scene, she said, Lynch would talk to them prior to it, and they would consequently be sympathetic and supportive. Lynch said that Arquette did not complain about the things she had to do. Nevertheless, the actress admitted, 'I would cry in between takes. I mean, I, I called David "Satan" one day. He didn't like that. I didn't really mean it, but it's heartbreaking. It's a very vulnerable thing.'

TRIVIA: The house in which the Madisons live in the film is owned by Lynch in real life; he had it remodelled specifically for the film. 'It was altered from the way it was when I bought it to fit the picture,' he reveals, 'and it was a pretty rare opportunity, because when you go on location, people don't really like you tearing out walls and rearranging the interior of the house, and the exterior as well. So we were able to do that, and then after that, the house got destroyed and built another way. So the *Lost Highway* house doesn't really exist any more.' In the film, the address is given as 7035 Hollis; in the script dated 21 June 1995, it is 442 Hollis.

Several character names were changed from script to screen: Alice Wyatt became Wakefield, Claire Dayton became Candace, Dr Mel Rogoff became Dr Smordin, and Captain Henderson became Captain Luneau.

When Fred dials his home telephone from the Mystery Man's phone, the tones denote the last three digits of his number are 666.

Richard Currey's novel *Lost Highway*, published in May 1997, is not related to Lynch's film in any way.

APOCRYPHA: Lynch likes to tell the story that, having met to discuss their ideas for *Lost Highway*, he and Gifford not only hated each other's ideas, but after discussing them, hated their *own* ideas as well. 'That's not true,' says Gifford. 'What really happened is that we wrote a first draft, and we put a lot of comedy into it, and basically we realised that wasn't going to work. If we were going to make a movie the way we'd talked about, it had to have much more gravity; it had to be a very serious picture throughout. We couldn't have wild and comic routines in it.'

Gifford recalls a character from the first draft called Little Uncle Paul, a blind man who visits the Dayton house for a family gathering, wanders off, and gets caught in automatically-timed lawn sprinklers that soak him to the skin. 'We realised that was all wrong for what we were trying to do,' he explains. 'Then I went off to Spain for a couple of weeks, and that gave us time to let it settle, reread the draft and see what we were doing . . . So then we got back to work and wrote what became the final screenplay for *Lost Highway*.' Gifford says that he and Lynch accepted these changes as part of the creative process.

Another oft-repeated story is that Lynch had originally considered filming what he called his '21st Century Noir Horror Film' in black and white. Not so, says Lynch. 'Some films are black-and-white films and some films are colour films,' he says. 'They tell you pretty much straight away. I love black and white, but *Lost Highway* wouldn't work in black and white, just like *The Elephant Man* wouldn't work in colour.'

It has also been suggested that the lighting in the earlier part of the film, which deals with Fred and his predicament, is different to that of the latter part of the film, following Fred's metamorphosis into Pete. Cinematographer Peter Deming denies that this was a conscious effort to distinguish the two stories (which are really one story), but was instead a consequence of the different locations in which each story took place.

AVAILABILITY: *Lost Highway* is available in the UK from Universal/4Front as a full-screen (4:3), budget-priced PAL VHS (053

4463), and in the US as both a full-screen (440 054 989-3) and a letterboxed (440 046 567-3) NTSC VHS. The latter also includes an impressive trailer for the *Lost Highway* soundtrack.

At present, the only letterboxed (2.35:1) English-language DVD available is a Region 2 Japanese DVD (PIBF-1023), with optional English subtitles. A letterboxed laserdisc (ID 3946 PG) is available in the US NTSC format, however.

The shooting script, prefaced by a Chris Rodley interview with Lynch (a slightly altered version of the one in *Lynch on Lynch*), and featuring some (though not all) of the scenes cut from the final film, is available from Faber and Faber.

FINAL ANALYSIS: In 1980, after completing just two features, Lynch said that 'if you put a little vagueness in a film, people wonder what's going on. But sometimes it's necessary. I've just touched the tip of the iceberg in exploring this. Done right, it could drive people wild – in a good way, an inspiring way.' With *Lost Highway*, Lynch was able to explore the rest of the iceberg, taking his desired approach to material that *feels* dense, vague – even, at times, confused – but actually boils down to a solid, straightforward – though hardly simplistic – psychological thriller, composed of traditional *film noir* elements with a seemingly supernatural twist.

Yet although *Lost Highway* – which, like their two stories for *Hotel Room*, is almost as much Barry Gifford's film as it is Lynch's – drove many people wild, it was mostly with confusion and frustration, provoked by the fact that it leaves a great deal open to interpretation, inviting the viewer to draw his or her own conclusions, which may, or may not, agree with Lynch's, or Gifford's – and would be no less valid if they didn't. With *Lost Highway*, as with *Eraserhead* and the Red Room/Black Lodge/convenience store elements of the *Twin Peaks* saga, the simplest interpretations are rarely, if ever, the most satisfying.

Now the cautious but welcome reappraisal of this superbly crafted and intensely satisfying film by audiences and critics who initially dismissed it suggests that Lynch's self-styled '21st Century Noir Horror Film,' which actually arrived at the tail end of the twentieth century, was, simply and appropriately, ahead of its time.

EXPERT WITNESS: 'I said, "David, I have some ideas about how this character should look." He said, "No, no, no! Just show me." [So] I went off with the make-up people, and I got into this whole weird, fuckin' Kabuki-looking guy with ears [sticking out] and stuff . . . I cut my fuckin' hair off, and I put a crack in the middle of it and all this shit. And the make-up people said, "You're going crazy, man! Nobody in this movie looks like that; everybody looks regular!" I said, "Leave me alone; just give me some shit." I put this black outfit on. I walked up to David, and he said, "Wonderful!" and turned around and walked away.' – actor Robert Blake (Mystery Man)

LYNCH ON *LOST HIGHWAY*: 'A 21st Century Noir Horror Film. A graphic investigation into parallel identity crises. A world where time is dangerously out of control. A terrifying ride down the lost highway.'

The Straight Story (1999)

35mm feature film / 111 mins / colour / live action

Directed by David Lynch
Written by John Roach & Mary Sweeney
Produced by Mary Sweeney, Neal Edelstein
Executive Producers Pierre Edelman, Michael Polaire
Music Composed and Conducted by Angelo Badalamenti
Costume Designer Patricia Norris
Production Designer Jack Fisk
Editor Mary Sweeney
Director of Photography Freddie Francis, BSA
Casting by Jane Alderman CSA, Lynn Blumenthal

CAST: Richard Farnsworth (*Alvin Straight*), Sissy Spacek (*Rose*), Harry Dean Stanton (*Lyle Straight*), Everett McGill (*Tom the John Deere Dealer*), John Farley (*Thorvald*), Kevin Farley (*Harald*), Jane Galloway Heitz (*Dorothy*), Joseph A. Carpenter (*Bud*), Donald Wiegert (*Sig*),Tracey Maloney (*Nurse*), Don Flannery (*Dr Gibbons*), Jennifer Edwards-Hughes (*Brenda*), Ed Grennan (*Pete*), Jack Walsh (*Apple*), Max the Wonder Dog (*Farm Dog*), Gil Pearson (*Bus Driver*), Barbara June Patterson (*Woman on Bus*), Anastasia Webb (*Crystal*), Matt Guidry (*Steve*), Bill McCallum (*Rat*), Barbara Robertson (*Deer Woman*), James Cada (*Danny Riordan*), Sally Wingert (*Darla Riordan*), Barbara Kingsley (*Janet Johnson*), Jim Haun (*Johnny Johnson*), Wiley Harker (*Verlyn Heller*), Randy Wiedenhoff (*Fireman 1*), Jerry E. Anderson (*Fireman 2*), John Lordan (*Priest*), Garrett Sweeney, Peter Sweeney, Tommy Fahey, Matt Fahey, Dan Fahey (*Boys in Truck*), Russ Reed (*Mt Zion Bartender*), Leroy Swadley (*Bar Patron*), Ralph Feldhacker (*Farmer on Tractor*)

ALTERNATIVE TITLE: The French title, *Une Histoire Vraie*, translates as *A True Story*, or *A Real Story*.

TITLE SEQUENCE: A crowded starfield fills the screen, the camera moving forward almost imperceptibly as the sound of cicadas slowly fills the ears. What follows is arguably the most bizarre, or at least incongruous, opening image of any David Lynch film: 'WALT DISNEY PICTURES PRESENTS A FILM BY DAVID LYNCH'. As the cicadas mix into Angelo Badalamenti's title theme, the rest of the titles play in simple white Helvetica letters over the star-filled background, until the image dissolves through to swooping helicopter shots of cornfields being harvested.

SUMMARY: 73-year-old war veteran Alvin Straight, who lives with his speech-impaired daughter Rose, has a fall at his home in Laurens, Iowa, deep in the American Midwest. Alvin stubbornly refuses his doctor's advice, and when he hears that his estranged 76-year-old brother Lyle has suffered a stroke, he decides to visit him. Against Rose's advice, he hooks a trailer up to his riding lawnmower and off on the 317-mile trip. After a false start and a replacement mower, Alvin embarks on the journey alone, meeting various rural folk along the way. Six weeks, a near-fatal accident and a serious breakdown later, Alvin pulls up at his brother's place, where after ten years of not speaking to each other, they finally find that no words are necessary: a brother's a brother.

SOURCE: Almost twenty years after *The Elephant Man*, *The Straight Story* would be Lynch's return to a film based on a true story about a unique and extraordinary individual. The remarkable story of Alvin Straight's 317-mile journey from Laurens, Iowa to Mt Zion, Wisconsin on a John Deere lawnmower first appeared in the summer of 1994. As co-screenwriter Mary Sweeney recalls, 'It was just one of those human-interest stories that everybody was picking up for a month or so. I can't really say what it was that grabbed me about it,' she adds, 'but it has something to do with this simple courage of human beings, of how you go through life and when you get to the end of your life you look back and say, "Wow, that was it?"' Sweeney immediately saw its cinematic potential, and approached Straight himself for the rights, only to find that they had already been snapped up by octogenarian producer Ray Stark, whose credits included *The Night of the Iguana* (1964), *The Sunshine Boys* (1975), the *Hotel Room*-style *California Suite* (1978) and *Steel Magnolias* (1989). Septuagenarian screenwriter Larry Gelbart (*Tootsie*, 1982) would write the script.

A disappointed Sweeney continued to monitor the project's progress throughout the making of *Lost Highway*, which she produced and edited. 'Literally years went by,' she says, 'and I just kept checking on the option.' When Alvin Straight died in 1996, Sweeney asked her lawyers if she could make the picture anyway, given that Straight's story was now effectively public domain. 'They said no – as long as somebody else has the option, it reverts to his heirs, and you'll still get stopped by these people if you try it. But the people with the option weren't actively doing anything with it, and Alvin died very unhappy about that, so his kids were very open to the notion of someone taking over the option.' When the option finally lapsed in February 1998, Sweeney snapped it up. 'Then,' she says, 'everything happened at a runaway-train speed.'

PRODUCTION HISTORY: Once Mary Sweeney owned the rights to Straight's story, she and childhood friend John Roach – a commercials director from her home town of Madison, Wisconsin ('a real party place,' according to the script) – began researching what would become their first screenplay. They spent time with six of Straight's seven children in Des Moines and they re-traced his route. Sweeney recalls, 'When we got to a place in eastern Iowa where he broke down and camped in somebody's yard for a week, we got a lot of good stuff. It all seemed like some sort of story about the human condition.' Upon their return, Sweeney says, the script was written very rapidly, 'although it wasn't necessarily easy to write.'

'John and I have made a pact that we don't reveal which parts of the story are based on real facts that we gleaned from the kids, or knew about the trip, and which parts are parts we made up,' Sweeney adds, 'but there are both things in there.' The key, she says – echoing Lynch's attitude to the story of John Merrick – was to find the fundamental truth of the story, even where it diverged from actual reality. 'In the course of writing it we definitely had a sense of respect for the truth of the situation, so to the extent that we embellished the story, it had to do with coming up with a story idea that would move along, because it's really just about a guy on a lawnmower taking a trip . . . But any choices we had between elaborating on the story or having enough story with just the truth, we always stayed with the truth.'

Having completed the script at the end of June 1998, Sweeney gave it to Lynch, with whom she had a long-standing professional and – as his live-in partner and mother of his youngest son, Riley – personal relationship. 'I was really giving it to him just to get his feedback on the script, because it was John's first screenplay and mine. We were completely shocked that he liked it and wanted to make it.' 'They showed it to me and that was it,' Lynch told the *Los Angeles Times*. 'It became, for me, very real. Sometimes you might think you want to do something, but nature – or whatever is out there – doesn't think that's a good idea and you get red lights. Sometimes you get a green light or a series of green lights. This was one of those times.'

'Suddenly, we had five or six different people who wanted to finance it,' Sweeney says. 'It was low-budget; it was David Lynch; it was a straight narrative – nobody was afraid of anything.' Not even Straight's family, who might have baulked at the idea of the director of *Eraserhead*, *Twin Peaks – Fire Walk With Me* and *Lost Highway* tackling the tale of their father's journey. 'They really weren't the kind of people who would even know who David was,' Sweeney explains. 'They're very rural, very decent Iowa people, and they wanted his story told, quite simply.'

Production on *The Straight Story* began in mid-September 1998, with the film-makers following Straight's route east, spending the harvest season in Iowa, and crossing the Mississippi into Wisconsin as the autumn colours reached their most beautiful. In each rural stop along the way – Laurens, New Hampton, West Bend, West Union, Clermont, Prairie du Chien and Mt Zion itself – the film crew lived and worked among the residents, giving the lie to fictional accounts of Hollywood productions in small Midwestern towns (most recently, David Mamet's *State and Main*, 2000). When the production left Laurens, The *Laurens Sun* bade a fond farewell with a half-page announcement that read, 'Thank you to cast and crew of *The Straight Story*. You have brought so much excitement and enjoyment to our lives!'

Actor Richard Farnsworth relished the opportunity to meet many of the people whose lives had been touched by Alvin Straight during his journey. 'They had a good word to say for the old man,' he recalled. 'He was very independent. He might not have had any money, but he didn't want anyone to know about it. He was a very hard-headed old guy. I might have played him a little softer than he was.' The actor also identified with Straight's physical condition. 'It kind of gives you a feeling of what he went through sitting on the [lawnmower] every day. It wasn't very hard for me to do, frankly. Even the dialogue seemed to go smooth for me. I am kind of limited [as an actor],' he added. 'I do rural things. I couldn't do a Philadelphia lawyer or a nuclear physicist. But the way it was written, it just felt fine.'

Principal photography wrapped in Mt Zion, Wisconsin, in October 1998, after just six weeks of filming – precisely the length of time it took Alvin to make his epic journey. As befitted such an emotional story, each member of the cast and crew took away fond memories of the production, from the special skeet shoot organised by the Laurens police department, to the ladies at Deb's Diner in Laurens who covered an entire wall of the restaurant with photographs of the filming, to the shared memories of those who had known Alvin – including the four individuals in as many different towns who claimed to have sold him his first riding mower!

Post-production was completed in time for *The Straight Story* to receive its world premiere on 21 May 1999, as part of the Official Selection, in competition, at the 52nd Cannes Film Festival. 'We didn't win anything,' Mary Sweeney says, 'but frankly nobody cared about that at all – except we all felt that Richard should have got Best Actor. But we had such a fantastic screening, and the outpouring of love was like the opposite experience of *Twin Peaks* [*Fire Walk With Me*], which really felt like an outpouring of hate. The approbation was so tangible that it didn't make any difference to us whether the film won anything or not.' Farnsworth was overwhelmed by the standing ovation he received. 'It was thrilling,' he told the *Los Angeles Times*. 'The standing ovation really got to me, I tell you. It went on and on. I couldn't get over it.' 'It was very intense and beautiful,' Lynch agreed. 'It was as if there was no festival. There was just a roomful of people [applauding].'

Six months later, at the film's London Film Festival screening, Lynch, Mary Sweeney, John Roach and Freddie Francis were present as Farnsworth received another standing ovation from an audience that included many former Lynch collaborators, including John Hurt, Freddie Jones and Dexter Fletcher.

'It was really really important to us to be emotional but not sentimental, which is really hard to do,' Sweeney commented, 'and thank God David directed it, because our script could so easily have turned into a schmaltzy glossy Hallmark version of this guy's life. He was a complex, not totally great guy, but on the other hand, there were great things about him.' Above all, Sweeney was grateful to have found a project that would display Lynch's tender-hearted, sweet side. 'For a long time, I've been looking for something that would go more in that direction,' she told the *Los Angeles Times*, adding: 'I love all of David's films. The edgy and dangerous films are also very valid. But dysfunction isn't the only thing out there. He is pigeonholed as the master of weird, but he is much more. I'm happy [now] that a lot of people will be able to enjoy the tremendous power he has as a film-maker.'

CASTING: Alvin Straight was 73 years old, and suffering from numerous ailments brought on by old age, when he made his courageous journey. Richard Farnsworth, the Oscar-nominated actor who would portray him, had just turned 78 and was even more infirm at the time filming began. Farnsworth had begun his illustrious career in 1937, making his feature film debut as a stunt horseman in *The Adventures of Marco Polo*, following this by driving chariots for Cecil B. DeMille's 1956 remake of his own 1923 epic *The Ten Commandments*, and doubling for Kirk Douglas in Stanley Kubrick's

Spartacus (1960). Almost forty years into his feature-film career, Farnsworth made his speaking debut in *The Duchess and the Dirtwater Fox* in 1976, and the following year earned a Best Supporting Actor Oscar nomination for Alan J. Pakula's *Comes a Horseman*. Major roles in *The Grey Fox* (1982) and *The Natural* (1984), and supporting roles in *The Two Jakes* and *Misery* (both 1990) followed, before Lynch lured him out of retirement for *The Straight Story*. 'I identified with the old guy,' Farnsworth told the *Los Angeles Times*. 'I've had a few hard knocks in my life. He was on a cane and I was on a cane. It worked fine.'

Sadly, *The Straight Story* would prove not only to be veteran actor Richard Farnsworth's finest hour, but also his final film. Some six months after earning his second Academy Award nomination, this time for Best Actor, the terminally ill octogenarian was found dead at his New Mexico home on 6 October 2000, from a self-inflicted gunshot wound. 'He was very ill in that movie,' his companion of the past eleven years, Jewely Van Valin, told the *Guardian*, 'but, phenomenally, he made it through. He didn't want the world to know he was sick.'

Actress Sissy Spacek had not worked with Lynch since her unofficial duties on *Eraserhead*; since then, she has received five Academy Award nominations and one Oscar, for a diverse range of roles in such films as *Carrie* (1976), *Coal Miner's Daughter* (1979), *Missing* (1982), *The River* (1984) and *Crimes of the Heart* (1986).

THE LYNCH MOB: Harry Dean Stanton, aged 74 at the time of *The Straight Story*'s release, had previously appeared in *The Cowboy and the Frenchman, Hotel Room, Wild at Heart* and *Fire Walk With Me*; octogenarian Freddie Francis photographed two earlier Lynch films, *The Elephant Man* and *Dune*; composer Angelo Badalamenti has worked on every Lynch feature film (and several television projects) since *Blue Velvet*; Patricia Norris worked as costume designer on *The Elephant Man*, and has designed the costumes and production for every Lynch project since *Blue Velvet*.

The long-term on- and off-screen relationship between Lynch and co-writer/co-producer/editor Mary Sweeney was not the only off-screen partnership behind *The Straight Story*: production designer Jack Fisk (*Eraserhead*'s Man in the Planet) and leading actress Sissy Spacek (thanked in the credits of *Eraserhead*) have been married for more than 25 years. Lynch and Spacek had even been brother- and sister-in-law, during the period when Lynch was married to Jack Fisk's sister, Mary.

The Straight Story was produced by Neal Edelstein, Lynch and Mary Sweeney's partner in a new company, The Picture Factory. Edelstein had previously produced several of Lynch's commercials, his contribution to *Lumière et Compagnie*, and *Mulholland Drive*.

Edelstein and Lynch are also partners in the PC entertainment enterprise Black Lacquer, and the web design initiative Substation.

MEMORABLE QUOTES
Dorothy: 'What's the number for 911?'

Rose: 'What did the doctor say?'
Alvin: 'He said I was gonna live to be a hundred.'

Alvin: 'When my kids were real little I used to play a game with 'em. I'd give each one of 'em a stick, one for each one of 'em, and I'd say, "You break that." Of course they could, real easy. Then I'd say, "Tie them sticks in a bundle, try and break that." Of course they couldn't. Then I'd say, "That bundle, that's family."'

Alvin: 'We had a scout, a little fella, name of Kotz. He was a Polish boy from Milwaukee. He'd always take recon and he was darn' good at it. We went by his word and he saved our skin many a time. He was a little fella. We'd broken out of the hedgerows. We were makin' a run across the open, and we come upon the woods. We started drawin' fire. I took my usual position and I saw something moving real slowly. I waited ten minutes, it moved again, and I shot. The movement stopped. The next day we found Kotz head shot. He'd been workin' his way back toward our lines. Everyone in the unit thought a German sniper had taken him. Everyone, all these years. Everyone but me.'

Alvin: 'There's no one that knows your life better than a brother who's near your age. He knows who you are and what you are better than anyone on Earth. My brother and I said some unforgivable things the last time we met, but I'm tryin' to put that behind me, and this trip is a hard swallow of my pride. I just hope I'm not too late. A brother's a brother.'

SOUND AND MUSIC: Just as *The Straight Story* is Lynch's most anonymous film in some respects, his music collaborator Angelo Badalamenti's score is the composer's most restrained work, using a variety of stringed instruments to capture the heart of the American Midwest, and only occasionally straying into *Twin Peaks* territory (notably over the opening titles and end credits). Thirteen tracks, comprising some 52 minutes of music, appear on the Windham Hill soundtrack (01934 11513 2), along with a quote from Lynch himself: 'Tenderness can be just as abstract as insanity.' Four songs featured in the film do not appear on the soundtrack: 'The Most Requested Song' (from *Strange Tales of the Late West*) by Middlejohn & John Neff;

'Y'Ready' and 'Solo Spin-Out' by the Radio Ranch Straight Shooters; and S. Fine's 'Happy Times', performed by Jo Stafford.

Once again, Lynch took due credit for sound design. The sounds of the countryside are almost omnipresent in *The Straight Story*, except when drowned by those of machinery (cars, trucks, the grain elevator and, of course, Alvin's lawnmower), or a lightning storm, or even the whoosh of hundreds of cyclists passing at close range on a country road. Lynch makes characteristic use of sound, notably in three scenes in which the camera stays at a distance from Alvin so that his conversation is almost inaudible. We cannot hear him because we, the camera, are too far away. Lynch's use of sound is equally abstract, but far more powerful, for the scene in which Alvin and Verlyn (Wiley Harker) share their experiences of the Second World War, as sounds of combat, not necessarily linked to the stories either of the two veterans relate, are mixed in with the conversation.

INFLUENCED BY: Freddie Francis's photographic rendering of the rolling Iowa cornfields recalls Terrence Malick's *Days of Heaven* (1978), which employed the talents of two of *The Straight Story*'s behind-the-scenes stars: production designer Jack Fisk, and costume designer Patricia Norris, for whom it earned an Academy Award nomination.

DÉJÀ VU: Watching the first images after the starfield title sequence, we could almost be in *Blue Velvet*'s Lumberton or Twin Peaks, as Lynch establishes Laurens, Iowa as Anytown, USA using various views, before leading us to Alvin Straight's house in a shot that remains one of Lynch's most Edward Hopper-like images. Later, Rose watches a little boy playing by a water sprinkler (*Blue Velvet*); the sound of the grain elevator recalls similar industrial noises in *Eraserhead* and *The Elephant Man*; the camera moving along the yellow lines down the two-lane blacktop gives a nod to *Lost Highway*; a *Twin Peaks* owl hoots in the trees as Alvin gabs with Crystal. The burning house is an image familiar from both *Wild at Heart* and *Lost Highway*, though here the circumstances are far more innocent. Finally, *The Straight Story* ends with a familiar Lynch device: a star-filled sky. As Alvin says, 'The sky sure is full of stars tonight.'

CUT SCENES: As always with a Lynch film, there was considerably more to *The Straight Story* than made it into the final cut. Uniquely, however, the editor, Mary Sweeney, was also one of the film's writers. 'I think one of the gifts I bring to screenwriting is my twenty years of editing,' Sweeney says, 'so there was a continuum there. But David is very clear about the fact that writers are not welcome on the set: he loved their script, but now it is his picture, thank you very much. So I never had my writer's hat on when I was editing it.'

Thus, despite having co-written the script, Sweeney did not find editing her own scripted scenes to be too painful. 'The film takes on a life of its own,' she explains, 'and every time you see it there are certain sour notes that don't really fit in, and you just start plucking them out. It started emerging that the scenes we left out were scenes that weren't quite as emotional as the rest of the film. The film emerged as a more emotional version of the script, I think. When I look back at what came out . . . a lot of the stuff that came out was humorous, and although it wasn't like we didn't want humour in there, it was just that weighing in the balance, and emotion won out every time.'

POSTER: The image on most posters was a long-distance shot of Alvin Straight on his John Deere mower, silhouetted against either a dawn sky (the US) or a burning sunset that graduates up into a starry sky (the UK). On the latter, the title appears in shaky style, hand-lettered by Lynch himself. 'We were talking about title styles,' says Film Four marketing coordinator Ivan Wormley, 'and Lynch said, "Something like this," and wrote the title on a hotel napkin. It was so perfect, we just scanned it right in.'

TRAILER: Disney's US trailer opens with shots of Iowa cornfields, accompanied by Alvin's speech about family. A 'WALT DISNEY PICTURES PRESENTS' caption follows, and after Alvin announces his intentions, the trailer follows his progress almost chronologically, with additional captions bearing the legend 'A FILM BY DAVID LYNCH' and several critics' quotes. The final caption reads 'HEADING YOUR WAY THIS FALL.'

Film Four's UK trailer opens with a close-up of Alvin's lawnmower starting up, and a simple white caption ('A FILM BY DAVID LYNCH') before editing a mostly chronological montage of images from the film, accompanied by dialogue that explains the story. Lacking any kind of narration, or captions that would have better contextualised the story, the trailer is perhaps too passive to be truly engaging.

WHAT THE PAPERS SAID: In the US, critics were understandably startled by the fact that *The Straight Story* was a David Lynch film, perhaps forgetting that his oeuvre included another relatively restrained true story: *The Elephant Man*. Despite the fact that *The Straight Story* was clearly less 'Lynchian' than any of his earlier films, many reviewers could not help but look for similarities between his first Disney-distributed film and his more disturbing works. In *Time*, for example, Richard Corliss opined that, far from being a rare kind of character for a David Lynch film, Alvin Straight was 'your basic Lynch hero: a Kyle MacLachlan type, as average as apple pie, who follows his obsessions to heaven or hell. The supporting cast is normal too – and thus vastly weird, because Lynch presents them, as he did the sickos of *Blue Velvet*, without comment or condescension.' Corliss further suggested that the story might have 'all the narrative momentum of a lawnmower pulling the Cheops pyramid up an alp' if it were not for the script's ability to find 'new ways to make rural decency dramatic.'

The *Los Angeles Times* critic Kenneth Turan was not so sure, calling the script 'fake-folksy' and full of 'bogus homilies and contrived folk-wisdom,' and suggesting that the film was 'too mannered and weird around the edges to be convincing. While Farnsworth would be right at home in a genuinely earnest and honestly sentimental effort like Joe Johnston's *October Sky*,' he added, 'the rest of what's on the screen would not. For despite its gee-whiz dialogue, the film can't live without classic Lynch oddities like sinister grain silos, an overweight sunbather carefully eating pink Sno-Balls, and a woman who seems primed to set a local record for number of deer hit by a single driver. There's nothing wrong with touches like these – Lynch used them brilliantly in *Blue Velvet* – but they clash with, rather than enhance, the kind of feeling Farnsworth is working so hard to convey.'

In the UK, *The Straight Story* was greeted rather more warmly, from the tabloids to the broadsheets. 'David Lynch's best film and a joy for ever,' enthused the *Daily Mail*'s Christopher Tookey, 'ranking among the greatest achievements in cinema.' 'Lynch gets humanist, and produces a gem,' wrote *Time Out*'s Geoff Andrew, who had trashed *Twin Peaks – Fire Walk With Me* and *Lost Highway* in the same publication. 'Atypically for the director, it's also told straight, in naturalistic, linear fashion, but for all that the elegant, faintly formal compositions and camera movements (courtesy Freddie Francis), the expert and subtle use of sound and music, and the wry, gently humorous take on the absurdities of small-town life make the film recognisably Lynchian. Farnsworth's easy, twinkle-eyed charm is a winner all the way, but it's finally the film's deceptive simplicity and unabashed warmth that make it one of Lynch's most artistically and emotionally satisfying movies.'

BOX OFFICE: In the US, *The Straight Story* opened on just seven screens on 15 October 1999, earning a per-screen average of $13,187 (significantly less than *Lost Highway*'s). Slowly, over the coming weeks, the film was rolled out across America, at a pace that Straight himself would probably have appreciated. Six months later, the film was still on wide release, its modest gross of $6.2 million making it Lynch's most successful picture since *Wild at Heart*. In the UK, *The*

Straight Story was released on 2 December 1999, grossing a disappointing £215,500 overall.

AWARDS: *The Straight Story* may have come up empty-handed at the Cannes Film Festival, but numerous awards and nominations were forthcoming during the following year. At the Academy Awards, Richard Farnsworth was nominated in the Best Actor category (Kevin Spacey won for *American Beauty*); he was also nominated (along with composer Angelo Badalamenti) for a Golden Globe Award; with Sissy Spacek for a Golden Satellite Award; for a Las Vegas Film Critics' Society Award (Lynch, Badalamenti, Spacek and Freddie Francis were also nominated); an Online Film Critics' Society Award (Badalamenti and Francis were also nominated); at the Chicago Film Critics' Association Awards (Lynch was nominated, along with *The Straight Story* for Best Picture); and at the Southeastern Film Critics' Association Awards. Farnsworth was more successful at the New York Film Critics' Circle Awards, where he and Freddie Francis both won; at the Fort Lauderdale International Film Festival, where Farnsworth won the Jury Award; and at the Independent Spirit Awards, where Lynch, Mary Sweeney, John Roach and Neal Edelstein were also nominated.

The Straight Story was honoured as Best American Film at the Bodil and Robert festivals, and won a British Independent Film Award for Best Foreign Film (English Language); it was also nominated as Best Family Feature Film (Drama) at the Young Artist Awards, Best Foreign Film at the Guldbagge Awards, and Best Art Movie at the Csapnivalo Awards. Lynch won the European Film Awards' Five Continents Award, and Best Director at the San Diego Film Critics' Society Awards. Finally, Freddie Francis was nominated at the Camerimage Awards.

Finally, in December 2000, *The Straight Story* was nominated by the Video Software Dealers Association as 'Sleeper of the Year', an award given to a title that performed better than expected on video.

CONTROVERSY: One would think that the so-called moral majority would celebrate Lynch's only G-rated film as exactly the kind of film Hollywood should be making. If so, think again. The watchdog website www.capalert.com gives its own ratings to films rated by the Motion Picture Association of America (MPAA), based on a different set of criteria. Incredibly, *The Straight Story* fell foul of four out of six of CAPAlert's own categories: Wanton Violence/Crime ('terror of runaway lawnmower down a hill with the rider'), Impudence/Hate ('six uses of the three/four-letter word vocabulary with none of the most foul words, a lie about personal health to daughter, [and an] attempt to cheat'), Sex/Homosexuality ('none noted'), Drugs/Alcohol ('drinking beer'), Offense to God ('nine uses of God's name in vain but without the four-letter word vocabulary') and Murder/Suicide ('none noted'). Overall, the website's report noted that, 'because of the flagrant use of God's name in vain, this movie earned a CAPAlert red light.'

APOCRYPHA: In April 1999, bestselling American author David Guterson (*The Bridges of Madison County*, *Snow Falling on Cedars*) published his third novel, *East of the Mountains*. Upon the release of *The Straight Story* six months later, several critics pointed out coincidental similarities between the two stories, which both concern 73-year-old veterans with disturbing memories of the Second World War setting out on a journey across America – one to see his ailing brother, the other to revisit the land of his childhood – that they hope to complete before succumbing to terminal illness. While the similarities are startling, and Guterson may have been influenced by the real-life story of Alvin Straight, neither product can be said to have been influenced by the other, since the periods of publication of *East of the Mountains* and production of *The Straight Story* were virtually concurrent.

AVAILABILITY: In the UK, *The Straight Story* is available from Film Four/VCI as a full-screen (4:3) PAL VHS (VC3835) and a letterboxed (2.35:1) Region 2 DVD (VCD0042), the latter also featuring a grainy, full-screen copy of the British theatrical trailer, and a seventeen-chapter scene index.

In the US, *The Straight Story* is available as a full-screen (4:3) NTSC VHS (ARV 3151). A letterboxed (2.35:1) Region 1 DVD (20452) is also available, featuring the US theatrical trailer but lacking the chapter stops that, on almost every other DVD, allow instant access to any given scene. Lynch briefly explained his reasoning on the sleeve: 'I know that most DVDs have chapter stops. It is my opinion that a film is not like a book – it should not be broken up. It is a continuum and should be seen as such. Thank you for your understanding.'

'Chapter stops are a pathetic joke,' Lynch explains. 'I don't know who first got that idea, but it caught on, and it's just my opinion that it's wrong. But if [people] have a tape they can just go to their favourite scene, or whatever they wanna do, but I don't believe in having it blocked out like that.'

The shooting script is available in the US from Hyperion Books.

FINAL ANALYSIS: Actress Sissy Spacek (Rose) once described *The Straight Story* as 'a four-mile-an-hour road picture,' and in this, Lynch's third road movie (after *Wild at Heart* and *Lost Highway*), the director takes the well-worn genre on a journey of its own, the floating camera and snail's-pace editing giving time for the simple pleasures of watching a breeze waft across a cornfield, or emotions play across a face. As with *The Elephant Man*, Lynch's earlier true-life portrayal of a sensitive soul trapped in a failing body, *The Straight Story* shows the director at his most restrained; with a few exceptions, he resists the temptation to 'do a David Lynch', and turn the film into an exercise in weird Americana, as a lesser director might have done with identical material. The remarkable story of Alvin Straight, as told by Lynch, is no less wonderful and strange than any of his other films.

EXPERT WITNESS: 'David called me up and said, "Sis, I've got this part. She's just beautiful." He didn't tell me very much, except that she was very special. I was intrigued and excited. When I got the script, I wondered why there were all these long spaces in the dialogue. Sentences would start, stop suddenly and start again. Then [Rose] came to the set to help me and everybody fell in love with her. She was the queen. She has some handicaps, but she lives in the moment and she's great fun to be around.' – actress Sissy Spacek (Rose)

LYNCH ON *THE STRAIGHT STORY*: '*The Straight Story* is an unusual film for me. But I was so moved by the screenplay that soon enough I found myself in Iowa. It doesn't matter if the story is true or not. It's a story. Everything is a story. This is a different world than I've been in, one in which nature plays a big part. And, although it appears to be calm, there are many things going on.'

Mulholland Drive (2001)

35mm feature film / colour / live action

Directed by David Lynch
Written by Joyce Eliason & David Lynch
Produced by Neal Edelstein, Joyce Eliason, Michael Polaire
Executive Producer David Lynch
Music Composed and Conducted by Angelo Badalamenti
Director of Photography Peter Deming
Edited by Mary Sweeney
Production Designer Jack Fisk

SOURCE: *Mulholland Drive* began as a collaboration between Lynch and Joyce Eliason, the celebrated television writer of such lavish productions as *The Last Don* (1997) and its sequel (1998). 'We started working together,' Lynch says. 'It was kind of a thing where we were gonna see how it was gonna work, and there were a lot of other people pushing it to work, and it didn't work,' he reveals. 'It started when it was gonna be kind of a spin-off of *Twin Peaks*, in the very beginning, but didn't go anywhere. Just the words "Mulholland Drive" always got something going, but I never knew what.'

PRODUCTION HISTORY: Lynch's previous relationship with the ABC television network had been a mixed blessing, with *Twin Peaks* giving the director his first taste of television, but the network ultimately killing it before its time. Lynch's next show for ABC, *On the Air*, was also axed, with only three of its episodes broadcast, following which Lynch angrily painted a plywood board with the legend 'I WILL NEVER WORK IN TELEVISION AGAIN.'

By 1998, however, with the network now owned by Disney, the studio that would distribute *The Straight Story*, Lynch and ABC were evidently willing to give each other another chance. For Steve Tao, the network's vice-president of drama programming, it was a chance to rekindle the kind of event drama seldom seen in series television since *Twin Peaks*'s first season. '*Twin Peaks* was like a young rocker who dies in an airplane crash – the early departure creates an even greater hunger,' Tao told the *New Yorker*. 'We're hoping to feed that hunger with *Mulholland Drive*. Quite frankly, there's a plethora of sameness on TV. David Lynch's television stands out.' For Lynch, it was the opportunity to return to a medium in which a story does not necessarily have to have a beginning, a middle and an end. 'I've never liked having to bend my movie scripts to an end halfway through,' he admitted. 'On a series you can keep having beginnings and middles, and develop story for ever.' Essentially, he explained, 'I was lured back because of a really strong desire to tell a continuing story in which you go deeper and deeper into a world and you get lost in that world. A pilot is open-ended, and, when it's over, you feel all these threads going out into the infinite which, to me, is a beautiful thing. It's like a body with no head.'

Thus, in August 1998, Lynch and Tony Krantz – the former CAA agent who introduced Lynch to Mark Frost, currently co-chairman and CEO of Imagine Television – pitched *Mulholland Drive* to Tao and network president Jamie Tarses. 'It was the best kind of pitch,' Tao recalled, 'where you're on the edge of your seat. I remember the creepiness of this woman in this horrible, horrible crash, and David teasing us with the notion that people are chasing her. She's not just *in* trouble – she *is* trouble. Obviously, we asked, "What happens next?" And David said, "You have to buy the pitch for me to tell you."'

What happened next was that ABC put up $4.5 million for a two-hour pilot, with Disney's Touchstone contributing a further $2.5 million on the condition that Lynch shoot a closed ending; if the series failed, Disney could then release the film as a feature in Europe, as Warner Home Video had done with *Twin Peaks*, or sell the overseas theatrical rights to the feature on a territory-by-territory basis, almost certainly for a tidy profit. Five months later, on 4 January 1999, Lynch turned in a ninety-two page script for the pilot. 'It [was] one of the fastest scripts we [had] ever read,' Tao recounted. 'We could see it.' Twenty-four hours later, Lynch had a green light.

Filming began in late February, using several Los Angeles locations – including the eponymous street itself – previously used in *Lost Highway*, but shot in a very different style. 'It's definitely a different look,' says cinematographer Peter Deming, who also worked on Lynch's earlier film. 'It's probably a little more rooted in reality, at least to begin with, and then it goes different places. It's a little more naturalistic, and although it's stylised, it's not as heavily stylised. There are parts of the story where we're outside, where we wanted it to be very sunny and very Californian,' he adds, 'and I guess comparisons to *Blue Velvet* are inevitable, because it's based on greens and blues and things like that. But there are definitely cheery parts and not-so-cheery parts as far as the exteriors go. But hopefully it has its own look.'

As the dailies began to come in, the network's nerves began to show. 'In dailies you have the wheat and you have the chaff. No one really knows what is wheat and chaff but me,' Lynch explained, 'and sometimes there's some bad chaff that they're seeing and that makes them stay awake at night and worry.' Already concerned about Lynch's casting choices, and many of the more obscure elements of the script, executives now questioned Lynch's pacing. 'In *Mulholland Drive*, you start off with seven minutes of a car accident, [and] someone stumbling around dazed,' actor Justin Theroux (Adam Kesher) told the *New Yorker*. 'I'm sure ABC is thinking, "Okay, we've just lost *x* million viewers."' Line producer Michael Polaire also had his doubts that the network would weather Lynch's eccentricities. 'It's great, but it's way out there for ABC,' he told the same publication during production. 'They'll probably think, "What the fuck is this?"' Polaire was right.

In late April, Lynch delivered his first cut to ABC. It ran two hours and five minutes in duration, prompting the director to suggest that the network run it in a two-and-a-half-hour time slot. The network would have preferred forty-four minutes; Krantz suggested a compromise: cutting it to eighty-eight. 'I thought you would love this so much you'd put it in a two-and-a-half-hour time slot,' Lynch told the network. 'That would be a beautiful thing. See, I love it. And Tony

[Krantz] genuinely loves it.' ABC, however, did not love it. 'They hated it,' Lynch recalled bitterly, vowing for the second time never to work in television again. 'They hated the story, the acting. They thought it was too slow, that's for sure. Basically they hated everything about it.'

Following receipt of detailed notes from ABC outlining changes that they recommended should be made, Lynch offered to cut thirty-seven minutes from the end of the first cut, ending the pilot episode earlier and saving the remaining footage for the first instalment of the series proper. Krantz was not so sure that this would address the concerns expressed in the network's notes. 'ABC and Disney had put $7 million into the show,' he told the *New Yorker*, 'and simply cutting the last thirty-seven minutes contradicted the spirit of ABC's notes entirely and would have been a slap in their faces.' The network's reaction continued to puzzle Lynch. 'In the feature-film world, I've had creative control since *Blue Velvet*,' he told the *New Yorker*. 'And in my mind it's not worth doing anything if you don't have that freedom. You have to do what you believe in.'

Nevertheless, realising that the future of the show was at stake, and that it was more prudent to lose the scenes than lose the series, Lynch and editor Mary Sweeney stayed up all night, reluctantly cutting whole scenes and eventually trimming the pilot down to 88 minutes – the perfect length for a two-hour time slot. Lynch complained, 'They want things to move fast, but it's like water-skiing: when you go fast, you stay on top – you never get below the surface.'

'Editing is strange,' Sweeney says. 'It's actually very easy to try taking things out, but it's very hard to know when you need to put things back. So that night was not that horrible. What was horrible was seeing the result a month later in the cold light of a restful day, as opposed to the day we handed it in.' In any case, the hasty re-edit did not appease ABC. Having originally considered *Mulholland Drive* for a Thursday-night slot – in which it would have been competing with NBC's double-threat of *Friends* and *ER* – ABC passed on Lynch's show, opting instead for *Wasteland*, the new show from Kevin Williamson, creator of the *Scream* movie franchise and *Dawson's Creek*. (Ironically, Justin Theroux had passed on Williamson's show to star in *Mulholland Drive*; in the event, *Wasteland* ran for only a few episodes before ABC cancelled it.)

For a while, the possibility remained that *Mulholland Drive* would be retooled and picked up for a mid-season replacement; failing that, ABC might recoup its investment by airing the feature-length version as a two-hour TV movie, a possibility that Lynch dreaded. 'What we didn't want to happen was for them to air the version that they had in their hands,' says director of photography Peter Deming, 'which was hastily cut down for arbitrary reasons. My hope was that if they were going to show it they would at least let David go back and create a two-hour version.' Despite these fears, however, Mary Sweeney admits that this version 'came pretty close to getting aired, and we were starting to move towards David being able to take his name off of it,' just as he had with the butchered television version of *Dune*. As it turned out, this proved unnecessary, since ABC chose not to broadcast *Mulholland Drive* in any format. The project looked lost for ever.

Then, in March 2000, it was widely reported that French entertainment conglomerate Canal Plus had made a bid for the shelved pilot whereby it would pay ABC $7 million for the rights, and provide $2 million of production funding for Lynch to film a new ending. Although Lynch had previously stated that he considered *Mulholland Drive* to be lost for ever, Canal Plus's generous offer led him to reconsider. 'When you're in the middle of something, it's not impossible to let go of [it],' Lynch explains. 'But it makes an injury if you don't finish something, and part of your mind is always going back to it if it's not finished. So I don't know whether it was being hopeful, or I had a feeling, but many people involved in the project had feelings that it wasn't gonna die.'

Thus, in late September and early October 2000, Lynch recalled several members of the cast and crew and filmed nine additional days of what Peter Deming describes as 'completely new material, that was not part of the original pilot script.' With the new scenes in the can, Lynch took a break to film a commercial for Sony's Playstation 2 before heading to Prague in December to record the music for what would now be a fully fledged theatrical feature, a hybrid of three separate elements. 'We had a closed ending for *Mulholland Drive* that we shot but never edited,' Sweeney explains. 'It was not part of the 88-minute *or* the two-hour version of the pilot; it was done for the same reason that we did it on *Twin Peaks*, which had to do with theatrical-release potential outside of the US. So the feature will not just be the pilot material, but also the closed ending – which is completely fantastic and much more like David's usual thing – and all the new material. I think it's a really fantastic hybrid.'

Deming agrees, adding that 'it probably goes in a different direction in the feature than it ever would on television, and the reasons for that will probably become obvious when you see it.' Sweeney says that, because the pilot material was structured for a television audience, 'its entertainment value is pretty darn high.' Overall, she says, 'It's really sexy; the girls are gorgeous; the guys are handsome; it's Hollywood and it's fun – like the fun parts of *Wild at Heart*, with a lot of black humour.'

Peter Deming elaborates, 'It's definitely similar to *Lost Highway* in that when it's over, it's very thought-provoking and open to interpretation. [With] *Lost Highway*, when the film ended, you had to kind of sit there and go back over a lot of things and try and put the pieces together. While the structure of *Mulholland Drive* is very different, the same kind of process occurs.' The cinematographer even found this to be the case with his own understanding of the story. 'When we actually viewed it for the first time, I was talking to Mary Sweeney about my interpretation, and it was completely different from some of her interpretations. So again it's, as David would probably say, like a painting where every interpretation is different, but they're all correct.'

CASTING: Lynch had originally considered Dexter Fletcher (*The Elephant Man*) for the role of director Adam Kesher, meeting with him in early 1999, while the actor was in Los Angeles to promote the US release of *Lock, Stock and Two Smoking Barrels* (1998). 'We talked about the last twenty years,' Fletcher says, 'but we didn't talk at all about the project. I tried to bring it up, but we just talked about Patrick Stewart or Freddie Jones.' Fletcher says that Lynch had not seen him in anything that had jogged his memory: 'He just remembered me from twenty years ago, so he must have thought, "I wonder what Dexter's doing now, and what he's like now?" and he called me in for it. I just think if he knows you and he's worked with you and likes you, then that door is always open.' After unsuccessfully auditioning for the role of *Ronnie Rocket*, and Paul Atreides in *Dune*, Fletcher missed out on *Mulholland Drive*, too. 'I suppose he decided I wasn't right for it,' he says. 'Maybe I was a bit different to how he imagined.' According to several sources, Lynch had also considered British actress Helen Mirren, with whom he had also discussed the part of Dorothy in *Blue Velvet*, for a role in *Mulholland Drive*.

Lynch had previously employed singers Sting (*Dune*), Chris Isaak, David Bowie (both in *Fire Walk With Me*) and Henry Rollins (*Lost Highway*) as actors; now it was the turn of long-time Lynch fan Billy Ray Cyrus, cast as the pool man, Gene, after his agent arranged a screen test.

THE LYNCH MOB: Lynch's fondness for casting familiar faces had begun to wane between the filming of *Fire Walk With Me* and *Lost Highway*, and *Mulholland Drive* features fewer of the director's regular collaborators than ever. Of the cast, only Michael J. Anderson (*Industrial Symphony No.1*, and all incarnations of *Twin Peaks*) and Scott Coffey (*Lost Highway*, deleted scenes in *Wild at Heart*) had worked with Lynch before, although Lynch's former producer Monty (now 'Monte') Montgomery also turns up in a cameo.

Behind the camera, more of Lynch's best-known collaborators were present: these included cinematographer Peter Deming (*On the Air, Hotel Room, Premonitions Following an Evil Deed, Lost Highway*), composer Angelo Badalamenti (*Blue Velvet* onwards), Jack Fisk (*Eraserhead, On the Air, The Straight Story*), editor Mary Sweeney (assistant editor on *Blue Velvet* and *Wild at Heart*, editor of *Twin Peaks* episode 2007, *Twin Peaks – Fire Walk With Me, Hotel Room, Lost Highway* and *The Straight Story*) and producer Neal Edelstein (*Premonitions Following an Evil Deed, The Straight Story*).

EXPERT WITNESS: 'I want to say that the people at ABC are terrible, awful, heinous people who kiss up to you when they think you might be a star and then drop you like a hot turd when they decide you won't be. But really they're just terribly frightened people who want to keep their jobs by giving audiences what they want. The audience testing that the networks do is in Middle America, and I picture these men and women who spend their time in McDonald's and bent over slot machines being brought into a small room to watch David Lynch and turn up their knobs if they like it. Those knobs are going to be arrow-headed to the ground. On that basis, ABC assumes that America wants *Wasteland* and not *Mulholland Drive*, which means that they assume America is stupid. The sad thing is they're probably right.' – actor Justin Theroux (Adam Kesher)

LYNCH ON *MULHOLLAND DRIVE*: '*Mulholland Drive*? I wouldn't know anything about that.'

In Dreams:
Films That Never Were

The Dream of the Bovine (ongoing)

Between *Hotel Room* and *Lost Highway*, Lynch spent eighteen months working with *Twin Peaks – Fire Walk With Me* co-writer Robert Engels on an original screenplay for an absurd comedy which, according to Engels, was about three characters who used to be cows. 'They're living in Van Nuys,' he told Chris Rodley, 'trying to assimilate their lives; trying to live with us. They look like people, but they're cows. They do cowlike behaviour. They like to watch cars drive by the house and stuff.' According to cinematographer Peter Deming, 'It was a pretty interesting piece. Kind of existential Marx Brothers.'

The Dream of the Bovine was initially conceived as an episodic television series. 'I wasn't doing anything,' Lynch explains, 'so I asked my friend Bob Engels if he wanted to work on some episodes with me for the Comedy Channel. This was when it was just formed. So we wrote three episodes, and then sort of realised that it was basically a feature.' According to Mary Sweeney, this was where the project started to unravel. 'I thought the first draft was really hilarious and very surreal,' she says. 'But it had a four-part structure because it was initially written as a four-episode idea. Now they were going to make it a film, but it was clearly not structured for a feature, so that was my only comment – that it structurally needed some work. And when they restructured it, it lost a lot of humour. I don't know what happened.' Lynch admits, 'In its rewrites, it got off-track, possibly. And then I reread some parts of the original, and there's definitely something there. I love it, you know? It should be very bad quality, whatever it is. Extremely bad quality. Which is not hard to do.'

'I really like *The Dream of the Bovine*,' he adds, 'but I wanted this guy, Ed Wright, who was in *Twin Peaks* as Mr Mibbler in the bank, and he was also in *Wild at Heart*. But then I heard he was in a rest home, and I really fear that he has passed away. He was a real gem, because he was pretty much completely deaf, and he was a natural. And those two elements . . . I could yell at him during a take, and he wouldn't even know where the voice was coming from. He was so much fun to work with. There were three characters in *The Dream of the Bovine* and he needed to be one, and Harry Dean Stanton needed to be the other, and then there was a guy named Max Perlich, and he would've been perfect. But then he started lifting weights and he passed from that physical perfection to something else.' So does Lynch think that *The Dream of the Bovine* will ever become a reality? 'It's not ready to go yet,' he hedges, 'but it could happen. It needs work, though, that's for sure. It's close but no cigar.'

Driven to It (abandoned)

Driven to It was never a project in which Lynch was directly involved, but an unrealised film for which he had generously offered to act as executive producer. According to *Twin Peaks* actor Dana Ashbrook (Bobby Briggs), 'It was a film I wrote with my best friend, Robert Bauer, who played Johnny Horne in *Twin Peaks*. It wasn't going to be like a hands-on kind of thing,' he adds, referring to Lynch's involvement, 'but it was so gracious of him to help us out.'

Dune II, a.k.a. Dune Messiah (abandoned)

Although half scripted, Lynch's proposed adaptation of Frank Herbert's second *Dune* novel was abandoned after the box office failure of *Dune*.

Frances (filmed by Graeme Clifford)

After the success of *The Elephant Man*, Lynch was tempted to reunite with the team behind that film – EMI, Brooksfilms, producer Jonathan Sanger and screenwriters Eric Bergren and Christopher De Vore – for another film based on the life of an extraordinary individual. This time, the subject of the biopic was Frances Farmer, the Broadway star and Hollywood starlet whose mental breakdown precipitated the collapse of her career, which ended ignominiously in a barbaric mental institution. The echoes of *The Elephant Man* were obvious, even though Farmer's afflictions were mental rather than physical. When Lynch passed on the project, the film became the directorial debut of editor Graeme Clifford, who would later direct episode 2005 of *Twin Peaks*. Released in 1982, *Frances* received a mixed critical reception, and although it earned actresses Jessica Lange (Farmer) and Kim Stanley (Frances's mother) Academy Award nominations, it is hard to resist wondering what Lynch might have made of the material, had he not been tempted by *Dune*.

Gardenback (abandoned)

Gardenback was the script outline Lynch submitted, along with *The Grandmother*, as part of his application to the American Film Institute's Center for Advanced Film Studies. He described it as 'an abstract film about adultery . . . but it's about other things, too.'

'When you look at a girl, something crosses from her to you,' he told *Cinefantastique*. 'And in this story, that something is an insect, which grows in this man's attic, which mirrors his mind. The house was like his head. And the thing grew and metamorphosed into this monster which took him over. He didn't become it, but he had to deal with it, and it drove him to completely ruining his home.' Although Lynch claimed that no one but him understood the Kafkaesque scenario, fellow AFI student Caleb Deschanel (who would later shoot three episodes of *Twin Peaks*) introduced Lynch to a producer who offered $50,000 if he could turn it into a feature. Although Lynch was overjoyed with his budget, it also constrained him. 'It had to be expanded to be a feature [and] that killed it for sure, because it became less and less abstract and more and more "normal" in a boring way.' Lynch knew he could not tell the story in a rational way, with regular dialogue. Lynch eventually abandoned the project in favour of the film he *really* wanted to make: *Eraserhead*.

Goddess: The Secret Lives of Marilyn Monroe

See *Venus Descending*.

I'll Test My Log with Every Branch of Knowledge (abandoned)

Lynch's first idea for a television series came to him during the production of *Eraserhead*, when he suddenly pictured Catherine Coulson as the star of a show called *I'll Test My Log with Every Branch of Knowledge*. Her character would be a widow whose husband was killed in a forest fire, and who now educates her young son by taking him and the log to experts in various fields of knowledge.

'Maybe on this particular day she calls a dentist, but she makes an appointment for her log. And the log goes in the dental chair and gets a little bib and chain, and the dentist X-rays for cavities, goes through the whole thing, and the son is also there. Because she is teaching her son through his observations of what the log is going through.' The project was a passing whim for Lynch; nevertheless, the idea of Catherine Coulson with a log must have taken root somewhere. Some fifteen years later, she would play Margaret Lanterman, the Log Lady, in *Twin Peaks*.

The Lemurians (abandoned)

'*The Lemurians* was a thing Mark [Frost] and I were going to do as a TV show,' Lynch told *Rolling Stone*, 'based on the continent of Lemuria, which was fictitiously thought of as a very evil continent. It was sunk way before Atlantis even rose; sunk because they were so evil.' The story begins when underwater explorer Jacques Cousteau inadvertently disturbs the long-dormant race of Lemurians during one of his expeditions. This, in turn, causes a leakage of essence of Lemuria, which becomes a threat to all the goodness in the world. Lynch recalled, 'We never wrote a script, it was just kind of a treatment. But it made us laugh.'

Lolita (apocryphal)

Despite rumours to the contrary, Lynch claims never to have been interested in an adaptation of Vladimir Nabokov's controversial novel *Lolita*, with or without John Hurt as Humbert Humbert. 'Total baloney,' Lynch demurs, happy to lay the rumour to rest. 'Why remake a perfect film?' he says of Stanley Kubrick's 1962 adaptation. 'One of my all-time favourites; a classic. Nobody can touch it. When they did it,' he adds, referring to Adrian Lyne's 1997 version, 'it was a joke. I refused to see it.'

The Metamorphosis (ongoing)

'I've wanted to do *The Metamorphosis* since the 70s,' Lynch says of Franz Kafka's celebrated short story, first published in 1913, about a clerk who wakes up one day in the body of a giant bug. The story's themes of alienation – Kafka was a German-speaking Jew living in Czechoslovakia – probably appealed to *Eraserhead*-era Lynch; yet, despite the fact that fellow Brooksfilms alumnus David Cronenberg has already used elements of the tale in his films *The Fly*

(1986) and *Naked Lunch* (1991), Lynch is not ready to let go of the project.

Although his own script adds a prelude describing 'parts of the day before' the transformation, it would otherwise be a faithful adaptation of the story, albeit set in what he describes as an Eastern European version of America, circa 1955 or 1956. Lynch fears it wouldn't be profitable, 'There's a lot of dialogue, and also a lot of *unintelligible* dialogue that I would need to subtitle. It would almost be like reading a book.'

One Saliva Bubble (abandoned)

Having worked together on the stillborn Marilyn Monroe project *Goddess*, a.k.a. *Venus Descending* (see below), Lynch and Mark Frost were ready to consider another collaboration. The resulting project was *One Saliva Bubble*, which Lynch has described as 'an out-and-out wacko dumb comedy [with] clichés one end to the other. Mark and I were laughing like crazy when we wrote it.' As Frost told *Empire* of the collaboration, 'David is somewhat inaccessible to other people and very solitary, but there was some chemistry between us and we had a lot of fun . . . We'd just sit in a room together – I'd sit at a computer because he doesn't really type – and just kind of hammer it out as we went along. It was like a badminton match, just knocking the dialogue back and forth. The thing I remember the most is laughing ourselves ill from some of the things we would think of.'

The widely circulated first draft of *One Saliva Bubble*, dated 20 May 1987, concerns the chain reaction of chaos and absurdity sparked by a bubble of saliva, which shorts out a top-secret military satellite, and ultimately causes many residents of a town to swap identities – though only a pet dog can tell. Lynch says that he came close to shooting what would have been the De Laurentiis-produced film 'right after *Blue Velvet*,' with a cast headed by Steve Martin and Martin Short, who had previously appeared together in John Landis's *Three Amigos*. (1986). 'I was casting it, we went location scouting, and I was going to shoot it. And then Dino's company went bankrupt.' It took three years for Lynch to reclaim the rights to the project, only to find that if the film was ever to be produced, the financiers would have to pay De Laurentiis a share of first profits, because of the development money he had already sunk into it.

Today, Lynch is not sure he would make *One Saliva Bubble* even if he could raise enough money to pay off De Laurentiis and finance the film. 'It hasn't really dated,' he says, 'and I could probably get [the money]. But I just don't have any interest in doing it.'

Red Dragon (filmed by Michael Mann as Manhunter)

Because of the aborted *Dune* sequels, Lynch was still effectively under contract to Dino De Laurentiis after *Dune*, and the veteran producer did his best to find a project that Lynch would take on. One such possibility was Walon Green's adaptation of Thomas Harris's serial-killer thriller *Red Dragon*, in which the infamous Dr Hannibal 'The Cannibal' Lecter makes his first appearance, unofficially assisting a retired police officer with the hunt for a ruthless killer nicknamed 'The Tooth Fairy' by the tabloid press. 'I was involved in that a little bit, until I got sick of it,' he told *Rolling Stone*. 'I was going into a world that was going to be, for me, real, real violent, and completely degenerate. One of those things: No Redeeming Qualities. The way I was thinking of it, I didn't want to let it into my country club.'

Instead, the film was directed by Michael Mann, and its title was changed to *Manhunter* prior to its 1986 release – one of many concessions Mann was forced to make to producer Dino De Laurentiis. Although Mann was able to produce something akin to a 'director's cut' for cable television, this longer, superior version has not been widely circulated. In the wake of the success of Jonathan Demme's *The Silence of the Lambs* (1991) – for which *The Elephant Man*'s Anthony Hopkins won his first Academy Award – and its belated sequel, *Hannibal* (2001), De Laurentiis announced plans to produce a brand new adaptation of *Red Dragon*. One cannot help but wonder if he will call on Lynch to direct it.

Revenge of the Jedi (filmed by Richard Marquand as Return of the Jedi)

In 1981, Lynch was offered the third instalment in George Lucas's epic *Star Wars* trilogy, then titled *Revenge of the Jedi*. He turned it down, reportedly because he had no interest in making a science fiction film, let alone one based on somebody else's material, and over which he would not have full creative control. (Ironically, he picked *Dune* instead.) The film was retitled *Return of the Jedi*, directed by Richard Marquand and co-edited by future Lynch collaborator Duwayne Dunham (*Blue Velvet*, *Twin Peaks*, *Wild at Heart*).

Ronnie Rocket (abandoned)

After the success of *The Elephant Man*, Lynch returned to a project he had been working on since *Eraserhead*, 'an absurd mystery of the strange forces of existence' entitled *Ronnie Rocket*. The eponymous hero of the story was a malformed creature with blank features and a bald head, who had been surgically altered against his will and now sported a shock of red hair. 'Shock' was the right word, for, as the surgeons discovered, Ronnie was able to conduct electricity, and needed to be plugged into the mains every fifteen minutes. 'Ronnie was like a man-made kid,' explains Dexter Fletcher, the *Elephant Man* actor who was Lynch's original choice for the title role, 'and these young people found him somehow, and they could plug him into the mains, and he would make these amazing sounds, and they started to use him as a musical instrument in their band.'

When Lynch realised that Fletcher had grown too large for the role, he placed an advertisement in *Variety*, effectively an open casting call. Three-foot-tall Michael J. Anderson, a former electronics expert working for NASA contractor Martin-Marietta, now working as an extra in music promos, saw the ad and sent Lynch a copy of a video about his work on the space-shuttle programme, and was promptly invited to lunch with Lynch. 'I met Michael Anderson in New York,' Lynch recalls. 'He showed up in a gold suit, and he was pulling a wagon, and it was really a great meeting. We got on great.' Potential financiers did not take too well to Lynch's unequivocally bizarre tale, however, not least because he refused to tell anyone what it was about. 'It's not a commercial picture,' he admitted to *Rolling Stone*. 'It's an American smokestack industrial thing – it has to do with coal and oil and electricity. It might be a picture that I would love, but I don't know if too many other people are going to dig it. It's very abstract.'

Nevertheless, in April 1991, *Ronnie Rocket* looked like it might finally make it into production, courtesy of Lynch's new three-picture deal with French financier CIBY-2000. Actor Michael J. Anderson – by now known to millions as the Man From Another Place in *Twin Peaks* – told the *New York Daily News* that he was 'deliriously happy' to be cast as the title character, '[who] has a limited awareness of normal reality but a large awareness of transcendental reality.' However, after making the first of his three films for CIBY, *Fire Walk With Me*, Lynch cooled on the project. 'After so many years, now I have the opportunity to make it if I want to,' he told the *Los Angeles Times* in May 1992. 'But when I read it, it doesn't do the things it should to me. I've lost the electricity in it; it's like a light bulb with no electricity.'

Today, Lynch admits that it has been 'a long time' since he last looked at *Ronnie Rocket*, and he feels that the moment to make it has truly passed. 'If I had gotten the money to do it right when I wrote it, I think it would've been a different story. And now the script got out,' he says, referring to the availability of several drafts on the Internet, 'and that really hurts me.' Not that people who have read the script would know what the film would be like, he says; after all, 'the script is only a blueprint. But at the same time, I like to keep things private. Those kinds of things, for sure.' Besides, he says, even if *Ronnie Rocket* did get made, he would probably have to search again for an actor to play the title role, 'as Mike Anderson is probably too old to play him'.

They Don't Dance Much (abandoned)

Around the time of their collaboration on *Hotel Room*, Lynch and Barry Gifford discussed a possible adaptation of James Russ's crime novel *They Don't Dance Much*, first published in 1940. The novel is a small triumph of style and storytelling, narrated by penniless small-town cotton farmer Jack MacDonald, who gets a job at a newly-built roadhouse run by ambitious local entrepreneur Smut Milligan, and winds up accessory to a murder.

According to Gifford, *Wild at Heart* producer Monty Montgomery commissioned him to rewrite an unsolicited adaptation that had already been written, with a view to offering it to Lynch. Dissatisfied with the existing draft, Gifford chose to start from scratch. 'I based it on the same main characters, but completely rethought the whole script,' he says. 'I really threw in a lot of things that I thought David would like because he was going to be directing it.' Montgomery had proposed Madonna for the role of Lola Fisher, a suggestion that led Gifford to rethink the story as 'a kind of musical, with these brothers working in the roadhouse who were musicians. I put in a whole subplot with this crazy greasy gangster who was involved with Smut, and his cohorts, Wilbur and Badeye, Widey and Shorty. I had a ballet that these insane women put on at the roadhouse, and it ended in a big conflagration. It was wild.' Too wild, in fact. 'I think it was a little too far out even for Monty and David, at the time. Maybe they thought my take on it was too off-the-wall, but I loved it and I got carried away.' Lynch, for his part, has no recollection of the project. 'I have zero idea about that,' he says.

Untitled Neil Gaiman radio project (abandoned)

In the mid-1990s, Lynch considered a collaboration with comics author Neil Gaiman (*The Sandman*) on a radio project. 'We came close to collaborating,' Gaiman confirms. 'It mostly never happened because of time, I think – neither of us had any at the same time. The original idea was to do an audio serial together,' he adds, 'something that used David's passion for soundscapes and mine for audio drama. We exchanged some faxes, and had some phone calls – the idea was to look at radio and at the web. But overall, the idea of doing an audio series was about as uncommercial as you can get in America today.' Lynch and Gaiman finally got together to talk about it, 'by which time David wanted to do it as a film, I think. (I say this as he described a number of purely visual sequences to me.) And then time got away from us. He was busy building a studio, I went off on a book tour and it never happened. It was a strange premise, one I still like very much,' Gaiman adds, 'and the characters were wonderful and strange as well. It's not impossible that one day it'll come back from the dead.' Indeed, elements appear in Gaiman's novel *American Gods*. 'I think Lynch fans will like *American Gods*,' he says. 'It was an eye opener for me seeing how much of it was [rooted] in the Herrick and Gunther project.'

'I talked to him one day,' Lynch admits, 'and nothing ever came of it. I can't even remember what the project was.' Luckily, Gaiman's memory serves him better. 'It was about an unsuccessful P.I., Herrick, who lived above a family's garage, and how one day the family vanished completely; and about a man named Gunther who lived in a trailer lined with silver paper to keep out evil rays and emanations, who could know the history of any object by touching it. I don't remember it as having a title, though.'

Untitled Nikola Tesla project (abandoned)

Between his true-life stories of Joseph Merrick and Alvin Straight, Lynch once considered making a film about Croatian-born physicist Nikola Tesla, who discovered the rotating magnetic field, the bases of most alternating-current machinery, and sold patent rights to his dynamos, transformers and motors. 'I'm fascinated by Nikola Tesla, like countless thousands of others,' Lynch explains; indeed, directors from Orson Welles to Terry Gilliam had tried in vain to bring his extraordinary story to the screen.

Lynch pursued the project for a number of years, but was constantly frustrated by the number of scripts already circulating in Hollywood. 'There's a lot of projects floating around, and I didn't like the mix of the projects, and I didn't like any of the scripts.' Instead, Lynch turned to the theatre, perhaps for a stage play with music by Angelo Badalamenti. 'We even wrote some pieces of music. Well, he wrote them, but I helped to inspire him to write them, and talked to him about a seven-part play. I never wrote anything down.' Lynch did, however, discuss the project with a researcher named Ely Roth, who was working for a Broadway producer. 'Ely did mountains of really good research on Nikolai Tesla,' Lynch adds, 'and every bit of his research had to be double verified, so everything that he got was able to be used. There was plenty of fuel there, but I don't know what will ever happen.' Lynch is not sure if the project ever had a title.

One possible reason for Lynch's fascination is that Tesla claimed to have come by ideas much like Lynch himself. 'One day he [had] a vision of an alternating-current generator,' he described. 'Every screw, every wind of wire was presented to him, and all he had to do was go into the shop and build it. Along with the vision came the understanding.'

Up at the Lake (abandoned)

Up at the Lake remains the most enigmatic of Lynch's unproduced projects, almost certainly because it is the one about which he has said the least. '*Up at the Lake* was an idea and I pitched it to Raffaella [De Laurentiis] at a lunch,' he says. 'An idea came to me, and she said, "You've gotta tell this to Dino."' Lynch did so, 'and he gave me some money, and that was the end of it, [because] that was the time that his company went bankrupt.' Lynch claims not to remember what the idea was about. 'I sort of remember,' he offers, 'but I never wrote it. I wrote parts of it, like fragments. It was a mystery and it involved a lake,' is as much as he will say. 'And woods. But it also involved a city, too.' What kind of city? 'A mental city. I don't even know what city would have fit the bill. It was northwestern, but not north-western like Twin Peaks.' More like Spokane, Washington, he suggests, with some industry and a lot of older residential areas. 'I lived in Spokane so I might have been picturing my remembrances.'

Venus Descending (abandoned)

One of Lynch's first proposed projects after *Blue Velvet* was an adaptation of Anthony Summers's bestselling biography *Goddess: The Secret Lives of Marilyn Monroe*, first published in 1985. Summers's book explored the psychology and motives of the actress, born Norma Jean Baker, who left behind her humble beginnings (ten foster homes as a child) and tragic upbringing (both her grandmother and mother ended up in insane asylums) to become America's greatest female icon. 'I, like ten trillion other people, liked Marilyn Monroe, and was fascinated by her life,' Lynch recalled. 'So when this came along I was interested. The producer said, "There's a young man who desperately wants to write this, would you wanna meet with him and maybe work together?" And I said OK,' Lynch adds. 'That's when Mark [Frost] and I first met.'

At the time, Frost was a television writer who had cut his teeth writing for *The Six Million Dollar Man* at the age of twenty, and had since earned an Emmy nomination for his work on the ground-breaking and long-running police drama *Hill Street Blues*. Frost remembered, 'I had a strange premonition on seeing *The Elephant Man* that I would some day work with David Lynch, so I was eager to explore the possibility. We hit it off immediately.' As Summers told *Wrapped in Plastic*, '[They] were exceedingly interested in the book, [which] was optioned on a full business basis.' Lynch says that he and Frost met with Summers; Summers says that Frost visited him at home in Ireland, borrowing some of his research files before returning to the US. In either case, Lynch and Frost set to work on a feature-film screenplay entitled *Venus Descending*, which thinly disguises the film's true-life subject behind the fictional identity of Rosilyn Ramsay.

The screenplay, dated November 1987, opens in 1962 with what purports to be a clip from one of Ramsay's films: 'A large shell slowly descends, as if in a dream, folding open, revealing a beautiful blonde actress, Rosilyn Ramsay, costumed as Botticelli's Venus.' (Strikingly similar to Uma Thurman's appearance in Terry Gilliam's *The Adventures of Baron Munchausen*, 1989.) The picture fades into documentary-style footage of the star's funeral, at which point the script introduces the present-day (1986) framing device, as British investigative journalist Simon Campbell attempts to uncover the link between Ramsay and Attorney-General Phillip Malloy, a thinly-veiled version of Monroe's alleged lover Bobby Kennedy. Although frustrated by the FBI's unwillingness to open their files, Campbell's investigation ultimately reveals what Summers put forward in his book: that Ramsay's (and thus Monroe's) descent into depression and drug addiction was precipitated by Malloy's (i.e., Kennedy's) ending of their affair. The script takes one daring step further, however, claiming that Malloy murdered Ramsay, covering his tracks with an apparent suicide/overdose; Summers's book merely placed Bobby Kennedy at Monroe's house on the day of her death.

'The more we went along, the more it was sort of like UFOs,' Lynch told *Rolling Stone*. 'You're fascinated by them, but you can't really prove they exist . . . Same thing with Marilyn Monroe and the Kennedys and all this. I can't figure out even now what's real and what's a story. It got into the realm of a biopic, and the Kennedys thing, and away from this movie actress that was *falling*. 'Besides,' he added, 'When we put in the script who we thought did her in, the studio bailed out real quick.'

Lynch and Frost may have abandoned the project at this point (though there is strong evidence to suggest that Frost continued to develop the project without his writing partner), but their fascination with the fallen icon remained. Although their writing partnership on *Venus Descending* initially led to unrelated collaborations such as *One Saliva Bubble* and *The Lemurians*, the ghost of Marilyn Monroe continued to haunt them, and when the idea of creating a television soap opera was mooted, the idea of an iconic blonde beauty whose murder sparks a lengthy investigation proved impossible to resist. *Twin Peaks* was born.

Woodcutters from Fiery Ships (abandoned)

'*Woodcutters from Fiery Ships* started out as being lyrics for a song that Angelo and I did, and then I expanded it out into a video game which never happened,' Lynch says of his stillborn CD-ROM project, the story of which he described in detail. 'Certain events have happened or are sort of happening in a bungalow which is behind another house in Los Angeles,' he explained. 'And then suddenly the woodcutters arrive and they take the man who we think has witnessed these events, and their ship is, uh, silver, like a 30s sort of ship, and the fuel is logs. And they smoke pipes.' Lynch saw the interactive project as less of a game than 'a conundrum thing – a beautiful kind of place to put yourself. You try to make a little bit of a mystery and a bit of a story, but you want it to be able to bend back upon itself and get lost, really get lost.' Sadly, it was the project itself that got lost. 'I've given up on video games,' he says, 'but I haven't given up on video for the Internet.'

You Play the Black and the Red Comes Up (abandoned)

You Play the Black and the Red Comes Up is an unremarkable pulp novel, written by Eric Knight under the pseudonym 'Richard Hallas', and first published in 1938. The story is told from the point of view of Dick, a down-at-heel Marine deserter who comes to California looking for his estranged wife and son, becomes involved in a hold-up that goes badly wrong and meets a famous movie producer named Quentin Genter. Through Genter, Dick gets mixed up in a pseudo-religious cult, and becomes enamoured of a beautiful and mysterious woman who washes up on the shore one night. After attempting to kill his live-in lover in order to be with the mysterious stranger, Dick is finally placed on Death Row for another murder that he *didn't* commit, earning a last-minute reprieve when Genter confesses to the crime.

'David was thinking of directing it at one time, he told me,' says Barry Gifford, who republished the novel under his Black Lizard imprint, and discussed a possible adaptation with Lynch and *Wild at Heart* producer Monty Montgomery. 'Monty himself wrote a screenplay based on the novel, which I have,' he adds, 'and then he talked to me about perhaps writing a new screenplay based on it. But nothing went further with that.' What was it that Lynch liked about it? 'Not that much,' Lynch admits. 'The first part of it I liked a lot, and then it kind of got a little hokey, you know, I'd say about the time [the girl on the beach] appeared. Some of that could have been kind of interesting, just the way it unfolded. I started writing something, but I never wrote anything to do with the book. I wrote a prelude, and then it died.' Adds Gifford, 'They talked about it seriously, as they talked about a lot of different projects, but it never came to anything.'

Organic Phenomena:
Paintings and Photographs
by Bret Wood

As a film-maker, David Lynch has established his place in the forefront of contemporary cinema, intrepidly following the path of his dark and sometimes strangely comic imagination, even on its course into psychologically deep, dauntingly uncommercial and critically treacherous waters. Lynch's talent lies in keeping the viewer ankle-deep in ever-shifting psychological and aesthetic sands, orchestrating eerie convergences of opposite extremes, in a surreal landscape where absolute meaning is never clear. The coalescences of rusted metal and white picket fences, of adult corruption and youthful innocence, of deception and truth, of explicit meaning and baffling metaphor have made Lynch perhaps the most noteworthy film-maker working in a decade characterised by tired self-referentiality, empty post-mod homages and too many mavericks gone mainstream.

These same qualities that distinguish his films apply to Lynch's artwork as well, and have earned him renown as a painter and photographer, with solo exhibitions at New York's Leo Castelli Gallery, Los Angeles's James Corcoran Gallery, Tokyo's Museum of Contemporary Art, Paris's Galerie Piltzer and the Sala Parpallo of Valencia, to name just a few. Lynch, who in his pre-film-making years studied painting at Boston's School of the Museum of Fine Arts and the Pennsylvania Academy of the Fine Arts, has also worked in printmaking after accepting an invitation by the Tandem Press to be a visiting artist, first in 1997 and again in 1999 (at which time he also experimented with photogravure). In certain regards a departure in style and process from his previous work, the prints nevertheless continue many of the themes and images that haunt his earlier compositions and also shed some of the awkward quirkiness that sometimes diminished the impact of his previous creations.

A dominant work among Lynch's recent prints – both in size and in beguiling power – is *The Eight Quarters* (1998), a non-representational composition four feet by eight which is presented in a varied edition of twenty. Like the mesmerising lyrics Lynch composed for Julee Cruise and the perplexing phrases scattered throughout *Fire Walk With Me*, the text, neatly engraved in rows across the ink-washed surface of the paper, offers a beautiful but ultimately indecipherable message to the viewer ('the eight quarters were resounding with noise and there was darkness everywhere'). From his earliest known work (see *Six Figures Getting Sick* and *The Alphabet*), text has been an integral visual ingredient for Lynch.

Lynch's oil canvases and ink-and-paper paintings generally include bits of tormented free association: written in a quivering hand or else tiny letters scissored from newsprint (like the 'R' under Laura Palmer's fingernail) and pressed onto the canvas's congealed surface. In these recent prints, the once oblique captions have evolved into cleaner, bolder lettering that should, judging by its commanding scale, pronounce absolute meaning upon the compositions. Instead, this authoritative wordage is just as cryptic as the minute messages integrated into Lynch's previous paintings. An untitled print, captioned 'Billy's Problem' (1997, one in a series of forty-one monoprints – collograph and woodblock printing on handmade paper), sandwiches between its overbearing words the rough silhouette of a handgun, a blocky question mark and, at the centre, an amorphous grey stain that foils all efforts at interpretation. This significant void – which could represent an unfocused alternative to the gun or might represent the ill-defined 'Billy' himself – recalls the blue rose, the Black Lodge, the Lumberton drug scam, the plight of Fred Madison and all the other impenetrable Lynchian mysteries that, like dreams evaporated upon waking, defy clear understanding and tidy resolution and thereby haunt the spectator long after the image has faded from view. In a less vaguely diagrammed rendition of 'Billy's Problem', another print depicts a somewhat human head with the gun aimed definitively at its temple. With his round hollow skull atop a slender stem of a body, Billy in the past was the subject of *Billy Was Halfway Between His House and the Sickening Garden of Letters* (1990) and *Billy Finds a Book of Riddles Right in His Own Back Yard* (1992), which distil the themes of textual conundra and organic mystery so elemental to Lynch's work.

The *Ricky Fly Board* (1997, a collage with flies and india ink on Rives BFK paper) is a revisitation of the 'Ricky Boards' and 'Bee Boards' pictured in Lynch's 1994 book *Images* and played for laughs during the artist's appearance on *The Tonight Show*. Gone are the tiny labels that once identified each mounted bee ('Dougie', 'Dave', 'Ed', 'Chuck', *et al.*) and drove the work into the territory of camp. This revised *Ricky Fly Board* conveys far more by saying much less. The mathematically precise yet unexplained arrangement of insects on a white field glows with the suggestion of hieroglyphic scientific activity – its meditation on symbolic meaning underscored by the artist's signature as '(thumbprint) = D.L.' – and is closer in form to the clinically morbid work of Damien Hirst than the tongue-in-cheek creation of a corn pone hobbyist.

In a similar revisitation of a previous work, Lynch took the painting captioned *Ant Bee Mine* (1992), which might have been dismissed as a valentine from one Mayberry bug to another, and re-envisioned it as *Ant Bee Tarantula* (1998), in which a disembodied head floats, vomiting, against a sea of grey that recalls the horizontally streaked backgrounds of his earlier, similarly monochromatic paintings. Like the confused but deeply significant etchings of a psychologically troubled child, *Ant Bee Tarantula* resembles the 'Billy' series and Lynch's earlier paintings that indulge a juvenile perspective to wrestle with the moods and mysteries of nightmare and the subconscious, the potent effects of which defy conscious, adult understanding.

In the early 90s, Lynch crafted a series of 11 x 14 paper-and-ink pieces that are, if anything, even more primordial than the paintings and prints; a gallery of scrawlings that are often little more than blots and scrapes and captions that range from the seemingly innocuous (*Fish Hot Bandaid* and *Wood Fly Ammo*, both 1992) to the clearly disturbing (*Bugs Are in Every Room – Are You My Friend?*, 1992). Lynch's textual child's-eye paintings bring to the adult consciousness those preadolescent tremors of dread that signal the approach of that terrifying condition known as maturity. *Dead Squirrel* (1988) captures the moment at which a child contemplates death, the title repeated five times in print – possibly in horrified denial, possibly a joyous incantation of discovery – on a bleak field of grey.

The source of Lynch's juvenile horrors is occasionally made explicit by the artist, who came of age during the Cold War and thus paints *Sputnik Over City Featuring the Letter A* (1986-9), *Dream of Night Bombing* (1990) and *Bomber* (1985), the last two featuring a sinister black jet releasing a payload of bombs onto placid nocturnal landscapes. The bomber as stark icon of war also haunts the enigmatic painting *So This Is Love* (1992) and hovers above the romantic wasteland of *Industrial Symphony No. 1*.

The stark blisters of paint and pasted-on captions of Lynch's canvases frequently allude to uneasy reactions towards the looming mysteries of adult sexuality. Lynch's films repeatedly raise the notion of idyllic teen love with its idealism and naivety, though usually this purity of spirit is besieged by the varied horrors of adulthood personified by maniacal men and grotesquely painted whores (e.g. *Blue Velvet, Wild at Heart, Lost Highway*). *Yeah and She Had Red Lips Too* (1989) is a textured patch of smudges amid a tranquil sea of grey. *Red Headed Party Doll (She Was About Sixteen Years Old)* (1990) posits a congealed humanoid figure with arms outstretched before a canted white cross – a sexual martyr long wandered from the straight and narrow. The broken and abused woman is a recurring figure in both Lynch's films and paintings. The splotched, mangled figure of *She Wasn't Fooling Anyone, She Was Hurt and She Was Hurt Bad* (1992) might well have been the shadow twin of Laura Palmer, or the car-wreck victim of *Wild at Heart* who searches for her purse while tugging at the loose scalp of a fatal head injury.

Even the series of erotic *Nudes and Smoke* photographs are tinged with the suggestion of sexual jadedness and an exhaustion of youthful energy. Worse, perhaps, than the inferno of unchecked desire represented by the sexually voracious villains of Lynch's universe is the purgatory of middle-aged domesticity in which life is constrained by an oppressive tedium and slavery to television (witnessed in the parents of *Eraserhead*, *Blue Velvet* and *Lost Highway*). Lynch's syndicated comic strip *The Angriest Dog in the World* (1983–92) captured this horrific mundanity by making the panels virtually identical from week to week, the only variation being in the dialogue balloons that emanate from the suburban home on the right side of the frame – while on the left a factory belches smoke continuously into the sky. Bill and Sylvia offer an ongoing exchange of inanity that induces their reptilian dog to strain at its leash with a steady growl from daylight to dark, 'bound so tightly with tension and anger, he approaches the state of rigor mortis', the same kind of emotional suffocation that would inspire the splotchy images of the troubled child that Lynch's paintings so vividly express. The dialogue ranges from the nonsensical ('Seventeen weeks until Christmas!') to the overtly comic ('Bill . . . I wonder if Farrah Fawcett is a water sign.')

The adult Lynch recalls his boyhood years as troubled, but hardly tormented. He had a fondness for drawing weaponry, particularly the Browning water-cooled machine gun, but was apparently oblivious to any darker meaning it might hold. While he showed a definite interest in drawing and painting as a child, it wasn't until the ninth-grade Lynch met Bushnell Keeler, the father of school friend Toby Keeler, that he saw this as an actual career option. From there, he studied painting at Boston's School of the Museum of Fine Arts and the Pennsylvania Academy of the Fine Arts. It was while at the Academy that Lynch's style evolved from a more colourful, naturalistic style into the darker, more abstract approach for which he is now known. The first such painting, *The Bride*, was of a woman performing her own abortion.

Production designer and long-time friend Jack Fisk recalled a formative moment when a moth became stuck in a still-wet painting, its death throes marking out a spiralling design on the canvas. The explicit references to menacing insects (which, significantly, like those beneath the grass in *Blue Velvet*, are not always visually evident) bring to the forefront another potent symbol in Lynch's work. His father, a research scientist for the Department of Agriculture, often experimented with tree diseases and insects, and this exposure to decay formed memories Lynch has frequently harvested. In much of Lynch's work, insects undermine the balance of society, evidenced in the beetles that churn beneath the manicured turf of Lumberton and the gargantuan insect that fills a domicile with its segmented body and a wet grey stain in a print captioned 'ant in house.' The resonant earlier painting *Shadow of a Twisted Hand Across My House* (1988) places a huge claw against an institutional-looking dwelling while a truck-sized grasshopper sits idly watching from across the canvas. A similar expression of a child's-eye paranoia of insects and adulthood (an apt description of many of Lynch's paintings of the 1988-93 period) is found in *Bugs Are in Every Room – Are You My Friend?* (1992). In a 1997 blending of art and parasites (originally entitled *Meat as a Face With a Bird and a Rat*), Lynch made a raw steak the centrepiece of a painting (flanked by two small carcasses), then allowed assorted insects to erode a good part of the meat before shellacking it in the desired state of decay.

Hand in hand with organic decay is the industrial erosion that surfaces in much of Lynch's work, such as the grisly tangle of adhesive bandages and sludge that constitutes *Garden in the City of Industry*, a 1990 painting. The clash of natural and industrial is treated with Zenlike clarity in the print *rain* (1997), in which an opaque cloud of tar drips thick black slugs across a blurred sun. *Boise, Idaho* (1989) pairs an outline of the place where Lynch spent much of his childhood with an inversion of the triangular-shaped state: a funnel cloud of pitch rising from a patch of what might be buildings or land. Appealing on one level to his sensory fondness for rust, soot and grime, it also expresses a horror of apocalyptic social decay perhaps best represented by Lynch's former home of Philadelphia; many of Lynch's most troubling memories originated while living in a high-crime area of the city.

Inspired by an image from *Premonitions Following an Evil Deed*, Lynch's film for the Lumière centennial project, *Woman in Tank* (1997) is a hypnotic composition that shares the bleak aesthetic of his *Industrial Photographs* series while echoing the artist's laboratorial curiosity hinted at by *Ricky Fly Board*. Within layers of grey murk (as if the entire scene were under fetid water), the figure of a woman is revealed trapped inside an enormous glass vat fed by a hose and suspended from a series of steel cables. The tableau succinctly voices the blend of horror and fascination that Lynch has for years evinced towards medical science and the freak show (and the grisly attributes they share). A man alongside the tank, gripping its controlling levers, might be a scientist, a carnival spieler or both. The exhibition of the Elephant Man (by doctor and showman alike) and the shrivelled specimens that float forgotten in glass jars on dusty shelves in Lynch's *Organic Phenomena* photographs suggest evidence of science's shameful failings rather than trophies of progress. In a photograph taken within an operating theatre now unsanitary with grime and tainted by darkness, an enormous lamp mounted above a dissection slab stares into Lynch's lens with a gaping black void, an empty eye socket no longer possessing the power to illuminate.

Among Lynch's most impressive non-filmic work are these sombre black-and-white photographs of industrial decay, dismal realities that easily find profundity without the often superfluous captions and quirky elements of his paintings. Electrical stations, nuclear cooling towers, broken glass, riveted steel bridges, chainlink fences, rusted fire escapes, smokestacks and traintracks, dark with soot and wet with rain beneath overcast skies, often filled with engulfing patches of black that devour light and reflect nothing. The barbaric medical procedures of *The Elephant Man*, the laboratories of horror of *Dune*, the debilitating equipment that imprisons Jeffrey Beaumont's father, all bespeak this aesthetic fascination with and dreaded distrust of medical science.

This clash of technology (be it antiquated, modern or futuristic) and the organic has also been used by Lynch in his *Dental Hygiene* photos, in which white latex gloves, plexiglass face shields and sterile instruments are just as sinister and invasive as the bone saw that lies waiting on a grimy tabletop – though certainly less aesthetically interesting. The fragility of the flesh, the malleability of the organic, is expressed in the masses of gum and gobs of paint that often represent the human form in Lynch's artwork and is a primary element of the Bacon-inspired *Six Figures Getting Sick* whose stomachs fill with blood and spill their contents, just before the heads themselves release bile down the length of the frame.

Among Lynch's 1997 monoprints are a series of portraits of gnarled and pitted faces that reflect the indelible impact Francis Bacon – specifically, his disfigured portraiture of the 1960s and 1970s – had upon Lynch's fine art, following his visit to Bacon's exhibition at the Marlborough Gallery in 1967. The primary difference between the two groups of portraits is that Lynch avoids the realistic facial features and clean lines that tend to show through the twisted and blurred surfaces of Bacon's headshots, favouring instead faces so misshapen that they are only vaguely human. The identical black-suited shoulders at the base of each composition are necessary signifiers that the bulbous shapes above are actually human, leading one to recognise the hollow craters as mouths, nostrils and eyes. At the same time, the suits convey the Lynchian duality by pairing formal attire with grotesque visages that alternately resemble smashed animal skulls and elephantine wads of dung and pitch. In the rich, dark paintings of his past, Lynch's humans assume an embryonic form, with skull-like bulbous heads, gaping lipless mouths, hollow eye sockets and bodies that taper into long snakelike legs (not unlike the multiple miscarriages of *Eraserhead*).

In a 1988 series of photographs (*Man With Instrument, Man Thinking, et al.*), the head of a toy policeman's body has been replaced with a swollen knot of chewing gum, devoid of human facial features, streaked with creases like one enormous furrowed brow. Photographs of melting snowmen taken by Lynch in his boyhood home of Boise, Idaho, express this same curious and dreadful phenomenon, as does a sculptural experiment in which Lynch moulded clay around a ball of turkey and cheese and fashioned it into the shape of a head, then watched as his favoured ants entered the mouth and eyes and steadily devoured the head from within. As these works attest, the head is an anatomical portion upon which Lynch concentrates the most energy, as it is the repository of consciousness, in all its wonder and horror, and the part most sensitive to damage – vividly expressed in **red cloud** and a print in which a head radiates surprise as a bullet passes through it. Head trauma abounds in his filmic work (*Dune, Blue Velvet, Twin Peaks, Wild at Heart, Fire Walk With Me*), while *Eraserhead* and *Wild at Heart* feature full-blown decapitations. In non-violent situations, Lynch routinely distorts heads by lens (*Dune, Blue Velvet, Wild at Heart, Lost Highway*) and by make-up (*Eraserhead, The Elephant Man*), indulging his obsession with facial disfigurement as a visual representation of interior anguish.

Many of the pieces in the monoprint series eschew the shoulders in their representation of disembodied heads. But in these prints, the heads are identified as such by more recognisably human features and, in some cases, large block letters spelling, simply, 'head'. Like uniform masks frozen in expressions of intense anguish, these more identifiable faces stare forward with eyes and mouths agape, sometimes paired with the same ambiguous ink stains that helped convolute *Billy's Problem*.

The smooth texture of Lynch's prints sharply contrasts with the gooey mire of his canvases, upon which are mounded oil paints, housepaints, roofing tar and such found objects as Band-Aids, dead animals and even cuts of beef. Texture is one of his paintings' strongest points and is diminished in photographic reproductions of his work. The backgrounds of Lynch's larger monochromatic paintings (which are generally in the range of five feet by six feet, painted between 1986-90) are usually varying shades of grey spread in horizontal blurs across the canvas, suggestive of a single frame of a camera's swish-pan, electrical interference on a video screen or the rippling waves of a polluted sea. Upon this common field are positioned stark emblems of confusion and dread.

Inspired by the action painters of the late 40s and the 50s, as well as such nonrepresentational artists as Mark Rothko, Lynch habitually paints by smearing, mixing and sculpting globs of paint until they (typically but not always) assume vaguely identifiable forms. More recently, however, Lynch has been drawn towards more clean and concise designs and textures. Living in a Frank Lloyd Wright home (the Beverly Johnson House), designed in the 60s and citing the influence of Ray and Charles Eames, Lynch's focus in personal environment is on space and simplicity. In exploring this aesthetic interest, Lynch has begun designing pieces of furniture that more closely resemble postmodern Italian works than the earthy, organic constructions one might expect.

For Lynch, wood is clearly a very special material with great personal significance, given his father's trade [forester]. Thus what appeared to be shallow kitsch in the billboards and wall-hangings of Lumberton, the panelled walls of the Great Northern or the chunk of wood wielded by the Log Lady in *Twin Peaks* are in fact expressions of the film-maker's genuine fondness for an organic substance that seems to resist the decay that haunts the flesh and steel of his other works. All of Lynch's furniture works indulge his sensual attraction to wood. Several, such as the *Club Table, Steel Block Table* and *Floating Beam Table*, have been presented at the Salone del Mobile in Milan and are now being manufactured for sale by the Swiss company Casanostra. The white backgrounds and often simple designs of Lynch's prints reflect this tendency toward a cleaner aesthetic, though he has sacrificed none of the darkness and grotesquerie that have for years characterised his work in various media. Even Lynch's furniture, as visually and tactilely pleasing as it may be, might be described as grotesque for its asymmetrical and strangely disproportionate design.

In these recent works, Lynch has expanded the breadth of his vision to yet another medium with great proficiency and achieved a level of artistic maturity exceeding that of his previous work. One hopes that he will continue to cultivate this facet of his work along with the higher-profile cinematic endeavours for which, at least for the present, he will continue to be known.

© Bret Wood 2001
With thanks to *Art Papers* magazine

Industry:
Other Works by David Lynch

In addition to the paintings and photographs covered in the preceding essay, 'Organic Phenomena', Lynch has been involved in the following media projects:

1982

Begins contributing weekly four-panel comic strip, *The Angriest Dog in the World*, to the *LA Reader*, which runs for nine years. Lynch has stated that they will be recycled on the Internet. 'We haven't quite figured out how they're gonna work, but you'll probably be able to blow them up and scroll,' he added.

1987

Hosts *Ruth, Roses and Revolvers*, a documentary about surrealist film-makers, made for the BBC's *Arena*.
   Co-produces (with T-Bone Burnett and Roy Orbison) new recording of Orbison's 'In Dreams' for new Orbison collection, *In Dreams: The Greatest Hits* (VGDCD 3514).

1988

Appears with girlfriend Isabella Rossellini in Tina Rathborne's romantic comedy *Zelly and Me*.

1989

Writes lyrics for all ten songs on Julee Cruise's debut album *Floating into the Night* (9 25859–2), co-produced with Angelo Badalamenti.

1990

Directs 60-second commercial for Yves Saint-Laurent's Opium fragrance, starring Heather Graham (*Twin Peaks, Fire Walk With Me*).

Photography by Frederick Elmes (*Eraserhead*, *Blue Velvet*, *Wild at Heart*), music by Angelo Badalamenti.

Directs commercial for Calvin Klein's Obsession fragrance, with Lara Flynn Boyle (*Twin Peaks*) and photography by Frederick Elmes.

Directs 'We Care About New York,' a 30-second black-and-white public-service announcement about the rat problem in New York, with photography by Frederick Elmes.

Directs the second music promo for Chris Isaak's 'Wicked Game', a combination of colour clips from *Wild at Heart* and black-and-white studio footage of Isaak and his band performing the song, with photography by Frederick Elmes.

1991

Directs 30-second promo for Michael Jackson's *Dangerous* album and tour, photographed by Stephen Ramsey using high-definition digital animation. Available on Michael Jackson video *Dangerous: The Short Films* (49164 2).

Contributes one-minute track 'Ants' to the album *Komm* by German group Mutter.

Directs music promo for British dance group Massive Attack's 'Unfinished Sympathy'.

Co-produces (with Angelo Badalamenti) Julee Cruise's cover version of 'Summer Kisses Winter Tears' for the soundtrack album accompanying Wim Wenders's *Until the End of the World*.

Co-produces documentary series *American Chronicles* with Mark Frost.

1992

Directs 'Who is Gio?', black-and-white commercial for Gio, Giorgio Armani fragrance.

Lynch/Frost produces documentary *Hugh Hefner: Once Upon a Time*.

1993

Directs four commercials for Japan's Georgia Coffee, starring Kyle MacLachlan, Mädchen Amick, Dana Ashbrook, Harry Goaz, Michael Horse, Kimmy Robertson and Catherine Coulson in their *Twin Peaks* roles. 'This wonderful Japanese actor whose name is Usami was looking for his girlfriend,' Coulson told *Wrapped in Plastic*. 'And he comes to Cooper to help him find her. There are all these clues, and they all have the letter "G" [for Georgia Coffee].'

Directs 30-second commercial for Barilla Pasta, starring Gerard Depardieu as the proprietor of a café who cooks for a little girl who has fallen off her bike, and is surprised when a beautiful young woman falls off her scooter.

Directs commercials for Alka-Seltzer Plus, Jil Sander ('The Instinct of Life') and Adidas ('The Wall').

Directs 'Revealed', breast-cancer awareness announcement for the American Cancer Society.

Writes and directs thirty videotaped introductions to the Bravo cable networks reruns of *Twin Peaks*, hosted by Catherine Coulson as the Log Lady.

Writes lyrics for eleven songs on Julee Cruise's second album, *The Voice of Love* (45390), co-produced with Angelo Badalamenti.

1994

Executive produces Michael Almereyda's *Nadja*, in which he makes a cameo appearance as a mortuary attendant.

Directs commercial for Karl Lagerfeld fragrance Sun Moon Stars, starring Darryl Hannah.

Lends name (as 'David Lynch presents') to Terry Zwigoff's *Crumb*, documentary feature about cult comic artist Robert Crumb.

Hyperion publishes *Images*, a hardcover volume of Lynch's photographs and paintings.

1995

Directs music promo for 'Longing' by Japanese recording artist Yoshiki, formerly of rock group X (a.k.a. X-Japan).

1997

Presents furniture collection at Milan's Salone del Mobile, available for sale through Swiss company Casanostra. 'One of them is this steel block table . . . It's a beautiful table, it's very pure, but it's not a successful table because it tips over.'

Directs commercial for Clear Blue Easy One-Minute home

pregnancy test, in which a woman waits to discover the results of her pregnancy test.

Directs four promotional spots for Sci-Fi Channel (US).

1998

Produces *Lux Vivens (Driving Light)*, an album of Hildegard von Bingen's music performed by Jocelyn Montgomery (wife of *Wild at Heart* producer Monty Montgomery) with sound by Lynch, John Neff and Mark Seagraves.

2000

Directs, and lends his voice to, 'The Third Place', a 60-second black-and-white commercial for Sony's PlayStation 2 (Europe), in which a young man (Lynch's former assistant Jason Scheunemann) enters 'the third place' where he meets a doppelgänger of himself, a bandaged man – and a talking duck!

Directs political infomercial for Reform Party presidential candidate John Hagelin. 'I voted for John Hagelin,' Lynch says. 'He's got a great mind. He's not a politician, but he'd make a great leader. He's solid.'

Sculpture of cow with severed head, Lynch's contribution to New York's art show CowParade NYC, is rejected. 'Don't you think when people tell you you're allowed to do whatever you want as long as it's not sexually "X"-rated that they should stand behind their word and show your cow?' Lynch complained.

2001

Launches website, davidlynch.com

Directs *Dumbland*, 'a very dumb cartoon', for Shockwave.com website. 'It's a series of short pieces, [each] 3–5 minutes long. 45 minutes of Flash animation, which is very crude, just black-and-white line drawings.'

Releases album of guitar-based music, with John Neff.

Index of Quotations
AI stands for Author's Interview

The Amputee

Eraserhead

51 'In biographical movies . . .' Sanger, AI.
52 'star artists . . .' Tom Norman, quoted in *World's Fair*, 24 February 1923 and *The Penny Showman: Memoirs of Tom Norman, 'Silver King'* by Tom Norman with George Barnum Norman, London, privately printed, 1985.
53 'My mother was going along the street . . .' John Merrick, quoted in *The True History of the Elephant Man* by Michael Howell and Peter Ford.
53 'There, I was confronted with John Hurt . . .' Percy G. Nunn, quoted in *The Elephant Man: The Book of the Film* by Joy Kuhn.
54 'Lynch was utterly in control . . .' Eisner, quoted in *Work in Progress*, New York, Random House, 1998.
54 'This was a major commercial picture . . .' Lynch, quoted in *Film Review Annual 1980*, edited by Jerome S. Ozer, Jerome S. Ozer Publishing, 1981.

Dune

57 'To make *Dune*, you must be crazy . . .' Dino De Laurentiis, quoted in *PM Magazine*, September 1983.
57 'I like to go into weird worlds . . .' Lynch, quoted in 'My Year on Arrakis' by Paul M. Sammon, *Cinefantastique*, September 1984.
57 'I was inspired by . . .' Lynch, AI.
58 '[Dino] wanted to make a science fiction film . . .' Lynch, quoted in *American Film*, December 1984.
58 'I can't say enough good things . . .' 'Frank was a very gracious person . . .' Lynch, AI.
58 'My first visit to Churubusco Studios . . .' Frank Herbert, quoted in *Eye*.
58 'the necessity to bribe Mexican officials . . .' Frank Herbert, *ibid*.
59 'I'd be directing the actors . . .' Lynch, quoted in 'The World According to Lynch' by Lizzie Borden, *Village Voice*, 23 September 1986.
59 'A mound of stuff had to go . . .' Lynch, quoted in *Lynch on Lynch*, edited by Chris Rodley.
59 'After *Dune* was released . . .' Jennifer Lynch, quoted in *For One Week Only: David Lynch*.
59 'I was beaten down badly . . .' Lynch, *ibid*.
59 'We sat down and chatted . . .' Fletcher, AI.
60 'We looked at people who were older . . .' Lynch, AI.
60 'We just hit it off . . .' Lynch, quoted in 'Diane, Let Me Tell You About Kyle MacLachlan' by Hilary De Vries, *Los Angeles Times*, 23 September 1990.
60 'I read a lot when I was a kid . . .' Kyle MacLachlan, *ibid*.
60 'She was a member of the genius club . . .' Lynch, AI.
60 'When I first read *Dune* . . .' Diane Witt, quoted in 'St Alia of the Knife,' *Starlog*, February 1985.
61 'One of the first things we started out with . . .' Tony Masters, quoted in 'Designing *Dune*,' uncredited, *Cinefantastique*, September 1984.
62 'What miniseries?' Lynch, AI.
62 'We added some of David Lynch's original footage . . .' Harry Tapelman, quoted in *Cutting Room Floor* by Laurent Bouzereau, New York, Citadel Press, 1994.
67 '*Dune* is a huge, hollow, imaginative . . .' quoted in *Variety*, 5 December 1984.
67 'No science fiction film . . .' David Ansen, quoted in *Newsweek*, 10 December 1984.
67 'Those critics (admittedly not many) . . .' David Denby, quoted in *New York*, 14 January 1985.
68 'You only think you've seen rotten . . .' Rex Reed, quoted in *New York Post*, 14 December 1984.
68 'a first half of bewildering exposition . . .' Anne Billson, quoted in *Time Out Film Guide Ninth Edition*, edited by John Pym, London, Penguin, 2000.

80 'Those celebrating the success . . .' Derek Malcolm, quoted in 'David Lynch: *Blue Velvet*,' *The Guardian*, 17 February 2000.
81 '*The Wizard of Oz* reshot . . .' 'It's interesting that the parents . . .' Ballard, quoted in *Moving Pictures*, BBC, 1996.
81 'Two innocent youngsters . . .' Ballard, quoted in *Moving Pictures*, BBC, 1996.
82 'I never really asked David what it meant . . .' MacLachlan, quoted in 'Diane, Let Me Tell You About Kyle MacLachlan' by Hilary De Vries, *Los Angeles Times*, 23 September 1990.
88 'That's the one scene in *Blue Velvet* . . .' Lynch, AI.
90 'the work of a genius naïf . . .' Pauline Kael, quoted in 'Out There and In Here' by Pauline Kael, *New Yorker*, 22 September 1986.
90 'a disturbing and at times devastating . . .' quoted in *Variety Movie Guide 1999*, edited by Derek Elley, London, Boxtree, 1999.
90 '*Blue Velvet* is revving up . . .' Billson, quoted in 'Cult Classic or Sex Shocker,' *Time Out*, 4 March 1987.
90 'a visually stunning . . .' Geoff Andrew, quoted in *Time Out*, 4 March 1987.
90 'the film that David Lynch's career . . .' Sean French, quoted in 'The Heart of the Cavern,' *Sight and Sound*, January 1987.
90 'This is an ugly, brutal, naive movie . . .' Barry Gifford, quoted in *The Devil Thumbs a Ride and Other Unforgettable Films*, New York, Grove Press, 1988.
90 'I didn't immediately adore it . . .' Gifford, AI.
91 'One hit from Frank . . .' Lynch, AI.
91 'David had a phrase . . .' Rossellini, quoted in *Some of Me*.
91 'because people have an idea . . .' Lynch, quoted in *Inner Views* by David Breskin.
92 'For Duwayne, this changed the whole context . . .' Gifford, AI.
92 'That's absolutely not true . . .' Lynch, AI.
92 'it wasn't an artificial bird . . .' Lynch, quoted in *For One Week Only: David Lynch*.
93 'I can describe working . . .' Rossellini, quoted in *Some of Me*.
94 'Surrealism . . .' Lynch, quoted in *Ruth, Roses and Revolvers*.

The Cowboy and the Frenchman

95 'That night I got an idea . . .' Lynch, quoted in *Inner Views* by David Breskin.
96 'I asked David what he was doing next . . .' Michael Horse, AI.
97 'zero interest . . . 'Actually, *The Straight Story* . . .' Lynch, AI.
97 'I tried to get it . . .' Lynch, *ibid*.
98 'I think it was a two-day shoot . . .' Frank Silva, quoted in *Wrapped in Plastic*.
98 'It's my only western . . .' Lynch, AI.

Industrial Symphony No.1

99 'We told them about this thing . . .' Lynch, quoted in promotional material for *Industrial Symphony No. 1* video release, 1990.
100 'It starts with a film clip . . .' Lynch, *ibid*.
100 'Each piece is one great mood thing . . .' Badalamenti, *ibid*.
100 'There's many, many, many things . . .' Lynch, *ibid*.
100 'They had me floating the whole time . . .' Cruise, *ibid*.
100 'The music's going along . . .' Lynch, *ibid*.
101 'David would come in . . .' Badalamenti, *ibid*.
101 'One of David's famous things . . .' Cruise, *ibid*.
102 'It wasn't from *Wild at Heart* . . .' Lynch, AI.
102 'A fifty-minute video . . .' Corliss, quoted in 'Czar of Bizarre' by Richard Corliss, *Time*, 1 October 1990.

Twin Peaks – Fire Walk With Me

179 'Laura Palmer is a victim of incest . . .' Lee, quoted in 'Laura Palmer Lives!' by Jeff Dawson, *Empire*, December 1992.
180 'We're booked into more than . . .' Taku Ushiyama, quoted in 'They Really Care Who Killed Laura Palmer' by Dana Lewis, *Los Angeles Times*, 21 June 1992.
180 'Sheryl Lee deserves an Oscar . . .' David Foster Wallace, quoted in 'David Lynch Keeps His Head,' *Premiere*, September 1996.
180 'The plot of the film dovetails . . .' Garcia, quoted in 'Laura Palmer's Phantasmagorical Fall from Grace' by Stephen Pizzello, *American Cinematographer*, September 1992.
181 'We never really see the Laura who was . . .' Lucas, quoted in 'One Chance Out Between Two Worlds: Notes on *Twin Peaks – Fire Walk With Me*' by Tim Lucas, *Video Watchdog*, March/April 1993.
182 'We were preparing for the [cabin] scene . . .' Walter Olkewicz, quoted in 'Prime Suspect Walter Olkewicz Talks!' by Jason Allan Haase, *Wrapped in Plastic*, August 1996.
183 'I love that film . . .' Lynch, AI.

On the Air

184 'It just came into my head . . .' Lynch, quoted in 'Television of the Absurd; *Twin Peaks* Co-Creators Try Again with *On the Air*' by Daniel Cerone, *Los Angeles Times*, 18 June 1992.
185 'I really have a respect . . .' Lynch, AI.
185 'They were very, very happy . . .' Lynch, quoted in 'Television of the Absurd; *Twin Peaks* Co-Creators Try Again with *On the Air*' by Daniel Cerone, *Los Angeles Times*, 18 June 1992.
185 'I've heard that summertime . . .' Lynch, *ibid*.
185 'Because it's a half-hour comedy . . .' Ferrer, *ibid*.
188 'it doesn't necessarily follow . . .' Chris Willman, quoted in 'Lynch Goes Bananas in *On the Air*,' *Los Angeles Times*, 20 June 1992.
191 'Directing *On the Air* . . .' Sanger, AI.
191 'I had a blast . . .' Lynch, AI.

Hotel Room

193 'The only rules . . .' Gifford, quoted in the preface to *Hotel Room Trilogy* by Barry Gifford.
193 'If I recall correctly . . .' Gifford, AI.
193 'with the admonition . . .' Gifford, quoted in the preface to *Hotel Room Trilogy* by Barry Gifford.
193 'We shot all of it on a stage . . .' Deming, AI.
195 'a hoary mainstream conceit . . .' Wallace, quoted in 'David Lynch Keeps His Head,' *Premiere*, September 1996.
195 '*Four Rooms* was stolen . . .' 'they wanted sexier . . .' 'The nice thing about *Hotel Room* . . .' Gifford, AI.
197 'definitely not for the tastes of typical travellers . . .' Chris Wellman, quoted in 'Lynch's "Hotel" Creepy and Funny,' *Los Angeles Times*, 8 January 1993.
200 'That was absolutely not a mistake . . .' Gifford, AI.
200-1 'David prefers the longer version . . .' 'I think it's a great lost directorial work . . .' Gifford, *ibid*.
201 'I loved *Hotel Room* . . .' Lynch, AI.

216 'I thought it was a wonderful scene . . .' Gifford, AI.

219 'While I regret having to lose things . . .' Sweeney, AI.

220 'beautifully made . . .' Kenneth Turan, quoted in 'Living for the Odd Moments Along Lynch's *Highway*,' *Los Angeles Times*, 21 February 1997.

220 'dazzling style . . .' Jack Kroll, quoted in 'Fast Lane to Nowhere,' *Newsweek*, 24 February 1997.

220 'Lynch's visionary, impressionistic approach . . .' Todd McCarthy, quoted in *Daily Variety*, 21 February 1997.

220 '*Lost Highway* isn't refuse . . .' Corliss, quoted in *Time*, 3 March 1997.

220 'has scattered moments . . .' Owen Gleiberman, quoted in 'Mild at Heart,' *Entertainment Weekly*, 21 February 1997.

220 'low on logic . . .' Peter Travers, quoted in 'The Lost Boys,' *Rolling Stone*, 6 March 1997.

220 'a staggering tour de force' Harry Harootunian, quoted in 'Lost and Found,' *Film Threat*, February 1997.

220 'a brilliant new film . . .' Steve Biodrowski, quoted in *Cinefantastique*, April 1997.

220 'the most breathless work . . .' Michael Atkinson, quoted in 'Dead Ends,' *Spin*, March 1997.

220 'the best kind of bad dream . . .' Graham Fuller, quoted in 'David Lynch's Wanton Weirdness,' *Interview*, February 1997.

220 'My rule of thumb is . . .' Lynch, quoted in *Entertainment Weekly*, 28 March 1997.

221 'the movie exploits Ms Arquette . . .' Janet Maslin, quoted in 'Eerie Visions with a Mood of Menace,' *New York Times*, 21 February 1997.

221 'sexually exploitative' Turan, quoted in 'Living for the Odd Moments Along Lynch's *Highway*,' *Los Angeles Times*, 21 February 1997.

221 'a particularly unsavoury creation' John Powers, quoted in 'A Creepy David Lynch Special,' *Vogue*, February 1997.

221 'Part of the reason I did this movie . . .' Patricia Arquette, quoted in *Pretty as a Picture: The Art of David Lynch*.

221 'I would cry . . .' Patricia Arquette, *ibid*.

221 'It was altered . . .' Lynch, AI.

222 'That's not true . . .' 'We realised that was all wrong . . .' Gifford, AI.

222 'Some films are black-and-white . . .' Lynch, AI.

223 'if you put a little vagueness in a film . . .' Lynch, quoted in *Film Review Annual 1980*, edited by Jerome S. Ozer, Jerome S. Ozer Publishing, 1981.

223 'I said, "David, I have some ideas . . ."' Blake, quoted in 'Mystery Man' by Steve Biodrowski, *Cinefantastique*, April 1997.

224 'A 21st Century Noir Horror Film . . .' quoted on title page of screenplay for *Lost Highway* by David Lynch & Barry Gifford, 21 June 1995.

The Straight Story

225 'It was just one of those human-interest stories . . .' Sweeney, AI.

225-26 'Literally years went by . . .' 'They said no . . .' 'Then, everything happened . . .' Sweeney, *ibid*.

226 'When we got to a . . .' Sweeney, *ibid*.

226 'John and I have made a pact . . .' Sweeney, *ibid*.

226 'I was really giving it to him . . .' Sweeney, *ibid*.

226 'They showed it to me and that was it . . .' Lynch, quoted in 'David Lynch, Mild at Heart' by Amy Wallace, *Los Angeles Times*, 12 September 1999.

227 'Suddenly, we had five or six . . .' 'They really weren't the kind of people . . .' Sweeney, AI.

227 'Thank you to cast and crew . . .' uncredited, quoted in production notes for *The Straight Story*, November 1999.

Mulholland Drive

In Dreams: Films That Never Were

Industry: Other Works by David Lynch

Bibliography

Books

Alexander, John. *Great Film Makers: The Films of David Lynch*. London, Letts, 1993.

Atkinson, Michael. *BFI Modern Classics: Blue Velvet*. London, British Film Institute, 1997.

Breskin, David. *Inner Views: Filmmakers in Conversation*, expanded edition. New York, Da Capo Press, 1997.

Carr-Gomm, Richard. *Push on the Door*. London, The Carr-Gomm Society, 1979.

Caspary, Vera. *Laura* (reprint of 1942 novel). New York, Pocket Books, 2000.

Chion, Michel. *David Lynch* (English edition, translated by Robert Julian). London, BFI Publishing, 1995.

Drazin, Charles. *Charles Drazin on Blue Velvet*. London, Bloomsbury, 1998.

Eisner, Michael. *Work in Progress*. New York, Random House, 1998.

Frost, Scott (as Dale Cooper). *The Autobiography of FBI Special Agent Dale Cooper: My Life, My Tapes*. New York, Pocket Books, 1991.

Gifford, Barry. *Hotel Room Trilogy*. University Press of Mississippi, 1995.

    Night People. New York, Grove Press, 1992.

    Wild at Heart. New York, Grove Press, 1990.

    The Wild Life of Sailor and Lula. Edinburgh, Rebel Inc, 1998.

Grobel, Lawrence. *Above the Line: Conversations About the Movies*. New York, Da Capo Press, 2000.

Hallas, Richard (Eric Knight). *You Play the Black and the Red Comes Up*. New York, Dell, 1938.

Herbert, Frank. *Dune*. London, Victor Gollancz, 1966.

Eye. New York, Berkley, 1985.

Hirsch, Foster. *Detours and Lost Highways: A Map of Neo-Noir*. New York, Limelight Editions, 1999.

Howell, Michael & Peter Ford. *The True History of the Elephant Man* (third edition). London, Penguin Books, 1992.

Kafka, Franz. *Stories 1904-1924*, translated by J. A. Underwood. London, Macdonald, 1981.

Kaleta, Kenneth C. *David Lynch*. New York, Twayne, 1993.

Kuhn, Joy. *The Elephant Man: The Book of the Film*. London, Virgin Books, 1981.

Lavery, David (ed.). *Full of Secrets: Critical Approaches to Twin Peaks*. Detroit, Wayne State University Press, 1995.

Lynch, David. *Images*. New York, Hyperion, 1994.

Lynch, David, and Barry Gifford. *Lost Highway* (screenplay). London, Faber & Faber, 1997.

Montagu, Ashley. *The Elephant Man: A Study in Human Dignity* (third edition). Lafayette, Acadian House, 1996.

Naha, Ed. *The Making of Dune*. New York, Berkley Books, 1984.

Naremore, James. *More than Night: Film Noir in its Contexts*. Berkeley and Los Angeles, University of California Press, 1998.

Nochimson, Martha P. *The Passion of David Lynch*. Austin, University of Texas Press, 1997.

Roach, John & Mary Sweeney. *The Straight Story: A Screenplay*. New York, Hyperion, 1997.

Bibliography

Rodley, Chris (ed.). *Cronenberg on Cronenberg*. London, Faber & Faber, 1995.
           Lynch on Lynch. London, Faber & Faber, 1997.
Ross, James. *They Don't Dance Much*. Boston, Houghton Mifflin, 1940.
Rossellini, Isabella. *Some of Me*. New York, Random House, 1997.
Sparks, Christine. *The Elephant Man* (novelisation). New York, Random House, 1980.
Summers, Anthony. *Goddess: The Secret Lives of Marilyn Monroe*. London, Victor Gollancz, 1985.
Treves, Sir Frederick. *The Elephant Man and Other Reminiscences*. London, Cassell & Co, 1923.
Woods, Paul A. *Weirdsville USA: The Obsessive Universe of David Lynch*. London, Plexus, 1997.
Zizek, Slavoj. *The Art of the Ridiculous Sublime: On David Lynch's* Lost Highway. Seattle, Chapin Simpson Center for the Humanities, 2000.

Documentaries

Cousins, Mark (presenter). *Scene by Scene with David Lynch*, BBC Television, 1999.
Keeler, Toby. *Pretty as a Picture: The Art of David Lynch*, 1997.
Lynch, David (presenter). *Ruth, Roses and Revolvers*, BBC Television, 1987.
Ross, Jonathan. *For One Night Only: David Lynch*, Channel 4, 1990.

Picture Credits

The following pictures are courtesy of The Ronald Grant Archive: Page 1, page 2 (both), page 3 (top), page 4 (both), page 7 (top and bottom).

The following pictures are courtesy of The Kobal Collection: Page 3 (bottom), page 6 (both), page 7 (middle), page 8 (both).

The pictures on page 5 are from the author's private collection.

Index